❧ Jewish Histories of the Holocaust ☙

MAKING SENSE OF HISTORY
Studies in Historical Cultures
General Editor: Stefan Berger
Founding Editor: Jörn Rüsen

Bridging the gap between historical theory and the study of historical memory, this series crosses the boundaries between both academic disciplines and cultural, social, political and historical contexts. In an age of rapid globalization, which tends to manifest itself on an economic and political level, locating the cultural practices involved in generating its underlying historical sense is an increasingly urgent task.

For a full volume listing please see back matter

JEWISH HISTORIES OF THE HOLOCAUST
New Transnational Approaches

Edited by
Norman J.W. Goda

berghahn
NEW YORK • OXFORD
www.berghahnbooks.com

First published in 2014 by
Berghahn Books
www.berghahnbooks.com

© 2014, 2017 Norman J.W. Goda
First paperback edition published in 2017

All rights reserved. Except for the quotation of short passages for the purposes of criticism and review, no part of this book may be reproduced in any form or by any means, electronic or mechanical, including photocopying, recording, or any information storage and retrieval system now known or to be invented, without written permission of the publisher.

Library of Congress Cataloguing-in-Publication Data

Jewish histories of the Holocaust : new transnational approaches / edited by Norman J.W. Goda.
    pages cm — (Making sense of history ; Volume 19)
ISBN 978-1-78238-441-0 (hardback) — ISBN 978-1-78533-343-9 (paperback) — ISBN 978-1-78238-442-7 (ebook)
    1. Holocaust, Jewish (1939-1945)—Historiography. 2. Holocaust, Jewish (1939-1945)—Personal narrative—History and criticism. 3. Holocaust, Jewish (1939-1945)—Influence. 4. World War, 1939-1945—Jewish resistance. I. Goda, Norman J.W., 1961- editor of compilation. II. Bartov, Omer, author. Voice of your brother's blood : biography of the town of Buczacz.
    D804.348.J49 2014
    940.53'18—dc23

                                                                            2014009646

British Library Cataloguing in Publication Data

A catalogue record for this book is available from the British Library.

ISBN: 978-1-78238-441-0 hardback
ISBN: 978-1-78533-343-9 paperback
ISBN: 978-1-78238-442-7 ebook

Contents

List of Illustrations — viii

Introduction — 1
    Norman J. W. Goda

Part I. Theoretical Overviews

Chapter 1. The Jewish Dimension of the Holocaust in Dire Straits? Current Challenges of Interpretation and Scope — 17
    Dan Michman

Chapter 2. The Holocaust as a Regional History: Explaining the Bloodlands — 39
    Timothy Snyder

Part II. New Approaches to Jewish Leadership

Chapter 3. An Overwhelming Presence: Reflections on Mordechai Chaim Rumkowski and His Place in Our Understanding of the Łódź Ghetto — 55
    Gordon J. Horwitz

Chapter 4. Similarity and Differences: A Comparative Study between the Ghettos in Białystok and Kielce — 73
    Sara Bender

Part III. Documentation, Testimony, and Experience

Chapter 5. Diaries, Testimonies, and Jewish Histories of the Holocaust   91
Alexandra Garbarini

Chapter 6. The Voice of Your Brother's Blood: Reconstructing Genocide on the Local Level   105
Omer Bartov

Chapter 7. "If He Knows to Make a Child…": Memories of Birth and Baby-Killing in Deferred Jewish Testimony Narratives   135
Sara R. Horowitz

Chapter 8. "Why Didn't They Mow Us Down Right Away?" The Death-March Experience in Survivors' Testimonies and Memoirs   152
Daniel Blatman

Part IV. Rethinking Self-Help and Resistance

Chapter 9. Documenting Catastrophe: The Ringelblum Archive and the Warsaw Ghetto   173
Samuel Kassow

Chapter 10. Integrating Self-Help into the History of Jewish Survival in Western Europe   193
Bob Moore

Chapter 11. Jewish Communists in France During World War II: Resistance and Identity   209
Renée Poznanski

Chapter 12. Freedom and Death: The Jews and the Greek *Andartiko*   224
Steven Bowman

Part V. Aftermath: Politics, Aesthetics, and Memory

Chapter 13. Contested Memory: A Story of a *Kapo* in Auschwitz— History, Memory, and Politics   241
Tuvia Friling

Chapter 14. Pressure Groups versus the American and British Administrations during and after World War II   250
Arieh J. Kochavi

Chapter 15. Traveling to Germany and Poland: Toward a Textual
  Montage of Jewish Emotions after the Holocaust   266
  Michael Meng

Notes on Contributors   282

Selected Bibliography   286

Index   292

Illustrations

Figure 6.1. Members of the Sipo outpost in Czortków, taken in 1942–43. — 106

Figure 6.2. A position of the Russian Army near Buczacz, 1916. — 111

Figure 6.3. Bridge over the Strypa River in wartime Buczacz. — 112

Figure 6.4. Infectious Diseases Hospital, Buczacz, 1917. — 113

Figure 6.5. UPA memorial on Fedor Hill, taken in 2006 by Sofia Grachova. — 121

Figure 6.6. Bandera monument in Buczacz, taken in 2008 by Omer Bartov. — 121

Figure 6.7. Jewish cemetery monument. — 122

Figure 6.8. Fedor Hill 1944 memorial, taken in 2003 by Omer Bartov. — 123

Figure 6.9. New Jewish cemetery memorial, taken in 2007 by Omer Bartov. — 123

Introduction

Norman J. W. Goda

Historiographical discussion on the Holocaust in the past twenty years has focused on several factors concerning Jewish responses to the Nazis' policy of mass murder. One concerns the recovery of Jewish voices themselves through contemporary documents, diaries, and postwar testimonies, and their integration into broader Holocaust narratives. Another more complicated problem is to discern what Jewish narratives ultimately mean for the history of the Holocaust and for the longer continuum of Jewish history itself. The fifteen essays in this volume include recent work by leading scholars in the field, mostly from North America and Israel. They provide signposts concerning these problems ranging from ways of thinking about regional history to Jewish political identity in extremis.

The context of this discussion is extensive, stretching back to the war itself and including a number of historiographical trends, some intertwined, some strangely separated by internal sequestrations within the historical profession. They cannot all be explained here, even in part, and indeed, whole volumes in recent years have been dedicated to the broader historiography of the Holocaust and related questions of sources and approaches, to say nothing of arguments on individual questions.[1] But a sketch may be useful in providing some background to the essays that follow.

A small example may draw a larger picture. The Trial of the Major War Criminals at Nuremberg in 1945–46 was the first international inquiry into the crimes of the Nazi state. As the Soviets prepared their part of the case, concerning Crimes against Humanity, they included on their witness list the noted Yiddish-language poet Avrom Sutzkever, who survived the formation and ultimate destruction of the ghetto in Vilna, long a center of Jewish culture.

Notes for this section begin on page 11.

He had seen a great deal. His mother and newborn son were murdered. He had helped to rescue Jewish manuscripts from YIVO and other repositories before Alfred Rosenberg's Einsatzstab could destroy them. He survived by joining the resistance. And he wrote poems conveying what he had seen, including one, "A Wagon of Shoes," which predates many later artistic representations of the Holocaust through the medium of suddenly ownerless shoes of all sizes and types. Sutzkever had indeed witnessed a cartload of shoes in December 1941, and recognized those having belonged to his mother.[2]

Sutzkever was determined to testify, but just as important to him was *how* he would do so. "I will go to Nuremberg," he wrote in his diary in the middle of the trial in February 1946. "I feel the crushing responsibility that I bear on this journey. I pray that the vanished souls of the martyrs will manifest themselves through my words. I want to speak in Yiddish, any other language is out of the question.... I wish to speak in the language of the people whom the accused tried to exterminate.... May it ring out and may Alfred Rosenberg crumble...."[3] Sutzkever seemingly hoped to reconstruct a history in its own language—a history that even antedated the Germans—and in front of the man who meant to destroy that very history. Nuremberg, of course, was the wrong venue. Sutzkever's testimony of nearly forty minutes (in Russian—no Yiddish translator could be found) has been virtually forgotten, as has the long silence at the beginning of the testimony, perhaps representing for Sutzkever the stifled Jewish voice.[4] The episode goes unmentioned in most book-length accounts of the famous trial, lacking the initial staying power of testimonies by Nazi witnesses, included Adolf Eichmann's assistant Dieter Wisliceny, Einsatzgruppe commander Otto Ohlendorf, and Auschwitz Kommandant Rudolf Hoess. The subsequent U.S. trial of twenty-four Einsatzgruppen officers in 1947 and 1948 included no Jewish witnesses at all, even after Dina Pronicheva, a survivor of the September 1941 Babi Yar massacre, testified repeatedly and powerfully in the Soviet Union.[5]

The fate of Jews during the Holocaust was ancillary to the questions for which the Allies wanted answers.[6] Even for the Soviets, Jewish testimony provided more in the way of useful international propaganda than it provided in terms of the guilt of individual defendants or in terms of serious historical inquiry under communism.[7] And indeed the questions that came to haunt Nuremberg also troubled historians in the Atlantic world after they turned to the Holocaust in the 1960s and the decades that followed. Why and when did the Nazis decide on the mass murder of Europe's Jews? How was this terrible project carried to fruition? What was the mentality of the killers themselves?

The well-known result has been a tremendous amount of research through the lens of the perpetrators, including pointed discourse over the most vital questions. The issue as to when and why the Nazi state turned from persecution to mass murder was the subject of the debate between "intentionalists," who saw a top-down, ideological decision made no later than March 1941 and driven by Hitler himself, and "functionalists," who viewed the decision as arising from failed forced emigration plans combined with institutional rivalries and apparent victory in the climactic war against the Soviet Union. In the 1990s, local studies by a new generation of German scholars suggested that no decision was "made" at all. Rather, a series of local decisions based on factors ranging from German resettlement patterns, labor needs, food supplies, and security concerns, while strangely devoid of a driving antisemitic impulse, emerged differently in variant locations, finally radicalizing and almost metastasizing into a continent-wide program.[8]

Equally vital is the discussion over perpetrator motivations. Its origins lie perhaps in 1946 with Eugen Kogon, who described the camp system as a machine that killed impersonally rather than through an individual "will to exterminate."[9] Hannah Arendt's *Eichmann in Jerusalem: A Report on the Banality of Evil* (1963) similarly painted Eichmann, a "desk murderer," as a part of a larger, unthinking bureaucratic machine.[10] Historians and scholars from other disciplines revisited the problem in the 1990s owing to the discussion over Christopher Browning's *Ordinary Men,* which, in examining a reserve police battalion, cited sociological and psychological pressures that turned seemingly normal men into murderers, and Daniel Goldhagen's *Hitler's Willing Executioners,* which reintroduced German antisemitism into the equation but badly overstated the case.[11] The result was a series of historical studies revisiting the mentality, but also the bureaucracy, of murder, much of which overturned Arendt.[12] But there also emerged a quest in the social sciences for the genocidal mindset on the ground, which could, theoretically, be applied to mass killings from Africa to Southeast Asia.[13]

The outpouring of research on Nazi Germany has had additional, beneficial effects, including the approach of *Alltagsgeschichte,* which has discovered broad support among ordinary Germans not only for the regime but also for its antisemitic policies including beatings, plunder, and deportation.[14] As Helmut Walser Smith has put it, the "vanishing point" in German history has shifted from 1933 and the question as to why the Weimar democracy failed, to 1941, when men in the state apparatus, in the field, and even in private homes seemingly embraced the notion of what Alon Confino calls "a world without Jews."[15] To be sure, the post–Cold War outpouring of explanations has sometimes been opaque. The explanation of the Holocaust as the outcome of "modernity" has left more questions unanswered than answered.[16] The inclusion of the Holocaust in a postcolonial rubric of "genocide studies" has located commonalities between episodes of mass killing, but it has also obscured the unique aspects of the Final Solution ranging from the imagination of a global Jewish conspiracy to the carrying of genocide even to areas the Germans had no intention of colonizing.[17]

And what of the Holocaust's Jewish history? As Dan Michman, one of the contributors to this volume, put it in 1997,

> Holocaust historiography, by now unimaginably extensive, deals with fragments or subtopics of the event itself.... Moreover ... what is usually being explained, is the persecution of the Jews—confiscation of their property, forced emigration, and, ultimately, murder. The explanations differ, variously emphasizing Hitler's desire for world domination, rabid eliminationist anti-Semitism, racism, the almost apocalyptic clash between Bolshevism and fascism, the modern bureaucratic state and economic modernization, and modernity itself; but all these theories share one characteristic: the subject of the analysis is one-dimensional—the persecution or murder—and the explanation is placed linearly in German and/or European history. The Jews are this perceived as an object, as 'raw material,' and of minor importance in any explanation of the 'event' as such.[18]

The problem is not the existence of Jewish sources or even of historical questions concerning the Jews. Thousands of Jews, for example, kept diaries during the war, and hundreds of these survive throughout the world in either published or unpublished form.[19] It is also true, as recent scholarship has shown, that the notion of postwar Jewish silence borne of trauma is a myth.[20] Philip Friedman, a Jewish historian born in Lviv, virtually established the field of Holocaust Studies as a Jewish endeavor beginning as early as 1944. First in Poland, then in Western Europe, and ultimately in New York, he established guidelines for collecting testimonies and documents, launched bibliographical projects, and wrote historical accounts of his own, all of which expressed an interest, not only in Nazi persecution, but the reactions of Jewish communities in Europe and the U.S., as well as the behavior of local gentile populations.[21]

Nor was Friedman alone. Laura Jokusch has recently shown that up to two thousand Jewish survivors in no fewer than fourteen countries undertook grassroots documentation efforts immediately after the war that collected everything from documents to diaries to letters to photographs, as well as thousands of written survivor testimonies and questionnaires. "Most notably," Jokusch says, "they pioneered the development of victim-focused Holocaust historiography."[22] *Landsmannschaftn* from destroyed shtetls, meanwhile, sponsored hundreds of Yizkor (memorial) books commemorating their lost communities in the decades following the war.[23] Thousands of additional recorded testimonies were eventually collected at Yad Vashem and, starting in the 1990s, at the U.S. Holocaust Memorial Museum, the Fortunoff Archive at Yale University, the Shoah Visual History Foundation in California, and in a number of other smaller repositories. Historians Donald Bloxham and Tony Kushner estimated in 2005 that there were roughly one hundred thousand victim testimonies of different types.[24] The U.S. Holocaust Memorial Museum has even begun to publish translated Jewish sources in the form of a comprehensive *Encyclopedia of Camps and Ghettos* and an important series of documentary volumes titled *Jewish Reactions to the Holocaust*.[25]

What to make of it all? Can it create a coherent history of the Jews during the Holocaust? Partly, the problem lies, as Michman says, in the questions most historians have asked. Another concerns the disparate and multilingual nature of the Jews themselves. Nazi ideology notwithstanding, there was no central Jewish directorate. Save for charity agencies such as the American Jewish Joint Jewish Distribution Committee, whose transatlantic reach could hardly alter the course of the killing, Jewish responses could only be local in nature.[26] Another problem still lies in difficulties concerning the assessment of Jewish sources. Raul Hilberg, whose *Destruction of the European Jews* (1961) provided the first comprehensive examination of the bureaucratic destruction apparatus, found Jewish sources problematic. They were, he argued, subjective in a way that official records were not.[27] German historian Martin Broszat was similarly skeptical. In 1963 he attacked a book on the destruction of the Warsaw Ghetto written by Joseph Wulf, who survived the ghetto and then Auschwitz. Wulf used the ghetto archive of Emanuel Ringelblum as well as postwar testimony to incriminate Wilhelm Hagen, a German health official in Warsaw in 1942, who later became president of the Federal Republic's Health Office. Wulf, said Broszat, employed "incoherent documentation," and was more emotional than objective in his assumption that Hagen willingly contributed to the extermination machine.[28] As late as 1987, Broszat made the same methodological arguments in an exchange with historian Saul Friedländer, characterizing German holocaust historiography as objective and scientific, while Jewish accounts were, from a scientific point of view, overly clouded by "memory" and "sorrow."[29]

Whatever problems existed in their assumptions, Hilberg and Broszat referred primarily to the contextualization of Jewish sources when describing the perpetrators, their motivation, and their place, active or passive, within the killing apparatus. Jewish historians besides Wulf, most notably Philip Friedman, indeed added perspectives on such questions in the years after the war. But Jewish historians also wrote on many other questions in the immediate postwar period, often more focused on Jewish history, ranging from family histories, to ghetto life in Warsaw, to partisan resistance, to Jews living under disabilities imposed by Vichy in Algeria.[30] Historians at YIVO, along with Israeli historians in the 1960s and 70s, performed more extensive monographic studies on the Holocaust that examined specific—and burning—questions concerning Jewish ghetto administration, Jewish society in major ghettos, the difficulties and formation of resistance movements among Zionist youth groups, and the reactions of Jews in the United States. These studies include German documentary sources and trial records, but also Jewish diaries and postwar memoirs as well as contemporaneous Jewish records when available.[31]

Yet there was, and there remains, a strange disconnect between Jewish perspectives and the aforementioned historiographical trends in North America and Europe. Michman refers to an "Israeli School" of Holocaust research, which not only examines Jewish reactions during the Holocaust years, but also identifies antisemitism as the driving force behind Nazi persecution and mass murder. By and large, Israeli historians are skeptical concerning functionalist arguments concerning bureaucratic determinants of genocide and regarding more recent arguments about local determinants as causative factors in mass murder.[32] Thus both Yehuda Bauer and Yitzhak Arad have recently measured local explanations for the Holocaust in the Soviet Union that emerged in Germany in the 1990s arguing that they unduly downplay the Nazis' worldview, which emanated from Berlin.[33] Arad's recent book, *The Holocaust in the Soviet Union* (2009), is a comprehensive history that uses German, Soviet, and Jewish sources to examine the interaction of German killing together with Jewish and Soviet responses. But Arad has no doubt that German extermination policies rested on ideological foundations, irrespective of the timing of different killing operations.

The gap between approaches is bridged in part by Saul Friedländer's masterful two-volume history *Nazi Germany and the Jews* (1997–2007), which calls for, and indeed shows, what might be accomplished through an approach that integrates the history of the Germans and the history of the Jews in the fateful years.[34] The time Friedländer spends on the Nazis, their ideas, planning, and mentalities, provides far more than a simple prelude to destruction. Friedländer gives us the concept of a "redemptive antisemitism" within the Nazi leadership along with an institutional, and yet personal, documentary sense of how ordinary Germans reacted to it, from the bureaucrats who obsessed over the proper interpretation of the Nuremberg Laws to the ordinary housewives who, during Kristallnacht, reveled in the despair of their once-fellow citizens. But Friedländer also, primarily through the use of Jewish wartime diaries, represents the Jews as something other than objects, and he does so throughout the European continent, particularly in his second volume, which covers the war years. As Mark Roseman puts it, Friedländer moves the Jews to center stage, whether in Berlin, Amsterdam, Paris, Warsaw, or Vilna. In so doing he paints the perpetrators through the terrified eyes of the victims. But he also demonstrates the critical inability of Jews to suspend their disbelief, thus adding to the explanation of the catastrophe, while providing an intimate look into the ways in which Jewish communities and individuals across the continent tried to function.[35]

The memories of survivors have received a more positive assessment in recent years in terms of their reliability and in terms of the variety of aspects on which they shed light. Though they must be read with care, particularly if recorded decades after the fact, they are all we have to reconstruct many types of events for which there are no other sources, and as Doris Bergen has pointed out, they, remain by and large unintegrated.[36] A deeper problem, however, is what David Engel has called an academic sequestration of the broader sweep of modern Jewish history from the years 1933 to 1945. Unlike historians of

Germany, who have struggled to place the Nazi period within the context of German history as a whole, historians of modern Jewry have viewed the Holocaust as an external rupture in their field of study. A reading backward of Jewish history from the Holocaust, so the argument goes, distorts rather illuminates the history of Jewish emancipation, acculturation, and economic development, to say nothing of Jewish politics from socialism to Zionism. Thus, says Engel, the Holocaust has never been integrated into the history of the Jews as it has been integrated into European history. Greater crossover, he says, would offer richer accounts of variant Jewish responses to mass murder, which ranged from the misreading of German intentions, to the acceleration of political and cultural fissures within Jewish communities, to various forms of spiritual, covert, and open resistance.[37]

There are exceptions to this trend, of course. Postwar Zionist readings of modern Jewish history typically questioned the validity of emancipation, while seeing the Holocaust, or something like it, on the horizon.[38] But other work manages to avoid the teleology. Marion Kaplan's scholarship, for instance, shows that the responses of German Jews to the Nazi onslaught, particularly within the family unit, had their roots in the successful Jewish acculturation of the imperial period.[39] Yehuda Bauer's *The Death of the Shtetl* looks at the destruction of Jewish life in the Soviet-Polish borderlands from a pre-1941 perspective, explaining that Polish and Soviet rule eroded Jewish existence before the Nazis' arrival, and that to one extent or another, these trends conditioned local responses to the German campaigns of murder.[40] Antony Polonsky's sweeping three-volume history of the Jews of Russia and Poland from 1350 through the end of the Cold War follows a similar trend, integrating further the ways in which Jewish responses to the Holocaust in Poland and the USSR were rooted in historical and political developments in the decades before the war.[41] But generally speaking, there remains much to think about with regard to the challenges of integrating the disparate strands of European history, Jewish history, and the history of the Holocaust, while also considering the variety of Jewish sources either not touched or not fully exploited.

The essays that follow certainly do so. Dan Michman, in an interpretive historiographical essay that seeks to understand current writing on the Holocaust, challenges recent trends in global scholarship that try to redefine and ultimately "tame" the event. It is insufficient, Michman argues, to place the Holocaust within the current rubrics of Genocide Studies, postcolonial paradigms of imperialism, or even more localized or regional studies of Eastern Europe's "Bloodlands." At its core, he argues, the Holocaust remains as Jewish as it was unprecedented, spanning the European continent and beyond, aiming at Jews in places where the Germans intended to settle, and in places, such as the Netherlands, where they had no interest in doing so. The nature of German antisemitism—which declared war against an imagined Jewish ethos as well as the Jews themselves—was not defined by region or imagined German settlement patterns, but by the existence of Jews themselves. Timothy Snyder, who coined the term "Bloodlands" to denote the contested region between Hitler and Stalin, and who has argued that the heart of the Holocaust lay in this place, remains somewhat skeptical. Fourteen million persons died in this region, most of them not Jewish, under the overlapping power of Stalin and Hitler. The masses of bodies cannot be explained by German antisemitism (or by German sources) alone, nor can they be adequately explained through a microhistorical approach, now fashionable in Germany, that examines local German policies to the exclusion of a broader, interethnic, and interpolitical regional history that predated the arrival in 1941 of German killing squads. Such a regional approach would of course enrich our understanding of the violence as a whole, but it would also enhance how we write the Holocaust in Eastern Europe, since Jews throughout the Bloodlands experienced Stalin before they experienced Hitler and his local collaborators in Lithuania, East Galicia, and elsewhere. As politically aware actors in their own right, their response to the policies of the former helped to condition their understanding and their response to the latter. They did not have the luxury, enjoyed by scholars, of sequestering regimes by nationality on the one hand and political ideology on the other.

Their disagreements aside, Michman and Snyder both pose challenges for future research. On the one hand the comprehensive uniqueness of Germany's war against the Jews cannot be minimized, lest it be misunderstood. On the other hand, it is the study of the Holocaust by locality within broader regions that provides us with a fuller mosaic of its smaller and larger pieces that make the whole richer, if not more easily researched and understood. In the meantime, we must find and then explain Jewish narratives not only within the unprecedented nature of German policies, but within the chronological context of Jewish politics, the Jewish understanding of interethnic relationships in Eastern Europe and beyond, and even perhaps Jewish lore. Here stands a steep challenge concerning sources as well as methodological approach, since we often confront sources that are fragmentary, isolated, or otherwise mutilated, themselves part of the destruction wrought by the war.

Yet the challenges can provide very rich rewards. Omer Bartov's essay takes a tightly local approach with the town of Buczacz that is also fully integrated in terms of interethnic relations and broad in terms of chronological scope. We must, Bartov insists, understand the long-term collective ethnographic and political biography on the local level, as we also recover lost history by critically using all available sources, even those that were viewed skeptically in years past, including postwar survivor testimonies and the rich yet vastly underused Jewish memorial books from Buczacz and elsewhere. In Buczacz, we can see not only the local dynamics of the Holocaust and its tangled prehistory. We also understand the insufficiency of "modernist" explanations that emphasize the dehumanization of the victims, for here they were killed face to face, as well as the somewhat facile explanations of genocide that accompanied the breakup of Yugoslavia in the 1990s, namely, that ethnic rivalries alone provide a disaster in waiting. Samuel Kassow's essay on Emanuel Ringelblum's almost miraculous Oyneg Shabbes archive in the Warsaw Ghetto argues something similar especially insofar as Ringelblum, as an historian of Poland's Jews, existed within a larger geographic, interethnic, and Jewish political milieu. Thus, aside from offering an invaluable source for the massive lost civilization of Warsaw's Jews, Ringelblum's archive cannot be understood properly without a sense of Ringelblum's prewar politics, based as they were on socialism, Zionism, and activism, an optimism for the future of Polish-Jewish relations, and a love and fascination with the ordinary within Jewish secular culture. Sara Bender's essay reminds us of the enduring value of comparative history. By juxtaposing the Białystok and Kielce ghettos, Bender demonstrates the importance of local political dynamics within Jewish communities themselves, and the importance of local Jewish leadership, which varied from ghetto to ghetto. Worlds of difference spanned the experiences of Herman Levy, the wholly ineffective chairman of the Kielce Judenrat, and Ephraim Barash, the more effective chairman of that in Białystok. The dynamics of the Jewish police also varied greatly in terms of corruption and origins. But, as Bender shows, the geography of the ghettos in terms of Jewish assets and the possibility of work mattered as well, helping to condition the responses of Jewish leaders. Stephen Bowman, in examining the Sonderkommando revolt in Auschwitz-Birkenau, argues that the Greek Jews leading the failed revolt perhaps did so under the shadow of Flavius Josephus himself, or at least medieval readings of Josephus, as well as nineteenth-century Greek lore, internalized by Greece's Jews, that emphasized a fight to the death. Bowman suggests that the Greek Jewish Birkenau revolt might one day, at least in a literary sense, take its place amid the Jewish canon of the Holocaust. Yet a broader and deeper Jewish historical narrative exists in Western Europe as well as in Eastern Europe. Bob Moore thus shows that Jewish self-help and escape networks in Western Europe, which must be integrated into the history of Jewish responses more broadly, absolutely hinged on contacts, connections, and relationships that existed before the war, even children's prewar summer camps. Thus in Belgium, as in the Bloodlands, the prewar history of Jews and their relationships with their neighbors must be understood if we are to grasp the Jewish experience of the Holocaust as a whole.

    Other essays within this volume discuss the value of different Jewish sources more directly. Some concern contemporaneous sources and the kinds of perspectives that they provide. Alexandra Garbarini's assessment of Holocaust diaries as sources separates them methodologically from postwar Jewish testimonies. In the first place, they include in many cases the voices of those who did not survive the Holocaust itself. Perhaps more importantly, they provide a unique window into what Jews in different regions, at least on an individual level, understood concerning the new parameters of their lives, and the place of the Jews in Hitler's Europe more generally, as well as their reading of German intentions, which remained in many cases opaque at least until 1943. Similarly, Renée Poznanski provides a deep reading of Jewish Communist writing in wartime France from a new, post–Cold War perspective. She grapples with problems of Jewish ethnic and political identity in the Communist resistance, arguing that within the intellectual straightjackets imposed by Communist orthodoxy, Jewish Communists like Joë Nordmann struggled to find the space to understand and narrate the unique place of the Jews in the thinking of the German and Vichy French authorities. Thus can the underground, more so than in past years, be defined as a conscious-yet-difficult Jewish, as well as leftist, narrative.

Other essays remind us of the value of postwar Jewish testimony, and what it can add to the known as well as the unknown. Gordon Horwitz's reassessment of Mordechai Chaim Rumkowski, the elder of the Łódź Ghetto, is based partly on relatively new postwar sources and assessments, which place Rumkowski's decisions more firmly within the context of German brutality. In reexamining Rumkowski, often viewed as the least admirable of Jewish leaders during the war, Horwitz reminds us of that which we still do not know about the man, but also of the problem that Rumkowski shared with most Jews—the fundamental inability to suspend his own disbelief. Daniel Blatman's account of the death marches in 1945 show the true value of postwar testimony, without which we would know little to nothing of these episodes, which together comprise the final phase of the Holocaust itself. But beyond this, Blatman discusses what evacuated Jews themselves understood, namely, that the marches meant an end to the terrible, but at least knowable, routines of Auschwitz, thus strangely and horribly augmenting the precariousness of survival. Sara Horowitz similarly provides a close and fascinating reading of postwar testimonies. In confronting what she labels "deferred memory," she discusses the most horrific and perhaps most repressed of recollections—the stifling and killing of infants in order to preserve the lives of Jews in hiding. Horowitz, in discussing the displacement of memory, also points to the ways in which it is, surely in this case, gendered, dealing as it does with eternal issues of maternity and paternity.

And finally, the essays in this volume concern the problematic nature of Jewish Holocaust memory in politics as well as in culture. Tuvia Friling's essay on Eliezer Gruenbaum confronts the controversial life and death of a Jewish-Communist-turned-Auschwitz-Kapo, whose father, Yitzhak Gruenbaum, was a leading Zionist and Israeli minister. The 1948 killing of Eliezer during Israel's War of Independence, probably by Israeli forces, was based on the assumptions of early survivor memory in Israel whereby the grey zones, later discussed by Primo Levi, simply did not exist.[42] The effort of the father to rehabilitate the son, even posthumously, revealed the fissures in Jewish society that reached back to the prewar period. Arieh Kochavi revisits the issue of Jewish pressure groups in the United States and Great Britain during and after the war, placing their pleas for rescue within the context of those of other pressures regarding everything from Allied POWs to Czech and Polish civilians to other displaced persons after the war. Finally, Michael Meng examines the ambivalent yet emotive power of film and text in postwar Germany and Poland, which represented Central Europe as a graveyard, but also as something living, containing everything from Polish scavengers searching for bits of gold in Birkenau in 1945 to overly emotive German manifestations of regret in our own years.

It is hoped that these essays will be useful to anyone interested in Jewish narratives during the Holocaust period, not only in terms of what happened to Jews, but with regard to the way Jewish sources might be read, analyzed, and integrated. I thank the contributors for their fine papers and for their patience and help during the editing process. I also thank Richard Breitman, Christopher Browning, Manuela Consonni, Olga Gershenson, David Engel, Nathan Stoltzfus, and Gerhard L. Weinberg for their thoughtful contributions and comments. Jack Kugelmass, the Director of the Center for Jewish Studies at the University of Florida was instrumental in bringing this work to fruition and had provided steady and friendly guidance to scholarship and programming at the University of Florida's Center for Jewish Studies. For their support of Jewish and Holocaust Studies at the University of Florida, I thank David and Nan Rich as well as Gary and Niety Gierson. For their generous support for Holocaust Studies at the University of Florida and of the discussions that made this volume possible, I reserve special thanks for Norman and Irma Braman. And lastly, for their love, patience, and unending support, I thank my wife Gwyneth and my sons Grant and Lucas.

Gainesville, Florida, 2014

Notes

1. A sample includes Michael R. Marrus, *The Holocaust in History* (Hanover, NH, 1987); Dan Michman, *Holocaust Historiography: A Jewish Perspective—Conceptualizations, Terminology, Approaches and Fundamental Issues* (London, 2003); Dan Stone, *Constructing the Holocaust: A Study in Historiography* (London, 2003); David Bankier and Dan Michman, eds., *Holocaust Historiography in Context: Emergence, Challenges, Polemics, and Achievements* (Jerusalem, 2008); Tom Lawson, *Debates on the Holocaust* (Manchester, 2010); Dan Stone, *Histories of the Holocaust* (New York, 2010); Dan Stone, ed., *The Holocaust and Historical Methodology* (New York, 2012); Boaz Cohen, *Israeli Holocaust Research: Birth and Evolution,* trans. Agnes Vazsonyi (New York, 2012).

2. International Military Tribunal, *Trial of the Major War Criminals before the International Military Tribunal, Nuremberg, 14 November 1945—1 October 1946* (Nuremberg, 1947–49), vol. 8, 306.

3. Annette Wieviorka, *The Era of the Witness,* trans. Jared Stark (Ithaca, 2006), 31–32.

4. Sutzkever's testimony almost surely did not turn out the way he had hoped, and his testimony in Russian might have been at the insistence of the prosecutors. See Christian Delage, "The Place of the Filmed Witness: From Nuremberg to the Khmer Rouge Trial," *Cardozo Law Review* 31, no. 4 (2009): 1087–12.

5. Karel C. Berkhoff, "Dina Pronicheva's Story of Surviving the Babi Yar Massacre: German, Jewish, Soviet, and Ukrainian Records," in *The Shoah in Ukraine: History, Testimony, Memorialization,* ed. Ray Brandon and Wendy Lower (Bloomington, IN, 2008), 291–317; Hilary Earl, *The Nuremberg SS-Einsatzgruppen Trial, 1945-1958: Atrocity Law and History* (New York, 2009).

6. Even when the Allies became interested in Jewish statements, it was for geopolitical reasons. In 1946, the Anglo-American Committee of Inquiry on Palestine interviewed Jews in Poland, Germany, France, Italy, and elsewhere to gauge the degree to which Palestine truly represented their only hope. U.S. counterintelligence agents also interviewed Jewish survivors in an effort to determine the degree to which Soviet agents had penetrated Jewish groups moving west from Poland and Romania. The counterintelligence aspect is an unexplored subject. On the Anglo-American Committee, see Amikam Nachmani, *Great Power Discord in Palestine: The Anglo-American Committee of Inquiry into the Problems of European Jewry and Palestine, 1945-1946* (London, 1987).

7. Vladimir Prusin, "'Fascist Criminals to the Gallows!': The Holocaust and Soviet War Crimes Trials, December 1945-February 1946," *Holocaust and Genocide Studies* 17, no. 1 (2003): 1–30. See also Ilya Altman, "The History and Fate of the Black Book and the Unknown Black Book," in *The Unknown Black Book: The Holocaust in the German-Occupied Soviet Territories,* ed. Joshua Rubenstein and Ilya Altman (Bloomington, IN, 2008), xix–xl.

8. Analyses of the literature include Jan Philipp Reemtsma, *Charisma und Terror: Gedanken zum Verhältnis intentionalistischer und funktionalistischer Deutungen der nationalsozialistischen Vernichtungspolitik* (Frankfurt, 1994); Stone, *Histories of the Holocaust,* 64–112. Representative works include Gerald Fleming, *Hitler and the Final Solution* (Berkeley, CA, 1984); Richard Breitman, *The Architect of Genocide: Himmler and the Final Solution* (New York, 1991); Philippe Burrin, *Hitler and the Jews: The Genesis of the Holocaust* (New York, 1994); Götz Aly, *"Final Solution": Nazi Population Policy and the Murder of the Jews,* trans. Belinda Cooper and Allison Brown (New York, 1999); Christian Gerlach, *Kalkulierte Morde: Die deutsche Wirtschafts- und Vernichtungspolitik in Weißrußland 1941 bis 1944* (Hamburg, 2000); Christopher R. Browning with Jürgen Matthäus, *The Origins of the Final Solution: The Evolution of Nazi Jewish Policy, September 1939-March 1942* (Lincoln, NE, 2004); Christoph Dieckmann, *Deutsche Besatzungspolitik in Litauen 1941-1944* (Göttingen, 2011). A synthesis of the recent German thinking is Peter Longerich, *Holocaust: The Nazi Persecution and Murder of the Jews,* trans. Shaun Whiteside (New York, 2010), which, despite its title, says very little from Jewish perspectives.

9. Kogon quoted in Nicolas Berg, *Der Holocaust und die westdeutschen Historiker: Erforschung und Erinnerung* (Göttingen, 2003), 570.

10. Hannah Arendt, *Eichmann in Jerusalem: A Report on the Banality of Evil* (New York, 1963).

11. Christopher R. Browning, *Ordinary Men Reserve Police Battalion 101 and the Final Solution in Poland* (New York, 1992); Daniel Jonah Goldhagen, *Hitler's Willing Executioners: Ordinary Germans and the Holocaust* (New York, 1996); Geoff Eley, ed., *The Goldhagen Effect: History, Memory, Nazism—Facing the German Past* (Ann Arbor, 2000); Leonard S. Newman and Ralph Erber, eds., *Understanding Genocide: The Social Psychology of the Holocaust* (New York, 2010). Owing to the Hamburg Institute of Social Research's *Wehrmachtsausstellung* of 1995, new work was also done on genocidal mindset in the German army. See Hannes Heer and Klaus Naumann, eds., *Vernichtungskrieg: Verbrechen der Wehrmacht* (Hamburg, 1995).

12. On the revision of the view of desk killers, see Bernard J. Bergen, *The Banality of Evil: Hannah Arendt and the Final Solution* (Lanham, MD, 1998); David Cesarani, *Becoming Eichmann: Rethinking the Life, Crimes and Trial of a "Desk Murderer"* (Cambridge, MA, 2006); Bettina Stangneth, *Eichmann vor Jerusalem: Das unbehelligte Leben eines Massenmörders* (Munich, 2011), and more generally Michael Wildt, *Generation des Unbedingten: Das Führungskorps des Reichssicherheitshauptamtes*

(Hamburg, 2002); Michael Thad Allen, *The Business of Genocide: The SS, Slave Labor, and the Concentration Camps* (Chapel Hill, NC, 2002); Catherine Epstein, *Model Nazi: Arthur Greiser and the Occupation of Western Poland* (New York, 2010).

13. For example, A. Dirk Moses and Dan Stone, eds., *Colonialism and Genocide* (London, 2007); Olaf Jensen and Claus-Christian Szejnmann, eds., *Ordinary People as Mass Murderers: Perpetrators in Comparative Perspective* (Basingstroke, 2008).

14. For example Peter Longerich, *"Davon haben wir nichts gewusst!": Die Deutschen und die Judenverfolgung 1933-1945* (Munich, 2007); Frank Bajohr and Dieter Pohl, *Massenmord und schlechtes Gewissen: Die deutsche Bevölkerung, die NS-Führung und der Holocaust* (Frankfurt, 2008); Peter Fritzsche, *Life and Death in the Third Reich* (Cambridge, MA, 2009).

15. Helmut Walser Smith, *The Continuities of German History: Nation, Religion and Race Across the Long Nineteenth Century* (New York, 2008); Alon Confino, *Foundational Pasts: The Holocaust as Historical Understanding* (New York, 2011).

16. Zygmunt Bauman, *Modernity and the Holocaust,* new ed., (Ithaca, NY, 2000). See arguments in Stone, *Histories of the Holocaust,* 113–59. See also critique in Yehuda Bauer, *Rethinking the Holocaust* (New Haven, CT, 2002), 68–96

17. See arguments in Stone, *Histories of the Holocaust,* 203–44; see also Donald Bloxham, *The Final Solution: A Genocide* (New York, 2009), and the Review Forum by Jürgen Matthäus, Martin Shaw, Omer Bartov, Doris Bergen, and Donald Bloxham in *Journal of Genocide Research* 13, no. 1–2 (2011): 107–52.

18. Michman, *Holocaust Historiography,* 59.

19. Alexandra Garbarini, *Numbered Days: Diaries and the Holocaust* (New Haven, CT, 2006); Alexandra Zapruder, ed., *Salvaged Pages: Young Writers' Diaries of the Holocaust* (New Haven, CT, 2004).

20. See especially the essays in David Cesarani and Eric J. Sundquist, eds., *After the Holocaust: Challenging the Myth of Silence* (London, 2012).

21. Roni Stauber, "Philip Friedman and the Beginning of Holocaust Studies," in Bankier and Michman, *Holocaust Historiography in Context,* 83–102.

22. Laura Jokusch, *Collect and Record! Jewish Holocaust Documentation in Early Postwar Europe* (New York, 2012), 9.

23. Sampled in Jack Kugelmass and Jonathan Boyarin, eds., *From a Ruined Garden: The Memorial Books of Polish Jewry,* 2nd ed. (Bloomington, IN, 1998).

24. Donald Bloxham and Tony Kusher, *The Holocaust: Critical Historical Approaches* (Manchester, 2005), 16

25. Geoffrey Megargee, gen. ed., *The United States Holocaust Memorial Museum Encyclopedia of Camps and Ghettos, 1933–1945,* 7 vols., (Bloomington, IN, 2009–); also see the museum's *Jewish Responses to Persecution,* 5 vols. (Lanham, MD, 2010–).

26. Standard studies are by Yehuda Bauer, *My Brother's Keeper: A History of the American Jewish Joint Distribution Committee 1929-1939* (Philadelphia, 1974); *American Jewry and the Holocaust: The American Jewish Joint Distribution Committee, 1939–1945* (Detroit, 1981).

27. Raul Hilberg, *Sources of the Holocaust: An Analysis* (Chicago, 2001), 47.

28. Berg, *Der Holocaust und die westdeutschen Historiker,* 594–99. Broszat referred to Joseph Wulf, *Das Dritte Reich und seine Vollstrecker: Die Liquidation der 500,000 Juden im Ghetto Warschau* (West Berlin, 1961).

29. Berg, *Der Holocaust und die westdeutschen Historiker,* 614.

30. Early Bibliography in Jokusch, *Collect and Record,* 283–85.

31. Representative works include Isaiah Trunk, *Lodzsher geto: a historishe un sotsyologishe shtudiye* (New York, 1962); Trunk, *Judenrat: The Jewish Councils in Eastern Europe under Nazi Occupation* (New York, 1962); Yitzhak Arad, *Ghetto in Flames: The Struggle and Destruction of the Jews in Vilna in the Holocaust* (Jerusalem, 1981); Yisrael Gutman, *The Jews of Warsaw, 1939–1943: Ghetto, Underground, Revolt,* trans. Ina Friedman (Bloomington, IN, 1982). The Yad Vashem International Historical Conferences were also key in the assessment of Jewish historiographical progress. See

for example Yisrael Gutman and Cynthia J. Haft, eds., *Patterns of Jewish Leadership in Nazi Europe, 1933-1945: Proceedings of the Third Yad Vashem International Historical Conference, Jerusalem, April 4-7, 1977* (Jerusalem, 1979).

32. Dan Michman, "Is There an 'Israeli School' of Holocaust Research?," in Bankier and Michman, *Holocaust Historiography in Context*, 37–65. Michman himself is an exception to this trend. See most recently his *The Emergence of Jewish Ghettos During the Holocaust* (New York, 2011), which questions the degree to which ghettos were a preconceived prelude to destruction.

33. Yehuda Bauer, *Rethinking the Holocaust*, 86–92; Yitzhak Arad, *The Holocaust in the Soviet Union* (Lincoln, NE, 2009), 131–32.

34. Saul Friedländer, *Nazi Germany and the Jews: The Years of Persecution, 1933-1939* (New York, 1997); idem., *Nazi Germany and the Jews: The Years of Extermination, 1939-1945* (New York, 2007). A helpful essay defining an "integrated" history of the Holocaust is Saul Friedländer, "An Integrated History of the Holocaust: Some Methodological Challenges," in Stone, *The Holocaust and Historical Methodology*, 181–89.

35. Mark Roseman, "Holocaust Perpetrators in the Victims' Eyes," in *Years of Persecution, Years of Extermination: Saul Friedländer and the Future of Holocaust Studies*, ed. Christian Wiese and Paul Betts (New York, 2010), 81–100.

36. Doris L. Bergen, "No End in Sight? The Ongoing Challenge of Producing and Integrated History of the Holocaust," in Wiese and Betts, *Years of Persecution, Years of Extermination*, 289–309. An early positive assessment on spoken testimony is Lawrence Langer, *Holocaust Testimonies: The Ruins of Memory* (New Haven, CT, 1991). More recent assessments include Henry Greenspan, *On Listening to Holocaust Survivors: Beyond Testimony*, 2nd ed., (St. Paul, MN, 2010); Thomas Trezise, *Witnessing Witnessing: On the Reception of Holocaust Survivor Testimony* (New York, 2013); and on various memory sources, Christopher R. Browning, *Collected Memories: Holocaust History and Postwar Testimony* (Madison, WI, 2003); Zoë Waxman, *Writing the Holocaust: Identity, Testimony, Representation* (New York, 2006), and and the essays in Jürgen Matthäus, ed., *Approaching an Auschwitz Survivor: Holocaust Testimony and its Transformations* (New York, 2009); Nancy R. Goodman and Marilyn B. Meyers, eds., *The Power of Witnessing: Reflections, Reverberations, and Traces of the Holocaust* (New York, 2012). An example of practical application is in Christopher R. Browning, *Remembering Survival: Inside a Nazi Slave Labor Camp* (New York, 2010).

37. David Engel, *Historians of the Jews and the Holocaust* (Stanford, CA, 2010). See also the review forum of Engel by Alexandra Garbarini, "Reflections on the Holocaust in Jewish History," David Cesarani, "On the 'War' Between Holocaust Historians and Jewish Historians," and Richard I. Cohen, "Writing Jewish History After the Holocaust," in *Jewish Quarterly Review* 102, no. 1 (2012): 89–111.

38. For example David Vital, *A People Apart: The Jews in Europe, 1789-1939* (New York, 1999).

39. Marion A. Kaplan, *The Making of the Jewish Middle Class: Women, Family and Identity in Imperial Germany* (New York, 1991); idem., *Between Dignity and Despair: Jewish Life in Nazi Germany* (New York, 2009).

40. Yehuda Bauer, *The Death of the Shtetl* (New Haven, CT, 2011).

41. Antony Polonsky, *The Jews in Poland and Russia*, 3 vols. (Oxford, 2010–12).

42. Primo Levi, *The Drowned and the Saved* (New York, 1988), 36–69; also Jonathan Petropoulos and John Roth, eds., *Gray Zones: Ambiguity and Compromise in the Holocaust and Its Aftermath* (New York, 2005).

Part I
THEORETICAL OVERVIEWS

CHAPTER 1

The Jewish Dimension of the Holocaust in Dire Straits?
Current Challenges of Interpretation and Scope

DAN MICHMAN

What exactly is "the Holocaust"? The endeavor to comprehend its exact nature and scope started during the period itself.[1] During some seven decades of research, many interpretations regarding the Holocaust have been proposed, and an enormous amount of data has been amassed. Yet in their eagerness to promote new interpretations, some scholars interpret new data in a way that dismisses or marginalizes important historical evidence and past interpretations. This undermines the proper mode of scholarship, by which later interpretations either acknowledge or convincingly challenge earlier depictions. Although old-fashioned positivism is passé, we need to understand what historical theoretician Chris Lorenz has called the "internal reality" of the past.[2] I am thus troubled by several recent scholarly trends that have become fashionable but that disregard essential aspects of the Holocaust and may distort future research. Indeed, these interpretations have posed a severe challenge to rethink what I would call "the core of the Holocaust."[3]

Problems of Terminology

We should first discuss terminology in order to establish how it emerged from general rather than scholarly discourse, to emphasize how unclear and fluid it really is and how this lack of clarity has influenced scholarship. *Shoah* (catastrophe or disaster) and to a lesser extent *Hurban/Churbn* (destruction) are the He-

---

Notes for this section begin on page 31.

brew words used in Jewish discourse designating the fate of the Jews during the Nazi era. *Hurban* (Yiddish pronunciation: *Churbn*) is a biblical word, later used for the destructions of the First and Second Temples.[4] *Holocaust,* a Greek word meaning "entirely burnt sacrifice," originally a term for pagan sacrifices, was used in the Greek version of the Bible to translate *korban 'ola,* and it was used in modern secular language to describe real or looming massacres.[5] It entered discourse during the 1950s, mainly in the English-speaking world to designate the Jewish catastrophe.

This latter development occurred with the first wave of scholarly research on the perpetrators, carried out mostly by German researchers. They concluded that antisemitism and anti-Jewish policies had not been just one of many facets of the Third Reich but that the "Jewish" ingredient had special importance.[6] The term h/Holocaust to designate the fate of the Jews during the Nazi period, in other words, emerged in non-Jewish circles. The worldwide attention given to the Eichmann trial in 1961 contributed to its spread, and during the 1970s and the 1980s the term entered other languages, especially following the 1978 U.S. television series *Holocaust.*[7] In 1985 Claude Lanzmann challenged the term's propagation through his documentary, titled *Shoah.* The Hebrew word became dominant in French, and from there penetrated other European languages.[8] Both terms are now in global use and compete in a sense. "Shoah," thanks to its Hebrew origin, designates only the fate of the Jews; "Holocaust"—because of the broad interest in the topic—is also used in many cases to include the persecution of the homosexuals, Sinti and Roma (gypsies), and increasingly all victims of the Nazi regime.[9]

There is another related term—"genocide"—coined by Raphael Lemkin and made public in his book *Axis Rule in Occupied Europe* in 1944.[10] Lemkin had already contemplated mass killing in the wake of the Turkish mass murder of the Armenians (1915).[11] A lawyer by profession, he used the term "genocide" not to explain the past (although he related to it) but to prevent what he saw as a recurring phenomenon. To apply as a legal concept, the definition had to include universal elements. Lemkin thus employed a social science model based on recurring patterns.[12] Genocide as a social science term thus functions differently from Holocaust or Shoah as historical terms.

This raises the question of the way these terms relate to each other. For Lemkin, what we now call the Holocaust was part of the many genocide(s) carried out by the Nazi regime. For several decades, when the term genocide was used, it was almost automatically identified with the Holocaust. But, from the early 1980s, scholars, many having studied the Holocaust first, delved into other cases that could be included in the growing field of genocide studies. Thus the idea of "Holocaust" *and* "Genocide" became from the 1990s the most common title for academic chairs outside Israel, mainly in North America. This idiom reserved a special place for the Holocaust, now related to the broader circle of genocide. But scholars searched for more cases to include in that circle; in recent comprehensive studies on genocide, one finds an enormous number of cases of mass murder from antiquity to today.[13] But does the expanding number of cases contribute to or obscure the comprehension of the phenomenon?

To distill common denominators from many cases from different times and places, one must deemphasize differing historical realities and contexts. Instead, one emphasizes, for example, common social and psychological factors to explain perpetrators. Specific characteristics of victim societies, meanwhile, become largely irrelevant precisely because they are so different. The inherent problems have led to contradictory observations. British genocide sociologist Martin Shaw complained in 2007 that genocide studies lack a clear, rigorous, sociological concept of genocide.[14] Historians Donald Bloxham and Dirk Moses said in 2010 that genocide studies are not historical enough, calling for "historicization and causation" on the basis of many cases.[15] The German historian Christian Gerlach concluded that "genocide" is a nonusable concept and suggested using "(extreme) mass violence" instead.[16] British historian Dan Stone—perhaps to "rescue" the concept of genocide—has limited it to "state-led mass murder."[17] But vagueness remains. Australian genocide scholar Colin Tatz states that "our maturing discipline needs to find a sense of collegiality, consensus on terminology, and yardsticks with which to measure scales, dimensions, and degrees of the crime."[18]

How should the Holocaust be viewed than within the current meanings of the term genocide? Yehuda Bauer first employed the notion of "the unique and the universal."[19] The Holocaust, he said, has unique features as a tragedy of the Jewish people, yet also possesses universal humanitarian implications, including the imperative to prevent future genocides. Bauer later changed the idea of "uniqueness" into "unprecedentedness," claiming that "significant factors render the Holocaust unprecedented but by no means unique." This unprecedentedness, according to him, lies in the role of Nazi ideology, and consequently, "the Holocaust can be defined as the most extreme case of genocide known to us to date—in other words, while it is part of a general picture of genocidal events, it contains unprecedented elements."[20] Christopher Browning, in a recent contribution to the *Oxford Handbook of Genocide Studies,* has written that, the Holocaust means "the *total historical experience of the Nazi persecution of the Jews,* culminating in the 'Final Solution.'" It was, however, the Final Solution that "gained an autonomy, priority, and singularity apart from all other persecutory and genocidal policies of the Nazi regime. Its goal was the total and systematic elimination of every last Jew—man, woman, and child—within the Nazi sphere of power, and was therefore a genocidal project that ultimately had no geographical limit…"[21]

Browning's statement ironically appears in a volume edited by Donald Bloxham and Dirk Moses, who have argued *against* uniqueness. Indeed Bloxham, in his 2009 book *The Final Solution: A Genocide,* states that "Between 5,100,000 and 6,200,000 Jews were murdered during the Second World War, an episode the Nazis called the 'final solution of the Jewish question.' The world today knows it as the Holocaust. The subtitle I have chosen for this book—*A Genocide*—uses the indefinite article not to diminish the magnitude of the Holocaust but to encourage the reader to think of it as a particular example of a broader phenomenon."[22] Yet Bloxham further calls the "uniqueness discourse" mere "rhetoric," and attributes it partially to Jewish theological interpretations and identity politics. Moses goes further, claiming, "whether similarities [between the Holocaust and other genocides] are more significant than the differences is ultimately a political and philosophical, rather than a historical question.... Uniqueness is not a category for historical research; it is a religious or metaphysical category."[23] However, this "anti-uniqueness" claim by Bloxham comes only sentences after his statement that "the scale, determination, and intensity of the Nazi pursuit of Jews across Europe is *exceptional* even within the annals of genocide,"[24] and this at the end of a study that puts the focus on the Holocaust. What, then, should we understand by his term "exceptionality," or by Browning's "singularity," except that there is apparently something in the case of the Holocaust that is impossible to ascertain in other examples of genocide? Note that two historians make these statements, which refutes Moses's statement that such a claim is ahistorical.

Indeed, in recent years something basic has changed in genocide research. Colin Tatz describes the growing problem: "Foremost is the challenge of finding a space for encompassing and embracing the Holocaust with some comfort. The judeocide is an ally, not an enemy, and not on the margins"![25] He sees enmity among genocide scholars toward Holocaust studies, partially resulting from "competition of victimhood" among scholars that reject the Holocaust's public and scholarly centrality. They are irritated by the notion of the "uniqueness" of one case, sometimes owing to political attitudes regarding the Israeli-Palestinian conflict.[26] But the real issue may lie in methodology: the social scientific approach of finding a model versus the historical approach of understanding a case through its many facets, and thus emphasizing specifics. Yet from the historian's view, it is precisely the *exceptional* dimension(s) of the Holocaust that should draw attention, while one still remains aware of their connections with other developments.

Problems of Geography

Amid debates over terminology, method, and uniqueness, historians have recently emphasized, somewhat problematically, Eastern Europe as the locus par excellence of the Holocaust. Research from the end of the 1940s through the 1980s focused on Auschwitz, which became an idiom, even replacing the term Holocaust (or Shoah) in philosophical and theological contemplations[27] and visual representations such as the iconic photo of the Birkenau gate.[28] The Auschwitz-centered view resulted from two circumstances. First, Holocaust research during the first decades after 1945 developed almost exclusively in the West, with an emphasis on Western and Central Europe, from which Jews had been deported primarily to Auschwitz. Secondly, Poland emphasized Auschwitz in national remembrance, claiming initially that about 4 million people from all over Europe—it did not emphasize the Jewishness of the victims—were annihilated there.[29]

After the fall of the Communist bloc in 1989 and the opening of its archives, research on the Holocaust in Eastern Europe and the Soviet Union burgeoned. The resulting picture of the Holocaust has become much broader and multifaceted. But the pendulum has swung too far. Eastern Europe has come to be seen by many not only as the location of a major part of the Holocaust, but also as its core. This results from the convergence of archival findings with the more general theoretical interpretations deriving from the concept of "genocide," relating specifically to colonialism, empire building, and the so-called "Bloodlands."

Jürgen Zimmerer was among the first to promote the idea that "colonialism served as an important source of ideas" for the Holocaust. As a German scholar Zimmerer was troubled that Germany carried out two twentieth-century murder campaigns: of the Nama and Herrero in German Southwest Africa and then of the Jews in the Holocaust. Though looking for links, he ultimately emphasized that Nazism was complicated and eclectic, and that "the murder of the Jews … stands out in many ways from other genocides."[30] But others took Zimmerer's line of reasoning further, becoming more "orthodox" regarding the link between colonialism and ensuing genocides in colonized territories.[31]

Thus Mark Mazower's *Hitler's Empire* (2008) interprets the Third Reich through the concept of colonial *Lebensraum*. The Nazis' main goal, Mazower argues, was to control Europe, and Hitler, he states, remained nothing more than "a Greater German nationalist."[32] Nazi empire building was a form of colonialism resulting from earlier examples. Here Mazower, like Zimmerer and others, links colonialism with Nazi genocide. But, as *Lebensraum* was in Europe's east, Mazower says that Eastern Europe "must lie at the heart of any account of the Nazi empire."[33] And here, Hitler's imperial fantasy caused, as a by-product, the deaths of "millions of Russians, Poles, Jews and Belorussians." In his 650 pages, Mazower does not mention persecution of the Jews in Germany in the 1930s until page 83, and here in an insufficient and hence distorted manner, which ignores the distinct nature of Nazi antisemitism and provides no framework for understanding why these persecutions happened. And so, the Final Solution is dealt with as distinct from the enormous anti-Jewish enterprise of the 1930s. It remains unclear *why* it was so important for the Nazi regime to get rid of the Jews in Germany, in Eastern Europe, and throughout the entire European continent. For Mazower, "the Jews certainly occupied a special place in the political demonology of the Third Reich" and that statement suffices in his eyes to explain what happened to them. Moreover, "the Germans had somehow stumbled into the great centers of east European Jewry," a consequence that, Mazower says, the Germans had not really foreseen. Finally, he emphasizes that the Jews "constituted only … one of the regime's ethnic targets."[34] Mazower adds that, "it was thanks to Nazism that German soldiers and civilians ended up dying in numbers that were probably not far short of the toll of the Final Solution itself."[35]

In his extremely popular book *Bloodlands,* Timothy Snyder adds to this trend.[36] The murder of the Jews occurred for Snyder in the context of broad, spiraling mass-killing actions carried out by the Hitler and Stalin regimes in a clearly defined time period (the 1930s and 1940s) and in a geographical area—the "Bloodlands"—stretching from western Poland to the Black Sea that both occupied. The Holocaust thus blurs into a bloody epoch in those "Bloodlands," and not elsewhere, because it resulted from "the Germans and the Soviets… [provoking] one another to ever greater crimes."[37] "These atrocities," says Snyder, "shared a place, and they shared a time…. To describe their course has been to introduce to European history its central event."[38] For Snyder too, Nazi anti-Jewish policies in the 1930s play no role of substance, and the non–Eastern European parts of the Holocaust are considered marginal.[39]

These studies add knowledge and thought-provoking angles, but they miss, and hence blur, some of Holocaust's essential characteristics. They identify the Holocaust as the very *act* of wholesale murder of the Jews, focusing on Eastern Europe, from 1941, and as part of a much broader array of genocidal acts. The Jews are thus simply another "enemy" or "inferior" ethnic group. Nazi anti-Jewish policies of the 1930s are not analyzed because they did not include genocide; non–Eastern European aspects of the Holocaust are viewed as marginal; "antisemitism" is understood simplistically as another group hatred, and the sheer intensity of the effort to eradicate the Jews is not explained. These studies further neglect analysis of the key terms in Nazi discourse and the unique phenomena of Jewish Councils and ghettos, and the broader perspective of Jewish history is ignored.

"World Jewry" and "the Jewish Spirit" as Indicating the Exceptional Dimension of the Holocaust

How, then, should we understand the Holocaust? How has recent scholarly research delved into its particulars? And what is the importance of Jewish history within the Holocaust as a whole? Jewish history has usually been interpreted as "Jewish reactions to" or "coping with" the persecutions. It is portrayed as an internal Jewish issue,[40] through which the essentials of the Holocaust—caused by perpetrators—cannot be approached.[41]

But Jewish history in the right sense, i.e., the history of Jewish society,[42] is of critical importance for understanding the obsession of the Nazis and their allies. One could start with the Jewish place in European culture and society and hence in the European mind. After the end of the eighteenth century the position of Jews underwent enormous changes. They adapted to the developing norms of European societies, increasingly integrating and even assimilating. In central and Western Europe their appellation was altered to Israeliten/israélites, meaning that they belonged to an "Israelite" religion, not to a Jewish ethnicity. Later in the Soviet Union the Jewish religion was suppressed, the Jewish communities dissolved, and the definition of Jews as a fully recognized "nation" denied.[43]

The point is that Jews in 1933 were not a cohesive entity and in many places no longer even Jews in the classic, historical sense. Scattered throughout Europe, they belonged to different and often quarrelsome religious denominations, different political parties, and different social strata, not even possessing a common language.[44] To me, here lies the weakness of most Holocaust explanations that relate to antisemitism as a clear and cohesive phenomenon or that simply tie antisemitism as another ethnic hatred to political, imperial, colonial, racial, nationalist, economic, or other lines of development culminating in yet another genocide. Most scholars have failed in this connection to employ the history of *mentalities* in order to understand the true mechanics of Nazi antisemitism.

For contrary to the fractured state of modern Jewish existence, Hitler and the Nazi *Weltanschauung* imagined a cohesive image of *der Jude* or *internationales Judentum* or *Weltjudentum*.[45] This aspect of "World Jewry" is key. "Jews" were not just an ethnic "other." For a millennium and a half they embodied throughout Christian Europe the ultimate rival in the claim for spiritual chosenness and superiority. Enmity toward the Jews was enmity toward the abstract spirit of Judaism. And in late modern Europe, in the age of secularization and modernization, and especially due to the social upheaval caused by the wide-ranging consequences of industrialism, this notion underwent transformation of which Nazism's view of the Jews and Judaism was the most extreme product.

"World Jewry" and the *jüdische Geist* were perceived by the Nazis, and many others throughout Europe, as conspiratorial, powerful, and cohesive forces that undermined the human spirit and the very existence of humankind. It could not be integrated. It had to be erased for the sake of human survival. This dimension was new (past views had it that the Jews had to be redeemed through conversion, reeducation, or adaptation, either by force or via a supervised gradual process), especially when it became an essential part of the political religion of a well-organized and powerful state.[46] Jews were not the only group persecuted by Nazi Germany, but they were perceived as most threatening. The Jews stood for the "unnatural," corrosive principle of human equality, which underlay the pernicious beliefs of Christianity, liberalism, democracy, internationalism, capitalism, and communism and undermined the hierarchical principle of nature.[47] In Nazi language, no other enemy was defined with the attribute *Welt-* or *internationales* unless it was another aspect of "Judaism" such as Bolshevism. As the SD (SS Security Service) expert Paul Zapp described it, Jewry was the "binding element of the obstacle front of all adversaries of National Socialism."[48] SS man Dieter Wisliceny, one of Adolf Eichmann's aides, further explained in 1946 in a revealing testimony that for Nazism "the world is directed by forces of good and evil. According to this view, the principle of evil was embodied in the Jews.... This world of images is totally incomprehensible in logical or rational terms [because] it is a form of religiosity that leads to sectarianism. Millions of people believed these things... something that can be compared only to similar phenomena from the Middle Ages, such as the mania of witches (*Hexenwahn*)."[49]

Thus the battle against Jews had a redemptive goal not just for Germany (to use Saul Friedländer's term, but going even beyond how he describes it)[50]—it had a goal to redeem *the world*. The Jewish spirit had to be exorcized. For Hitler and his grand vision of restructuring the world on the principle of race, the war against the Jews became a central obsession, accompanying his political career throughout.[51] This obsession combined with the sense of "emergency" was critical. In Hitler's first political writing of September 1919 he described the Jews as *Rassentüberkülose* ("race-tuberculosis"),[52] a lethal disease threatening humankind; this was a hybrid racist/medical terminology, which linked the possible treatment of such a disease with the public health needs. His view was expressed most clearly in his well-known *Reichstag* speech of 30 January 1939, when he foretold that in another world war, "the result will not be the bolshevization of the earth, and thus the victory of Jewry, but the annihilation (*Vernichtung*) of the Jewish race in Europe!" And in his political testament, written on 29 April 1945 shortly before his suicide, he called on future generations "to fight mercilessly against the poisoners of all the peoples of the world, international Jewry."[53] Similarly, Heinrich Himmler in his well-known speech at the *SS-Gruppenführertagung* (meeting of senior SS officers) in Posen on 4 October 1943 described the Jews as a *Bazillus* (Bacillus).[54]

The murder of close to 6 million was the result of the uncompleted scheme that was called "The Final Solution of the Jewish Question," although many more Jews were targeted, and a considerable number of non-Jews also died because of it. Moreover, the murder of the Jews was one, albeit the most salient, result of what we now call "the Holocaust," the Holocaust being a much larger obsession—to liberate Germany first, Europe afterward, and the world in the end from the undermining "Jewish spirit" and its carriers, the individual Jews.[55] One needs to listen to the terms that Hitler, and later Himmler, used when they spoke openly and did not resort to the bureaucratic euphemisms *Auswanderung, Räumung, Aussiedlung, Umsiedlung,* etc.: they did not say *Ermordung* (murder)—but rather *Vernichtung* (annihilation), i.e., turning the Jews into "*nichts,*" nothing.[56] Similarly, Jewish ideas such as equality had to be *vernichtet*— the books or cultural artifacts carrying these ideas, even when written by non-Jews, had to be removed from libraries and homes, burned (as Goebbels did on 10 May 1933)[57] or (as Einsatzstab Rosenberg did in the 1940s) collected and concealed—in order to keep some physical remnants in a well-guarded "safe," accessible in the future only to a handful of faithful Nazis.[58]

In 1933 the road was opened to materialize the vision. But how could a vague goal—"*Entfernung der Juden überhaupt*" ("the total removal of the Jews") be achieved? Hitler was not involved in the daily shaping of anti-Jewish policies. Although he followed the issue closely, he did not even set up a "special committee for Jewish affairs."[59] Yet it is precisely this conundrum that is so important. In *Mein Kampf* (1924) Hitler contemplated the different types of personalities directing society: (1) the theoretician, who knew "how to shape ideas," (2) the *Programmatiker,* the implementer of ideas, and (3) the leader, who knew how to lead the masses. He explained that the combination of the theoretician and the leader in one person is "the rarest thing to find on the globe; such a combination creates the distinguished [or pre-eminent] personality."[60] Hitler viewed himself as this personality. He left the role of the *Programmatiker* to others. This proved in the end—at least regarding the Jewish issue—to be successful.

Hitler's visions of the need to combat *der Jude* and the global threat of *das Judentum* took shape through trial and error in which broadening circles played a role. These circles included not only the German bureaucracy—whose part was emphasized by Raul Hilberg and "functionalist" historians and whose mode of working was so well defined by Ian Kershaw as "working towards the Führer"[61]—but many beyond it, first in Germany, later in every occupied and allied country. Most puzzling is the rapid eagerness to join in, especially since the Nazi state existed for only twelve years and ninety-eight days. In historical terms this period was an explosion of violence. Yet it was not an explosion without a reason: it was the result of the combination of Hitler's charismatic impact and the widespread varieties of antisemitism, glued together by readiness to embrace simplistic, conspirational explanations resulting from deep economic and political crises.[62]

Hitler, one of history's most transformational leaders, infused the Nazi state and its anti-Jewish project with uncommon energies.[63] Policies evolved through zigzags, with the bureaucracy sometimes moving in contrary directions based on differing interpretations of Hitler's will. Indeed a myriad of antisemitisms were in play, since Hitler's goal of total removal of the Jews was interpreted in different ways. And, since "the Jew" represented many things in those varying antisemitisms, the development of Nazi policies was "twisted," often unfocused, though continuously escalating, because the essential thread was the obsessive search for a "solution." Christopher Browning has described the persecution of Jews in Germany in the 1930s as "aimed at excluding them from both the German *Volksgemeinschaft* and German soil" and including "civic death," "social death," and "economic death."[64] These "deaths" were *not* consecutive stages of a gradual development (as Raul Hilberg has argued)[65] but parallel—sometimes competing, sometimes hitting dead ends, but ultimately complementary. They were all part of the enterprise for which the term "the Holocaust" should be used. Yet they also included aspects of German "self-purification" from "Jewishness." Thus philosopher and jurist Carl Schmitt in 1936 called upon the German legal profession to fight against the "Jewish spirit" that had polluted German legal thought,[66] and the Deutscher Sprach-Verein (German Language Association) embarked on an *Entjudungskampf* of the German language.[67]

But it was supposedly the physical Jews themselves who disseminated the Jewish poison. A major problem was therefore the identification of "the Jew"—bridging the gap between images and reality. Hilberg interpreted the definition of the Jews, formulated already in April 1933 (and redefined in November 1935) as a tool to enable the regime to operate against its Jews. This is true from a bureaucratic point of view. However, one must note the deeper meaning of "definition." In the context of the whole period one can see the beginning of a meticulous process of identification (through census and marking) that continued in every place annexed or occupied by Germany.[68] It was carried out by the local authorities, by Jewish Councils, or with the help of local collaborators. Wherever the Nazis ruled, *Israeliten* and nonpracticing Jews, including converts, had to be turned again, in public and legal discourse, into "Jews" (*Juden, juifs, joden*).

This changed vocabulary was part of the effort to turn the Jews into a coherent entity, thus reversing modern Jewish history. In many places in the occupied Soviet Union, where Jewish communal life had been entirely suppressed by Communist authorities, Jewish communities were forcibly reconstructed in the form of ghettos by the Germans, only to be destroyed.[69] In short, the Nazis needed to re-create "the Jews" as a visible entity to fit their anti-Jewish image. Only thus would the imagined enemy become real, ejected from society, and exorcized from the world. This aspect was unequalled in the treatment of other targeted "enemies" and "inferior" groups.

Another immensely important aspect of the Holocaust is the economic persecution of the Jews, a field still in need of research.[70] Instead of viewing expropriation as a *stage* in the escalating process of persecution (as is the case in Hilberg's paradigm), one should understand it as one of the attempts to "remove the Jews."[71] Only thus can one understand why economic persecution was so comprehensive, preceding the Final Solution, and not just a by-product of it, as is the case in other genocides. Moreover, amazing as it may sound given everything known about the "machinery of destruction," the Final Solution never possessed a designated budget! Rather each "participant" was to cover his part financially from his own resources. This led, among other things, to the confiscation of Jewish bank accounts and properties, as well as to bargaining over costs of deportation between the SS and the German railways.[72]

Another aspect of major importance for the understanding of the Holocaust is that it was not solely a German enterprise. Unlike other genocidal patterns, this was not a clash between two entities. The German paradigm was studied by a variety of neighboring peoples and governments. Even in the 1930s it helped radicalize other forms of antisemitism. But probably the outstanding example is Romania. Over three hundred thousand Jews were murdered or starved to death as a result of the Romanian government's initiatives.[73] In most occupied countries meanwhile, state apparatuses willingly contributed to the Nazi project.[74] This was especially so in Western European countries that had recognized Jews as equal citizens since the late eighteenth century.[75] Thus the Dutch Supreme Court in October 1940 did not challenge the German order for the introduction of the "Aryan clause" (i.e., declaring that a person was of pure Aryan descent) into preconditions for serving in the civil service, despite the fact that the Supreme Court's president, Lodewijk E. Visser, was a Jew who was thereby forced to leave his position.[76] This phenomenon was not restricted to state bureaucracies: it encompassed civil organizations and individuals.[77]

The escalation to wholesale murder had the war as its context as the aforementioned scholars have argued. But it was far from a sudden explosion. The war itself was driven by ideology centered on "international Jewry."[78] German bureaucrats and intellectuals, searching for the sources of Jewish vitality, encountered the cultural stereotype of the *Ostjude*. The despised image of the Eastern European Jew developed in the nineteenth century. In the Third Reich's world of images, the *Ostjude* was perceived as the source of Jewish power.[79] Thus, although the invasion of Poland in September 1939 had the apparent political trigger of Danzig, the invasion's higher purpose was greater. The initial conquest of *Lebensraum* signaled an advanced stage of struggle against "the well" of world Jewry. This conviction is expressed in a variety of documents. The Nazis believed that strangling Polish Jewry could dry up American Jewry, which would weaken the threat of the United States.[80] Therefore, the invasion of Poland was a quantum leap in anti-Jewish policies.[81]

If the *Judenpolitik* of the invasion of Poland had meant a war against the demographic and spiritual source of Judaism, then the war against the Soviet

Union, unleashed in June 1941, was destined to be not simply an imperialistic war, but the apocalyptic struggle against the "Jewish idea." The Soviet Union was the bulwark of "Judeo-Bolshevism." Bolshevism was one of the bluntest forms of that Jewish idea, which Hitler openly expressed in his infamous speech on 30 January 1939, which he and others quoted later several times: "Today I will once more be a prophet: If the international Jewish financiers in and outside Europe should succeed in plunging the nations once more into a world war, then the result will not be the bolshevisation of the earth, and thus the victory of the Jews, but the annihilation of the Jewish race in Europe."[82] Both the Soviet state and its carriers, the Jews, had to be eliminated. This stage thus represented a further crystallization of the war against the Jews. Again Hitler laid down a general vision without specifying exactly how it would be achieved, and implementation materialized through the creativity of an enormous legion of helpers.[83] Toward the end of 1941 the European-wide Final Solution crystallized and, as Dan Diner described it, "the disposition for genocide turned retrograde [from the eastern killing fields], and moved westward, in paradoxical reverse to the direction of German expansion."[84] Hitler discussed extending the project beyond Europe, into the Middle East, in his conversation with the Grand Mufti of Jerusalem in November 1941.[85]

This extreme vision was not Hitler's alone. For example, in an academic meeting on *Die Judenfrage* (The Jewish Question) at Jena University in the summer of 1943, the organizer, Professor Theodor Scheffer, stated that "the fact that the Jewish Question has been solved to a large extent in the Reich itself does not mean for us that we finished with it; it is a world question to which this war and its constantly fiercer battles are related."[86] Thus murder was not dependent on the war. Rather the war derived from the "world Jewish Question." Furthermore, in the beginning of August 1941, immediately after Hermann Göring commissioned Reinhard Heydrich to check the feasibility of a *"Gesamtlösing der Judenfrage"* (31 July 1941), Eichmann ordered the Reichsvereinigung der Juden in Deutschland to provide him with statistics of *world* Jewry, including data for every city in the United States and for the different regions in Palestine, such as the Galilee and the Negev.[87]

If the military campaigns of 1939 and 1941 enabled the breaching of existing moral codes, then the mental escalation toward murder can be sensed even before 1939. Göring noted during the well-documented meeting of senior officials on 12 November 1938, two days after *Reichskristallnacht,* that, "We cannot let them die from starvation.... The Jew must have the possibility to buy food or socks." Here Heydrich replied: "We only have to decide, if we want it or not."[88] Heydrich, who belonged to the elite core of the SS, already had a more radical mindset. The context was simply not yet ripe. But the psychology of extermination became a basic element of the many "little" executors of the grand vision. In 1943 a German clerk replied to the request of an extremely disabled Dutch Jewish soldier for exemption from deportation owing to his condition: "A Jew is a Jew," he wrote, "with or without legs, and if we will not win [the war] against the Jews and eliminate them, then they'll eliminate us...."[89]

The Essential Input of Jewish History

Yet the depiction of the Holocaust above is still based on the perspectives of the perpetrators. The specific nature of the Holocaust cannot be fully grasped without integrating detailed insights gained through the perspective of Jewish history. The historical development of the Jews in modern Europe, and how the Nazis imagined that place, has been mentioned. Yet there are other Jewish or Jewish-centered perspectives that are critical, a few of which I mention here because they challenge current interpretations based on paradigms of genocide studies, colonialism, the Bloodlands, and so on.

One concerns the strange Nazi indifference toward Jewish religious life. The first major, countrywide anti-Jewish action after the Nazi rise to power, the 1 April 1933 boycott of Jewish businesses, fell on Sabbath, on which, according to the Jewish religion, Jews are not allowed to work. The Nuremberg Laws of 1935 prohibited intermarriage, to which the *halakhah* (Jewish religious law) is also opposed. Meanwhile, free prayer and other religious and cultural activities in synagogues were allowed to continue in Germany throughout the 1930s and in many occupied countries thereafter. The lack of any official policy toward Jewish religious practice puzzled me years ago.[90] Yet Nazism was simply uninterested in one of the most obvious representations of Judaism. Its own perception of the Jewish spirit was detached from the way Jews perceived their own culture. Nazi antisemitism had diverged from past religious anti-Judaism. Thus the Nazi drive against the Jews simply does not fit that part of Lemkin's definition of genocide that relates to culture and religion.

Another example relates to Jewish self-organization. An example from the field of medicine is illuminating. With the segregation of the Jews in Warsaw shortly after the occupation and the establishment of the Warsaw Ghetto at the end of 1940, a complex Jewish medical and sanitation infrastructure came into being, including hospitals, clinics, outreaching medical services, and medical research. Similar infrastructures emerged in other ghettos and Jewish settings in Germany, the Netherlands, and elsewhere. This happened because Jews had been at the forefront of the medical profession prior to the Nazi era and because they knew how to organize, institute, and maintain such projects. Moreover, antisemitism in general and its Nazi form in particular perceived Jews as anomalous: Jews did not deserve to live, but possessed medical capabilities on which the Nazis could count when separating them from general infrastructures. They let the Jews organize themselves, confident that the Jews would establish infrastructure to cope with medical hardships. Indeed, next to the denigrating view, the Nazis admired Jewish skills. This conundrum is unequaled—in fact, nonexistent—in the annals of other recorded genocides.[91]

A third example is the help and rescue extended to Jews either by gentiles or by Jews themselves within occupied Europe. Given the continental scope of the Final Solution and the fact that only the Jews were targeted in their entirety, there was always "a third actor" in the field—those often called bystanders—who were not part of the anti-Jewish endeavor. In rough terms, they could either join the Nazis, remain uninvolved, or assist Jews. Such assistance might even occur in the "Bloodlands," thus underscoring the difference of the fate of Jews compared with other groups. Jews, for example, could not hide persecuted Communists or resistance fighters. This unique situation served after the Holocaust as the catalyst for the creation of the Yad Vashem Righteous Among the Nations commemorative program.[92] In non-Holocaust genocides, such as the Armenian, there were also rescuers—but not from a third "unaffiliated" group, only from the persecuting group.[93]

To what extent, then, do the recent interpretations of the Holocaust contribute to our understanding of it? My sense is that they seek to "tame" the Holocaust, in part by imposing a rigid pattern based on broader paradigms that ignore its unique details. Yet the Holocaust continues to attract varied scholarly attention precisely because of its extreme dimensions of human behavior. Holocaust scholars can indeed benefit from an array of analytical tools. But tools remain tools: if they become sanctified or fetishized, or are too rigorously imposed on the multifaceted materials of history, they undermine true comprehension.

In the Vilna Ghetto, Abba Kovner and his circle in the HaShomer HaTzair Socialist underground youth movement proclaimed on 1 January 1942 that a comprehensive murder campaign of all European Jews was emerging, not just in the Bloodlands, but throughout Europe.[94] More than one thousand miles away in Amsterdam, my aunt, Dr. Leny Jakobs-Melkman, wrote on 19 October 1942—three months after the beginning of the deportations from the Netherlands—in a letter to a non-Jewish acquaintance that "The Jews are to be eradicated [*uitgeroeid* in Dutch] and it is such foolishness to think that you will be the only one or one of the few who will not be eradicated. And yet you have to believe in that nonsense because it is the only way to keep one's spirits up. The possibility of winning the race against the end of the war seems to become smaller by the day."[95] And so, two ordinary European Jews, descendants of families that had lived for centuries in Europe, at two edges of Europe, east and west, were very much aware that the Jewish fate was essentially different than that of their surrounding, occupied societies. They lacked tangible information about the factual scope of the Nazi enterprise, and they lacked access to Nazi records and the array of Jewish sources that historians can now use. But they clearly sensed then what we as historians should understand now about the very core of the Holocaust in which they found themselves.

Notes

1. Dan Michman, *Holocaust Historiography: A Jewish Perspective. Conceptualizations, Terminology, Approaches and Fundamental Issues* (London, 2003), 335–36; Samuel D. Kassow, *Who Will Write Our History? Emanuel Ringelblum, the Warsaw Ghetto, and the Oyneg Shabes Archive* (Bloomington, IN, 2007), esp. 145–208, 225–83.

2. Chris Lorenz, "Historical Knowledge and Historical Reality: A Plea for Internal Realism," *History and Theory* 33, no. 3 (1994): 297–327.

3. I focus on scholarly research, not the arena of public memory. For a study of the field of memory that discusses this topic, see Daniel Levy and Natan Sznaider, *The Holocaust and Memory in the Global Age* (Philadelphia, 2006).

4. Haya Lipski, "The Term 'SHOAH': Meaning and Modification in the Hebrew Language from Its Beginnings and to This Day in the Israeli Society" (M.A. thesis, Tel Aviv University, 1988); Dalia Ofer, "Linguistic Conceptualization of the Holocaust in Palestine and Israel, 1942-53," *Journal of Contemporary History* 31, no. 3 (1996): 567–95; Dan Michman, "Waren die Juden Nordafrikas im Visier der Planer der 'Endlösung'? Die 'Schoah' und die Zahl 700.000 in Eichmanns Tabelle am 20. Januar 1942," in *Die Wannsee-Konferenz am 20. Januar 1942: Dokumente, Forschungsstand, Kontroverse*, ed. Norbert Kampe and Peter Klein (Cologne, 2013), 379–97.

5. Jon Petrie, "The Secular Word 'HOLOCAUST': Scholarly Sacralization, Twentieth Century Meanings," http://www.berkeleyinternet.com/holocaust/ (accessed 19 March 2014).

6. On this development, see Dan Michman, *Holocaust Historiography*, 338–39.

7. Gerald Green, *Holocaust* (New York, 1978); Hazel Guild, "Germany and the TV *Holocaust*," *Variety*, 23 May 1979; Judith E. Doneson, *The Holocaust in American Film* (Philadelphia, 1987).

8. Claude Lanzmann, *Shoah* (Paris, 1985). For the choice of the term Shoah as the title of the film and for its broad impact, see Claude Lanzmann, *Le Lièvre de Patagonie* (Paris, 2009), ch. 21.

9. For instance, the title chosen in 1981—three years after the screening of *Holocaust*—for the Dutch translation of Frank Rector, *The Nazi Extermination of Homosexuals* (New York, 1981), was *Homo Holocaust* (Amsterdam, 1981); and the subtitle of Radu Ioanid's study *The Holocaust in Romania* reads: *The Destruction of Jews and Gypsies Under the Antonescu Regime, 1940-1944* (Chicago, 2000).

10. Raphael Lemkin, *Axis Rule in Occupied Europe: Laws of Occupation, Analysis of Government, Proposals for Redress* (Washington, DC, 1944). See the works on Lemkin cited in Israel W. Charny, *Encyclopedia of Genocide* (Santa Barbara, 1999); Donald Bloxham and A. Dirk Moses, eds., *The Oxford Handbook of Genocide Studies* (Oxford, 2010), 19–41.

11. Raphael Lemkin, "Les actes constituant un danger general (interétatique) consideres comme delites des droit des gens," October 1933, in Prevent Genocide International, http://www.preventgenocide.org/fr/lemkin/madrid1933.htm (accessed 19 March 2014).

12. See Dan Stone, "Raphael Lemkin on the Holocaust," in *The Origins of Genocide: Raphael Lemkin as a Historian of Mass Violence*, ed. Dominik S.J. Schaller and Jürgen Zimmerer (London 2009), 95–106. Genocide scholar Barbara Harff identified in an initial structural model six principal factors for distinguishing between failed states between 1955 and 1997 that had genocides or "politicides" and those that did not. See Barbara Harff, "No Lessons Learned from the Holocaust? Assessing Risks of Genocide and Political Mass Murder since 1955," *American Political Science Review* 97, no. 1 (2003): 57–73. Harff's list now has over sixty variables in three categories (Harff's presentation at the Holocaust and Genocide Symposium, Israel Academy of Sciences, 2–4 Sep-

tember 2012). Mental aspects, which are hard to measure but still important in historical analyses, are absent from her list.

13. Israel W. Charny, ed., *The Widening Circle of Genocide* (New Brunswick, NJ, 1994); Robert Gellately and Ben Kiernan, eds., *The Specter of Genocide: Mass Murder in Historical Perspective* (New York, 2003); Ben Kiernan, *Blood and Soil: A World History of Genocide and Extermination from Sparta to Darfur* (New Haven, CT, 2007).

14. Martin Shaw, *What is Genocide?* (Cambridge, 2007), 4. Shaw strives for a definition and understanding of genocide through the "structure of the conflict," not through the intentions of the perpetrators. This is a questionable approach from a historical perspective, downplaying intentions as a motivation, since causation is essential in historical explanation. A major problem from a sociological point of view remains that there is no commonly accepted definition of genocide; see http://en.wikipedia.org/wiki/Genocide_definitions (accessed 19 March 2014).

15. Donald Bloxham and A. Dirk Moses, "Editor's Introduction: Changing Themes in the Study of Genocide," in Bloxham and Moses, *Oxford Handbook of Genocide Studies*, 5–12.

16. Christian Gerlach, *Extremely Violent Societies: Mass Violence in the Twentieth-Century World* (New York, 2010).

17. Dan Stone, "Beyond the Auschwitz Syndrome," *Patterns of Prejudice* 44, no. 5 (December 2010): 454–68. Another version of this article is in *History Today* 60, no. 7 (2010)—http://www.historytoday.com, 5, from which the quotes here are taken. An alternative term used is "state-sponsored mass murder." See Meredith Hindley, "Executing the Twentieth Century, H-Net reviews," December, 2004, https://www.h-net.org/reviews/showrev.php?id=10038 (accessed 19 March 2014).

18. Colin Tatz, "Genocide Studies: An Australian Perspective," *Genocide Studies and Prevention* 6, no. 3 (2011): 232.

19. Therefore, the volume of articles published in 2001 in honor of Bauer was titled *The Holocaust: The Unique and the Universal. Essays Presented in Honor of Yehuda Bauer*, ed. Shmuel Almog et al. (Jerusalem, 2001).

20. Yehuda Bauer, "Holocaust Research—A Personal Statement," in *The Holocaust: Voices of Scholars*, ed. Jolanta Ambrosewicz-Jacobs (Krakow, 2009), 23, 25. See also Bauer, "Holocaust and Genocide—Two Concepts or Part of Each Other?" (lecture of 23 April 2009, reported by Raz Segal), *Strassler Center for Holocaust & Genocide Studies at Clark University, 2008-2009 Year End Report*, http://www.clarku.edu/departments/holocaust/PDFs/yearendreports/2009annualreport.pdf (accessed 19 March 2014). Bauer also formulated the *Declaration of the Stockholm International Forum on the Holocaust* (January 2000), where it is stated that, "the unprecedented character of the Holocaust will always hold universal meaning," and that "humanity [is] *still* [my emphasis] scarred by genocide, ethnic cleansing, racism, anti-Semitism and xenophobia." http://archivio.pubblica.istruzione.it/shoah-itfitalia/allegati/stoccolma_en.pdf.

21. Christopher R. Browning, "The Nazi Empire," in Bloxham and Moses, *Oxford Handbook of Genocide Studies*, 420–21. My emphasis.

22. Donald Bloxham, *The Final Solution: A Genocide* (New York, 2009), 1.

23. A. Dirk Moses, "Conceptual Blockages and Definitional Dilemmas in the 'Racial Century': Genocides of Indigenous Peoples and the Holocaust," *Patterns of Prejudice* 36, no. 4 (2002): 18.

24. Bloxham, *Final Solution*, 1. My emphasis.

25. Tatz, "Genocide Studies: An Australian Perspective." Bloxham and Moses, in their introduction to *Oxford Handbook of Genocide Studies*, 3, also point to the fact that "the relationship between study of the Holocaust and study of genocide warrants reflection, because it has been both negative and positive, characterized variously by synergies, processes of self-definition by mutual exclusion, and occasional resentment." The very fact that there are two separate volumes of the *Oxford Handbook* series, one for Holocaust Studies and one for Genocide Studies, is a case in point. See Peter Hayes and John K. Roth, eds., *The Oxford Handbook of Holocaust Studies* (Oxford, 2008).

26. This is clearly demonstrated in the recent debate between the British genocide sociologist Martin Shaw and Brown University Holocaust and genocide historian Omer Bartov. Shaw,

who does not hide his political inclination, states that the fate of the Palestinian Arabs in 1947–48 resulting from their war with the Palestinian Jews (he mistakenly refers to "Israel" before May 1948) should be included in the scope of Genocide Studies. Bartov shows the scholarly deficiencies of this argument. See "The Question of Genocide in Palestine, 1948: An Exchange between Martin Shaw and Omer Bartov," *Journal of Genocide Research* 12, no. 3 (2010): 243–59.

27. For example Richard L. Rubenstein, *After Auschwitz: Radical Theology and Contemporary Judaism* (Indianapolis, IN, 1966).

28. Probably the most extreme scholarly representation of this tendency is Zygmunt Bauman, *Modernity and the Holocaust* (Ithaca, NY, 1989).

29. The origins of the incorrect 4 million number lay with the Soviet Extraordinary State Commission that investigated crimes committed at Auschwitz. See Franciszek Piper, "The Number of Victims," in *Anatomy of the Auschwitz Death Camp*, ed. Yisrael Gutman and Michael Berenbaum (Bloomington, IN, 1994), 61. For more on Auschwitz as an icon see Tim Cole, *Selling the Holocaust. From Auschwitz to Schindler: How History is Bought, Packaged, and Sold* (New York, 1999); Joachim Neander, "The Image of Auschwitz in History Politics," *Holocaust and Modernity* 9, n. 1 (2012): 54–84 [in Russian with English summary].

30. Jürgen Zimmerer, "The First Genocide of the Twentieth Century: The War of Destruction in South-West Africa (1904–1908) and the Global History of Genocide," in *Lessons and Legacies*, vol. 8, *From Generation to Generation,* ed. Doris Bergen (Evanston, IL, 2008), 58. See also Dan Stone, *Histories of the Holocaust* (New York, 2010), 222–42. In my eyes Stone is not critical enough of the "colonial" school of interpretation.

31. Dirk Moses has used the "colonial paradigm" in a different and sophisticated, but to me unconvincing, way. He writes:

> The Holocaust was not a classical case of "colonial genocide," that is, of a colonizer destroying the colonized. Nevertheless, the colonial experience was relevant to the fate of the Jews. German Jews were killed *as colonizers* [Moses's emphasis] who had—in the Nazi imagination—dominated Germany and led it to the brink of extinction. Eastern European Jews had to die because they provided the "breeding ground" for those colonists. Simultaneously, Hitler regarded Germans as a colonizing people. His administrators and soldiers were taught to think of eastern Jews in terms of colonial stereotypes: as dirty, lazy and uncivilized. For that reason they had no place in greater Germany's future.

Dirk A. Moses, "Colonialism," Bloxham and Moses, *Oxford Handbook of Genocide Studies,* 77. First, Eastern European Jews were not viewed as colonizers but as invaders, a stereotype going back to late nineteenth-century antisemitic thought; they "had to die," as I will explain, because of their being viewed as a disease and as the breeding ground for Jewish ideas. Similarly, the images of Eastern European Jews were not shaped by the colonial tradition, but by that of antisemitism traced back to the Middle Ages, emancipation debates, and more. These images, moreover, were not unique to Germany.

32. Mark Mazower, *Hitler's Empire: How the Nazis Ruled Europe* (New York, 2008), 5.

33. Mazower, *Hitler's Empire,* 4.

34. Mazower, *Hitler's Empire,* 368–415; quote from 414.

35. Mazower, *Hitler's Empire,* 12. A similar interpretation is Anton Weiss-Wendt, "Introduction: Toward an Integrated Perspective on the Nazi Policies of Mass Murder," in *Eradicating Differences: The Treatment of Minorities in Nazi-Dominated Europe,* ed. Anton Weiss-Wendt (Newcastle, 2010), 1–22.

36. Timothy Snyder, *Bloodlands: Europe Between Hitler and Stalin* (New York, 2010).

37. Snyder, *Bloodlands,* 380–81.

38. Snyder, *Bloodlands,* 380.

39. Indeed, according to Snyder, "the Germans brought Jews from elsewhere to the bloodlands to be killed." Snyder, *Bloodlands,* viii. Of course, many Jews were also killed outside the

Bloodlands as defined by Snyder. Snyder also ignores the Nazi persecution of Jews in Tunisia and Libya.

40. See most recently Stone, *Histories of the Holocaust,* and Tom Lawson, *Debates on the Holocaust* (Manchester, 2010).

41. Michman, *Holocaust Historiography,* 59–88.

42. "Jewish History" is a well-established field of research. Timothy Snyder misunderstands "Jewish history" as the fate of the Jews as designed by the hands of their persecutors. See his subchapter titled "The Test: *Bloodlands* as Jewish History" in his response to critics: "The Causes of the Holocaust," *Contemporary European History* 21, no. 2 (2012), 149–68.

43. Dan Zhits, "The Jewish People and Jewish History in the National Soviet Conceptualization," *Bulletin of the Arnold and Leona Finkler Institute of Holocaust Research* 8 (Ramat-Gan, 1998), 32–56 [Hebrew]; Benjamin Pinkus, *Russian and Soviet Jews: Annals of a National Minority* (Jerusalem, 1986), 151–82 [Hebrew].

44. Michman, *Holocaust Historiography,* 59–88. Hannah Arendt depicted the Jews in Europe since the mid nineteenth century as being a "non-national element in a world of growing or existing nations." Hannah Arendt, *The Origins of Totalitarianism* (London, 1962), 22. Zygmunt Bauman followed up by saying that "by the very fact of their territorial dispersion and ubiquity, the Jews were an inter-national nation, a non-national nation…. *The Jews were not just unlike any other nation; they were also unlike any other foreigners.*" Bauman, *Modernity and the Holocaust,* 52 [Bauman's emphasis]. For a thorough analysis of European Jewry in the 1930s, see Bernard Wasserstein, *On the Eve: The Jews of Europe before the Second World War* (London, 2012).

45. For instance, Hitler, in his seminal speech of 30 January 1939, on the occasion of the sixth anniversary of his ascendance to power, prophesized about a possible war, to be unleashed by "*das internationale Finanzjudentum.*" For an elaboration on the terms "world Jewry" and "international Jewry," and their contexts and importance, see Jeffrey Herf, *The Jewish Enemy: Nazi Propaganda during World War II and the Holocaust* (Cambridge, MA, 2008). For an example of the usage of this vocabulary see the speech of the *Hauptbefehlsleiter der NSDAP im Generalgouvernement,* Friedrich Schmidt, on 9 March 1942 in Kraków, about an "anti-Jewish war of extermination" (*einem antijüdischen Vernichtungskampf*). The war is a struggle against "Weltjudentum," "Weltmarxismus," "Weltkapitalismus der Plutokraten," and "Weltbolschewismus"; the "Vernichtung Adolf Hitlers und des deutschen Volkes" turned for the "Weltjuden … zu einer Frage des Entweder-Oder geworden" (into an issue of "either-or"); "Aus schöpferischer Gemeinschaft zum Sieg," *Krakauer Zeitung,* 10 March 1942.

46. See Philippe Burrin, "Political Theology: The Relevance of a Concept," *History and Memory* 9, no. 1–2 (1997): 321–49; Michael Burleigh, "National Socialism as a Political Religion," *Totalitarian Movements and Political Religions* 1, no. 2 (2000): 1–26; Uriel Tal, *Religion, Politics and Theology in the Third Reich: Selected Essays* (London, 2004).

47. In *Mein Kampf,* Hitler condensed the myriad of antisemitic ideas into a package. The "Jewish idea" undermined the world of ideas, but "the Jew" undermined humankind. The Jewish presence in person or idea had endless disguises: a capitalist one, a Marxist or Bolshevik one, a liberal, religious, or Zionist one, etc. The war against this creed was therefore of apocalyptic dimensions. In *Mein Kampf,* Hitler expressed the following thoughts:

> The Jewish doctrine of Marxism [the equality of all human beings] rejects the aristocratic principle of Nature and replaces the eternal privilege of power and strength by the mass of numbers and their dead weight. Thus it denies the value of personality in man, contests the significance of nationality and race, and thereby withdraws from humanity the premise of its existence and its culture. As a foundation of the universe, this doctrine would bring about the end of any order intellectually conceivable to man. And as, in this greatest of all recognizable organisms, the result of an application of such a law could only be chaos, on earth it could only be destruction for the inhabitants of this planet.

If, with the help of his Marxist creed, the Jew is victorious over the other peoples of the world, his crown will be the funeral wreath of humanity and this planet will, as it did thousands of years ago, move through the ether devoid of men.

Eternal Nature inexorably avenges the infringement of her commands.

Hence today I believe that I am acting in accordance with the will of the Almighty Creator: *by defending myself against the Jew, I am fighting for the Work of the Lord* [my emphasis].

Adolf Hitler, *Mein Kampf* (Munich, 1925), 60; English translation *Documents on the Holocaust*, ed., Yitzhak Arad et al. (Jerusalem, 1981), 22.

48. Das "verbindende Element für die Querfront aller Gegner des Nationalsozialismus"—quote from his educational essay "Das Judentum als tragendes Element der weltanschaulichen Gegnerfront." See Konrad Kwiet, "Paul Zapp—Vordenker und Vollstrecker der Judenvernichtung," in *Karrieren der Gewalt. Nationalsozialistische Täterbiographien,* ed. Klaus-Michael Mallmann and Gerhard Paul (Darmstadt, 2005), 254–55.

49. Dieter Wisliceny, "Bericht," Bratislava, 18 November 1946, Yad Vashem Archives, M-5/162, 8ff. See Dan Michman, "Täteraussagen und Geschichtswissenschaft: Der Fall Dieter Wisliceny und der Entscheidungsprozess zur 'Endlösung'," in *Deutsche, Juden, Völkermord. Der Holocaust als Geschichte und Gegenwart,* ed. Jürgen Matthäus and Klaus-Michael Mallmann (Darmstadt, 2006), 209–10. On the identification of Jews with the devil in Christian tradition see the still valuable study of Joshua Trachtenberg, *The Devil and the Jews* (New Haven, CT, 1943). On the historical alleged connection between Jews and witchcraft in medieval and early modern Europe see Ronnie Po-Chia Hsia, "Witchcraft, Magic and the Jews in Late Medieval and Early Modern Germany," in *From Witness to Witchcraft: Jews and Judaism in Medieval Christian Thought,* ed. Jeremy Cohen (Wiesbaden, 1996), 419–33.

50. Friedländer makes clear distinction between "persecution" as the earlier phase of Nazi policies, and "extermination" as the later (second) phase; his entire book is divided into two volumes carrying those different terms, and his reasoning is explained in the introduction to *Nazi Germany and the Jews: The Years of Persecution, 1933-1939* (New York, 1997), 1–6. Hitler, he says, "was driven by ideological obsessions that were anything but the calculated devices of a demagogue; that is, he carried a very specific brand of racial anti-Semitism to its most extreme and radical limits. I call that distinctive aspect of his worldview 'redemptive anti-Semitism'; … It was this redemptive dimension, this synthesis of a murderous rage and an 'idealistic' goal, shared by the Nazi leader and the hard core of the party, that led to Hitler's ultimate decision to exterminate the Jews"; "the peculiar frenzy of the Nazi apocalyptic drive against the mortal enemy, the Jew, … give[s] both universal significance and historical distinctiveness to the 'Final Solution of the Jewish Question'" (3–6). Friedländer speaks about an apocalypse, embodied in the Final Solution, which was by itself the radical result of a racial antisemitic ideology focusing on "the Jew" from a racial perspective. Although I agree with him regarding the apocalyptic element, I will try to show in the following that Hitler's and the radical Nazi vision in general went beyond that.

51. Ian Kershaw, *Hitler. 1889-1936: Hubris* (New York, 1999), 125.

52. Eberhard Jäckel, ed., *Hitler. Sämtliche Aufzeichnungen 1905–1924* (Stuttgart, 1980), 89.

53. Arad et al., *Documents of the Holocaust,* 134–35, 162.

54. "Wir wollen nicht am Schluss, weil wir einen Bazillus ausrotten, an dem Bazillus krank werden und sterben" ("We do not want, in the end, because we destroy a Bacillus, to be infected by this Bacillus and to die")—"Rede des Reichsführer-SS bei der SS-Gruppenführertagung in Posen am 4. Oktober 1943," in International Military Tribunal, *Trial of the Major War Criminals before the International Military Tribunal, Nuremberg, 14 November 1945–1 October 1946* (Nuremberg, 1948) [hereafter *TMWC*], vol. 29, Document 1919-PS, 146. English excerpt and translation in Arad et al., *Documents on the Holocaust,* 345.

55. Jewish religious life under the Nazi regime was much less under attack than Jewish

participation in all other spheres of life—administration, culture, economy, etc.; see Michman, *Holocaust Historiography*, 251–69.

56. Another term is "*ausrotten*" (extinguish).

57. On book burning see Werner Treß, *Wider den undeutschen Geist: Bücherverbrennung 1933* (Berlin, 2003).

58. Peter M. Manasse, *Verschleppte Archive und Bibliotheken. Die Tätigkeit des Einsatzstabes Rosenberg während des zweiten Weltkrieges* (St. Ingbert, 1997); Jan Björn Potthast, *Das jüdische Zentralmuseum der SS in Prag: Gegnerforschung und Völkermord im Nationalsozialismus* (Frankfurt, 2002).

59. David Bankier, "Hitler and the Policy-Making Process on the Jewish Question," *Holocaust and Genocide Studies* 3, no. 1 (1988): 1–20.

60. Adolf Hitler, *Mein Kampf* (Munich, 1935), 650–51.

61. Kershaw, *Hubris*, 527–91, esp. 529–31.

62. Wolfram Meyer zu Uptrup, *Kampf gegen die, 'jüdische Weltverschwörung': Propaganda und Antisemitismus der Nationalsozialisten 1919 bis 1945* (Berlin, 2003).

63. Bernard M. Bass discusses transformational leadership in *Leadership and Performance* (New York, 1985).

64. Browning, "The Nazi Empire," 420–21.

65. Michman, *Holocaust Historiography*, 16–20.

66. Carl Schmitt, "Die deutsche Rechtswissenschaft im Kampf gegen den jüdischen Geist: Schlußwort auf der Tagung der Reichsgruppe Hochschullehrer des NSRB vom 3. und 4. Oktober 1936," *Deutsche Juristen-Zeitung* 41 (1936): cols. 1193-99.

67. Thomas Pegelow Kaplan, "Rethinking Nazi Violence: Linguistic Injuries, Physical Brutalities, and Dictatorship Building," unpublished paper at the international conference "Violence and Politics in Germany: Origins and Consequences of Nazism," Bar-Ilan University and Tel Aviv University, 13–14 January 2013.

68. The most meticulous and precise one was probably the one carried out in the Netherlands in January 1941: *Statistiek der Bevolking van Joodschen Bloede in Nederland* (Gravenhage, 1942).

69. Dan Michman, *The Emergence of Jewish Ghettos During the Holocaust* (New York, 2011), 102–21.

70. An important conference, "Spoliés! Aryanization and the Spoliation of Jews in Nazi Europe (1933-1945)," on 1–3 June 2010 in Grenoble, France, attempted to find a broad and integrative view of the economic persecutions of the Jews by Nazi Germany and its allies; the proceedings have not yet been published. Significant contributions to the understanding of the economic aspects involved in the persecution of the Jews have been provided by Adam Tooze, *The Wages of Destruction: The Making and Breaking of the Nazi Economy* (London, 2006).

71. At the opening of the infamous meeting of Nazi senior officials on 12 November 1938, Göring stated that "das Problem in der Hauptsache ein umfangreiches wirtschaftliches Problem ist" ("the problem is in the main a large-scale economic matter"); Stenographische Niederschrift der Sitzung im Reichsluftfahrtministerium am 12. Nov. 1938, Doc. 1816-PS, in *TMWC*, vol. 28, 499. For important ideological and practical aspects of the ejection of the Jewish influence from the economy (in German discourse of the time called *Entjudung*), see Avraham Barkai, *From Boycott to Annihilation: The Economic Struggle of German Jews 1933-1943* (Hanover, NH, 1989); Hans-Christian Petersen, "Judenbild und Wirtschaftsleben: Über Nationalökonomen im 'Dritten Reich'," in *Kapitalismusdebatten um 1900: Über antisemitisierende Semantiken des Jüdischen*, ed. Nicolas Berg (Leipzig, 2011), 85–109.

72. Raul Hilberg, *Sonderzüge nach Auschwitz. Dokumente zur Eisenbahngeschichte* (Mainz, 1981).

73. Jean Ancel, *The History of the Holocaust in Romania* (Lincoln, NE, 2011); Simon Geissbühler, *Blütiger Juli. Rumäniens Vernichtungskrieg und der vergessene Massenmord an den Juden 1941* (Paderborn, 2013).

74. A desideratum in Holocaust historiography is a comprehensive and integrated study of the European-wide involvement of state bureaucracies in this enterprise. Some insight regarding

one country, France, can be gained from the recent publication "L'antisémitisme français sous l'Occupation," *La Revue d'Histoire de la Shoah,* no. 198 (March 2013).

75. A thorough comparative view of this aspect is included in Pim Griffioen and Ron Zeller, *Jodenvervolging in Nederland, Frankrijk en België. Overeenkomsten, verschillen, oorzaken* (Amsterdam, 2011). For the case of Belgium see also Bob Moore, *Victims and Survivors: The Nazi Persecution of the Jews in the Netherlands 1940-1945* (London, 1997), 57; Rudi van Doorslaer et al., eds., *Gewillig België. Overheid en Jodevervolging tijdens de Tweede Wereldoorlog* (Antwerp, 2007).

76. Lou de Jong, *Het Koninkrijk der Nederlanden in de Tweede Wereldoorlog,* vol. 4b (Gravenhage, 1972), 764–65;

77. This is an enormous phenomenon. For a sense of it in places far away from each other—Poland and France—see Jan Gross, *Neighbors: The Destruction of the Jewish Community in Jedwabne, Poland* (Princeton, 2001); Tal Bruttmann, *La logique des bourreaux, 1943-1944* (Paris, 2003); Jan Grabowski, *Hunt for the Jews: Betrayal and Murder in German-Occupied Poland* (Bloomington, IN, 2013).

78. Gerhard L. Weinberg, "Two Separate Issues? Historiography of World War II and the Holocaust," in *Holocaust Historiography in Context: Emergence, Challenges, Polemics and Achievements,* ed. Dan Michman and David Bankier (Jerusalem, 2008), 379–401.

79. Michman, *Emergence of Jewish Ghettos,* 45–89.

80. An October 1940 directive banning Jewish emigration from the General Government, quoted in a memorandum of Eckart, dated 23 November 1940 and addressed to the district governors in the General Government, explained that "The continued emigration of Jews from Eastern Europe [to the West] spells a continued spiritual regeneration of world Jewry, as it is mainly the Eastern Jews who supply a large proportion of the rabbis, Talmud teachers, etc., owing to their Orthodox-religious beliefs, and they are urgently needed by Jewish organizations active in the United States, according to their own statements. Further, every Orthodox Jew from Eastern Europe spells a valuable addition for these Jewish organizations in the United States in their constant efforts for the spiritual renewal of United States Jewry and its unification. It is United States Jewry in particular, which is endeavoring, with the help of newly immigrated Jews, especially from Eastern Europe, to create a new basis from which it intends to force ahead its struggle, particularly against Germany." English translation in Arad et al., *Documents on the Holocaust,* 219.

81. See Dan Michman, "Why Did Heydrich Write the *Schnellbrief?* A Remark on the Reason and on its Significance," *Yad Vashem Studies* 32 (2004): 433–47; Jochen Böhler, *Auftakt zum Vernichtungskrieg: Die Wehrmacht in Polen* (Frankfurt, 2006).

82. English translation in Arad et al., *Documents on the Holocaust,* 134–35.

83. This aspect is by now well established by an enormous body of research carried out since the downfall of communism in Eastern Europe; first and foremost see Christopher R. Browning (with Jürgen Matthäus), *The Origins of the Final Solution* (Lincoln, NE, 2004), 213–423; Peter Longerich, *Holocaust: The Nazi Persecution and Murder of the Jews,* trans. Susan Whiteside (Oxford, 2010), 179–255.

84. Dan Diner, "The Irreconcilability of an Event: Integrating the Holocaust into the Narrative of the Century," in *Remembering the Holocaust in Germany, 1945-2000: German Strategies and Jewish Responses,* ed. Dan Michman (New York, 2002), 103.

85. Browning, *Origins of the Final Solution,* 406. There are two versions of the meeting between Hitler and Amin al-Husseini. Browning quotes one, the other is to be found in David Yisraeli, *The German Reich and Palestine* (Ramat-Gan, 1974), 308–11 [Hebrew]. For a discussion of the dynamics of the evolution of the scope of the Final Solution beyond Europe, see also Michman, "Waren die Juden Nordafrikas im Visier der Planer der 'Endlösung'?"

86. Uwe Hoßfeld et al., eds., *Kämpferische Wissenschaft. Studien zur Universität Jena im Nationalsozialismus* (Cologne, 2003), 530–31.

87. See Michman, "Waren die Juden Nordafrikas im Visier der Planungen zur 'Endlösung'?"

88. *TMWC,* Doc. 1816-P, vol. 27, 535.

89. "Jud ist Jud, ob mit, oder ohne Beine, und wenn wir den Juden nicht besiegen u. ausschalten, dann schaltet er uns aus." document reprinted in René Pottkamp, "'Jud ist Jud'," in *Uit de Kelders van het NIOD,* ed. David Barnouw et al. (Amsterdam, 2012), 58–59.

90. Michman, *Holocaust Historiography,* 263.

91. Miriam Offer, "The Medical Services in the Warsaw Ghetto During the Holocaust: Its Organization and its Medical and Ethical Challenges in Historical Context" (Ph.D. diss., Bar-Ilan University, 2009) [Hebrew], esp. 345–50.

92. On the close relations that could evolve between rescuers during the Holocaust and Jews, see Daphna Ben-Yosef, "Rescuers and Survivors—The Second Phase: Romantic Relationship between non-Jewish Rescuers and Holocaust Survivors after World War II" (Ph.D. diss., Bar-Ilan University, 2011) [Hebrew].

93. Yair Auron brings an example of a Turk who rescued Armenians, and calls him a Righteous Among the Nations. Yet the Yad Vashem category explicitly uses the term Nations in plural. The rescuer whom Auron mentions should be called a "righteous Turk." Similar cases, where people of the persecuting group help people of the persecuted group, obviously happened in other cases of genocide too. See Yair Auron, *Genocide: In Order Not to Be Among the Silent* (Tel Aviv, 2010) [Hebrew], 121–23.

94. Dina Porat, *Beyond the Reaches of Our Souls: The Life and Times of Abba Kovner* (Tel Aviv, 2000) [Hebrew], 80–102, esp. 91.

95. Hans Ziekenoppasser, "Een Stem uit het Verleden," *Nieuw Israëlitisch Weekblad* 27, 6 April 2012, 69–70.

CHAPTER 2

The Holocaust as a Regional History
Explaining the Bloodlands

TIMOTHY SNYDER

In early spring 1933, as the weather warmed and the soil softened, a Ukrainian man dug his own grave. By this time about 2 million inhabitants of Soviet Ukraine had already died of starvation in Joseph Stalin's deliberate campaign of hunger. The man hoped to maintain his individual dignity. The bodies of those starved to death in Soviet Ukraine in early 1933 would be found later in a field or by the road. Each corpse would be thrown into the back of one of the carts that came every week or so. Then the body would be buried in mass graves along with many people unknown to the deceased, and in some place where his or her family, if there were any surviving family members, would never be able to find it. So he dug his own grave.

In April 1940 a Polish army officer, like many other officers in the Polish army, kept a diary. Most Polish officers during the war were reservists—people with a university education, who, by definition, were called up in 1939. This was an age of letters, and educated people kept diaries. The second to last entry of this officer's diary reads: "They asked for my wedding ring which I…" and then it trails off. It does not trail off, I believe, because the officer found it difficult to talk about his wife. Nor does it trail off because the symbol of the wedding ring meant so much to the officer. He was at a place called Katyn, and he rightly suspected that he would soon be executed. He probably knew that the Soviet NKVD officers, in whose custody he was, were asking for his valuables preparatory to killing him. So, his diary entry ends most likely because he hid his wedding ring so they would not find it. Almost certainly they did. But his diary was also found on his body after it was exhumed a couple of years later and we have it.

Notes for this section begin on page 50.

In September 1942, the surviving Jews of Kovel, a town now in Western Ukraine, were locked inside the synagogue. At the time Kovel was in German-occupied eastern Poland. It was late enough in the events that we call the Holocaust that Kovel's Jews knew what would soon befall them. They would be taken out and shot. And so, locked in their synagogue, they left messages with bits of porcelain or with glass or with stones, scratching messages on the walls. One young woman, speaking for herself and her two sisters, left a message for her mother. It said, "We are so sorry you could not be here with us." This sentiment might seem strange under the circumstances, but it conveys something fundamental about the Holocaust that we forget: people tended to want to be with their families. The last line reads: "we kiss you over and over." When the Soviets drove the Germans from Kovel, in 1944, a Soviet officer found and recorded these words in the synagogue. The Soviets used the Kovel synagogue as a grain silo thereafter.[1]

These were three of about 14 million people who were murdered as a matter of Nazi or Soviet policy in the years 1933 to 1945 in the region that I call the Bloodlands.[2] In the past generation, the study of the fate of the people who lived in these lands—today's Poland, Ukraine, Belarus, western Russia, and the Baltic states—has taken a decided turn toward the local. We have no national histories of the Holocaust in most of these countries, and my book was the first to discuss the Holocaust on the lands where it took place. It arose, from among many other impulses, the conviction that we must, I believe, consider the regional history of mass killing even as we make the move to examine mass killing on the more local level. My specific concern in our consideration of the history of mass killing, and specifically of the Holocaust, is that we have imported the preoccupations of now-unfashionable macrohistories into the now-fashionable microhistories, without first adequately applying what we must come to learn about the middle level, the meso-level, the region, the zone where the global and the local factors meet.

A region is not always what we think. Usually we consider regions according to groups of provinces, or states, or empires, or perhaps if we are very adventurous, as zones on the border of two empires. But if our subject is mass killing, we should define a region as where mass killing took place. The "Bloodlands" are a fairly significant area, but compared to all of the territory that the Germans and the Soviets ruled from 1940 to 1942—territory stretching from France to Siberia, they are actually quite small and compact. Nevertheless, the vast majority of German and Soviet killing happened precisely here. In the entire stretch of territory controlled by one regime or the other, some 17 million people were deliberately killed by the two regimes between 1933 and 1945. But of that 17 million, 14 million died in the Bloodlands region. We need to understand this region in order to understand the victims and the regimes that killed them.

There must be something about this place, it would seem, or something about events that happened in this place, that made it distinctive. Three seemingly distinct conceptual geographies return us to the same place. The first I have already stressed: 14 million people in all, an astonishing number, died here. Second, this is where the entirety of the Holocaust took place.[3] Most Jews killed here lived here because this territory was, once, the world homeland of the Jews. We tend to think of Jewish history in an unterritorial way, but there was indeed a place, here, where more Jews lived than in any other. Finally, the Bloodlands were where German and Soviet power overlapped. Both regimes were present. There were many places where the Nazis ruled and Soviet power did not extend: most of Germany itself, France, the Low Countries, and so on. Meanwhile, most of the Soviet Union was never touched by German power. Places that were touched only by German or Soviet power were difficult, desperate places, but they were not nearly so dangerous for Jews and for everyone else as the places where both of these states were present. We thus face three necessarily related questions: why did the Holocaust happen? Why were so many non-Jews killed in the same places where the Holocaust happened? And why did this killing happen on lands that were touched by both Nazi and Soviet power?

The introductory claims have been simple matters of chronology, geography, and arithmetic, none of which is the least bit controversial or contested. But if Christopher Browning is correct, and he is, that this was the greatest moral and demographic catastrophe in the history of Europe, why has it never been seen in this way? Why have we not noticed? On the lands where about 5.4 million Jews were deliberately killed in the Holocaust, during the years when Hitler was in power more than 8 million people who were not Jews were also killed as a matter of deliberate policy. Even if all one studies is the Holocaust, one must still explain why there were so many other bodies, so to speak, lying about. It has taken a lot of methodological trouble to ignore those bodies: the 5 million victims of German policies of starvation and German "reprisals," as well as the 4 million victims of Soviet policies of starvation and Soviet terror. It is a trend that must be undone in the name of common sense and historical explanation, and not least in the name of respect to everyone concerned. But there is also work that must be done before we can seriously consider performing microhistories throughout the region.

Imagine a crime scene in an apartment building. Five people, clearly all belonging to one family, have all been murdered. Another five people, who do not seem to belong to the same family, also seem to have been murdered by the same person. Still another four people, not belonging to the same family but apparently killed by someone else, are also in the apartment building. A police officer filing a report would presumably mention all of the murders and would presume that there was some relationship between all of the killings. There are powerful reasons why we do not see the history of the Bloodlands in this way. First, we understand history nationally, as the history of the Jews or the Poles or the Ukrainians or the Russians or the Germans, and we also use the language of our one group as though it held all the lessons to their history. Each national history casts its own villains and heroes. If we push national histories together, they repel each other. Nor can we simply drop a book of Polish history on top of a book of Jewish history on top of a book of German history and Ukrainian history and get a history of Eastern Europe. Each national history operated according to its own logic. One of the problems with microhistory, as it is often written now, is that it simply replicates the problems and the assumptions of national history rather than confronting them.

Given the way that the world is still structured, with national states and national educational systems and national memory ministries and so on, a national way of understanding these events prevails in a seemingly natural and straightforward, but ultimately unhelpful, way. I say "ultimately unhelpful" because it cannot answer key questions. National history is very good at asking questions that it cannot answer, at bringing us to doorways through which we then must pass on our own, without its assistance. Consider the elemental questions: why were the victims the victims? Why were we the perpetrators the perpetrators? Why did others stand by and do nothing? National history asks these morally urgent questions, but it cannot provide answers because the answers transcend national narratives. We do not like to think about the problem in this way. Nations, we think, have sovereign histories. This is the very traditional assumption that slips through from macro- to microhistories.[4]

The other difficulty in studying regional history lies in the bipolarity of modern mass politics. The tendency since the French Revolution, strengthened by the experience of fascism and anti-fascism, is to apprehend politics in terms of left and right. We tend to understand the Soviet Union and Nazi Germany in these terms, as if the essence of the regimes themselves had little contact with one another. If we were only interested in ideas, it would be plausible, though perhaps not advisable, to write a book about National Socialism and not mention the Soviet Union or vice versa. However, if the subject is the Holocaust or ethnic cleansing or mass killing in the most afflicted part of Europe, we cannot keep the USSR and Nazi Germany apart. These two regimes, different as they were in terms of ideas and systems, had territory in common. In the Bloodlands, the places both regimes ruled, everyone made contact with both systems. Everyone who lived in this territory, so long as they lived, compared these two systems because they had to. As historians, we have the luxury of separating the two systems as if they did not overlap geographically. To do so falls within our comfort zones of national narratives and left-right politics. But history is fundamentally uncomfortable. Although the Germans now lead the way in Holocaust history, we cannot count on this problem being solved in

Germany. In Germany, national and the political problems profoundly reinforce each other, which means that politically careful public discourse and historically valuable scholarship keep their distance one from the other. It seems safest to write national history, because it seems necessary to preserve the peculiarities of German history, a negative *Sonderweg*.[5]

How might we undo this trend and write a history that has a chance of truly describing and explaining these terrible events? What might a truly regional history look like? What is the preparation that is truly necessary before we make the move to microhistory? Any sound interpretation of events of such scale must work as global history, rather than simply against national and ideological histories. I have tried to avoid national exceptionalism in my work, not because nationalism is unimportant, but because I have sought that larger framework. National history stops at the point where it cannot answer its own questions, and pretends that this is the end of history; we must go further. *Bloodlands,* although very much about Jews, Poles, Lithuanians, Ukrainians, and Russians, does not start from Jewish, Polish, Lithuanian, Ukrainian, or Russian history. This may seem like a simple point, but in fact it is not.

If we proceed from the question as to why 14 million people were killed in the region, we begin from a very different point than traditional Jewish history narratives do. If we were to start from Jewish narratives, we might ask what the Holocaust has in common with the Khmelnitsky Uprising or the history of pogroms. If we start from the framework of Polish history, we would ask what Katyn has in common with the failed Polish uprisings of the nineteenth century. And histories of national suffering do not take us very far.[6] The sweep of Ukrainian history cannot explain why 3 million Ukrainians were deliberately starved in 1933. The same point can be made about perpetrators. A German history that plots a course of teleological murder works just as poorly, though events from 1933 to 1939 remain important in explaining the German turn to murder.

I suggest that we proceed from the lives and deaths of everyone who was in the region. These regional experiences, much more than our conventional national paradigms, prepare us more properly for microhistorical approaches. There was a larger calamity of which the Holocaust was the worst and distinct part, and we must explain all the parts on the basis of Jewish and non-Jewish experiences. These experiences will attune us to the German and Soviet (and other) policies that we must account for. If we think back to the apartment house with the imaginary crime victims, such an approach is simply intuitive. If we know that the Holocaust happened in the time and place where so many other people died, the way that those people died, why they died, might have something to do with why so many Jews died. At the very least, we must be sure we understand these experiences before we seek to write microhistory. Otherwise we run the risk of attributing national motivations to others simply because we are ignorant of the crucial structures of experience, or of misunderstanding national motivations when they are indeed the relevant ones.

In other words, we can think of regional history as the necessary intellectual exercise that prepares us for microhistory. It can help us see that the mental habits that national and ideological history permit are not really acceptable in the history of atrocity. One of these mental habits is that of dialectics. There are at least three such exercises that have clouded our understanding of these events. The first is a Soviet apologist dialectic, which reads: "Granted, the Soviet authorities killed millions of civilians in the 1930s. But the Red Army won the Second World War." This is a logical non sequitur. But the deeper problem of method is this: we simply cannot explain why something happened in 1933 by referring to events in 1945. The second is the Nazi apologist dialectic, which borrows from Ernst Nolte's notion that the Nazis, in comparison with the Soviets, were not so bad after all.[7] The Nazi and Communist systems were not in some sort of fatal Hegelian relationship. They were distinct political orders animated by very different leaders with very different ideas. They sometimes competed, sometimes cooperated, and sometimes interacted. Just when and how they interacted is an empirical question, not one to be resolved by intuitions developed by dialectical thinking and in more or less complete ignorance, in Nolte's case, of the history of Eastern Europe and the Soviet Union. But it is one that we must resolve before we undertake serious microhistory, since the localities touched by the Holocaust were generally also touched by Soviet power, but cannot themselves provide the sources we need to see the larger patterns.

A third dialectic is that of decadent liberalism, that of our own moment, fairly common among historians of Germany writing in English. This is the notion that, since the Soviets and the Germans were so different, somehow they met in the middle of Europe and cancelled each other out. The visual image of this dialectical myth is the Red Army's liberation of Auschwitz, which somehow is supposed to allow us to think that the two regimes were not in contact with each other, or were each other's dialectical opposites. Indeed, the Red Army liberated Auschwitz—after waiting about an hour's drive away for several months while the Nazis gassed the Hungarian Jews already in Auschwitz and the Jews of the Łódź Ghetto, Theresienstadt, and Slovakia who were deported there while the Red Army waited. The Soviets had no policy to rescue Jews, and their Polish Communist clients set about memorializing Auschwitz (once they had ceased using it as a camp) as a site of universal (not Jewish) suffering.

The reason, I think, why we find this last dialect comforting is that it would allow us to proceed with microhistory just on the basis of what we think we know about German history. If the German national narrative is a sufficient explanation of the Holocaust, then all we need to do is export familiar actors, motivations, and concepts to places beyond Germany. Or, in an even more deplorable error, we can use only German language sources as we try to ascertain what happened in these localities, thereby risking that Nazi colonial thinking shapes our own analysis. Far from undoing the consequences of previous occupations, later occupations exacerbated them. Understanding the Holocaust means understanding that Jewish survival rates were lowest in zones of multiple occupation.

I emphasize regional history as method, but not to the exclusion of ideas. Ideas, Nazi or Stalinist, are a standard explanation of mass killing. But ideas do not kill anyone on their own. If East European antisemitism killed just by virtue of being East European antisemitism, there would be no Jewish history. Alone, it cannot explain the Holocaust any more than air alone can explain a tornado. Ideas, to be lethal, must be incorporated by institutions. In the case of the Holocaust an antisemitic state made war on its neighbors, where Jews lived, and destroyed the states where Jews had been citizens. The Holocaust took place in a kind of stateless zone. Collaboration, in the sense of cooperation with policies of killing that come from the outside, simply cannot be explained by ideology alone, not because there was so little collaboration, but because there was so much. Collaboration only makes sense if we can answer the question: "collaboration with what?" Almost no one aspires to become a collaborator. Collaboration can only happen when a foreign power animated by a certain ideology becomes present. If it happened here, many of us would collaborate because that is what people tend to do. So, the question of collaboration must also begin with the question of the meaning of the destruction of prewar institutions by Soviet or Nazi power, and then ask which institutions, animated by which ideology, are present in the region at the crucial moments.

If we wish to make a plausible connection between ideas and actions, we must also grasp how these institutions, Soviet or Nazi, understood time. One way in which Stalinism and Nazism differed was the manner by which they understood the past and the future. For Soviets in the Stalinist era, the revolution that mattered was that of 1917. It was in the past. Stalin viewed himself—while industrializing, collectivizing, controlling land, and in carrying out policies of terror—as securing socialism in one country. All of the Soviet killing occurred in the decade before the war, and almost all of it was within Soviet borders. For Hitler, revolution meant something different. It could only happen in the future, and during war. Hitler, Himmler, Heydrich, and the rest understood that the only way they could transform society the way they wanted to was through war.

German historians have indeed led the way in seeing that both ideologies had economic components. Each—when we scrape away the ideological expression on which we tend to focus, also contained projects for global transformation that in practice had a certain regional emphasis. National Socialism centered on racial war in which the Jews were to be eliminated, but it also looked to the economic project of colonizing much of Eastern Europe. It sought to balance the industrial modernity in Germany with pastoral peaceful countryside from which the Germans could remove everyone else and purify themselves.[8] Soviet ideology was one of class war, but Stalinist class war had a desired endpoint: a Socialist, industrialized society in which the state took control of agriculture and use it to modernize. Control of the countryside and the peasants meant control of agricultural profits to finance industry. While Nazism envisioned an anti-modern bucolic utopia, Soviet ideology sought to modernize a backward country. Both ideologies also set their regional aims within a global vision. The Nazis imagined a true global war to be won against the British and the Americans, and a world in which all Jews would be eliminated or be under their control. The Soviets too had a global view. Their revolution, they thought, came early, but other revolutions would eventually follow in a world revolution. In the meantime, they aimed to collectivize agriculture while industrializing. These two sets of visions, which we tend to compartmentalize intellectually, intersected in a place, above all in Ukraine. And though we as historians tend to separate ideas, the people who matter in this story had no such luxury. Thus Jews from Ukraine, when asked to recount their lives as Holocaust testimony, very often begin by discussing the deliberate Soviet famine of 1933. Ukrainians, meanwhile, remember being starved by both regimes.

Thus the region faced two very different, but fantastically ambitious, neo-colonial projects. It is not surprising that so many died here. Nor is it surprising, given that both ideologies fixated on fertile soil, that the primary method of mass murder in the 1930s and 1940s was starvation. The two regimes could cooperate on one important matter: the destruction of independent Poland. From the point of view of both Moscow and Berlin, Polish statehood was awkward and paved the way for the Soviet-German alliance in 1939. But Hitler and Stalin could not agree about Ukraine. For Germany, Ukraine was the breadbasket needed to balance industry. For the Soviets, Ukraine was the breadbasket needed to build industry. The purposes and the ideologies were different, as were the visions. But the land is the same and only one regime could control it.

What did it all mean for the Jews? Two major preconditions were met for a Holocaust to take place, and a regional approach helps us to see them both. The first was Nazism's special enmity to the Jews, in which all German failures were the Jews' doing. Nazi antisemitism also touched—and this is the second precondition—the lands where Jews lived. Nazi antisemitic ideas alone could not have brought about a Holocaust; only one-quarter of one percent of Germany's population was Jewish in 1939. When the Holocaust eventually occurred, 97 percent of its victims were people who did not know the German language and who lived beyond Central and Western Europe. The Jews were predominantly an Eastern European people. There were not very many Jews in Western Europe; even if all of them had been killed—including those rescued in Denmark—these calculations would be essentially the same. Jews were killed en masse in the places where they lived in high numbers. To understand how it could happen, we must understand the special German enmity toward Jews, but also why there was such a conflict in the world homeland of the Jews.

This is an argument that is not explicitly in *Bloodlands,* but it helps to explain, I think, why the book works as regional history. The book goes through each of these killing policies in turn, beginning with the famine in Soviet Ukraine and the two policies of the Great Terror in the Soviet Union, namely, the mass murder of politically suspect peasants and the mass murder of politically suspect ethnic minorities. The 1939 Nazi-Soviet alliance is especially important because it moved Soviet power westward, allowing the Soviet Union to incorporate eastern Poland and the Baltics. German power here became truly murderous. With the invasion of Poland, the Einsatzgruppen went into action. World War II, meanwhile, might have begun in some other way, but the fact that it began with the Nazi-Soviet alliance was very telling and important, not just for the non-Jewish nations in whose national histories it looms large, while usually being completely absent in histories of the Holocaust.

Poles, Lithuanians, Latvians, and Estonians all especially want us to remember the Nazi-Soviet alliance because it destroyed their states. Ironically, though, the destruction of these states mattered more for the Jews than for anyone else. In general terms, and here Hannah Arendt was absolutely right, the fate of the Jews in World War II rose and fell with the nation-states.[9] A Jew's chance of survival depended on the degree and character of state destruction. The Holocaust began where the state was twice destroyed, first by the Soviet Union and then by Nazi Germany. But we can extend this point. Jews in parts of Europe where state institutions were removed or displaced had a one in twenty chance of survival. Jews in places where state institutions remained, even if that state was a Nazi ally—Romania, Italy, Hungary, Bulgaria—and even if that state was Nazi Germany itself, had a one in two chance of survival. A 50 percent survival rate is horrible and worse than the survival chances of any other national group in World War II. But it is hugely better than 5 percent. Given the centrality of the state to political thought in general and Jewish political thought in particular, it is surprising how little attention we pay to the destruction of states in 1939 and after. I fear that it is one of many ways that our view of mass killing has been, so to speak, "Nazified." We see only Eastern European ethnicities, rarely Eastern European institutions. One of the dangers of microhistory is that it allows us to overlook prewar institutions, whose destruction (and sometimes perversion) was a crucial part of the history of the Holocaust.

I try also to explain how the Holocaust occured in regional terms. The Nazis believed from the beginning that the Jews had to be eliminated from Europe. But how were the Nazis to do this? At first they considered deportation, imagining the General Government as a dumping ground. This was not very satisfactory. They turned next to Madagascar, off the southeast African coast, which seemed plausible after the defeat of France. But a maritime deportation required British acquiescence, which was not forthcoming. Another idea was to deport the Jews to their Soviet ally; Eichmann contacted Moscow and asked the Soviets to take 2 million Jews. The answer, unsurprisingly, was negative. Finally, the project centered on driving the Jews eastward with the invasion of the Soviet Union. This idea was a fourth iteration of the Final Solution.

When the Germans invaded the Soviet Union in June 1941, they realized the limitations of their own ambitions, thus escalating and accelerating the Final Solution, now the murder of Jews, as the war continued. The Germans initially thought they would destroy the Red Army and the Soviet state in nine weeks, starve 30 million Soviet citizens in the first winter, begin a general colonization policy in which they would starve and move tens of millions more people and, as I already said, resolve the Jewish problem. But the Red Army resisted, the Soviet state did not collapse, and the Germans could not starve people to the extent they had hoped—though they starved very large numbers. The Jews, meanwhile, were supposedly responsible for every defeat and identified with the Soviet state besides. They were killed in large numbers for the first time when the invasion began and then again as the offensive renewed in the autumn. At some point between the fall of 1941 and the spring of 1942, Hitler communicated the policy that Jews, wherever they lived, were to be killed. This was the fifth iteration of the Final Solution—what we call the Holocaust.

Regional history brings some air into the Hitlerian vacuum. It helps us to understand the progression of the Holocaust where written orders are scarce. The Baltics are especially important, particularly Lithuania and Latvia. But what happened there only makes sense if we have the whole region in view. The Holocaust in the sense of the mass murder of Jews began in Lithuania for several reasons. The German army's failure to take Leningrad was one factor. Another was Lithuanian collaboration enabled by the prior Soviet destruction of the Lithuanian state. The Germans, seen as liberators, could pick and choose among Lithuania's troubled and decimated political class. Many Lithuanians who had in fact collaborated with Soviet power collaborated with the Germans to cleanse themselves of having done so. Double occupation meant double collaboration.[10]

What is, and what is not, regional history? The approach, although it may permit comparisons, is not simply a comparative approach. We do not yet know all we need to know about either the Nazis or the Soviets. One of the most important aspects of each regime was the design of each on Eastern Europe and the way the two regimes encountered each other there. So my approach is more about overlap and interaction than comparison. I think that we have a lot of work to do before we can make meaningful comparisons. But if we do not allow ourselves to compare, we are in no position to say anything of interest or persuasive about the Holocaust or about any of these crimes.

After all, if one claims that the Holocaust was worse than any other atrocity, one makes a comparison. It would be best if it were an informed one. Very often it is not. So while my own approach is not chiefly comparative, it is also clear that the taboo on historical comparisons to the Holocaust makes serious historical work in this field impossible. We cannot, after all, police our own minds. If we know that the Soviets carried out policies of ethnic mass killing before the Nazis, we have made a comparison willing or not. If we know that the Soviet Gulag system had over a million people in 1939 and German concentration camps in that year had about twenty thousand, we have also made a comparison. And the problem further resides within the sources themselves. Anyone who has spent time with Holocaust survivor testimonies knows that Jews compared power systems in Eastern Europe, just like everybody else who lived through one and anticipated another. If one remembered Soviet rule, one also had every reason to wonder what it would be like when the Germans came and to plan accordingly. Responses ranged from fleeing to building bunkers to making friends with local notables. Comparison thus runs through the sources as an inherent part of the history. We should not prevent comparisons that people in that time and place could not. To place a taboo upon comparison is to deny the lived experience of almost all of the victims and survivors of the Holocaust.

The hesitation about comparison concerns the fear of minimizing one experience by bringing in another. But this problem works in multiple ways. Many critics say that my book minimizes Stalinism, because I make Stalinism seem rational and because I lower the estimate of those killed by the Stalinist system.[11] The Holocaust, of course is another matter. Historians of the Holocaust have argued that, though Stalinism killed more people in aggregate, the Holocaust remains distinct as the only attempt to exterminate an entire population.[12] Yet in fact the Soviets did not kill more people than the Germans. And within the Bloodlands, the Holocaust alone killed more people than all Soviet policies of mass killing put together. Here the Holocaust was not only qualitatively but quantitatively worse. And it is regional history that permits us to see this. It is the most radical defense of the unprecedented character of the Holocaust, precisely because it considers all of the policies of mass killing. Transnational history allows for firmer conclusions than national history, and regional history delivers findings that we need as we shift from the macrohistorical to the microhistorical level.

The macrohistorical level is in some sense more important, since killing was a result of policy. The micro level indeed allows us to apprehend experience in part. But we cannot apprehend experience fully if we do not know what the victims knew, if our methods prevent us from seeing what was most important to them, if we do not understand the full setting. I hope that my approach places the victims at the center of the story more clearly: lost neither in the heights of the history of decision making, nor in the haze of local history without broader context.

History as a humanity must recognize that numbers are not just quantitative but qualitative. Large numbers are made up of small numbers—units of one where the one is not just a generic person or a generic Jew. That individuality, which we have to remember, also has to count. The difference between zero and one, in other words, is a kind of infinity and it is our job to recall that infinity over and over again because if we cannot and we do not have the sense for what was lost then we have not done our work as humanists. So in that spirit I name the people I mentioned at the beginning, because of course each of the 14 million people murdered had a name. The Ukrainian who dug his own grave, his name was Petro Veldii. The Pole who kept a diary was Adam Solski. And the young Jewish woman who scratched a note to her mother on the wall of the Kovel synagogue a few hours before she was shot was Dobcia Kagan.

Notes

1. For the primary sources see Timothy Snyder, *Bloodlands: Europe Between Hitler and Stalin* (New York, 2010). I begin with the same anecdotes in a response to German critics. In that text, written in German, I am chiefly concerned with the issues of comparison rather than with the issue of the starting point for microhistory, but I use some of the same arguments there as here. Both texts began with notes from a lecture that I delivered in Germany. "Das Bild ist größer, als man denkt. Eine Antwort auf manche Kritiken an *Bloodlands*," *Journal of Modern European History* 11, no. 1 (2013): 1–22.

2. *Bloodlands* has subsequently been published in thirty-five other languages, including the languages of the region it concerns—in this historiographical sense, it has become regional history.

3. If the Holocaust is understood as the German policy of killing all Jews under German control. Romanian policy was also to kill Jews; including the Romanian killings increases the number of Holocaust victims from c. 5.4 million to c. 5.7 million. Notably, almost all Romanian killing of Jews took place on lands that were either lost to the Soviet Union in 1940 or were taken from the Soviet Union by Romania in 1941. For recent treatments see Jean Ancel, *The History of the Holocaust in Romania*, trans. Yaffah Murciano (Lincoln, NE, 2011); Simon Geissbühler, *Blutiger Juli: Rumäniens Vernichtungskrieg und der vergessene Massenmord an den Juden 1941* (Paderborn, 2013).

4. I make these claims as a practitioner of microhistory who was led to conclude that some of the essential features of local killing episodes could only be described and explained at a higher scale. See for example three of my articles on the fates of Jews, Ukrainians, and Poles that preceded, and for me necessitated, *Bloodlands*: "'To Resolve the Ukrainian Problem Once and for All': The Ethnic Cleansing of Ukrainians in Poland, 1943-1947," *Journal of Cold War Studies* 1, no. 2 (1999): 86–120; "The Causes of Ukrainian-Polish Ethnic Cleansing, 1943," *Past and Present* 179, no. 1 (2003): 197–234; "The Life and Death of West Volhynian Jews, 1921-1945," in *The Shoah in Ukraine: History, Testimony, and Memorialization*, ed. Ray Brandon and Wendy Lower (Bloomington, IN, 2008), 77–113.

5. This is the theme of Timothy Snyder "The Problem of Commemorative Causality in the Holocaust," *Modernism/Modernity* 20, no. 1 (2013): 77–93.

6. While it is difficult to retrodict from lachrymose histories in general, there can be particular precedents that are worthy of attention. In the case of the Holocaust, the generation of the

Judeo-Bolshevik trope during the Russian Imperial expulsions of the Jews, the October Revolution, and the civil wars is obviously of significance. For the necessary background see Oleg Budnitskii's important 2005 study, now translated into English as *Russian Jews Between the Reds and the Whites, 1917-1920*, trans. Timothy J. Portice (Philadelphia, 2012). See also Eric Lohr, *Nationalizing the Russian Empire: The Campaign against Enemy Aliens during World War I* (Cambridge, MA, 2003). Similarly, it does help to understand that the historical basis of violence in rural Ukraine was the effort to control fertile territory. See the classic treatment by Daniel Beauvois, *La bataille de la terre en Ukraine: les Polonais et les conflits socio-ethniques, 1863-1914* (Lille, 1993).

7. What Nolte and his contemporary critics had in common was the treatment of the entire issue as a matter of German ethics and German history. For discussions see Charles Maier, *The Unmasterable Past: Holocaust, History, and German National Identity* (Cambridge, MA, 1987); Peter Baldwin, ed., *Reworking the Past: Hitler, the Holocaust, and the Historians' Debate* (Boston, 1990).

8. The turning point was probably Christian Gerlach's *Kalkulierte Morde: Die deutsche Wirtschafts- und Vernichtungspolitik in Weißrußland 1941 bis 1944* (Hamburg, 1999). See also Gerlach's *Krieg, Ernährung, Volkermord: Forschungen zur deutschen Vernichtungspolitik im Zweiten Weltkrieg* (Hamburg, 1998).

9. This is an argument that appears throughout her writings: in *Eichmann in Jerusalem*, in the *Jewish Writings*, and in *Origins of Totalitarianism*. In the last, for example, she writes: "the Jews, the only non-national European people, were threatened more than any other by the collapse of the system of nation-states." She sees statelessness as a result of the extrusion of Jews from the rule of law or from the state itself, but the main source of statelessness was the destruction of states themselves. Mark Mazower approaches this argument not from the experience of Jews but from the history of international law in in his *Hitler's Empire* (New York, 2008) and before that in Mark Mazower, "An International Civilization? Europe, Internationalism, and the Crisis of the Mid-Twentieth Century," *International Affairs* 82, no. 3 (2006): 553–66. The thread he is following is Czesław Madajczyk, "Legal Conceptions in the Third Reich and its Conquests," *Michael: On the History of Jews in the Diaspora* 13, no. 3, (1993): 131–59. The masterful source text of Majdanczyk is Alfons Klafkowski, *Okupacja niemiecka w Polsce w świetle prawa narodów* (Poznań, 1946). This powerful response to Carl Schmitt and his German colleagues, composed, astoundingly, during the war itself, is, unfortunately, not translated and thus not generally known.

10. Christoph Dieckmann's recent history of the Holocaust in Lithuania will come to be seen, I believe, as one of the major studies of the Holocaust itself. Though it is concerned with one (major) case, it is unsurpassed in its use of primary sources and in its conceptual range. *Deutsche Besatzungspolitik in Litauen 1941-1944* (Göttingen, 2011).

11. As practically every Eastern European reviewer has noticed.

12. Yehuda Bauer's formulation of the Holocaust as "unprecedented" seems well chosen. See Bauer, *Rethinking the Holocaust* (New Haven, CT, 2002), 39–67.

Part II

NEW APPROACHES TO JEWISH LEADERSHIP

CHAPTER 3

An Overwhelming Presence
Reflections on Mordechai Chaim Rumkowski and His Place in Our Understanding of the Łódź Ghetto

GORDON J. HORWITZ

Rumkowski Imagined

In 1963, Moshe Pulawer, a successful Yiddish actor and survivor of the Łódź Ghetto, appended to his memoir a small play. Its subject is Chaim Rumkowski, leader of the beleaguered Jewish community in Łódź and the man who, then as now, inescapably, has been associated with its burdens and its fate. The play consists of but one act. The setting is the ghetto. It is late at night on the eve of the impending deportation of the young children of the ghetto in September 1942. The scene takes place outside the dormitory of a ghetto orphanage in the Marysin quarter. Already the orphans are in their beds. Outside in the darkness, a worried Rumkowski, still awake, is pacing, deep in thought. He passes beneath the windows where the children sleep; from time to time he peers inside. All at once, he perceives a voice speaking in the darkness. A mysterious figure appears: it is Rumkowski's conscience, though to Rumkowski it remains a stranger.

    Forthrightly, Rumkowski's conscience insists that he now must do the right thing: in the face of the German order to surrender the children, Rumkowski, as a leader, must not obey. Like his courageous counterpart, Adam Czerniaków, chair of the Jewish Council in Warsaw, the voice tells him he too must refuse to relinquish the children of the ghetto, even at the cost of his life. Argumentative even in the face of promptings of his own conscience, Rumkowski declines, rejecting any other approach than his chosen course, preserving the ghetto

---

Notes for this section begin on page 69.

and rescuing lives even at the cost of others. Admonishing him a final time, the phantom vanishes. Still pondering, sensing a chill, Rumkowski departs the stage. At last, a narrator relates that on the following day the young children of the ghetto were indeed deported, never to return. The curtain falls.[1]

Whatever he might have thought of the portrayal, it is unlikely that Rumkowski—a man accustomed to his leading role in the life of his community—would have been surprised to be the centerpiece, not to say the inspiration, for artistic representations of his burdened solitude. Seeking recognition, elevating his person above all others, he wished to be portrayed as he saw himself: the indispensible leader upon whom the fate of the ghetto depended. Examples of this trait are many. In 1942, a ghetto artist famously depicted him thus: dressed in suit and tie, his ample white hair well combed, Rumkowski towers above the ghetto against the backdrop of the moonlit sky. Bent forward before an open book, fingertips pressed to his brow, he contemplates the suffering of the dead and dying. Their anguished spirits, reflections of his deepest concern, are projected onto the heavens. Below him in the darkness the ghetto, marked by its high bridge and the nearby towers of the church looming over Kościelny Square; all is deserted save for the presence of a German sentry and a passing service vehicle. Its headlights, two cones of light, radiate forward as it proceeds south along Zgierska Street toward the heart of the city. The ghetto sleeps; Rumkowski, awake, keeps a lone vigil, hovering above his people through the night.[2]

A Matter of "Disbelief"

To all who remembered him, and to all who study the Łódź Ghetto, Rumkowski inevitably comes to mind. An object of unavoidable interest to his contemporaries, his place in history assured through the survival of an extensive record of his words and deeds, reinforced yet further by the still-emerging observations of those who knew him, Rumkowski remains an overwhelming presence. To think of the ghetto is also to revisit his controversial leadership. The ambiguity of his policies as head of a Jewish community in peril, the internal contradictions in his character, not to say evident hypocrisy of his status as both courageous protector and alleged predator of the young, continue to demand scrutiny. The ambiguities also extend to his role as local potentate, engaged in sincere and hard-fought efforts to secure the lives of as many of his people as possible, while also gladly banishing his enemies from the ghetto to share in the fate of the deported.

The Łódź Ghetto, as it was lived, and as it is remembered, is unthinkable with Rumkowski left out of the picture. But, overbearing as he once was, clamoring as he once did for the attention and respect of his fellow Jews, has he come too much to overshadow the history of the ghetto? If so, what cost has his overwhelming presence exacted on our understanding of the ghetto and the fate of its people? How might we move beyond his dominant position in order to further our understanding of the ghetto and its place in the Nazi vision of a world from which Jews were to disappear forever?

To ask these questions is in no way to discount Rumkowski's place at the top of the internal administrative hierarchy of the ghetto; nor is it to underplay Rumkowski's achievements in organizing the labor potential of the ghetto in the service of its long-term survival. Nor should we easily discount the will he displayed in playing for time, clinging, to the bitter end, to a "strategy of 'rescue through labor,'" long after, apart from temporary accommodation to the requirements of the war economy, the Nazi regime increasingly jettisoned productionist considerations in favor of a policy of total annihilation.[3] Regarding this catastrophe and Rumkowski's failure to avert it, however, there is much bitterness. Long has he been the object of contested, polarized interpretations, called to account as a self-interested betrayer of his own people. On rarer occasions he is viewed as a misunderstood, potential savior.[4] Indeed, Rumkowski—the man who from its inception took a guiding hand in shaping the ghetto, and who, in the worst of moments stood squarely in the fatal crosswinds of life and death—is deservedly at the center of considerations whenever attention turns to understanding the ghetto and the fate of its inhabitants.

But was Rumkowski really in a position to alter the final outcome? The Germans who oversaw the ghetto entrusted him with wide-ranging powers internal to the life of the ghetto. Beset as he was by responsibilities and the pressures of dealing with his overseers, Rumkowski took to wielding his received authority with no small satisfaction, and in doing so grew confident in his abilities and in his mission. He never tired of reminding the captive ghetto community of his indispensability and that upon unwavering fulfillment of his strategy of rescue through labor depended their survival. And, on the whole, the overburdened ghetto population concurred.[5] But instrumental as Rumkowski was in giving shape to the day-to-day life of the ghetto and in helping secure its continued existence until very late in the war, where it counted most—in preventing the destruction of the ghetto and the final slaughter of its people—his vaunted authority proved little more than a chimera, at the very least an exceedingly weak force, as easily revoked as it had been granted. Rumkowski was, as he had been from the start, ultimately subordinate to the overwhelming and greater power of the ghetto's German masters; they alone decided the fate of the ghetto and its subject population.[6]

If we are to advance our understanding of the ghetto, it may be time to adjust our perspective beyond Rumkowski; new questions, particularly directed to probing the emotional responses to the unprecedented circumstances of the ghetto and the annihilation of its population, may point the way. In this effort we may begin more consciously to enter a realm that to contemporaries was marked by what Alon Confino, in reference to a revealing phrase drawn from Saul Friedländer's recent masterful narrative of the Shoah, has suggestively referred to as "the historical sensation of disbelief."[7] In their daily lives, and, most acutely during the several waves of deportation that, beginning in 1942, punctuated the history of the ghetto, the Jews of Łódź experienced and witnessed a series of unprecedented, shocking episodes. Stressful, unfamiliar, and seemingly inexpressible encounters with threats to life destabilized the community, tearing at its social fabric, forcing both the ghetto leadership and the community into confronting things unimaginable, things that, according to "one's immediate perception of the world" and its ways, were never meant to be.[8]

I wish to posit, if only tentatively, that an aspect of the overwhelming attention to Rumkowski in narratives of the Łódź Ghetto may be one, but by no means the only, powerful instance of that same "sensation of disbelief" that marked the experience of the ghetto as a whole. Contemporaries grappled with the disbelief that of all people it was this man who played so singular a role in their fate, and it has troubled posterity as well. But if Rumkowski, for all his peculiarity and particularity, evoked something of the sensation of "strangeness"—to borrow a related term from Confino—of the events with which he was associated, this may be part of a much wider and deeper phenomenon.[9] For to its inhabitants the ghetto was nothing if not an anomalous place, and their disbelief extended far beyond consideration of this eccentric fellow, Rumkowski, who came to dominate their world. And what of the perpetrators, and the bystanders? They all, from radically differing perspectives than those who inhabited the ghetto, were bound to experience something of a "sensation of disbelief" of their own in the face of unprecedented events to which they were either participants or witnesses. Did not these experiences leave evidence of having stirred, or having found a source in their own underlying perceptions and imaginings?[10]

The Failed Protector

Apart from the sheer theatricality of his outsized person, the image of Rumkowski, this unlikeliest of failed protectors of the community, as we are reminded time and again, was bound up with the fate of the children of the ghetto. Children were his life's work, the source, for good and for ill, of his reputation and standing in the community. And in the ghetto too, Rumkowski's stature was measured, in his eyes and those of others, in relation to his own favored image as their advocate and defender. Amid the many daily spoken and unspoken tragedies, it was the removal of the young children in September

1942 that stands out as determinative of judgments of Rumkowski. The episode defined him, casting a cold light on his failings as a leader and as a man. Oskar Rosenfeld—noting what was being said of Rumkowski in the aftermath of this mournful episode—confided to his diary that the one unforgivable stain upon Rumkowski's record as leader of the ghetto was his having seen to the removal of the youngsters from the Marysin homes in September 1942.[11] As Moshe Pulawer's aforementioned theatrical portrayal reminds us, it was precisely because of Rumkowski's chosen role as protector of the children that his failure of courage in this instance stood glaringly in contrast to the decision of his counterpart in the Warsaw Ghetto, Adam Czerniaków, who, when faced with the same circumstances only weeks before, took his own life.

In confronting the German order to surrender the children, it appears that Rumkowski was no less dismayed, and left to struggle with his own deeply felt "sensation of disbelief." During the long weeks of spring and summer preceding the September roundup, Rumkowski had intimations of the danger ahead. News of anguished separation of young children from their parents had accompanied the arrival of survivors of the dissolved provincial communities already transferred into the ghetto.[12] In response, and in the hope of maximizing their prospects for survival during this period, Rumkowski was keen to integrate the young into the labor force as rapidly as possible.[13]

Hans Biebow, director of the Gettoverwaltung—the German municipal bureau charged with administering the ghetto—was fully aware of Rumkowski's strategy and did not like it. "The severe decline in output of the various departments in recent months should be traced to the steady decline in nutrition," Biebow informed the Gestapo on 11 June 1942. "Importantly, however, output has also decreased because the Elder of the Jews has begun to sabotage the work systematically by removing good skilled workers from the factories ... and replacing them with children aged eight to fourteen who, of course, cannot do what is needed. There are departments in the ghetto where only children are working ..."[14] The ghetto was increasingly on edge, and by 23 June, the ghetto *Chronicle* noted that "rumor of a supposed forthcoming resettlement of children up to the age of 10 still persists."[15] As mounting concern crystallized into reality, what followed later that summer came even to Rumkowski as a terrifying shock.

Recently we have learned a bit more of the circumstances surrounding the demand placed upon Rumkowski to submit to the removal of the young children of the ghetto and the pressures he faced. Arnold Mostowicz, for one, a compelling eyewitness, speaking on camera for the 1998 film, *Fotoamator,* by the young Polish film maker, Dariusz Jabłoński, noted that once faced with the order to deport the young children of the ghetto Rumkowski had assembled doctors of the ghetto to solicit their advice. What should be done? Mostowicz recalled that among the doctors there was overwhelming agreement that there was no choice but to comply with the order.[16] Most significant to our theme is the diary of Estera Daum, published only in 2008.¹⁷ Daum was one of Rumkowski's office assistants in his Central Secretariat on Bałut Market, and her account indicates that, just days prior to the terrible week of terror in September 1942, Rumkowski had been subject to physical intimidation, leaving him, afterward, altogether devastated. He pleaded with the Germans on behalf of the children. His arguments were rejected, and in the most harrowing fashion.

Daum emphatically suggests that Rumkowski came to know whom he was dealing with: for the man before whom he plead his case was none other than *Amtsleiter* Biebow, who was to demonstrate on this occasion—and it would not be the last—the limits of their decidedly unequal "partnership" in maintaining the ghetto. With the turn to mass killing in 1942, and long after, Biebow, as mercurial a figure as any to emerge from the surviving record, hardened in his dealings with Rumkowski. Initially fastidious in his deportment and outwardly polite in his demeanor toward Rumkowski and his staff, over time Biebow increasingly veered into erratic behavior. In this instance, the mask of propriety fell with suddenness. This would not be the sole instance when Biebow demonstrated the brutal underside of his nature and that of the regime he loyally served.¹⁸

For Rumkowski, a critical, a revealing signal of what was soon, unbelievably, to befall the ghetto, was delivered at the end of August 1942. Ms. Daum was a witness. From an office adjoining that of Rumkowski, she overheard Rumkowski in private conversation with Biebow. She recorded hearing Rumkowski—from a distance his voice sounding to her ears slightly muffled—speaking of the children. In response, Biebow angrily rebuffed his interlocutor for advancing this "trite argument," pointedly reminding Rumkowski that it had been owing only to Biebow's "personal influence" that the children had been spared thus far. Twice Biebow barked out to Rumkowski a barely distinguishable order. And then, to Ms. Daum's astonishment, upon reaching the threshold of the office and knocking—she had been called earlier to deliver to Rumkowski a requested document—she came upon the following scene: Biebow stood directly behind Rumkowski, who was bent forward onto the desk. She thought she might well have seen Biebow, whose arm was raised menacingly above Rumkowski, possibly while brandishing a gun, though she could not be certain of that one additional detail. But another detail struck her with clarity: for an instant, she and Rumkowski, who was still bent over the desk, had locked eyes. In this terrifying state, he seemed to be looking up at her, dumbfounded, as if neither knowing what to make of this, nor knowing what to say or do.¹⁹ He was helpless, and, given the compromising position he had been forced to assume and the implied menace of further escalation toward greater violence, Rumkowski could have been left in no doubt that Biebow was engaging in as determinative a demonstration of the power relations defining their dealings as any he had heretofore experienced.

Only days after this disturbing encounter, on the eve of the deportation order, Rumkowski prepared to address the ghetto, informing them of the German demand to surrender for deportation the elderly and the young children. To his staff Rumkowski appeared to be in a state of near "collapse." "He was not the same man." By the evening preceding his anguished oration, Estera Daum, aware of his deteriorating mental state, encountered him in his office once again, contemplating what to say, at a loss to find words appropriate to the occasion. A "blank sheet of paper" lay before him on the desk. She is said to have recalled him asking if she thought him "a monster."[20]

We have long known of the anguished words Rumkowski publicly uttered on the tense afternoon of 4 September 1942, pleading with the parents of small children in the ghetto to yield to the terrible logic of German demands, and fragmentary echoes of the response of those parents in response to his words remain embedded in the most moving accounts of this moment and the days of terror to follow. To read of these events in the words of the masterful eyewitness and ghetto chronicler, Josef Zelkowicz, is to enter a realm of terrifying factuality, to be sure, yet one marked time and again by some variant of that same "sensation of disbelief" evident to any and all within sound of Rumkowski's voice that terrible September afternoon.[21] To experience the terrifying round-ups that followed, Zelkowicz wrote, was to encounter circumstances beyond all "logic" in which "one's faculty for reason no longer functions." Even if one might find a way to express "everything that your eyes may have seen, your ears have heard, and your human heart has felt," Zelkowicz went on to state, "You will not believe it even though you have personally heard and sensed it, because your limited intellect cannot grasp it."[22] And yet, because this most critical moment in the history of the ghetto concerned the fate of the children, and, in part, because it was Rumkowski, of all people, who played so prominent role in offering them up for destruction, questions persist, matters are left unsettled. Is there more to say? Here others venture forth in the hope that imagination might further illuminate the darkness.

Rumkowski as "The Emperor of Lies"

In a most recent foray, Steve Sem-Sandberg, a Swedish writer born of the 1950s, has come forward with a massive volume containing a fictional portrait of Rumkowski and the world of the Łódź Ghetto. The work draws inspiration and factual support from the ghetto's extensive evidentiary base of archival documentation, supplemented by published and unpublished recollections and memoirs of the ghetto's survivors. The portrait would seek to lift the veil obscuring Rumkowski's private thoughts and actions, with an eye toward shining a sensational light on the recesses of the man's conflicted soul. Here the very essence of the often-considered moral ambiguities of Rumkowski, entailing doings both private (and hidden) and public, has proven an irresistible lure for a writer determined to explore the still opaque core of his being. Readers are asked to follow the writer to the heart of an almost unbelievable inner darkness within.

Sem-Sandberg is acutely conscious of divide between the documentary record and what lies beyond; therein he finds a rich field for imaginative exploration. As a writer, he is sensitive to these very "gaps in the recording of events, places where reliable evidence is thin on the ground."[23] He plausibly speculates that Rumkowski's contemporaries inside the ghetto may have known more about Rumkowski than they dared put to paper, and "that the fiction, or perhaps rather the *editing* of the fiction, of the ghetto had begun even before the German occupation came to an end."[24] Touching upon what must appear the most intensely rendered, and disturbing, of explorations of Rumkowski's suspected depravity, he ponders this gap, stating: "It applies also to the exact circumstances surrounding Rumkowski's adoption of a child from one of the ghetto's children's homes, and his relationship with that child."[25]

Sem-Sandberg notes that, "the fact that Rumkowski systematically abused the orphans is exceptionally well substantiated," offering as evidence the unsettling account of Lucille Eichengreen, a young woman who as a resident of the ghetto befriended others who described to her their own experiences and their awareness of Rumkowski's predatory ways. In addition, Ms. Eichengreen courageously wrote of being personally traumatized by the man's crude and unwelcome advances.[26] For his part, Sem-Sandberg interprets Rumkowski's actions "as manifestations not so much of Rumkowski's sexual predilections as of his constant need to assert his power and authority at all levels in the ghetto. In a world where the only options were survival and subjection, the role of sexuality is hard to define but should not be underestimated."[27] Indeed, taking note of Rumkowski's relations toward women, the historian Andrea Löw has similarly indicated that, "the combination of power and sexuality even within ghetto society seems to be a larger problem than previous research would suggest."[28]

How are we to explore this? There are hazards, to be sure. Anxious as he is to fill in the gaps in the record, Sem-Sandberg does not really possess direct evidence of the nature of Rumkowski's relationship to his adopted child. What follows in Sem-Sandberg's account, among the most distressing in his imagined portrayal of Rumkowski, is based entirely upon conjecture. But at what cost? Can we say that the memory of this youngster has not been injured in this case, for what if the writer has surmised incorrectly, seizing upon a child of the ghetto (the real and known name of Rumkowski's actual adopted son is but slightly altered in the fictional text), shaming his memory and his spirit, even if in the interest of a perceived, previously unspoken truth? As Simon Schama posited in response to this work, given the depth and breadth and texture of the available documentation, any such venture into the transformation of the record into fiction, should evidence, as a prerequisite, decidedly more in the way of sensitivity than mastery of literary technique alone can offer.[29]

At the same time it is worth noting that Sem-Sandberg saw fit to surround his sensational elaboration of Rumkowski's colorful persona with extended sketches of the daily lives of lesser-known personages in the ghetto and its disparate neighborhoods. Some of these secondary characters, including individuals close to Rumkowski's inner circle, are based to greater or lesser degree upon the available record, supplemented with imagined characteristics and invented situations. Here too, the author's fictional portrayals outrun available historical evidence, yet his effort to probe relatively unexplored aspects of daily life inside the ghetto may prove a worthy reminder that—however overshadowed by lingering fixation on Rumkowski—there do remain important and little-explored aspects of the spheres of privacy and the intimate that, when examined in greater depth, may deepen our understanding of life in the Łódź Ghetto.

Clear-eyed with respect to the irrevocable wartime destruction "of the great bulk of Jewish records, including private diaries and letters," Raul Hilberg late in his career drew attention to what he referred to as "a persistent reluctance to approach the subject of interpersonal relations among the Jewish victims."[30] Indeed, it is in the realm of matters most personal—touching upon emotions felt within the bonds of the family and within the private sphere of intimacy between men and women most particularly—that the prosaic life in the ghetto was experienced. The available literature on the Łódź Ghetto has long provided tantalizing suggestions of the myriad ways in which the exigencies of life in the ghetto impinged most agonizingly upon the personal areas of daily existence. The diary of David Sierakowiak, for one, offers insights into the searing, hidden conflicts in which hunger and scarcity tore at the unity of families in the ghetto.[31] Jonathan Friedman, for another, has helped point the way toward the critical evaluation of oral testimonies of survivors of Łódź and of other ghettos on the topics of courtship, wedlock, birth, and sexuality.[32] In this regard, we cannot but recall that Oskar Rosenfeld, in addition to his prewar career as a cultural critic, had also achieved some success as an author of fiction.[33] With a writer's eye for the telling, intimate detail, in his notebooks, at last published only in 1994, he attended closely to the unusual ways ghetto life touched upon intimacy between men and women, often rendered at a glimpse. Rosenfeld, for instance, would recall young women of the ghetto admiring themselves in the reflected glass of "dirty windowpanes," attentive to their hair, makeup, and dress.[34] At the same time he did not flinch in taking note of the disconcerting loss of common distance and privacy as men and women of the ghetto coped with having to encounter one another in the primitive latrines that they were compelled to share. "A well-manicured female hand holds the door when one wants to open it inadvertently," he would note on one occasion. "It belongs to a beautiful young girl I had seen in the office." In this way, Rosenfeld provides a sense of the unexpected ways the ghetto offered up fleeting reminders of how weakened some established boundaries governing interactions between the sexes had become.[35]

More to the point of our discussion, however, would be to explore ways in which the "sensation of disbelief," or at the very least, an unsettling sense of the alien and unfamiliar, found expression in the distorted setting of the ghetto, touching upon matters most private. Notably, Rosenfeld also sensed the disturbing interplay of power and eros, catching sight, as he further records, of "so-called dignitaries" and ghetto policemen, married men among them, shamelessly out for a stroll in the ghetto with their girlfriends.[36] Of Rumkowski, he would note that from the balcony of his residence he enjoyed summoning young women, spotted on the street below, to come up to his apartment. On one occasion in which a married woman refused his entreaty, members of the Jewish police retaliated by entering and trashing her residence.[37] Less overtly, from the oral testimony of a prominent ghetto administrator, we learn how, catching sight of an attractive woman on the street, he instructed a ghetto policeman assigned to him to arrange for the young woman to meet him for a private gathering late at night; the encounter led to courtship and marriage.[38]

Sometimes acting as facilitators in meetings initiated at the request of their superiors, at least some Jewish policemen took available advantage of their access to ghetto women. Anatol Chari, a surviving member of the ghetto's elite Sonderkommando, has written with directness of his own experiences, acknowledging that among the many privileges he enjoyed as a member of this unit—above and beyond access to enhanced rations, superior housing, and freedom from initial waves of deportation—were the opportunities afforded Jewish policemen in winning the attentions of young women and receiving from them the favors of intimacy. One of the young men, he recalled, enjoyed boasting of his many conquests.[39] More disturbingly, in the summer of 1944 the ghetto diarist, Jakub Hiller, recorded having been approached by a young woman, distraught and in tears, relating how under the pretext that compliance might lead to sparing them feared removal from the ghetto, Jewish policemen had been assaulting women held in the ghetto's Central Prison, a staging area for deportations.[40]

The Germans: The Ghetto and the Awakening of the Sinister Imagination

Whatever abuses of power characterized the behavior of some in positions of authority within the ghetto, it was the Germans who in their dominance indulged in actions especially menacing in nature. Along the path toward destruction of the ghetto population, close contact with the Jews of the ghetto undoubtedly provided sinister confirmation of German power over the disposition of Jewish bodies. According to testimony delivered at his postwar trial, only months following the drunken outburst in June 1944 in which he had beaten Rumkowski severely, Biebow went on to assault the young daughter of a ghetto physician. As she struggled to resist his unwanted advances, Biebow tore at her dress and, firing his gun, wounded her in the eye. Soon thereafter, she, her father, and the rest of her family were deported.[41] In addition, Biebow is reported to have ordered Jewish women assigned to ghetto clearance operations to undress after work so that while he passed through their quarters he might view them thus exposed.[42] For Dr. Ernst Zirpins, director of the Litzmannstadt Criminal Police, the ferreting out of hidden valuables from the captive Jewish population of the ghetto yielded not only startling insights into the seeming ingenuity of ghetto residents in illegal concealment of their valuables, but offered unchallenged access to the most intimate spaces of the female anatomy. "Naturally, the conditions to which the Jews in the ghetto are subject are not especially luxuriant," Zirpins wrote in October 1941. "Whereas prior to the creation of the ghetto they displayed a malicious smile and even revealed delight in the creation of this Jewish state in miniature, today the picture has somewhat changed." Experience had revealed that Jews had been known to cloak valuables in piles of unwashed, used clothing and even conceal them within the hidden recesses of their bodies. The Criminal Commissar went to great lengths to advise his officers to expect to find Jewish women concealing paper currency in the tightly wound braids of their hair, and jewels in brassieres and used sanitary wrappings, and, with the aid of bandages, taped to the skin beneath their breasts. "The activity of the Criminal Police in Litzmannstadt is, to be sure, a job conducted under the most unfavorable, difficult, and filthy conditions imaginable," Zirpins would write, "yet on the other hand, in breaking new ground, as varied as it is interesting, it is above all professionally rewarding, even satisfying."[43] For inclusion as the final image in a remarkable series of color slides he fashioned from his own visual record of the ghetto, Walter Genewein, an accountant loyally serving under Biebow's administration, selected a chilling image: viewed at a remove, a crowd of Jewish men are seen to shower under water sprayed from a network of pipes overhead. The men worked in the warehouses at Pabianice, a Gettoverwaltung-administered facility, where their grim task was to sift through and sort the belongings of those deported to their deaths in Chełmno. A caption the photographer assigned to this final image reads, simply, "Pabianice Juden-Bad." "Jewish bath." As one team of scholars have noted, the chilling image, strategically placed at the end, may have symbolized for initiates a means of indulging, perhaps not without shared amusement, their common understanding of the fate of the Jews.[44]

Sinister imaginings, worthy of further study, have left unmistakable traces in the visual and literary documents of the ghetto era. Among the work of an unknown photographer assigned to Reserve Police Battalion 101 who, in the winter of 1940–41, assisted in patrolling the ghetto perimeter, we find a chilling set of nighttime images of slick black cobblestones, of headlights stylishly transformed by time-lapse imagery, streaking past the branch office of the Litzmannstadt Gestapo across from Bałut Market in the heart of the ghetto. Another member of that same reserve police unit, immersed in the solitude of standing guard outside the ghetto on long winter nights, would be inspired to compose a poem in which he likened snow lying on the ground near the ghetto perimeter to "a burial shroud" and nearby buildings to objects seemingly "banished by death."[45] Encountering in May 1942 a young SS lieutenant in a provincial town near Łódź, the town's mayor was struck by the brazenness of the officer's approving revelation that the fate of recently deported Jewish population was death. The mayor was struck by the sadistic satisfaction with which he related that the killing was proceeding and limited only by the "capacity" of one of the recently established killing installations. The junior officer specifically went on to describe in detail the killing procedure and functioning of one of the gas vans.[46] Whatever disbelief the mayor may have still harbored at the hearing of this revelation was soon settled into increasing confirmation. A day later he had occasion to visit Biebow's headquarters in Litzmannstadt, as Łódź then was known, on official business. Astonished, with a sense of intensifying unease he was taken aback at the sight of staggering quantities of jewelry and other confiscated valuables, some being at that moment examined under the careful eye of expert technicians, others placed in brimming bowls, still more held for safekeeping in basement storage closets where the collected objects were stacked "to the ceiling."[47]

In the months prior to the September 1942 roundup, a disquieting "sensation of disbelief" attached most tellingly to accumulating rumors and evidence of the tragic fate of those deported from the Łódź Ghetto and surrounding Jewish communities of the Warthegau during the first half of the year. Foreboding overshadowed the ghetto, giving rise to speculation, entailing worry and concern for one's fate and that of loved ones, unsettling thoughts commingling the rumored and the known, the improbable and the menacingly possible. To cite but one example: well documented are the efforts of the courageous ghetto photographer, Mendel Grossman, compelled to wander amid and photograph the puzzling bundles of feather bedding, material vestiges of the already deported, delivered into the ghetto in the spring of 1942.[48] Zelkowicz, likening the swirl of feathers to a snowfall in June, sensed something uncanny and sinister in the air.[49] A like concern marked the subtext of the ghetto *Chronicle* as it took note of the disturbing return of personal effects traceable to Jews deported that spring and shipped back to the ghetto for sifting and recycling.[50] Soon thereafter, the *Gettoverwaltung,* as we know from a surviving document, delivered to Rumkowski an improbable request: might the ghetto possibly have in its possession a bone grinder, specifically mentioning that the device was to serve the needs of the Sonderkommando in Kulmhof (Chełmno). According to Estera Daum, the request arrived in Rumkowski's secretariat, and was brought to his attention, at a time when Kulmhof and Auschwitz had become an object of discussion among persons in her circle of acquaintance.[51] As Isaiah Trunk would note, by the summer of 1942, even within the general population "the atmosphere became ever more tense" and dispiriting, made worse by "the shocking stories about the dreadful outrages during the deportations from a series of ghettos in the Łódź region, particularly the bloody deportation in Zduńska Wola on 24–25 August 1942, about which the surviving remnants sent into the Łódź Ghetto spoke."[52]

Even if Rumkowski was then yet unaware of the precise details of the method of destruction awaiting the children about to be swept away along with the aged, similarly targeted during the terrible days of September 1942, by the time of his anguished address to the ghetto population, as Yisrael Gutman reminds us, apprehension that deportation meant death was widespread.[53] Sensing the impending danger, he had done all within his power to shield the children through their accelerated integration into the workshops, hoping in this way to demonstrate of their utility and worthiness to serve and to live. As he had done for the ghetto as a whole, now directly on their behalf, he hoped to win a reprieve from his German masters through appeal to the logic of an ongoing, productive Jewish contribution to the German war economy. Biebow and his German allies within the provincial Nazi party organization and the German defense establishment, each profiting from or gaining material advantage from the fruits of ghetto labor, were willing to keep the ghetto going for a time.[54] But at a moment when the Final Solution was well under way, during that terrible summer of 1942, the children were expendable. Rumkowski might ponder, and he might plan, stepping up his training of young workers and integrating them into the factories and workshops. But once the Germans found them unfit for larger tasks and a drag on scarce resources, their lives were forfeit, and were to be hauled away like so much scrap. As Michal Unger reminds us, as important as Rumkowski was in organizing the ghetto and keeping it up and running as a going concern, and for a remarkably long time, he was but "an insignificant part of this huge machine" that, ultimately, functioned so long as it suited the interests of the German authorities, and no longer.[55]

Rumkowski—and After

The ghetto, it need hardly be stated, was a place ruled by a hard and unforgiving reality. That in its sheer peculiarity it should have left traces in the imagination of victim and perpetrator alike, however, cannot escape our attention. Nor can we overlook all the attention lavished upon the person of Rumkowski. His well-documented aspirations, his wishes and his dreams, understandably, have occupied our attention for quite some time. Tantalizingly, some think that in plumbing to the depths the riddle of his troubled soul, the "secret of the ghetto"—the phrase is drawn from Rosenfeld—would be revealed at last.[56]

In part, the fictionalizing of his person begins with Rumkowski himself. A self-promoter of grandiose aspirations, even in his own time, Rumkowski evoked myths, not least those of his own making. Demanding favorable attention, even in his worst moments, he fantasized lasting confirmation of his favored image as the beneficent leader. In his irrepressible self-regard, he took imaginative solace in knowing, whatever his personal fate, he would live on in the thoughts of posterity. He "sees himself in *historical* perspective," Rosenfeld, observing him closely, noted; "he sees himself as a kind of Shabbatai Zvi, but a genuine one who will hold out to the end without fail. Sees himself becoming a hero in Jewish history."[57] Among Rumkowski's most revealing fantasies was an image of one day parading the surviving remnant of the ghetto through the gates to freedom.[58] To the contrary, many of the Jews of the ghetto, notably the unprivileged, excluded from his special protection and favor, in brief, all who felt victimized by Rumkowski's unequal and heavy-handed rule, had their own dream: that one day Rumkowski would have to answer for his deeds.[59] Imagining his own future, Rumkowski appears to have considered the prospect; as in life, his imagined response to his future accusers would be one of defiance: "So what will be?" he is said to have confided, "I think I will save some of the Jews. All my work here is to save as many as possible. Afterwards ... if I survive, let them try me. Let them! I don't care."[60]

Long after the war, yet another survivor of the Łódź Ghetto composed a play in which Rumkowski is at last compelled to answer for his actions as leader of the ghetto before the law.[61] According to the script, upon arrival at Auschwitz, former residents of the ghetto, now inmates assigned to the unloading of the transport, beat him severely. Rumkowski tries desperately to shield his face from repeated blows while above him an angry circle of Jewish onlookers, enjoying the spectacle, hurl scorn. Amused, but only for a while, SS guards order Rumkowski taken away to be killed.[62] Upon his death, the higher powers, unable to resolve his fate, condemn Rumkowski's spirit to wander restlessly between heaven and earth. Decades pass. A reexamination of his case is ordered. Rumkowski is summoned before a heavenly tribunal: judges, prosecutor, defender, and officers of the court, angels all, and above each, a halo, await the arrival of the defendant. Two figures, clothed in dark attire, accompany Rumkowski to his seat.[63] Called upon to speak in open court, Rumkowski is submissive, striking a pose of quiet humility. "Naturally, in administering the ghetto I made many mistakes, but I tried my best."[64] Acknowledging his susceptibility to the temptations that came with power, he insists on the correctness of his course of action. Knowing firsthand the might and cruelty of the German authorities, he would not risk the certain destruction of the ghetto by encouraging open resistance. Aware of the fate of the Jews of Warsaw, he still believed that, through unswerving demonstration of its usefulness to the Germans, the Łódz Ghetto, an "exception," would be spared.[65] In the end, having listened to the arguments for and against, the judge eschews issuing a conclusive judgment, failing to condemn Rumkowski for all time. Instead, his spirit is ordered once again to wander between heaven and earth. Perhaps there will come a time when humankind has learned to make an end to persecution and war and accord life the value it deserves. Only then, his judge declares, might his restless soul at last find desired elevation to a "higher" realm.[66]

To the very end Rumkowski clamored for recognition, asserting that he was "*a piece of Jewish history.*"[67] Indeed so. To be sure, as Primo Levi reminded us, to examine Rumkowski and his career is to come upon a disturbing example of the folly of grasping at and wielding power, however debased and revocable.[68] Yet his is still not the only story to tell. As we continue to delve into the strange, and for all its reality, seemingly "unbelievable" world of the ghetto, let us not overlook its ability, in its own time and in our own, to challenge the historical imagination. In the pursuit of understanding of the phenomenon and in giving shape to new narratives, as both Saul Friedländer and Alon Confino remind us, historians would do well to attend closely to instances of the strange, the unthinkable, and the all but inconceivable. Encountering within the record any of numerous instances of this recurring "sense of belief," we may well be touching upon "a defining characteristic of the period."[69] Understandably, Rumkowski, most especially, in his person and in his unavoidable association with truly shattering events, has long served as a startling embodiment of this wider phenomenon. But let us not also permit his well-illuminated image to cast too great a shadow. "Rumkowski *was* the ghetto." So proclaims the novelist.[70] But in truth the Łódz Ghetto, and the community of Jews who experienced it in all its bitterness, did not begin or end with Rumkowski; neither should our widening understanding of it begin and end with him alone.

Notes

1. Moshe Pulawer, *Geven iz a geto* (Tel Aviv, 1963), 180–85.

2. See reproduction in Alan Adelson and Robert Lapides, eds., *Łódz Ghetto: Inside a Community under Siege* (New York, 1989), opposite 130.

3. See Dan Diner, *Beyond the Conceivable: Studies on Germany, Nazism, and the Holocaust* (Berkeley, CA, 2000), 117–37, esp. 123, 125, 134, 136; Michal Unger, "Jewish Forced Labor in the Lodz Ghetto and Its Influence on German Policy," in *Fenomen getta łódzkiego 1940–1944,* ed. Paweł Samusia and Wiesław Pusia (Łódz, 2006), 180–82.

4. On the viewpoint of one of his more outspoken defenders, see Abraham Cykiert, "The Uniqueness of the Lodz Ghetto and Rumkowski," in Samusia and Prusia, *Fenomen*, 129–34. Vigorous refutation of Cykiert's opinion, and a decidedly critical view of Rumkowski, may be found in Julian Baranowski, "Chaim Mordechaj Rumkowski——Kollaborateur oder Retter?," in *Der Judenmord in den eingegliederten polnischen Gebieten 1939-1945,* ed. Jacek Andrzej Młynarczyk and Jochen Böhler (Osnabrück, 2010), 301–10.

5. On this broader compact, see Unger, "Jewish Forced Labor," 181–83.

6. Unger, "Jewish Forced Labor," 181–83.

7. Alon Confino, *Foundational Pasts: The Holocaust as Historical Understanding* (New York, 2012), 59–60; Saul Friedländer, *Nazi Germany and the Jews, 1939-1945: The Years of Extermination* (New York, 2007), xxvi.

8. The phrase is from Friedländer, *Years of Extermination,* xxvi. "'Disbelief' here means something that arises from the depth of one's immediate perception of the world, of what is ordinary and what remains 'unbelievable.'" See also Confino, *Foundational Pasts,* 61–64.

9. Confino, *Foundational Pasts,* 52, 60.

10. Of note, on the discussion of the contributions of cultural historical approach suggested, most recently, by Confino, see Dan Stone, "Holocaust Historiography and Cultural History," *Dapim* 23 (2009): 52–68, followed by the commentary of Dan Michman, Carolyn Dean, Wendy Lower, Federico Finchelstein, and Dominick LaCapra, 69–93.

11. Oskar Rosenfeld, *In the Beginning was the Ghetto: Notebooks from Łódź,* ed. Hanno Loewy, trans. Brigitte M. Goldstein (Evanston, IL, 2002), Notebook H, 196.

12. See, for example, Lucjan Dobroszycki, ed., *The Chronicle of the Łódź Ghetto 1941-1944,* trans. Richard Lourie and Joachim Neugroschel et. al. (New Haven, CT, 1984), entry for 20 May 1942, 183–84. Here the chroniclers took note of the tragic separation of young children from their parents during selections in the nearby town Brzeziny.

13. "Creation of new workshops" to provide "easy work for children and old people" was a significant theme in Rumkowski's address to the ghetto on 31 May 1942. "The problem of work ran like a red thread the Chairman's entire speech." Dobroszycki, *Chronicle,* 194–95.

14. Cited as "Summary of a meeting between Biebow and the Gestapo on June 11, 1942," quoted in Unger, "Jewish Forced Labor," 182.

15. Dobroszycki, *Chronicle,* entry for 23 June 1942, 210.

16. *Fotoamator* (Photographer) (1998), dir. Dariusz Jabłoński, Apple Film Productions, English version trans. Alina Skibinska and Wolfgang Joehling.

17. Elżbieta Cherezińska, *Byłam sekretarką Rumkowskiego: Dzienniki Etki Daum* (Poznań, 2008). A thoroughgoing analysis of the diary of Estera Daum awaits scholarly comparison between the original and published versions. On the background to its publication and its published format see the editor's comments: Cherezińska, "Od autorki," in *Byłam sekretarką Rumkowskiego,* 6, 17–20, 369.

18. On 16 June 1944 Biebow stormed into Rumkowski's office and physically assaulted him, sending Rumkowski to hospital. Dobroszycki, *Chronicle,* entries for 16 June 1944, 17 June 1944, 504–5.

19. Cherezińska, *Byłam sekretarką Rumkowskiego,* entry for 24 August 1942, 213–14.

20. Cherezińska, *Byłam sekretarką Rumkowskiego,* entry for 12 September 1942, 217–18.

21. Josef Zelkowicz, *In Those Terrible Days: Notes from the Łódź Ghetto,* ed. Michal Unger, trans. Naftali Greenwood (Jerusalem, 2002), 249–83.

22. Zelkowicz, *In Those Terrible Days,* 354–55.

23. Steve Sem-Sandberg, *The Emperor of Lies* (New York, 2011), 648.

24. Sem-Sandberg, *Emperor of Lies,* 648.

25. Sem-Sanberg, *Emperor of Lies,* 648–49.

26. Lucille Eichengreen, *Rumkowski and the Orphans of Łódź,* with Rebecca Camhi Fromer (San Francisco, 2000).

27. Sem-Sanberg, *Emperor of Lies,* 649.

28. Andrea Löw, *Juden im Getto Litzmannstadt: Lebensbedingungen, Selbstwahrnehmung, Verhalten* (Gottingen, 2006), 505.

29. Simon Schama, "The Emperor of Lies," *Financial Times,* 15 July 2011. Here, the reviewer notes, "The fact that so much of the book turns on the fate of children only makes its failure of tenderness the more distressing."

30. Raul Hilberg, "Incompleteness in Holocaust Historiography," in *Gray Zones: Ambiguity and Compromise in the Holocaust and its Aftermath,* ed. Jonathan Petropoulos and John K. Roth (New York, 2006), 89.

31. David Sierakowiak, *The Diary of David Sierakowiak: Five Notebooks from the Lodz Ghetto,* ed. Alan Adelson, trans. Kamil Turowski (New York, 1996), entry for 5 September 1942, 219–20. See also the discussion in Michal Unger, "The Status and Plight of Women in the Łódź Ghetto," in *Women in the Holocaust,* ed. Dalia Ofer and Lenore J. Weitzman (New Haven, CT, 1998), especially 137–39.

32. Jonathan Friedman, "Togetherness and Isolation: Holocaust Survivor Memories of Intimacy and Sexuality in the Ghettos," *The Oral History Review* 28, no. 1 (2001): 1–16.

33. Hanno Loewy, "Editor's Introduction," in Oskar Rosenfeld, *In the Beginning Was the Ghetto: Notebooks from Łódź* (Evanston, IL, 2002), xv–xvi.

34. Rosenfeld, *In the Beginning,* Notebook B, "Face of the Ghetto, June 1942," 44.

35. Rosenfeld, *In the Beginning,* Notebook G, entry for 5 March 1943, 161–62.

36. Rosenfeld, *In the Beginning,* Notebook G, 23 February 1943, 159. See also Notebook H, entry for 8–9 July 1943, 195.

37. Rosenfeld, *In the Beginning,* Notebook H, entry for 6 May 1943, 189.

38. Interview with Bert Fleming, 15 May 1996, United States Holocaust Memorial Museum Archive [hereafter USHMMA]. RG 50.030*0365.

39. Anatol Chari, with Timothy Braatz, *"Undermensch": Mein Überleben durch Glück und Privilegien",* trans. Franka Reinhart (Munich, 2010), 62–66, 68.

40. Diary of Jakub Hiller, YIVO Institute for Jewish Research, RG 1400, Box M7, folder 16, entry for 4 July 1944. Also noted in Andrea Löw, "Ordnungsdienst," in Samusia and Pusia, *Fenomen,* 164.

41. Jerzy Lewiński, ed., *Proces Hansa Biebowa* (Warsaw, 1999), testimonies of Dr. Leon Szykier and Dr. Michal Eliasberg, 93, 127.

42. Testimony of Dr. Michał Eliasberg, in Lewiński, *Process,* 127–28. See also the account of Binna W., quoted in Friedman, "Togetherness and Isolation," 12.

43. Dr. [Ernst] Zirpins, "Das Getto in Litzmannstadt, kriminalpolizeilich gesehen," *Kriminalistik: Monatshefte für die gesamte Kriminialistische Wissenschaft und Praxis* 15, no. 10 (1941): 111–12.

44. Florian Freund, Bertrand Perz, and Karl Stuhlpfarrer, "Bildergeschichten-Geschichtsbilder," in Hanno Loewy and Gerhard Schoenberner, eds., *"Unser einziger Weg ist Arbeit: Das Getto in Łódź 1940-1944* (Frankfurt, 1990), 56, and image 393, on 142.

45. USHMMA, photos courtesy of Michael O'Hara, in Gordon J. Horwitz, *Ghettostadt: Łódź and the Making of a Nazi City* (Cambridge, MA, 2008), among images following 180.

46. Alexander Hohenstein, *Wartheländisches Tagebuch aus den Jahren 1941/42* (Stuttgart, 1961), entry for 12 May 1942, 258–62, especially 259–61.

47. Hohenstein, *Wartheländisches Tagebuch,* entry for 13 May 1942, 263–64.

48. Arieh Ben-Menachem, in Mendel Grossman, *With a Camera in the Ghetto,* ed., Zvi Szner and Alexander Sened (Tel Aviv, 1970), 103–4.

49. Josef Zelkowicz, "Inem lager fun altshik," 17 August 1943, YIVO, RG 241/no. 895.

50. Dobroszycki, *Chronicle,* entries for 30 May 1942, 31 May 1942, 190–91,

51. Cherezinska, *Bylam sekretarką Rumkowskiego,* entries for 8 June, 13 July, 16 July, 1942, 201–2, 207–9.

52. Isaiah Trunk, *Łódź Ghetto: A History,* trans. and ed. Robert Moses Shapiro (Bloomington, IN, 2006), 239.

53. See the discussion in Yisrael Gutman, "Introduction," in Trunk, *Łódź Ghetto,* xlix–liii.

54. Unger, "Jewish Forced Labor in the Lodz Ghetto," in Samusia and Pusia, *Fenomen,* 182.

55. Unger, "Jewish Forced Labor," 182–83. The phrase appears on 183.

56. See illustration in Oskar Rosenfeld, *Wozu noch Welt: Aufzeichnungen aus dem Getto Łódź,* ed. Hanno Loewy (Frankfurt, 1994), 137.

57. Rosenfeld, *In the Beginning,* Notebook 15, 207. Emphasis in original.

58. Rosenfeld, *In the Beginning,* Notebook H, entry for 12 May 1943, 189.

59. Arnold Mostowicz speculates that even had Rumkowski succeeded in his efforts to preserve the ghetto until a miraculous liberation and rescue of those still alive on the eve of its dissolution in the summer of 1944, he would have been either "hanged on the spot or torn to pieces" by survivors ill-disposed to forgive him, recalling those who died, whether succumbing to conditions inside the ghetto or through deportation to their destruction, on his watch. Arnold Mostowicz, *Der Blinde Max oder Passierschien durch den Styx* (Berlin, 1992), 132–33.

60. Solomon Uberbaum, quoted in Shmuel Huppert, "King of the Ghetto: Mordecai Haim Rumkowski, the Elder of [the] Łódź Ghetto," *Yad Vashem Studies* 15 (1983): 150.

61. Ray Eichenbaum, "Das Verfahren gegen M. H. Rumkowski," in Eichenbaum, *Romeks Odyssee: Jugend im Holocaust,* trans. Herbert Kolmer and Vladimir Vertlib (Vienna, 1996), 117–70.

62. Eichenbaum, "Das Verfahren," 117–23. On the still-uncertain details of Rumkowski's death in Auschwitz, see Löw, *Getto Litzmannstadt,* 483 and Michal Cechinski, "How Rumkowski Died," *Commentary,* May 1979, 63–65.

63. Eichenbaum, "Das Verfahren," 130–31.

64. Eichenbaum, "Das Verfahren," 139.

65. Eichenbaum, "Das Verfahren," 148–49.

66. Eichenbaum, "Das Verfahren," 168–69.

67. Rosenfeld, *In the Beginning,* Notebook 15, 208. Emphasis in original.

68. Primo Levi, *The Drowned and the Saved,* trans. Raymond Rosenthal (New York, 1988), 67.

69. Confino, *Foundational Pasts,* 54; Friedländer, *Years of Extermination,* xxvi.

70. Sem-Sandberg, *Emperor of Lies,* 458.

CHAPTER 4

Similarity and Differences
A Comparative Study between the Ghettos in Białystok and Kielce

SARA BENDER

Scholarly work published in the last two decades on daily life and individual fates of Jewish communities in Poland during World War II and the Holocaust have played an important role beyond their historical information and conclusions.[1] Individual studies also afford historians a broader view of life in the various ghettos, enabling them to determine differences and similarities in an effort to understand the factors that determined ghetto experiences. In examining a wide range of essential characteristics, it is clear that each Jewish community—from the beginning of the German occupation until its final destruction—possessed distinctive features.

In a recent review of three studies on the Jews of Łódź, historian Samuel Kassow notes the primary components of Jewish history in the ghettos. "The ghettos established by the Nazis," he writes, "…take on various characteristics. This stemmed from a wide variety of factors. What was the nature of local Jewish society before the war? What were the aims of the local German authorities and how much power did they have? Was the ghetto located in the General-gouvernement, in the Reich or in the newly occupied Eastern territories? Did an existing economic base and a skilled labor-force facilitate the development of workshops and industry? What room for maneuver did the local Jewish leadership have…?"[2]

Comparative thinking is thus essential. Since I have written about the Jewish communities in Białystok and Kielce, I have chosen to compare the common features as well as the differences between these two ghettos. I will focus on cen-

---

Notes for this section begin on page 86.

tral issues such as Jewish leadership, life in the ghetto, the Jewish police, relations with the occupation authorities, and the final destruction of these communities.

From the Beginning of the Occupation to the Establishment of the Ghetto

Located in southeastern Poland, Kielce suffered aerial bombardment on the fourth day of the war. It was occupied by the Wehrmacht on 5 September 1939. Military rule ended on 25 October, at which time the Jews of the city were placed under civil administration, which in turn lasted until 5 April 1941. Kielce was one of the three major cities—along with Radom and Częstochowa—in the Radom District, established in late October 1939 as one of the four districts of the Generalgouvernement. On the eve of the war, some eighteen thousand Jews resided in the city, constituting about one-third of the entire population.[3] In the interwar period, the Jews of Kielce belonged mainly to the middle and lower classes and, with the exception of a small group of wealthy individuals, the majority was quite poor.

For twenty-two months, from the outbreak of the war to the end of June 1941, Białystok, in eastern Poland, was under Soviet rule as a result of the Ribbentrop-Molotov Pact. Before the war, Białystok was the second largest textile manufacturing center in Poland after Łódź and, on the eve of the war, it had at least fifty thousand Jewish residents—about half of the entire population. While its Polish residents lived on the outskirts of the city, most of the Jewish residents lived in the city center. It was a varied population consisting of bourgeoisie, intelligentsia, businessmen, and traders, as well as workers. Thousands of Jewish refugees, who had arrived in Białystok from central and western Poland in the early months of the war, were expelled by the Soviets to the interior of the USSR. The Germans occupied Białystok on 27 June 1941 during Operation Barbarossa after the Jews of Kielce had already been confined in a ghetto for three months. Within two weeks of the capture of Białystok, the Germans burned or shot some seven thousand of the city's fifty thousand Jews.[4] Białystok became the central city in the Białystok District, the final borders of which were established by the Germans in late 1941. The district was divided into seven subdistricts. By September 1941, after the mass murder of Jews in the first months following of the invasion of the Soviet Union, the district had a Jewish population of about one hundred and fifty thousand.[5]

The Appointment and Performance of the Judenrat

In November 1939, the Germans appointed 53-year-old Dr. Moshe Pelc chairman of the Judenrat of Kielce. Pelc was presumably recommended by Polish members of the city council due to his involvement in Polish society in the city, his prominence within the Jewish community, and his good command of German. He had served as a military physician in World War I, settled in Kielce with his family in 1919, and specialized in pediatric medicine. Everyone in the Jewish community knew him as the physician of the Jewish Gymnasium and director of the orphanage and the old-age home.[6] The minutes of a Judenrat meeting held on 10 December 1939 reveal that many of those mentioned as members of the Judenrat were well-known public figures in the city's Jewish community.[7] Like most of the Judenräte in the Generalgouvernement, the Judenrat of Kielce established a large bureaucratic apparatus. From its inception and throughout the entire occupation, it concerned itself with matters such as food, employment, housing, health, sanitation, religion, burial, education, welfare, and so on. Eventually, it also assumed responsibility for areas beyond traditional Jewish experience in the Diaspora, such as prisons and Jewish police.

Kielce's Jewish leaders faced financial difficulties from the start. Among the first expenditures were two "contributions" (ransom payments) that the Germans demanded from Pelc, just as they had from most Jewish communities in the occupied territories. The first contribution imposed on Kielce's Jews amounted to one hundred thousand złoty and the second to five hundred thousand złoty.[8] Other Judenrat leaders in the Radom district understood the need to keep money in the Judenrat treasury. Thus Josef Diamant of Radom in October 1939 negotiated the ransom payment with the Germans and succeeding in converting part of the payment to one thousand men's suits and sets of linen to be sewn by Jewish tailors for the SS. Leon Kupinski of Częstochowa presented various excuses and managed to convince the Germans to decrease the demanded sum. Pelc, however, paid the German ransom in full, completely emptying the coffers of the Jewish community.[9]

From December 1939, the Germans began large-scale seizures of Jewish property in Kielce, transferring it to German ownership. Among the businesses in Kielce transferred to German trustees were four quarries, a barrel factory, a brick factory, a feather-processing plant, a wooden goods factory, a steel foundry, a paper factory, a glass factory, and the city's marble industries.[10] On the eve of the war, Jews owned 61 percent of the city's shops and small businesses. Within a few months of the initial German occupation, only 32.3 percent of the shops in Kielce remained in Jewish hands.[11] Since most of the Jews of Kielce had engaged in commerce and peddling, the impact on the economy of the city was significant and, before long, commerce came to a standstill, resulting in shortages of goods.

Within six months of the occupation, thousands of Jewish refugees also flooded into the city. They came from the areas of western Poland annexed to the Reich, such as Pomerania, Upper Silesia, and the newly created Warthegau. Three thousand more refugees arrived in August 1940 from Kalisz and

Kraków.¹² Due to the Judenrat's inability to collect taxes from the wealthier members of the community and the Judenrat's complete lack of funds, Pelc was unable to cope with the thousands in need of assistance, whose numbers were constantly increasing. Pelc further lacked leadership abilities. Growing problems combined with criticisms from members of the community convinced him that he was unsuited for the position.

In the summer of 1940, after eight months as chairman of the Judenrat, Pelc resigned, citing poor health. He recommended that the Germans appoint his deputy, Herman Levy, to replace him. Sixty years old at the time of his appointment, Levy was a man of means and public standing, who lived with his family in Kielce and owned a large furniture factory as well as various properties in and outside the city. On the eve of the war, he was active in the Jewish community, a member of the board of the Great Synagogue and a city councilman. He had a reputation as a philanthropist, was head of the wood-traders' association in Kielce and the broader district, and favored close cooperation with Poles. Most of the Jews of Kielce knew Levy as a prominent industrialist with contacts and influence, and his appointment encountered no opposition from the occupation authorities.¹³

When he took up the position in August 1940 (officially appointed in late 1940), Levy was determined to meet the challenges faced by the community leadership. Determined to improve the lives of the poorest Jews, he immediately made changes in the Judenrat departments. Levy was more dynamic than Pelc, and in the new Judenrat he included representatives of all segments of Jewish society in Kielce, including of the thousands of refugees. The Judenrat's ten departments included a financial department, charged with drawing up a budget, determining levels of taxation, and registering taxpayers.¹⁴

But on 31 March 1941, just as Jewish life in Kielce seemed to have attained a certain degree of stability—for nineteen months most Jews continued to live in the homes they had inhabited before the war—the German district governor Karl Lasch ordered the establishment of a ghetto in the city. Within five days all of the Jews were ordered to move to the "Jewish Quarter" and were prohibited from residing outside the ghetto.¹⁵

To make matters worse, another one thousand refugees arrived from Vienna on the eve of the ghetto's establishment, bringing the ghetto population to twenty-seven thousand. For the ghetto itself, the Germans chose the poorest, most miserable part of the city. Most houses had only a single story and lacked running water or sewage. Nearly twenty-eight thousand Jews were now packed into six hundred structures on twenty-six streets, in unbearably crowded, life-threatening conditions. On 5 April 1941, the ghetto was enclosed within a wooden and stone fence with barbed wire, nearly ten feet high. Signs posted every few yards said, "Closed Area. Entry Forbidden" in a number of languages. Near the ghetto's five gates were signs bearing the legend "Jewish Quarter," and after the ghetto was sealed it was declared an infected area, off-limits to everyone without exception.[16]

In Białystok, as in Kielce, it appears that the Polish mayor recommended the city's chief rabbi, Gedaliah Rosenman, to the Germans as the Judenrat chairman. Rosenman passed the position on to Efraim Barash, who held the position until the ghetto's liquidation in August 1943. A native of Wołkowysk who served as community president there, Barash settled in Białystok with his family in 1934.[17] From his first day as head of the Judenrat in Białystok, Barash understood that he had to chart a policy that served the interests of the Germans while protecting Białystok's tens of thousands of Jews, toward whom he felt a heavy responsibility. Barash was joined by twenty-three other members, mostly known public figures and active members of Białystok's Jewish political parties. At the Judenrat's first meeting, on 2 August 1941, it was decided to establish thirteen departments, each with a different area of responsibility. New departments were added as the Judenrat's sphere of activities widened.[18]

Unlike Kielce and many other towns in the Generalgouvernement in which ghettos were established in the spring of 1941, the ghettos in the eastern territories conquered by the Germans in the summer of 1941 were established within a short time. This was surely related to Berlin's decision to murder the Jews in the east, made even before Operation Barbarossa. On 26 July 1941, just one month after the city was taken, the German authorities in Białystok ordered Barash to establish a ghetto.[19] When Barash discovered that the Germans had designated Białystok's most impoverished areas for the ghetto, he tried to convince the Germans to establish the ghetto in the city center—where the factories and workshops were and where most of the Jews lived and worked. Thanks to these efforts, the ghetto was established in the city center, including more streets and a number of large, stone buildings.[20] On 1 August 1941, the ghetto's two gates were closed, imprisoning forty-three thousand Jews inside.

Both in Kielce and in Białystok, the position of chairman of the Judenrat entailed broad responsibilities for the provision of essential services under conditions of shortage and dwindling resources, imposed on the Judenrat all at once, with no organizational or professional preparation. The ability of the head of the Judenrat to deal with these increasingly pressing matters put the Judenrat to the test while, at the same time, determining the nature of communal life under German occupation.

In the Ghetto

The transition to the ghetto in Kielce brought about a further deterioration in Jewish public life. It severely affected remaining Jewish businesses, most of which remained outside the ghetto. Due to the particularly harsh conditions and treatment at workplaces outside the ghetto, and the fear of abduction to an unknown place of work, many Jews were deterred from going to work. Six weeks after the establishment of the ghetto the Germans began distributing special work permits to Jews who worked in essential jobs outside the ghetto—in the railway, the quarries, flour mills, feather-processing plants, and so on. Since most of these jobs were physically very demanding and workers found them hard to bear, some disappeared to avoid returning to work. Despite the Jewish refugees in Kielce, who were doomed to starvation if they failed to go out to work, the Judenrat found it difficult to meet the labor quotas.

Most preferred to seek work within the ghetto.[21] Some businesses were already within the ghetto confines and other Jews managed to transfer their businesses to the ghetto and opened shops and workshops. At the end of 1941, there were factories and workshops of various kinds operating in the Kielce Ghetto, including tinsmithing, upholstery, paving stones, metalwork, glaziery, carpentry, paint manufacture, dyeing, leather-working, shoe-making, etc. But even in aggregate, Jewish businesses in the Kielce Ghetto provided employment for but a few hundred Jews. Hunger was rife and many Jews were prepared to accept work of any kind within the ghetto, but the number of available jobs was much smaller than the number of those in search of employment.[22] The shortage of work became a severe problem. The gap between those with money in their pockets and the destitute thousands grew more acute, even though some began to live on their savings.

In the meantime the shortage of running water, an inadequate sewage system, and lack of medicine and sanitation facilities meant that typhus and tuberculosis reached epidemic proportions. Within a few weeks of the establishment of the ghetto, the supply of clothing was insufficient and there was also a severe shortage of food, since Poles were barred from entering the ghetto. Jews sold the clothing from their backs in exchange for a piece of bread. Children, their bellies swollen from hunger, picked through the garbage. The shortage of fuel meant that many suffered from cold. Jews died every day and the despair continued unabated.[23]

According to the statistics of the Judenrat's labor department for the months of July–August 1941, only 60 percent of the 5,300 Jewish men registered in the ghetto as fit for work were actually employed: 2,500 outside the ghetto and, in the ghetto itself, 320 as craftsmen and 400 for the Judenrat administration, including the Jewish police.[24] The unemployment rate for women was much higher, primarily due to the physically demanding nature of the work available. Very few women worked outside the ghetto, with the exception of day-laborers, generally employed in cleaning, laundry, or weeding. The proportion of women who worked inside the ghetto was probably less than a quarter of their total number. On this subject, Gertrude Zeisler, a refugee from Vienna, wrote in a letter dated 7 November 1941: "If there were only a chance of finding some kind of work. Unfortunately, it is impossible, especially for women. My friend tried to harvest potatoes for one day. She gave up, although she is a younger and more industrious worker than me. In the evening, she was on the verge of collapse and all she had accomplished was to ruin her last dress and shoes.... The world looks very gray."[25]

Herman Levy, who was a meek and accommodating man, meticulously carried out German orders in his capacity as Judenrat chairman. He was unable to mitigate the German decrees such as demands for supply of Jewish manpower for labor before the establishment of the ghetto, prohibition of trade with the gentile population, the prohibition of schools in the ghetto, and so on. Worse, tax collection stopped almost completely with the creation of the ghetto. Levy and his Judenrat colleagues tried a number of sporadic activities to help ease the suffering of the ghetto's inhabitants, such as the fumigation of homes and clothing, the vaccination of children against smallpox, the setting up of free coffee stations and two soup kitchens, as well as a committee to help the poor. But without financial resources the Judenrat was unable to cope with the severe shortages in the ghetto that affected every aspect of life and was forced to rely on charitable donations, which were also limited.[26]

Efraim Barash, on the other hand, earned his position of unchallenged leadership in the Białystok Ghetto by stressing certain basic principles. First, he realized that without funds in the Judenrat coffers, the ghetto's existence would be in grave danger. To confront the expected financial crisis, Barash appointed Dov Berl Sobotnik, who had a talent for resolving complicated financial problems, to head the Judenrat's financial department. Not long after the establishment of the ghetto, the Judenrat began collecting taxes and was consistently tough with those who tried to evade their responsibilities. The wealthy who refused to pay were imprisoned by the Jewish police and generally paid what was asked after a day or two in jail.[27]

Barash also understood that work was the key to survival—an intensive work strategy accompanied his policy throughout the whole period of occupation. It was Barash who decided to create factories in the ghetto, based on the premise that making the ghetto a productive place with cheap labor that could serve German interests would prevent future deportations. The idea gained momentum and garnered support both among the members of the Judenrat and among a considerable proportion of the ghetto's Jews. At the time, the underlying concept was logical and virtually impossible to contest.

The Białystok Ghetto became a sort of labor camp, not unlike the Łódź Ghetto. Białystok's ghetto factories and workshops produced shoes, clothes, barrels, rope, cigarettes, electrical appliances, hats, alcohol, chemicals, gloves, felt goods, brushes, boots, uniforms, suitcases, soda water, metals, wooden clogs, soap, haberdashery, knitted goods, wagons, leather, starch, fur, chemical dyes, cotton wool, toys, furniture, blankets, and medical dressings. The ghetto also had a laundry, a glass polishing plant, an upholsterer, sewing workshops, a blacksmith, and a saddler. Although most of the manufactured goods were designed for the German army's use, some were also sold on the private market.[28] At the same time, Barash became convinced that benefits derived from Jewish labor by the German ghetto rulers improved the attitude of the latter, and that the Białystok Ghetto would survive the war. By virtue of his prestige, integrity, education, and standing, he swept many along with him.

The Judenrat's efforts to stabilize the Białystok Ghetto economy bore fruit. It did not suffer from starvation. Effective food distribution, legal trade permits, food factories, and the conversion of vacant lots into vegetable gardens not only saved the ghetto residents from starvation but actually rendered their lives tolerable. Although at the time, January 1943, the Białystok Ghetto numbered about forty-one thousand residents—an easy number to feed compared with large ghettos such as Warsaw and Łódź—only a highly efficient economic administration could prevent dire shortages and serious economic hardships.[29] Memoir writers and survivors from Białystok confirm that throughout the year and a half of the ghetto's existence, until the *Aktion* of February 1943, daily life gradually stabilized and became tolerable relative to life under the yoke of occupation.

Optimism in Białystok was reinforced by two other factors, ironically related to deportations. First, in January 1943, Białystok's Jews realized that although the tens of thousands of Jews in the district, from towns like Grodno, Łomża, Sokółka, Grajewo, Wołkowysk, and others,[30] had been deported to Treblinka and Auschwitz between November 1942 and January 1943, the Białystok Ghetto had been left untouched. Second, in February 1943, when the Germans deported eight thousand of Białystok's own Jews to Treblinka and murdered two thousand more on site, they kept a promise to Barash, whereby they did not deport the workers and their families who had hidden in the factories during this *Aktion*.[31] The very fact that by February 1943 about twenty-nine thousand Jews in the Białystok Ghetto were the sole surviving Jews in the entire Białystok district reinforced Barash's certainty that a partial *Aktion* would suffice to appease the Germans, and that the remaining Jews would survive. The Jews in the ghetto, whose faith in Barash only increased, shared his conviction.

Following the February *Aktion,* Jewish public life in the Białystok Ghetto quickly returned to a familiar course. The hundreds of ghetto inhabitants who had previously ignored Barash's appeals to go to work learned their lesson from the *Aktion,* changed their minds, and began to see the factories as a relatively safe haven. The factories filled with young children and adults over sixty, heeding the Judenrat's calls and flooding the ghetto factories with manual labor, the demand for which continued to grow. A report on the labor situation in the ghetto in early March 1943 stated that, of its 29,000 Jewish inhabitants, 17,080 Jews were employed in factories inside and outside the ghetto, while

11,000 children, elderly, infirm, and otherwise disabled were unfit for work.[32] As a result of the efficient organization of the ghetto following the *Aktion,* the number of German orders for industrial products grew, and there was also an improvement in the inhabitants' economic circumstances.

Ironically, the overall feeling in the ghetto on the eve of its destruction was optimistic. As Haika Grosman, an activist in the ghetto underground, put it: "April [1943] has gone, and May has exploded into our lives with its sweet promise. Spring has come and gone, to be replaced by the summer of 1943. February's blood has been washed away by the spring showers, and the puddles of water have dried in the sun. The ghetto is quiet. Each day, workers leave for the workshops and factories. Each day Jews obediently leave the ghetto to serve their German masters."[33]

Jewish Police—Jüdische Ordnungsdienst

In addition to their role as Jewish "order service," Jewish ghetto police had judicial authority and, as in most of the ghettos, the authority to carry out sentences. The Jewish police formed a Judenrat department, often subordinate to the Judenrat chairman, although the limits of its criminal and administrative judicial authority varied from ghetto to ghetto. In Kielce, matters were different. With the transition to the ghetto in April 1941, control over the Jewish police was assigned to the Schupo (Schutzpolizei)—part of the German Security Police—which selected eighty Jewish policemen, mostly from Jewish refugees from Vienna and Łódź, although some local Jews and refugees from other parts of Poland were also included.[34] In early 1942, the number of Jewish policemen was increased to 120. Bruno Schindler, a German Jew who had arrived in Kielce from Łódź, was appointed chief of the Jewish police, and an Austrian refugee by the name of Gustav Spiegel was made his deputy. They wore dark blue uniforms, peaked caps, and armbands with the words "Jewish Order Police," and carried wooden or rubber truncheons.[35] In Kielce in particular, the Jewish police was under the very close and dominant supervision of the Schupo, receiving its orders directly from the commanders of the Schupo and the Gestapo, though technically part of the Judenrat.

Feeling protected by the authorities, the Jewish police took advantage of their position and, since most were refugees from Austria and Germany, they treated the Jews of Kielce as *Ostjuden*—wretched Polish Jews.[36] From survivor testimonies we further know that, relative to the prevailing hunger and poverty in the ghetto, the Jewish police lived lives of luxury and profligacy and engaged in drinking bouts at the ghetto's restaurants and canteens.[37] Some beat up lawbreakers, and going above and beyond the Germans' requirements. Policemen also were exempt from taxes, received increased food rations, demanded and received bribes from Jews, and even extorted money. On the whole, they were perceived throughout the ghetto as corrupt, and the entire Jewish public feared them and regarded them as an integral part of the German authorities in charge of the ghetto. Levy, head of the Judenrat, was unable to restrain the Jewish police, and it seems he made no effort to rid it of corruption.

The Jewish police force in Białystok, formed with the establishment of the ghetto there, numbered two hundred young Jewish men, mostly from the middle class: "educated, high school graduates, merchants, and anyone who was a member of the intelligentsia."[38] Yitzhak Marcus, a well-known and respected industrialist, was appointed chief of the ghetto police. In the first nine months, threatening and dangerous elements operated within the police force, terrorizing both the inhabitants and the Judenrat and jeopardizing continued reasonable existence within the ghetto. Barash was aware of the situation, but waited for a suitable time to convince the chief of police to denounce the corruption and dismiss those involved. In June 1942, Barash carried out a purge of the police ranks, during the course of which more than twenty corrupt policemen were sent to labor camps.[39] Afterward the Jewish police force was placed under the exclusive control of the Judenrat presidency and, in keeping with Barash's efforts to maintain high moral standards in the ghetto, the Jewish police refused to collaborate in the *Aktion* of February 1943, disobeying German orders to round up the Jews from their homes. Although they were severely beaten and accused of sabotaging the evacuation, the Jewish police threw off their hats and left the hunt for the Jews to the Germans themselves.[40]

Relations with the German Authorities

Barash cultivated good relations with the German police officials who oversaw the Białystok Ghetto, thereby mitigating or even abrogating some of the harsh decrees against its inhabitants. Through these Germans, Barash developed direct contacts, primarily with military officials from the German Armaments Ministry, whom he asked—employing the method of influence from lower to higher ranks—to intervene on the ghetto's behalf in Berlin. Barash's efforts resulted in an unending stream of visits by important German figures and even German committees from Königsberg and Berlin, to see Jewish industries and their products.[41] It was a type of foreign policy with the declared purpose of proving to the Germans that the Jews of Białystok were useful elements that were worth keeping. Barash strove to turn the local commanders into advocates on behalf of the ghetto, who conveyed its advantages even to the upper echelons in Berlin. He thereby hoped to buy time, and bring his ghetto safely to the end of the war.

Dr. Wilhelm Altenloh, the chief of the Security Police (KdS) overseeing Białystok, surely updated Barash regarding German plans for the future of the Jews in the district and town. Jewish and non-Jewish sources, including Mordechai Tenenbaum's diary, Haika Grosman's memoirs, the testimony of Barash's secretary Hadassah Shprung, Szymon Datner's historical research, and comprehensive legal material, show that Barash made every effort to forge ties with the local German authorities.[42] Shprung's testimony shows that throughout the ghetto's existence, Barash frequently paid visits to Gestapo officials. After a year of dealing with German officials, Barash knew who could be bought and who could not. He always brought valuable items to meetings with the Germans, such as a diamond, a gold coin, or on one occasion a valuable Persian rug, which he spread on the floor of the commander's office upon his arrival at local Gestapo headquarters.[43] At the very least, Barash's efforts bought time. In early October 1942, the Reich Main Security Office in Berlin ordered the Security Police in Białystok to evacuate twelve thousand Jews from the ghetto. The inspector of the German arms industry in the Białystok District (named Froese), and the deputy head of the civil administration in the district, (named Brix) both appealed to Berlin later in the month to spare the ghetto.[44]

Kielce was less equipped for such appeals. Security Police and SS in charge of the Kielce Ghetto were regularly present there, terrorizing its inhabitants. A series of zealous, bloodthirsty commanders viewed every Jew as a dangerous enemy, and neither Pelc nor Levy found a way to negotiate with the occupation authorities, or to create—through the ghetto commanders—a tolerable framework for thousands of Jews in conditions of terrible hardship. There is no evidence that Levy ever thought to convince the Germans, as had Barash, that cheap ghetto labor in return for food deliveries was to their benefit. Rather he accepted the situation too quickly, doing everything he could to satisfy the occupation authorities. Michael Weichert visited the Kielce Ghetto a number of times as head of the "Jewish Social Self-Help organization" based in Kraków and especially active in Warsaw.[45] He later testified that the Germans made Levy's life miserable, tormenting him and forcing him to take part in lavish meals in the city, at which exposed waitresses circulated among the tables.[46]

The Liquidations

The terrible life of the Kielce Ghetto ended quickly. Between 20 and 24 August 1942, seventeen months after its establishment, it was liquidated in three *Aktionen*. The evacuation was extremely brutal. Kielce's Jewish police ordered the thousands of Jews out of their homes. As disoriented Jews rushed in panic through the streets en route to the deportation point, German police struck them with whips, truncheons, and rifle butts while setting dogs on them. Since the number of freight cars that had arrived could not hold all of the deportees, the Germans shot twenty-five hundred Jews—the elderly, infirm, disabled, and children—on the spot. Bodies covered the ghetto's streets. The bulk of Kielce's Jews met their deaths in the Treblinka death camp. Following the selections and evacuation of the ghetto, the Germans left about two thousand Jews in a small part of the ghetto in order to clean up the area and collect all the possessions the Jews left behind. Levy and his family were included in this group. This small ghetto was a kind of labor camp and in late May 1943 was closed down. The majority of the seventeen hundred Jews left at the time were transferred as slave laborers to three industrial plants in the city of Kielce; about five hundred were sent to other slave labor camps in the Radom District.[47]

The liquidation of the Białystok Ghetto occurred with no previous warning. On 15 August 1943 special evacuation forces arrived from Lublin. Summoned to Gestapo headquarters, Barash was told that Białystok's Jews were to be transported, together with their families and industrial machinery, to work in Lublin. The Germans explained the transfer by pointing to the extensive industrial infrastructure existing in Lublin, under which conditions the productivity of the Jewish workers would certainly increase. Barash, confident of his own powers of persuasion, made one last attempt to get the order rescinded. But this time he faced Germans he did not know who could not be bargained with, begged, or bribed.[48]

In the final week of August 1943, without any help from the Jewish police, twenty-seven thousand Jews were deported from the Białystok Ghetto. Ten thousand of them, who had undergone early selection and were deemed unfit for work, were sent to Treblinka and Auschwitz. About fifteen thousand were sent to forced labor in the Majdanek network of concentration camps. About 1,250 Jewish children were sent to Theresienstadt to be exchanged for German prisoners.[49] A few hundred more hid in the ghetto, and about a thousand more remained in a smaller ghetto, ordered to collect all of the Jewish property and the industrial machines, which were sent to Lublin. About a month later, they too were sent to Lublin, and thus the Jewish community of Białystok, too, came to an end.[50]

Conclusions

The Kielce Ghetto is remembered as one of many ghettos annihilated during Operation Reinhard in the summer of 1942. The Białystok Ghetto is remembered as a story of persistence. Ultimately, life in the ghettos of Poland depended upon two main factors: local German commanders and Judenrat chairmen, whose primary role under a more benign occupation would have been limited to the orderly tax collection and the maintenance of an honest police force. These two tasks had the potential to create tolerable conditions for ghetto Jews. In Białystok there was a relatively unusual combination. The Germans and Ephraim Barash shared common interest in maintaining the ghetto's existence for the duration of the war. Barash bribed the Germans lavishly, and German administrators knew that overseeing the ghetto was preferable to military service on the eastern front. In an effort to buy time, Barash saw himself as a mediator in the tradition of Jewish intercessors who saved their people from destruction throughout history. He could not accept that an ideology would drive the Germans to destroy the Białystok Ghetto. An intelligent regime, he thought, would not murder its slaves. Barash, like most Jewish community leaders, could not understand that German policy was not based on utilitarian or rational considerations, and that in the long run, the Jewish fate would be determined by Nazi fanatics in Berlin.

In Kielce, Levy was more unquestioningly obedient to the Nazis. Worse, he failed to keep corruption in check, particularly within the aggressive regime of Kielce's Jewish police. The combination of German commanders who never ceased to inflict suffering on the Jews, and a corrupt internal Jewish administration controlled by the Jewish police, most of whom were not locals and lacked empathy for the Jews of Kielce, resulted in deterioration of life in the Kielce Ghetto to the depths of degradation and misery. In the struggle for survival in Kielce, there was no lack of scoundrels, informants, bribe takers, and thieves, who believed that every means, even the most despicable, was legitimate as long as it enabled them to survive another day. Jews came to suspect one another. Jewish decency and morality disappeared. Judenrat employees and Jewish police extorted money from ghetto inhabitants, and for payment, Jews even led the Germans to places in which their fellow Jews had hidden goods.

Levy managed to improve the social conditions in the ghetto for a short time and, in certain periods, even increased the Judenrat coffers. But many of Kielce's survivors blamed Levy for Kielce's devastation, complaining in their memoirs that his personal storehouses were filled with food, that he colluded with the corrupt police, and that he dutifully carried out German orders. Pelc, who was deported to Auschwitz on suspicion of collaboration with the Polish intelligentsia in Kielce, was murdered in the camp in 1941—even before the establishment of the ghetto. Herman Levy was suspected of having procured false documents and, in January 1943, was murdered by the Germans, in the Kielce cemetery, together with his wife and two sons. Barash and his wife and son were murdered during Operation Erntefest, on 3 November 1943, in one of the Majdanek camps, along with thousands of other Jewish slave laborers.

Notes

1. Tikva Fatal-Knaani, *Grodno Is Not the Same* (Jerusalem, 2001); Sara Bender, *The Jews of Białystok During World War II and the Holocaust*, trans.Yaffa Murciano (Hanover, NH, 2008);Yehuda Bauer, *The Death of the Shtetl* (New Haven, CT, 2009); Michal Unger, *Lodz: The Last Ghetto in Poland* (Jerusalem, 2005) [Hebrew]; Sara Bender, *In Enemy Land: The Jews of Kielce and the Vicinity During World War II—1939-1945* (Jerusalem, 2012) [Hebrew].

2. Samuel Kassow, "The Case of Lodz: New Research on the Last Ghetto in Poland," in *Yad Vashem Studies* 35, no. 2 (2007): 245.

3. Abraham Wein, ed., *Pinkas Hakehillot. Encyclopedia of Jewish Communities: Poland*, vol. 7, *Lublin and Kielce Districts* (Jerusalem, 1999), 496; Krzysztof Urbański, *Zagłada ludnośći zydowskiej Kielc 1939-1945* (Kielce, 1994), 53; Krzysztof Urbański, *Kieleccy Żydzi* (Kraków, 1992), 151; Adam Massalski and Stanisław Meducki, *Kielce w latach okupacji hitlerowskiej 1939-1945* (Ossolineum, 1986), 56.

4. Yad Vashem Archive [hereafter YVA], TR-10/823 (Wuppertall Trial), 26–97; Szymon Datner, *Pamięci 200,000 Żydow województwa białostockiego wymordowanych przez Niemców* (Łódź, 1946), 12–13. See also Christopher R. Browning, *Ordinary Men* (New York, 1992), 11–12; Heiner Lichtenstein, *Himmlers grüne Helfer* (Frankfurt, 1990), 77–78;YVA, TR-11/I 0116, 50-51. This estimate is based on a later assessment by the Judenrat.

5. Bender, *Białystok*, 98–103.

6. Pelc's son later described him as a strict and principled man, whose stubbornness got him into trouble with Jews and Poles alike. See Yochanan Peltz, *Zichronot* (Memoirs) (1990), a family booklet (in the author's possession). *Al beiteinu she-harav—Fun der khoruver heym* (editor not noted) (Tel Aviv, 1981), 76–78. See also Jan Sikorski,"Dr. Moyzesz Pelc," *Przegląd Lekarski* 45, no. 1 (1988): 180–81; Alice Birnhak, *Next Year God Willing* (New York, 1994), 6–11.

7. United States Holocaust Memorial Museum Archive [hereafter USHMMA], RG 15.031/12752.

8. Urbański, *Kieleccy Żydzi*, 150;Wein, *Pinkas Hakehillot*, vol. 7, 235; Mildred (Mania) Feferman-Washof, *The Processed*, memoirs written in 1945–1946 (USHMM Library, and in the author's possession), 11; Urbański, *Zagłada*, 50. According to Mosze Bahn's testimony in YVA, M-49E/66, the second contribution amounted to 1 million złoty. Most sources, however, cite the figure five hundred thousand.

9. *Pinkas Hakehillot*, 538; Sebastian Piątkowski, "Judenraty w dystrykcie radomskim," *Biuletyn Kwartalny Radomskiego Towarzystwa Naukowego* 33, no. 1 (1998): 62.

10. For a detailed list of the nationalized factories see the Kielce State Archive (Archiwum Państwowe w Kielcach) [hereafter APK], Documents pertaining to the city of Kielce:Verordnung über die Beschlagnahme des Vermögens des früheren polnischen Staates innerhalb des GG, APK, 15/11/1939, VBIGG (1939), 37; Verordnung über die Errichtung einer Treuhandstelle für das GG, vom 15/11/1939, APK,VBIGG I (1939), 36.

11. Adam Massalski and Stanisław Meducki, *Kielce w latach okupacji hitlerowskiej 1939-1945* (Ossolineum, 1986), 100; Urbański, *Zagłada*, 50; Feferman-Washof, *The Processed*, 8.

12. YVA, JM/3535, K44, 29-30; Adam Rutkowski, "Martyrologia, walka i zagłada ludności żydowskiej w dystrycie radomskim podczas okupacji hitlerowskiej," *Biuletyn Żydowskiego Instytutu Historycznego*, no. 15–16 (1955): 76.

13. Urbański, *Zagłada*, 64.

14. *Gazeta Żydowska*, no. 32, 1940 (*Gazeta Żydowska* was the Jewish newspaper published in the area of Generalgouvernement, with the permission of the German authorities. It began publishing in late 1940, with its main editorial office in Kraków);Wein, *Pinkas Hakehillot*, vol. 7, 497; Urbański, *Zagłada*, 62–63.

15. APK 03/2643, Anordnungsblatt für die Stadt Kielce, no. 7/1941, 2–5. See also YVA TR-10/911, 25;YVA M-49E/85, Testimony of Moshe Medlow, 1; APK 03/2640—Anordnungsblatt für die Stadt Kielce, no. 7/1941, 10.

16. YVA, 03/2985, Testimony of Jechiel Alpert, 5; YVA, M-49.E/66, Testimony of Mosze Meir Bahn; Urbański, *Zagłada*, 84; Testimony of Waclaw Ceberski, in Eugeniusz Fąfara, *Gehenna Ludności Zydowskiej* (Warsaw, 1983), 90.

17. Bender, *Białystok*, 104–5.

18. Nachman Blumental, *Darko shel Judenrat* (Conducts and Actions of a Judenrat, Documents from the Białystok Ghetto) (Jerusalem, 1962), 2, 549.

19. Bender, *Białystok*, 103.

20. YVA M-11/17, Peysekh Kaplan, "*Der Khurbn Bialystok*" (The Destruction in Białystok), March 1943; YVA, M-11/18, Kaplan, *Der Yidnrat in Bialystok* (The Judenrat in Białystok), March 1943, 16. See also Srulke Kot, *Khurbn Bialystok* (The Holocaust in Białystok) (Buenos Aires, 1947), 30.

21. *Gazeta Żydowska*, no. 97, 1941.

22. See YVA, 03/2983, Testimony of Jechiel Alpert, 5; *Gazeta Żydowska*, nos. 80 and 99, 1941.

23. Bender, *Kielce*, 145–55.

24. *Gazeta Żydowska*, no. 99, 1941.

25. Gertruda Zeisler, *I Did Not Survive: Letters from the Kielce Ghetto* (Jerusalem, 1981), 10.

26. Bender, *Kielce*, 165–67.

27. Bender, *Kielce*, 119–22.

28. Bender, *Kielce*, 129.

29. See Blumenthal, *Darko shel Judenrat*, 219, 221, 225; YVA, M-11/18, Kaplan, *Der Yidnrat in Bialystok*, 2–3.

30. Bender, *Białystok*, 169–72.

31. Bender, *Białystok*, 197–203.

32. Mordechai Tenenbaum-Tamaroff, *Dappim min ha-Delekah* (Pages from the Flames), new ed. (Jerusalem, undated), 75–76.

33. Haika Grosman, *Anshei ha-Mahteret* (The Underground Army) (Tel Aviv, 1965), 260.

34. Bundesarchiv—Außenstelle Ludwigsburg, testimonies of survivors from Kielce, taken by police investigators in various countries, including Israel, Argentina, the United States, Canada, Australia, and West Germany, to be used in the Kielce Trial, II 206 AR-Z 157/60 (StA. Darmstadt 2 Js. 1752/64 u.a), Testimony of Avraham Meir (24 March 1966).

35. Feferman-Washof, *The Processed*, 21; Urbański, *Zagłada*, 64; YVA M-49/E/66, Testimony of Mosze Meir Bahn,

36. According to Szaja Zalcberg, everyone knew that the Judenrat chairman Herman Levy had a cellar full of food. See YVA, M-49/E/1705, Testimony of Szaja Zalcberg. Alice Birnhak, who worked for the Judenrat, wrote in her memoirs that Levy increased his personal wealth in the ghetto, as did the Jewish police. See Birnhak, *Next Year God Willing*, 173, 185. Interview with Rafael Blumenfeld, January 2001 (author's archive). See also Testimony of Mosze Meir Bahn, in Fąfara, *Gehenna*, 75–77.

37. Bender, *Kielce*, 143–45, 148–50.

38. Kot, *Khurbn Bialystok*, 32. See also D. Klementinowsky, *Lebn un Umkum in Bialystoker Geto* (New York, 1946), 39–40; Blumental, *Darko shel Judenrat*, 187–91; Raphael Reizner, *Der Umkum fun Bialystoker Yidntum 1939-1945* (Melbourne, 1948), 93–94.

39. Bender, *Białystok*, 135–38.

40. Tenenbaum-Tamaroff, *Dappim min ha-Delekah*, 66. See also Kot, *Khurbn Bialystok*, 59.

41. Bender, *Białystok*, 131–32.

42. Interview with Szymon Datner in Warsaw, April 1983.

43. Testimony of Hadassah Shprung Levkowitz, 1983, 1991 (author's archive).

44. Tenenbaum-Tamaroff, *Dappim min ha-Delekah*, 53. See also YVA, Testimony of Fritz Friedel, written in prison in Białystok, 12–13 June 1949, Israel Police, Department for the Investigation of Nazi Crimes, Bureau 06, Israel Police 1505, 21.

45. The "Jewish Social Self-Help" organization (Yiddisher Sozyaler Aleynhilf—Zydowska

Samopomoc Społeczna), was established in April 1940 in Warsaw, with headquarters in Kraków. The organization would become an autonomous institution, operating with German permission.

46. YVA, M-49/E/66, Testimony of Mosze Meir Bahn.

47. Bender, *Kielce,* 181–98.

48. Testimony of Fritz Friedel, YVA, 1505, Department for the Investigation of Nazi Crimes, Israel Police Bureau 06, Manuscript of Fritz Friedel, 12-13.6.1949. See also Berl Mark, *Der Oyfshtand in Bialystoker Geto* (Warsaw, 1950), 375.

49. Bender, *Białystok,* 269–73.

50. Bender, *Białystok,* 250–58, 264–76.

Part III

DOCUMENTATION, TESTIMONY, AND EXPERIENCE

CHAPTER 5

Diaries, Testimonies, and Jewish Histories of the Holocaust

ALEXANDRA GARBARINI

Jewish histories of the Holocaust place Jews at the center of historical narratives as the subjects of Holocaust history.[1] Yet ever since the Holocaust has become central to histories of twentieth-century Europe, historians have overwhelmingly devoted themselves to the study of perpetrators (the main exception being Israeli Holocaust historiography in Hebrew). Jewish victims of the Nazis' "Final Solution to the Jewish Question" are more readily slotted into the role of objects of history, as the more or less helpless civilians who found themselves acted upon by powerful German agents of domination and destruction.

In recent years, however, a shift is detectable. Scholars have begun to regard the history of the Nazis' Jewish victims as worthy of critical analysis in its own right. While acknowledging that European Jews were ultimately unable to counter the forces intent on eliminating them, historians also increasingly look upon Jews not merely as the objects of Nazi exterminatory policies but as historical subjects who responded in complex ways to their persecution and murder. Scholars investigating Jewish responses to the antisemitic policies and actions of the Nazis and those who cooperated with them, among other topics, have focused on the commitment of European Jews—individually and collectively, during the war and in the immediate postwar years—to documenting their experiences of victimization. The scholarship on Holocaust testimonies has cast light on the extent of this phenomenon and on those who spearheaded contemporary documentation projects, the results of which became the core collections of several substantial archives devoted to the history and memory of the Holocaust in Europe and Israel.[2]

Notes for this section begin on page 102.

This essay sets out an argument about the importance of one particular type of source material for writing Jewish histories of the Holocaust: diaries. There are two questions I address in the following pages. The first concerns theoretical and methodological issues surrounding the use of diaries by historians: How should historians use and analyze diaries? The second question concerns more strictly historical issues: What aspects of the history of the Holocaust do diaries open to view and make available for analysis? Without in any way denigrating the value of autobiographical sources produced after the war, I argue that there is value to parsing Jewish testimonial literature on the basis of the context of production. I do not seek to characterize retrospective accounts as "unreliable" and contemporaneous accounts as "authentic."[3] Instead I put forth the potentially paradoxical assertion that all autobiographical texts are reliable *and* mediated (indeed, this claim describes all sources used by historians). If we understand reliability not in black-and-white terms but in terms that allow for qualification, then the obvious question for any source is to think creatively about what it may be trusted to reveal. Diaries permit historians to pose the dual question how the persecution and mass murder of European Jews were understood at the time by the very people designated as victims—and how do we understand such events today and, on the basis of our present understanding, analyze contemporaneously produced sources? Ultimately, the theoretical/methodological and the historical are linked. How we conceptualize and approach diaries as sources has fundamental implications for how we understand the past and what we understand about it—for discerning Jewish understandings, and thus for writing Jewish histories of the Holocaust.

Theoretical and Methodological Issues

I argue for the importance of disaggregating diaries from autobiographical texts produced after the war. Diaries are typically lumped together with other Jewish autobiographical sources produced in the postwar years, all of which scholars conventionally refer to as "testimonies." The categorization of diaries as testimonies emphasizes over all other factors, first, the identity of the author as a Jewish Holocaust victim; second, the autobiographical nature of the texts; and third, the intentionality that underlay these sources' production—that they exist because their authors chose to recount their own experiences in order to contribute to a broader understanding of the history of the Holocaust.[4] Yet there are other characteristics of these sources of potentially greater historical significance that are occluded by the category "testimonies." When we conflate diaries with postwar testimonies and memorial literature, crucial aspects of the Jewish history of the Holocaust are lost to view.

"Testimonies" is not a synonym for "diaries." Indeed, diaries offer different insights and raise different source criticism issues. Historians must be attuned not only to authorship (to the relationship of the author to the object of writing) but also to time and the context of production. If, as Paul Ricoeur has argued, "truth is time-dependent" in narratives, then diarists wrote in a state of what he called "prefiguration" and "figuration," when the goal of narrative is to understand and respond on the basis of one's understanding. Survivors' retrospective point of view, or "refiguration," leads to the reordering of the significance of events based on their knowledge of outcomes. Whereas a survivor's story is "pulled toward its future," that of a diarist writing during the war is "pushed onward by its past."[5]

In analyzing diaries as distinct from survivors' recountings, the significance of time and the context of textual production are also usefully conceptualized in terms borrowed from Reinhart Koselleck. The events of 1940 or 1943 may "have occurred once and for all, but the experiences which are based upon them" are not fixed and keep changing because they stand in relation to a different totality of experience.[6] Diarists and survivors do not share, in Koselleck's words, the same "space of experience," the same historical past and present circumstances. Nor do they share the same "horizon of expectation," the same sense of the future they were living toward. The "horizon of expectation" before diarists' eyes differed markedly from what in the end actually occurred, which became the "space of experience" of survivors as they reflected back on their past. Moreover, the "expectations of the future" held by survivors at war's end helped to shape how they recalled their experiences during the war. Those expectations were wholly different, of course, from the expectations during the war, which themselves changed as the war progressed. Attending to how diarists' changing sense of the future during the war influenced their experiences and interpretations of the present in their diaries enriches historians' knowledge and understanding of Jews' historical experiences.

Clearly diarists did not have the concepts at their disposal that memoirists would later have and use. Texts produced after the war are "mediated by the full knowledge of the horrors of the camps—conditions that were not known at the time," as Zoë Vania Waxman put it.[7] For Jews writing during the war, the Holocaust did not exist in their minds as a singular historical event, as a concept that unified European Jews' disparate wartime experiences under different political and military authorities, German and non-German. Nor were diarists' narratives shaped by or premised upon the fact of their own individual survival. Indeed, a shift is detectable in diaries as far as the expectations people articulated for individual and Jewish collective survival are concerned. In diaries written before 1942 or 1943, individual survival was in question whereas the survival of European Jewish communities in some form was a given. After

1943, and certainly after the war, the possibility and later the fact of individual survival became overshadowed by awareness of the millions murdered, even if individual survival took on symbolic meaning for some as proof that Hitler's "Final Solution" remained incomplete.[8]

To call attention to diarists not having had at their disposal the concepts and knowledge that developed later is not tantamount to saying that diaries are unmediated or truer than postwar accounts. The absence of a "temporal filter" between Jews' experiences of persecution and mass murder *and* the moment in which they documented those experiences does not make diaries more straightforward or reliable.[9] Diaries do not speak for themselves. Historians must employ the same critical methods in reading diaries that they employ in interpreting other sources. Diary writing entails narration, imposing order on experiences. Diary entries have themes, derived from diarists' own reading and earlier experiences. For these reasons, diaries require analysis, synthesis, and framing.[10] They need to be read in the context of the history of diary writing, European Jewish history, and individuals' biographies—as well as in conjunction with other sources produced contemporaneously with the unfolding events later known as the Holocaust. After all, depending on the individual, diarists had murky or elaborated ideas about truth, evidence, history, justice, about Jewish identity, European culture, political ideologies, God, man, and the self. In the course of their writing they appropriated, adapted, contested, and rejected wholesale concepts in their heads. Those concepts derived from before the war and during, from reading history, literature, and sacred texts, from personal experiences, family and local ties, no less than collective frameworks of belonging. Diarists certainly had their own sense of the historical significance of the events through which they were living. Their writing was an outgrowth of that sense, reflected that sense, and was mediated by the concepts they employed.

Foregrounding the importance of diaries' contemporaneity as compared to their autobiographical quality means that diaries help reconstruct "what happened." But even more so, diaries make an unparalleled contribution to understanding what Dan Michman has described as the "micro dynamics—i.e., the changes—in cultural perceptions and concepts throughout the period between 1933 and 1945."[11] They make visible that which was fleeting, what people thought and did in the here-and-now, whether or not it had tangible impact on the future. The past, in other words, is not just composed of events; it is also composed of "the realm of the possible," the perhapses and might-have-beens that help define historical agents' "space of experience" and "horizon of expectation."[12] Examining what people invested with meaning and what they imagined expands historians' notion of Jewish agency beyond simply understanding decisions Jews made that helped them survive or perish. Limiting historical importance to actions that had life-or-death consequences reduces people's experiences to a binary outcome. We need to consider the depth and breadth of Jews' experiences so that their lives do not become "epiphenomena" of the catastrophe.[13] Diaries and other documents produced during the war reveal meanings Jews imparted to their lives, their worlds, and the experiences they were undergoing. What is more, diary writing did not just reflect or convey what an individual already knew to be true but also formed part of an individual's effort to render their present suffering meaningful.

New Jewish Histories of the Holocaust

These theoretical and methodological considerations set up a discussion of aspects of the Jewish history of the Holocaust that diaries open to view when we read them separate from testimonies. For one, diaries reveal that even during the war, philosophical and literary issues that became central to postwar reflection on the meaning and implications of the Holocaust—and that seemed to be predicated on the concepts elaborated and historical knowledge accumulated after the war—were already emerging. Perhaps most intriguing is that we can trace the articulation of such issues to Jewish diarists who had no way to piece together the European-wide scale of what was occurring. Jewish diarists' struggles to represent their experiences and their sense of themselves as knowledgeable in the absence of that big picture are highly suggestive. For whereas Holocaust historians traditionally consider knowledge as accretive and thus show a preference for sources that convey a broader perspective (particularly those produced by German government officials), a careful reading of Jewish diaries suggests a different form of knowledge and valuing of the micro.[14] Indeed, it seems more appropriate to regard diarists, not as myopic and unperceiving, but as sophisticated thinkers and worldly-wise despite their isolation.

Lucien Dreyfus (born 1882, Westhouse, Alsace; died 1943 [?], Auschwitz-Birkenau) is one example of a diarist who did not comprehend the full scope of the ensuing Nazi extermination of the Jews. But he nonetheless reached similar conclusions to some postwar leftist thinkers and Orthodox Jewish commentators about the political-moral and theological implications of what would come to be known as the Shoah. A teacher at a lycée in Strasbourg and editor of the most prominent Jewish organ published in Alsace and Lorraine, the weekly *La Tribune Juive,* Dreyfus had espoused throughout his adult life the conviction that the Jewish and French aspects of his identity were complementary.[15] The French Third Republic's collapse and the new Vichy regime's anti-Jewish policies called into question his identity as equally French and Jewish and, what was more, provoked him to question the fundamental morality of Western civilization.[16] In his diary entries, he lamented the disappearance of the humanitarian instincts of European bourgeois society, and he became convinced that "the success of the patron of Berchtesgaden [Hitler] can only be explained by the complicity of the entire European bourgeoisie who shared his antipathies or exploited them."[17] He conjectured that, ultimately, the bourgeoisie's hateful instincts and need "to be superior to their fellow man" had fueled disdain for the stranger and made war a necessity.[18] Thus France's renunciation of universalist principles and the return of war to Europe was tantamount to a betrayal of Dreyfus's dearly held faith in France.

During the first three years of the war, Dreyfus's diary entries testify to his sense of helplessness in the face of human malevolence and his turn to God and theodicy to rescue hope in justice and morality. Having abandoned rabbinical school as a young man, he now looked to the eternity of divine justice in order to explain the deep causes of Jews' wartime suffering. Religious faith filled the void created by Dreyfus's disillusionment with France and Western civilization. He explained: "These ideas correspond to my temperament, and if in these notebooks I occupy myself with nothing other than the highest principle of man, the fact is that the rest of what preoccupies my loved ones, even the war, is nothing vis-à-vis the problem posed by the Bible. There is a God who punishes and rewards.... I will not seek to convince those opposing, but I intend to keep intact the spiritual traditions that date back to Sinai."[19] To account for Jewish suffering, he returned to a traditional Jewish view of history. Beginning with the Bible, Jews injected history with meaningfulness. God was radically other, his ways inscrutable, and yet human history offered clues about how God judged his creations' exercise of free will. Dreyfus thus resorted to theodicy in his attempt to make known God's reasons for "punishing" the Jews.[20] He speculated that Jewish assimilation had provoked God's wrath.

When Dreyfus heard reports (from sources he did not specify) beginning in July 1942 about mass murders of Jews in Poland, his reliance on "spiritual traditions" to explain Jewish suffering was not shaken. Moreover, the news that first reached him in Nice about the massacre of seven hundred thousand Polish Jews only confirmed his belief that the entire Western world shared responsibility for "the catastrophe of this war."[21] "Everyone is guilty," he declared.[22] From his perch on the Mediterranean coast, he did not possess knowledge of the European-wide extent of the genocide of Jews then underway, but he still regarded Western civilization as having become morally bankrupt. He attributed its decline to modern society's abandonment of religion, and wartime events proved to Dreyfus that religion was as necessary to human society in modern times as before. "The decline of the religious idea facilitated the explosion of anti-Jewish hatred and the catastrophe of this war.... That which does not agree with science and human reason can all the same be indispensable to life in society. It is necessary to prove that science and reason have in themselves destructive tendencies, and this reflection forces a person to the necessity of recognizing a [higher] authority."[23] Dreyfus assigned responsibility for the war and the murder of Jews to liberal enlightened society (the proponents of "science and human reason") as well as to the obvious perpetrators, the Nazis. He determined that science and reason were themselves harmful, and this conclusion led him to despair of the possibility that human beings would create a just society without religion.

It is perhaps curious to twenty-first-century readers of Dreyfus's diary that the murder in Poland of hundreds of thousands of Jews did not strike him as unprecedented or as requiring explanation beyond what he took to be the hideous nature of human beings. By contrast, he regarded the betrayal by the French regime in Vichy, by dispossessing Jews of their rights as French citizens, as having broken a covenant between the French and the Jews. The latter occurrence called for a larger explanation; it constituted, in his eyes, divine reprisal for the sinfulness of French Jews, although it also attested to the moral bankruptcy of secular democracy. Yet the killings in Poland he understood to be in line with the pogroms from the past: "They speak of 700,000 Jews killed in Poland and the surrounding area. This figure is not necessarily an exaggeration. In proportion to the number of Jews dispersed world-wide, it is not as many as during the epoch of Chmielnicki persecutions."[24] Strikingly, he did not regard the mass murder of Polish Jews as qualitatively different from, or even as surpassing in scale, other instances in history in which Jews were killed en masse.

Dreyfus was wrong, of course. The "Final Solution" had no parallel in Jewish history. At a remove from events in Poland and having limited information, Dreyfus could not grasp the enormity of the unfolding extermination of European Jews, much less that he and his wife would soon be caught in the SS dragnet to share the fate of Polish Jewry.[25] Yet incorrect though he was, his diary remains an invaluable source. Rather than read Dreyfus's diary to take stock of Jews' ignorance and to try to pinpoint if and when he came to understand "the Holocaust" as we now understand it, a close reading of Dreyfus's diary reveals the sophistication of his thinking about these events as they were unfolding, in spite of his lack of complete knowledge. Moreover, Dreyfus's deepened belief is barely represented in the historical literature on Jewish responses to the Shoah—especially given his identity as a bourgeois, acculturated west European Jew—even though he was far from exceptional; there were other victims who became more believing Jews during the Holocaust.[26] Furthermore, his theological interpretation of the meaning of Jewish wartime suffering was common among Orthodox Jews during and after the Shoah.[27] And at the same time that the reinforcement of Dreyfus's religious faith is a less familiar story, his questioning of Western civilization and humanist values has become central to post-Holocaust discussions.[28] Many Holocaust victims and survivors shared his sense of the betrayal of liberal enlightened society.[29] His disillusionment with France and the European bourgeoisie, as well as his refusal to exonerate France from culpability in the persecution of the Jews, anticipated the leading postwar interpretations of Vichy France and the Allies. This aspect of Dreyfus's analysis was trenchant, even if some of the answers he arrived at seem incongruous, in particular that he maintained his trust in God rather than becoming deeply cynical or nihilistic.

In contrast to Dreyfus, diarists writing in Poland in the context of the mass killings of 1942 and 1943 came to believe they faced a historically unprecedented situation. Writing about their experiences for a postwar audience made manifest their sense of the unrepresentability of their experiences. That recognition only deepened their alienation from the outside world, i.e., their intended audience. The reflections and worries articulated by Margarete (Grete) Bolchower (née Presser; postwar, Holländer) in her diary serve as an example of the struggles many Jewish writers articulated in attempting to document their experiences during the war. Again we find that issues, which gained theoretical significance in discussions among postwar writers and historians of the Holocaust, emerged earlier, before the conceptual and historical awareness of "the Holocaust" became consolidated. Bolchower's diary entries also demonstrate the importance of reading diaries analytically, with an awareness of literary devices and influences.

Bolchower was a German-speaking Jewish woman from Cieszyn in Silesia, on the Polish-Czech border. When the war began in 1939, she fled with her husband and only daughter to her husband's parents' home in Czortków, in eastern Galicia. After the Germans replaced the Soviets as overlords in Czortków in June 1941, Bolchower's husband, Marek, was killed in an *Aktion*. She placed her daughter Sonya in hiding with a Ukrainian peasant family, and she escaped the liquidation of the Czortków Ghetto and went into hiding herself in 1943 with two other Jews in a sheep stall on a Polish farmer's property. Once there, she began keeping a diary.

In her diary entries, Bolchower sometimes reflected on the impossibility of conveying Jewish wartime experiences to outside readers. In an entry of 30 July 1943—the first week of her diary—she admitted her "great predilection for adventure novels" and explicitly—and sarcastically—she identified her wartime experiences with that genre of writing: "Life has done me the favor and bestowed upon me the most improbable adventure."[30] The adventure metaphor imparted a kind of familiarity to her circumstances, as if she were now a protagonist in one of those stories. It became a way for her to render her experience comprehensible to others. In some instances, she presented her experiences with the tropes of the adventure genre, clearly recognizing their suspense value, and she employed recognizable literary devices to embellish them. But in other moments, Bolchower noted that the adventure model did not fit. Jews' wartime experiences were both more extreme than fictional adventure stories and full of terror instead of thrills: "The kitschiest adventure film, the craziest sensationalist novel is boring compared with our present life. If someone were to film it all, it would be the most interesting, sit on the edge of your seat film! For us it is only horrible, since it is unfortunately the bitterest reality [and] means the fight for our bare existence."[31] Bolchower emphasized how different the perspective of the Jewish insider was from that of the outsider. For Jews, not only were their experiences far removed from a generic adventure, but the genre was inadequate as a structure for Bolchower to understand or communicate her experiences.

Bolchower was concerned that the readers of her diary would not be able to empathize with Jews' experiences. Indeed, like other diarists, she feared not that Jews' experiences would remain unknown by the outside world but that they would never be emotionally assimilated by anyone else. Bolchower was confident that "[w]hen this horrible war finally ends, surely thousands of books will be written. But I do not believe that anyone who has not experienced it first-hand could feel a fraction of the incomprehensible horror, of the uninterrupted terror, the helplessness, and the powerless rage in which we have, already for over two years, lived?"[32] Bolchower was like so many other diarists who did not believe that their efforts to communicate their experiences would bridge the experiential chasm between them and the outside world. Many of them feared (in a way distinct from but related to the concerns of later scholars) that their diaries falsely transformed their experiences into narratives—distorting their experiences rather than facilitating a deeper understanding of what they had lived through and been made to suffer.

At the same time, Jews who wrote during the war about their experiences regarded the written word as extraordinarily powerful even if it was ultimately an insufficient medium.[33] And so, Jews like Bolchower continued to record diary entries, even as they despaired of the efficacy of the representations they were creating, even as they felt they were embarking on a quest doomed to fail. They insisted that futility or despair be offset by the hope that something of the reality of their experiences would be imparted in and through their diaries.[34] In trying to represent their experiences in writing, many Jews continued to hope that those experiences might yet be rendered meaningful because they would be known, remembered, invoked, and utilized in the pursuit of justice and knowledge after the war. This was one of their survival techniques. Bolchower herself survived the war, as did the other two Jews with whom she hid. Her daughter, Sonya, died, apparently of disease.

These near-sighted first-person documents, then, are rich sources that demonstrate Jews' struggles to make their lives meaningful in the midst of catastrophe—a catastrophe that they understood in local terms, on the basis of their past and present experiences, their understandings of history, literature, and human nature, and also their expectations of the future. Indeed, diaries allow us to recognize that the individually and collectively constituted "horizons of expectation" of Jews living during the war included anticipated futures different from what has come to be known as the Holocaust. Diaries allow us to identify and understand those horizons.[35] The Jewish historical commissions and other documentation projects to which survivors remained dedicated in the aftermath of the Holocaust and beyond exist on a continuum with these wartime documentation efforts. But there are insights to be gained in considering, independently as well as on a continuum, the diaries, testimonies, and other forms of documentation created by Jewish victims in distinct historical moments.

Thus far, my reading of Lucien Dreyfus's and Grete Bolchower's diaries could be seen as pushing backward our periodization of certain issues, from the postwar years to the war years themselves. At the same time, Bolchower's articulation, in 1943, that an unbridgeable chasm had opened up between Jewish victims and the outside world would appear to reinforce the notion that it was the mass killings of Jews beginning in the second half of 1941 that precipitated Jews' sense of rupture. By way of conclusion, I want to share some provisional thoughts about how a consideration of diaries separate from postwar literature and in conjunction with other contemporaneous literature can bring renewed attention to what came *before* and why such an undertaking is historically significant.

For it turns out that, at the end of 1940, before the onset of genocide, Jewish commentators expressed the inadequacy of language to capture early wartime Jewish experiences in Poland. Two examples will suffice. At the end of 1940, the *American Jewish Year Book* of the American Jewish Committee, consistent with its standard format, devoted Part II of its contents to country reports chronicling the significant events and developments that had touched the lives of Jewish communities across the globe during the preceding year. Uncharacteristically, however, the report on "Poland" did not launch directly into a chronicle of major developments but commenced with a quote from Habakkuk I:5: "A work is done in your days, / which ye will not believe though it be told." In so doing, the unattributed report writer framed the condition of Polish Jewry as having taken on biblical proportions. Readers were made to pause before being allowed to continue with their summary reading of the various situations in which their fellow Jews found themselves across much of Europe. The magnitude of the crisis of Polish Jewry in the beginning of the war, the sense of unprecedented catastrophe that was underway and the extent to which they were being abandoned to their fate, was further driven home to readers in the report's introductory paragraph: "The story of the Jews in Poland during the past year is the story of what is probably the greatest tragedy in the entire history of Israel.... Facts and figures, names and dates, become but inadequate symbols and shrunken garments. Three million broken lives cannot be set down on paper."[36] This sense of the inadequacy of language and even of numbers to represent the suffering of Polish Jews after a year and a half of German occupation indicates that a sense of rupture in Jewish history predated the onset of genocide. The author of this entry from the 1940 edition of the *American Jewish Year Book* suggested that Polish Jewry could not be restored to its former condition.

Richard Lichtheim, the Jewish Agency representative in Geneva, penned a report in December 1940 that offered a similar interpretation of the historical significance of the suffering of Polish Jews. As with the *American Jewish Year Book,* Lichtheim's report predated the onset of Polish Jews' systematic mass murder. He reflected on the larger implications of the circumstances of Jews in Poland, elsewhere in Europe, and around the globe. Perhaps informed by his firsthand exposure to the extermination of Armenians by the Ottoman Empire during World War I, he expressed the conviction that, whether or not a new calamity struck European Jews, the events of the last few years meant that the European Jewish future would look entirely different from the past. In so many words, he, too, argued that recent events constituted a fundamental break with the previous course of Jewish history, that the return of what had been was no longer possible.[37] These commentators did not anticipate "the Holocaust." Rather, they stressed the unprecedented nature of the Jewish suffering and displacement that had already occurred, especially in Poland. Subsequent developments have tended to overshadow that historical reality and perception. Thus, diaries and other contemporaneous documents contribute to our understanding of gradations of experience and perceptual differences, including a sense of historical rupture and unprecedented suffering that developed prior to and not in the wake of the genocide that we have come to call the Holocaust.

Examples such as these from the first year and a half of the war underscore the importance of analyzing the phenomenon of contemporaneous "bearing witness" in diaries and related sources in connection to what came before rather than, or at least separately from, what came after. To understand why Jews in so many parts of German-occupied Europe responded to their persecution and impending extermination during the years 1939 to 1945 by producing written accounts of their experiences and collecting accounts of the experiences of others, to understand why Grete Bolchower continued to force herself to write, to understand why other diarists, like Yitzhak Katzenelson, who described diary writing as "scraping running sores day by day," forced themselves to write, necessitates disaggregating Holocaust-era sources from postwar sources in order to analyze what concepts of justice, violence, truth, and evidence underpinned Jews' documentation efforts in this period. It is widely recognized that bearing witness to mass atrocities and the horrors of war did not originate with the Holocaust. Historians Jay Winter, Omer Bartov, David Engel, Samuel Kassow, and Laura Jokusch, and literary scholar David Roskies, among others, have written about modes of expression that developed in the era of World War I and point the way toward the testimonial practices of the Holocaust era.[38] Already a generation before, in the nineteen-teens and -twenties, people of different backgrounds who had experienced violence firsthand developed strategies of documentation and publication. The struggle of Grete Bolchower—her worries about representation—was not new to Jews writing after the mass deportations and killings from 1942 onward. These were familiar tropes of anxiety that were discussed and weighed over a generation before the Holocaust. The tradition of atrocity documentation was well established by the generation of Bolchower's parents.

Conducting research on these earlier practices and representations can contribute to bridging what historian Alon Confino recently characterized as "the daunting interpretative gap between the anti-Jewish persecution of the prewar years and the subsequent almost unimaginable total extermination."[39] The different perspectives offered by diarists—their near-sighted perspectives—in combination with the retrospective, far-sighted documents of survivors, give us a richer, fuller understanding of what we have come to know as the Holocaust.

Notes

1. Since the exchange of letters between Martin Broszat and Saul Friedländer in 1987, what ought to stand at the center of histories of the Nazi era remains a matter of contention. For Broszat and Friedländer's essays on the historicization of the Nazi era and subsequent correspondence, see Peter Baldwin, ed., *Reworking the Past: Hitler, the Holocaust, and the Historians' Debate* (Boston, 1990), 77–134. For a recent debate in which the centering of victims' experiences features prominently, see the review forum about Donald Bloxham, *The Final Solution: A Genocide* (Oxford, 2009), in *Journal of Genocide Research* 13, no. 1 (2011): 107–52, particularly the contributions by Omer Bartov (121–29) and Doris Bergen (129–34) and Bloxham's response (135–48).

2. A few examples of such scholarship include: Alexandra Garbarini, *Numbered Days: Diaries and the Holocaust* (New Haven, CT, 2006); Samuel D. Kassow, *Who Will Write Our History? Emanuel Ringelblum, the Warsaw Ghetto, and the Oyneg Shabes Archive* (Bloomington, IN, 2007); Laura Jokusch, *Collect and Record! Jewish Holocaust Documentation in Early Postwar Europe* (New York, 2012).

3. Thus, my argument is entirely distinct from that of historians of a different generation who expressed distrust toward Jewish retrospective accounts of the Holocaust because of factual inaccuracies contained therein. Lucy S. Dawidowicz, for example, described the tedium entailed in the process of "separating the documentary wheat from the epitaphic chaff." Lucy S. Dawidowicz, *The War Against the Jews, 1933-1945* (New York, 1975), 438. Yisrael Gutman wrote in a similar vein as Dawidowicz. In the preface to his book, *The Jews of Warsaw*, Gutman commented: "A scholar cannot afford to ignore such diversified works, which contain extremely important authentic material. On the other hand, he cannot ignore the fact that a large portion of this literature suffers from a number of drawbacks." Such drawbacks include factual errors and "a very personal and idiosyncratic viewpoint." Yisrael Gutman, *The Jews of Warsaw, 1939-1943: Ghetto, Underground, Revolt,* trans. Ina Friedman (Bloomington, IN, 1982), x.

4. On different types of evidence and historians' privileging of indirect, or unintentional, sources, see Marc Bloch, *The Historian's Craft,* trans. Peter Putnam (New York, 1953), 60–69. For a discussion of Marc Bloch's differentiation of evidence in relation to testimonies in particular, see Devin Pendas, "Testimony," in *Reading Primary Sources: The Interpretation of Texts from Nineteenth- and Twentieth-Century History,* ed. Miriam Dobson and Benjamin Ziemann (New York, 2009), 226–27.

5. Paul Ricoeur, *Time and Narrative,* vol. 1, trans. Kathleen McLaughlin and David Pellauer (Chicago, 1984), discussed in Wallace Martin, *Recent Theories of Narrative* (Ithaca, NY, 1986), 66, 72–76.

6. Reinhart Koselleck, "'Space of Experience' and 'Horizon of Expectations': Two Historical Categories," in *Futures Past: On the Semantics of Historical Time,* trans. Keith Tribe (Cambridge, MA, 1985), 273–75.

7. Zoë Vania Waxman, *Writing the Holocaust: Identity, Testimony, Representation* (New York, 2006), 56.

8. For a fuller discussion of the chasm of 1942–43 in Jewish diarists' understanding of individual and collective survival, see Garbarini, *Numbered Days,* ch. 5.

9. On the concept of a "temporal filter," see Pendas, "Testimony," 238.

10. On this point, I am in agreement with Amos Goldberg, "The Victim's Voice and Melodramatic Aesthetics in History," *History and Theory* 48, no. 3 (2009): 222. Nicholas Stargardt makes a similar point about the need for historians to employ "normal types of analytical scrutiny" in interpreting survivors' testimony in: "The 'Final Solution'," in *Twentieth-Century Germany: Politics, Culture, and Society, 1918-1990,* ed. Mary Fulbrook (New York, 2001), 152–53.

11. Dan Michman, "Introducing More 'Cultural History' into the Study of the Holocaust: A Response to Dan Stone," *Dapim* 23 (2009): 75. For a discussion of how historians should approach reading diaries that accords with my own, see Christa Hämmerle, "Diaries," in *Reading Primary Sources: The Interpretation of Texts from Nineteenth- and Twentieth-Century History,* ed. Miriam Dobson and Benjamin Ziemann (New York, 2009), 141–68.

12. Hannu Salmi, "Cultural History, the Possible, and the Principle of Plenitude," *History and Theory* 50, n. 2 (2011): 172–73, 183.

13. This phrasing is borrowed from psychologist Henry Greenspan, in his remarks at the Rutgers University Conference: "Testimonies, Personal Narratives, and Alternative Tellings: An Interdisciplinary Perspective," 27–28 March 2011. I am grateful to him for permission to quote him. Greenspan elaborates on this idea in *On Listening to Holocaust Survivors: Beyond Testimony,* rev. ed. (St. Paul, MN, 2010), 77–79.

14. The classic example is Raul Hilberg's monumental work, *The Destruction of European Jews,* rev. and expanded ed. (New York, 1985).

15. Consonant with the ideology of "Franco-Judaism," Dreyfus espoused in his published and unpublished writing that it was possible for French Jews to "have Jewish souls, [while] speaking the French language." United States Holocaust Memorial Museum Archive [hereafter USHMMA], Dreyfus, 17 September 1925, RG 10.144.02. All translations from the French are my own. On "Franco-Judaism," see Vicki Caron, *Between France and Germany: The Jews of Alsace-Lorraine, 1871–1918* (Stanford, CA, 1988), 9. On the related concept of "republican Judaism," see Pierre Birnbaum, *The Jews of the Republic: A Political History of State Jews in France from Gambetta to Vichy,* trans. Jane Marie Todd (Stanford, CA, 1996).

16. See Dreyfus's entries from 20 December 1940 and 16 March 1941, USHMMA, *Cahier* A, RG 10.144.04; 23 June 1942, 4 July 1942, and 6 July 1942, *Cahier* C, RG 10.144.06.

17. Dreyfus, 16 March 1941, USHMMA, *Cahier* A, RG 10.144.04.

18. Dreyfus, 14 May 1941, USHMMA, *Cahier* B, RG 10.144.05.

19. Dreyfus, 18 June 1941, USHMMA, *Cahier* B, RG 10.144.05.

20. Yosef Hayim Yerushalmi, *Zakhor: Jewish History and Jewish Memory* (Seattle, 1982), 8.

21. Dreyfus, 6 July 1942, USHMMA, *Cahier* C, RG 10.144.06. Dreyfus recorded the news about the murder of seven hundred thousand Jews in Poland in an entry for 4 July 1942 (USHMMA, *Cahier* C, RG 10.144.06).

22. Dreyfus, 4 July 1942, USHMMA, *Cahier* C, RG 10.144.06.

23. Dreyfus, 6 July 1942, USHMMA, *Cahier* C, RG 10.144.06.

24. Dreyfus, 4 July 1942, USHMMA, *Cahier* C, RG 10.144.06.

25. On 25 October 1943, Lucien Dreyfus and Marthe Dreyfus were trapped by an SS unit led by Aloïs Brünner in the village of Clans, in the département of Alpes Maritimes, along with

twenty-five other Jews who been hiding in Clans. First deported to the transit camp Drancy, the Dreyfuses were sent on to Auschwitz-Birkenau on 20 November 1943 on transport number sixty-two. Most likely because of their ages they were gassed upon arrival. The transport list was reprinted in Serge Klarsfeld, *Memorial to the Jews Deported from France 1942-1944: Documentation of the Deportation of the Victims of the Final Solution in France* (Paris, 1983). A memorial plaque in the village of Clans lists the names of all the Jews rounded up that day, including the Dreyfuses.

26. Reeve Robert Brenner's interviews with 708 Holocaust survivors in Israel in the 1970s revealed that approximately 5 percent underwent a transformation from being atheists to religious believers that they attributed to their experiences during the Holocaust. Brenner, *The Faith and Doubt of Holocaust Survivors* (New York, 1980), 119.

27. The most visible postwar proponent of this view was Rabbi Yoel Taitelbaum, the leader of the ultra-Orthodox Satmar movement, who published *And It Pleased Moses (Vayo'el Moshe)* in 1952, cited in Amos Funkenstein, *Perceptions of Jewish History* (Berkeley, 1993), 307–8. On the variety of expressions of Orthodox faith and observance during and in the wake of the Shoah, see Steven T. Katz, Shlomo Biderman, and Gershon Greenberg, eds., *Wrestling with God: Jewish Theological Responses during and after the Holocaust* (New York, 2007), esp. part 1.

28. The best-known works are Max Horkheimer and Theodor W. Adorno, *Dialectic of Enlightenment* (New York, 1997); Zygmunt Bauman, *Modernity and the Holocaust* (Ithaca, NY, 1989); George M. Kren and Leon Rapoport, *The Holocaust and the Crisis of Human Behavior* (New York, 1980).

29. On Holocaust victims questioning Western civilization, see Dominick LaCapra, *History and Memory after Auschwitz* (Ithaca, NY, 1998), 9.

30. Bolchower's diary is catalogued at Yad Vashem Archives under her postwar married name, Holländer. For that reason, I use Holländer in the author citations in the notes here and below, although in the text I refer to her by her married name during the war, when she wrote her diary. Margarete Holländer, 30 July 1943, Yad Vashem Archives [hereafter YVA], RG 033, File 774, 12. All translations from the German are my own.

31. Holländer, 14 December 1943, YVA, RG 033, File 774, 83.

32. Holländer, 30 July 1943, YVA, RG 033, File 774, 12.

33. Perhaps the most extraordinary statement to this effect can be found in "The Last Stage of Resettlement is Death," an anonymous report written after the mass deportation of Jews from the Warsaw Ghetto, in *To Live With Honor and Die With Honor!.. Selected Documents from the Warsaw Ghetto Underground Archives "O.S."* ed. Joseph Kermish (Jerusalem, 1986), 704.

34. Their extensive efforts at documentation and preservation strongly counter Robert Braun's conclusion that it is "futile to speak about the 'reality' of the past as an object of study." Robert Braun, "The Holocaust and Problems of Historical Representation," *History and Theory* 33, no. 2 (1994): 175.

35. Koselleck, "'Space of Experience' and 'Horizon of Expectations': Two Historical Categories."

36. "Review of the Year 5700—Poland," *American Jewish Year Book 5701* 42 (1940): 365.

37. Letter by Richard Lichtheim, Geneva, Switzerland, to Dr. Leo Lauterbach, Jerusalem, Palestine, 11 December 1940, in *Jewish Responses to Persecution*, vol. 2: *1938-1940*, ed. Alexandra Garbarini, with Emil Kerenji, Jan Lambertz, and Avinoam Patt (Lanham, MD, 2011), 483–84. For a discussion of the perception of unprecedented suffering among Jewish commentators at the end of 1940, see Garbarini et. al., *Jewish Responses to Persecution*, vol. 2, xxvi–xxvii, 476–77.

38. David Roskies, *Against the Apocalypse: Responses to Catastrophe in Modern Jewish Culture* (Cambridge, MA, 1984), esp. ch. 6; Omer Bartov, *Murder in Our Midst: The Holocaust, Industrial Killing, and Representation* (New York, 1996), ch. 2; Jay Winter, *Remembering War: The Great War Between Memory and History in the Twentieth Century* (New Haven, CT, 2006), esp. ch. 11, 238–45; Laura Jokusch, *Collect and Record!*; David Engel, *Historians of the Jews and the Holocaust* (Stanford, CA, 2010), 122–27.

39. Alon Confino, "A World Without Jews: Interpreting the Holocaust," *German History* 27, no. 4 (2009): 558.

CHAPTER 6

The Voice of Your Brother's Blood
Reconstructing Genocide on the Local Level

OMER BARTOV

And God said to Cain: Where is Abel your brother? And he said: I don't know; am I my brother's keeper?
And He said: What have you done? The voice of your brother's blood is crying to me from the ground.

—Genesis, 4:9–10

Most people think of the Holocaust as an event of industrial killing, symbolized by Auschwitz: a vast undertaking of streamlined, anonymous mass murder. In fact, half of the total victims of what the Nazis called the "Final Solution of the Jewish question" did not die in extermination camps; they were killed in their own homes and streets, cemeteries and synagogues, in nearby hills, forests, and ravines. The killing was neither anonymous nor streamlined: the murderers often knew their victims by name and saw them face to face just before they shot them; their deaths were bloody, gruesome, and accompanied by many instances of gratuitous cruelty. The killers were not only German police and SS, or only Germans of any description, but also members of other ethnic groups from the victims' own regions and towns, often people they had known for years as classmates and colleagues and neighbors. There was nothing secret about these events: they were public, routine spectacles in which everyone played one role or another.[1]

Perpetrator behavior is often explained as the consequence of dehumanization: the obstacle to the killing of innocents is removed by perceiving them as nonhuman.[2] This view of mass murder allows us to avoid any discussion of

---

Notes for this section begin on page 124.

the ghastly encounter between the killers and the killed, clearing the way for detached analyses of decision making and the logistics of genocide. I have never bought into this argument. But in order to examine its veracity, I decided to investigate the Holocaust in an entirely different way—not from the prism of Berlin, and not strictly through the eyes of either one side or another. Instead, I chose to reconstruct the event in its entirety as it occurred in a single site.

Selecting the site had to do with its representative value and the availability of sources. Eventually I picked a town whose name was familiar to me but about which I knew very little. Buczacz, located in interwar eastern Poland and now in western Ukraine, was the birthplace of Nobel Prize Laureate Shmuel Yosef Agnon, whose stories I had studied in school in Israel.[3] It was also, as it happens, my mother's hometown, although I had no intention of writing a family history. I was intrigued, however, by the notion of writing a biography of a town, a history through the eyes of the protagonists; in this sense my personal link to Buczacz clearly motivated me. The tension between analytical detachment and empathetic understanding was therefore built into my research project from its very origins.

No fewer than sixty thousand Jews were murdered in the area of Buczacz and Czortków, a nearby town in which the Security Police (Sicherheitspolizei or Sipo) outpost charged with this task was based. Accompanied by mistresses and wives, children, and parents who came to enjoy the rural surroundings,

Figure 6.1. Members of the Sipo outpost in Czortków, taken in 1942–43. Generallandesarchiv (GLA) Karlsruhe, 309 Zugang 2001, 42-871, photograph no. 26.

these twenty to thirty policemen led a comfortable existence, captured in hundreds of photographs kept in West German court archives.

They were ably assisted by up to 350 Ukrainian auxiliary policemen (organized in Schutzmannschaft or Schuma units), along with local German and Ukrainian gendarmes, as well as Jewish policemen recruited into the so-called Ordnungsdienst and paid by the Jewish Council (Judenrat).

From the local perspective, the Holocaust in Buczacz was a series of extremely violent roundups—referred to as *Aktionen* or *akcje*—assuming at times the character of communal massacres. About half of the approximately ten thousand victims were transported by train to the Bełżec extermination camp, where they were gassed; the other half were killed in situ. This reflected the fate of the five hundred thousand Jews who were living in the entire region, known as Eastern Galicia before World War I and designated as Distrikt Galizien by the occupying Germans in 1941: about two hundred fifty thousand Jews were gassed in Bełżec, while the rest were shot next to where they lived. Most of this massive bloodletting was accomplished within eighteen months in an area measuring less than half the size of the state of New York.[4]

For the Jews, Buczacz was a shtetl, as were many other similar towns in Eastern Europe. But the notion of a shtetl as a purely Jewish town was in truth a figment of Jewish lore rather than a reflection of historical reality. The quaint *shtetl* featured in Marc Chagall's paintings and the stories of Sholem Aleichem never actually existed.[5] The highest ratio of Jewish inhabitants in Buczacz during the modern era was reached in the second part of the nineteenth century, when Jews constituted over two-thirds of the town's population, the rest being Poles and Ukrainians. By the eve of World War I, massive emigration caused by growing poverty, as well as increasing numbers of Christian town dwellers, had diminished the ratio of Jewish inhabitants to somewhat over half of the total.[6] This was a characteristic pattern throughout Eastern Galicia, where rural Ukrainians constituted the majority of the population, while Poles and— especially in the smaller and mid-sized urban settlements—Jews dominated the towns and cities.[7]

This mix of populations meant that the German genocide of the Jews took place within a complex and increasingly volatile web of ethnic, religious, political, and national affiliations. In implementing the "Final Solution" throughout Europe, the Germans adapted with terrifying agility to vastly different local circumstances. Yet these circumstances largely determined the manner, speed, and scope of the killing, as well as its effects on the rest of the population.[8] In studying the Holocaust on the local level, we discover that the category of bystanders becomes meaningless. When an invading power joins forces with local elements to murder a segment of the population, there are only degrees of engagement, ranging from full cooperation to utter rejection. Within that context we can identify a prevalent gray zone: some who hide the persecuted also denounce them; some of the killers also shelter potential victims; some of the collaborators turn to resistance. Claims of indifference or passivity appear absurd, unless they encompass watching one's neighbors being shot, and then taking over their property.

The Germans marched into lands with a long history of both coexistence and conflict. That history had little to do with the occupiers, yet by necessity it played a part in the implementation of genocide. Even before World War I, Galicia had been a site of contestation between Poles and Ukrainians, whose origins can be traced back to the 1600s. Four centuries of Jewish settlement in the area also left a legacy of often uneasy relations and occasional outbursts of violence. The conduct of all local protagonists during World War II was therefore in some measure governed by collective memories and acquired perceptions and norms of behavior.

Buczacz allows exploration into the deep roots of local genocide. We can reconstruct mass murder in a single site and examine competing postwar narratives in judicial discourse, memory, and commemoration. Such a study is a collective "biography," in that it allows generations of Buczacz residents to speak out. To be sure, this is a schizophrenic "biography," since these voices from the past often speak in very different registers about themselves and their neighbors. But it is also a representative "biography," because it stands for an entire universe of similar towns and regions in Europe's eastern borderlands, a world that was wiped out and forgotten.[9] The interest in that world cannot reside only in the manner and causes of its destruction. It was rich and varied by its own right. We know so little of it because the voices of its inhabitants have been silenced. By letting them speak again, a careful, in-depth local study can exemplify the richness of what had been lost even as it investigates the reasons for the disaster. To the extent that we can conjure Buczacz back to life, the tragedy of its assassination is better comprehended. It is difficult to mourn a life one never knew; it is harder to accept the loss of a life intimately shared.

The final eruption of external and fraternal violence in World War II seemed to many both shocking and inevitable. But that is reading history backward. To be sure, there had been much prior talk in nationalist as well as technocratic circles about the need for the "unmixing" of incompatible peoples, creeds, or races.[10] But no one in 1941 could have anticipated the scale and horror of what came to pass. Still, the question must be asked: why did such unprecedented and gruesome violence seem at the same time to be a natural outcome of past events? Was this "a problem from hell," as was said about the genocide in 1990s Yugoslavia, an expression of endemic, unstoppable violence?[11] Were the various ethnic groups just waiting for the right moment to leap at each other's throats? This view is as inaccurate of Slobodan Milošević's Yugoslavia as it is of towns such as Buczacz in the 1940s. It implies that some societies are just prone to violence and there is little that more civilized nations can do about it. The fact is that while there was indeed an internal potential for violence, it was triggered by outside invaders, often representatives of those very same self-proclaimed higher civilizations, whose goals, determined independently from the peoples they occupied, could only be achieved by sword and blood.

The province that came to be called Galicia following the Austrian annexation of southeast Poland in 1772 had not experienced major outbreaks of violence since the early eighteenth century and remained relatively calm until World War I.[12] And yet, when the Germans arrived on the scene in July 1941, they needed to do very little, at times nothing at all, to incite violence.[13] This shift from coexistence to conflict can be understood in part through a detailed local history that traces the roots of this precarious interethnic balance from the very foundations of a town such as Buczacz in the late Middle Ages to its final destruction as a multiethnic community in World War II. In doing so, this local history re-creates the widely diverging narratives of the past told by Poles, Ukrainians, and Jews throughout the intervening centuries. These starkly different stories about the town they shared were not necessarily antagonistic; often each group simply ignored the others as it wove its own tales of history and myth, memory and legend. Yet the ever present and powerful underlying assertion of cultural, spiritual, and material difference did end up creating a sense of an essential and unbridgeable divide between the groups.

Concentrating on a single town makes it possible to use a wide variety of sources in order to re-create its evolving social and cultural fabric over time and then to zoom further in and meticulously reconstruct the violent events of its final destruction in all their complexity. One might have expected only a thin documentary record and even fewer individual accounts for this remote Galician town. In fact, official documentation by the Austrian, Polish, and Nazi regimes is plentiful, albeit riddled with prejudice and political bias. Early "voices" of the town's residents come from local histories and tourist accounts, collections of tales and legends, several diaries and memoirs, works of fiction and journalism—all reflecting their writers' individual and collective religious, social, ethnic and ideological perspectives. As we enter the town's final agony, official documentation thins out and the voices of its people multiply a hundredfold, becoming ever more desperate, shrill, and tortured. Polish residents deported by the Soviets in 1939–41 deposited valuable testimonies now stored at the Hoover Institution at Stanford University. A few diaries by Jews and Christians have been retrieved from archives or private hands. Hundreds of testimonies given by Jewish survivors from as early as 1944 to as late as the 1990s were found at the Jewish Historical Institute in Warsaw, Yad Vashem in Jerusalem, the Fortunoff Archive at Yale University, the United States Holocaust Memorial Museum in Washington, DC, and the Shoah Foundation at the University of Southern California. The records of West German trials of former Nazis, as well as judicial documentation from East Germany, Poland,

and the Soviet Union, contain vast amounts of information on individuals' involvement. Interviews with current and former residents of Buczacz; published accounts and memoirs, and not least, the remarkable memorial book of Buczacz—all of these provide us with a cacophony of voices that must now be finally orchestrated into a single narrative, filled with contradictions, holes, and unanswered questions, to be sure, and yet richer than anything we have had until now.[14]

Some voices reach us with force and clarity from the even more distant, opaque past. Natan Hanover's *The Abyss of Despair,* a vivid eyewitness account of the devastation wrought by Bohdan Khmelnitsky and his Cossacks in the 1648 uprising against Polish rule, tells of the Polish and Jewish citizens of Buczacz fighting side-by-side on the city's walls.[15] The German tourist Ulrich von Werdum, who visited Buczacz in 1672, wrote that despite the town's destruction by Ottoman troops, Buczacz had "been largely rebuilt, especially by the Jews, who are very numerous in this town."[16] That year the Peace of Buczacz was signed under the giant linden tree on a hill overlooking the town—where it still stands—between the Turkish Sultan and the Polish King. But only four years later the French traveler François-Paulin Dalairac reported that following more fighting, "the Turks [had] accomplished a lasting destruction" of Buczacz.[17]

Yet the town was rebuilt once again. When Dalairac returned in 1684, he observed that the Ruthenian peasants had put up their shacks "next to the gate of the city and under the guns of the castle," while within the walls "live only Jews and some Poles."[18] This was to remain the demographic and occupational pattern for the next two hundred years. The eighteenth century witnessed a period of peace and prosperity. Ruled by the immensely rich and notoriously eccentric Mikołaj Potocki—a patron of religion and the arts, a womanizer, a drinker, and a brawler—Buczacz gained its impressive town hall and monastery. It also experienced the arbitrary power of a grand Polish magnate: as the poet Zygmunt Krasiński wrote, Potocki "shot women on trees and baked Jews alive."[19]

Much of what we know about the early history of Buczacz comes from an account published in 1882 by the priest and historian Sadok Barącz, a fanatical Roman Catholic and devoted chronicler of Armenian origin.[20] Many of the documents he cites were subsequently destroyed. Another ardent collector was the writer Agnon, whose sprawling posthumous account of Buczacz overflows with tales of Hasidic rabbis and traitorous followers of the "false Messiah" Sabbetai Zvi. Agnon's eighteenth-century Buczacz seems to have nothing in common with that of Barącz save for their identical location.[21]

The Jewish Enlightenment, or Haskalah, which promoted modern education and social integration, promised to facilitate greater Jewish-Christian interaction.[22] And, indeed, some *maskilim* from Buczacz ended up as university-trained scholars, assimilationists, or Zionists.[23] But in the course of the nineteenth century, as nationalism began to infiltrate people's lives, it also introduced new criteria for distinguishing between one group and another. By the late 1800s the central question was: to whom does the town, the region, the state, naturally and by right belong? As Poles and Ukrainians grappled with each other over ownership of Galicia, the Jews, who could only shift alliances from one group to another, found themselves in an increasingly precarious no-man's-land.

Until World War I, the Habsburg Empire managed relations between ethnic-national groups in Galicia relatively effectively; heated rhetoric rarely transformed into physical violence. Instead, nationalism pushed for greater literacy and stimulated cultural activities, political engagement, and economic progress. All this changed dramatically in the Great War and the national-ideological struggles that followed it. Little has been written on the effect of the fighting in the East on such ethnically mixed communities as Buczacz. The devastation was on a scale not seen since the seventeenth century. Tens of thousands of soldiers were killed in close proximity to Buczacz, which was occupied twice by the Russians and remained close to the front for much of the war.

The Russian occupation also brought with it murderous pogroms. The unpublished diary of Antoni Siewinski, headmaster of the boys' school in Buczacz and an antisemitic Polish nationalist, provides an unparalleled, albeit deeply

Figure 6.2. A position of the Russian Army near Buczacz, 1916. Central State CinePhotoPhono Archives of Ukraine (TsDKFFA): 0-184874.

biased, view of his town under the first Russian occupation.²⁴ Just as Siewinski fled in the face of the second Russian offensive of summer 1916, the Russian Jewish soldier Aba Lev arrived in Buczacz on the heels of a victorious Cossack unit. The town, he wrote, presented a "terrifying picture of destruction, vandalism, and cruelty." He went on to describe the gruesome consequences of the pogrom that had just occurred there.²⁵ The author, playwright, and ethnographer, S. Ansky (Shloyme Zanvl Rappoport), remembered today mostly for his play *The Dybbuk,* visited Buczacz in early 1917. As he wrote in his extensive account of the Russian occupation, passing through "scores of large avenues" in Buczacz that had been "destroyed and burned down," he was stuck by the "tragic scene of the dead city."²⁶ Rare surviving Austrian and Russian documents and photographs of wartime Buczacz confirm these impressions.²⁷

The end of World War I did not bring peace to Galicia. As the Austro-Hungarian Empire collapsed, Ukrainians and Poles began fighting over the province.²⁸ In the course of the conflict, which the Poles quickly won, numerous Ukrainian atrocities against Polish civilians were widely reported.²⁹ Meanwhile a series of Polish pogroms against Jewish communities prompted the establishment of two international commissions of inquiry. Much of the anti-Jewish violence was linked to allegations that the Jews were taking the wrong side in the conflict, not taking any side at all, or professing Zionism. Whichever it was, the Jews clearly did not fit into the Polish or Ukrainian visions of a new nation-state.³⁰

Figure 6.3. Bridge over the Strypa River in wartime Buczacz. Österreichisches Staatsarchiv (ÖSA) / Kriegsarchiv (KA): 6500AT-OeStA/KA BS Portraits L I, "Bildersammlung."

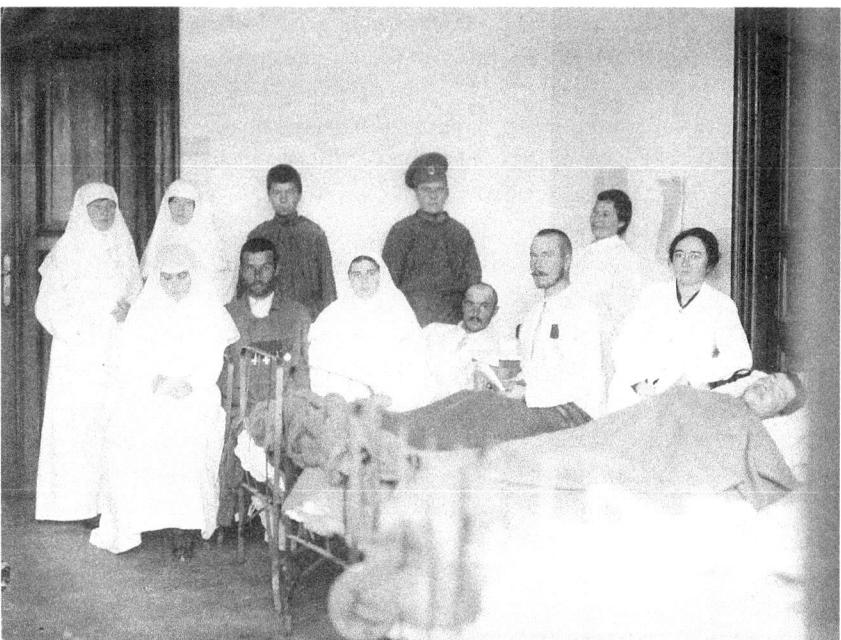

Figure 6.4. Infectious Diseases Hospital, Buczacz, 1917. Dr. Etel Zeigermacher, private collection, with permission. I would like to thank Dr. Etel Zeigermacher's son, of Melbourne, Australia, for providing me with the photos of the hospital where his mother served as a medical doctor in Russian-occupied Buczacz during World War I.

Following yet another war, this one between Poland and Soviet Russia over the postwar boundaries of the two states, these national, ideological, and interethnic conflicts left a bitter legacy of resentment, suspicion, and rage.[31] Ukrainian hopes to set up an independent state had been dashed as they found themselves under Polish rule; Polish attempts to colonize the region were met with violent Ukrainian resistance, which led to even more oppressive policies; and Jewish aspirations to integrate into Poland encountered popular and official opposition. By the 1930s, the Organization of Ukrainian Nationalists (OUN), established in 1929, was becoming increasingly radicalized, not least under the influence of Nazi Germany;[32] the Polish authorities were instituting antisemitic measures;[33] and growing numbers of young Jews drifted toward socialism and Zionism.[34]

A mass of police reports, political pamphlets, personal letters and diaries, and postwar memoirs reflects some of these trends in Buczacz.[35] The town remained politically and culturally vibrant throughout the interwar period. It had far more restaurants and hotels, cafés, and bars than one can find there today.[36] Such figures as the historian of the Warsaw Ghetto, Emanuel Ringelblum, and the "Nazi hunter" Simon Wiesenthal began their lives there.[37] Yet the mood was growing darker. Agnon, who visited Buczacz in 1930, saw a Jewish community in decline.[38] Many were leaving. Communist party cells were the only spaces where all three ethnic groups interacted without hindrance, but they had their own violent potential.[39] Many younger Ukrainians were joining the OUN; some of them would later show up on lists of the Schuma auxiliary police units recruited by the Germans. Postwar investigations and trials show them as participating in the murder of their Jewish and Polish neighbors.[40]

When the Soviets took over Galicia in 1939, a brief moment of exhilaration and hope was followed by two years of political terror and economic collapse. Driven by suspicion of enemy nationalities, social classes, and integral nationalists, the Soviets deported tens of thousands of Poles, Jews, and Ukrainians. This was oppression on an entirely new scale, followed by the mass execution of mostly Ukrainian political prisoners, just as the Germans attacked in late June 1941.[41] These state-ordered murders greatly exacerbated interethnic animosity and played into the hands of the invading Nazis, who were quick to blame them on the Jews while posing as liberators from so-called Judeo-Bolshevism. The ensuing massacres of Jewish populations can be traced back directly to Soviet policies and Nazi propaganda, though their deeper origins stretch back at least to World War I.[42]

As anti-Jewish violence became a daily routine in German-occupied Buczacz, this community of increasingly fragile coexistence was transformed into a community of genocide. Not all protagonists conformed to the roles assigned to them in conventional accounts: if many younger members of prewar Ukrainian nationalist organizations became direct participants in Nazi extermination policies, some older conservative Ukrainian political and religious leaders tried to prevent the violence.[43] While prewar Polish elites had supported the exclusion of Jews, they appear to have been more likely to shelter Jews or at least to sympathize with them than either their Ukrainian neighbors or Poles in the Polish heartland, not least because they also became targets of violence and ethnic cleansing. Conversely, Ukrainians sheltering Jews could also be seen by patriotic neighbors, local priests, and OUN sympathizers or members as betraying the national cause of creating a Pole- and Jew-free Ukraine.[44] If many peasants clearly took part in the killing, some poor peasants living on isolated farms hid Jews for little or no compensation.[45] Finally, while the Germans targeted Jews as a group, the Buczacz Jewish Council and police were notorious for their corruption and despised as tools of the Gestapo.[46] Yet several Jewish police officers eventually joined the resistance.[47]

Between fall 1942 and summer 1943 the vast majority of the Jews of Buczacz and the surrounding towns and villages were murdered. Most of the killing occurred during four roundups organized by Sipo personnel from Czortków and accomplished with ample local assistance. Mass shootings occurred primarily in two sites on either side of the town—the Fedor Hill, behind the magnificent Greek Catholic Basilian Monastery, and the Baszty Hill, where the ancient Jewish cemetery was located. The last *Aktion* in June 1943 targeted the town's Jewish police, some of whose members fought back and escaped to the forest.[48] Survivors of these massacres were mostly either hidden by local villagers or employed in the few remaining labor camps and farms scattered around this region.

Then, in spring 1944, the territories surrounding Buczacz erupted into a wave of horrific and increasingly chaotic violence. The German Wehrmacht, forced to retreat from parts of Eastern Galicia in March, counterattacked the following month and drove back the Red Army. Buczacz was again under German rule. Of the approximately eight hundred Jewish survivors who had come out of hiding after the first liberation, only a hundred were still alive when the Red Army returned in July 1944. In the intervening months, this remote region of Eastern Europe became the scene of mayhem and devastation, cruelty and suffering, a last frenzied upheaval after three years of total war and genocide. The Czortków Sipo outpost and its Ukrainian auxiliaries continued to hunt down and murder Jews until it was finally dismantled in early 1944.[49] As the Gestapo vacated the scene, some local German officials, along with commanders of retreating combat units, actually protected the remnants of the Jewish population from local militias and roaming bandits, disbanded Ukrainian auxiliary police, and murderous villagers.

Throughout this period, even as the Red Army and Wehrmacht were slaughtering each other, the Ukrainian Insurgent Army (UPA)—the military arm of the more radical faction of OUN led by Stepan Bandera—which had already carried out a vast ethnic-cleansing operation against the Poles in the neighboring province of Volhynia, engaged in similarly bloody actions in Galicia; any surviving Jews the UPA encountered were also murdered.[50] Here, too, the retreating Germans helped save the Poles of the eastern territories, loading them into trains heading toward the relative safety of Poland's heartland. When the Soviets finally broke through the German lines in July, they launched a massive liquidation operation geared to uproot military and political Ukrainian nationalist organizations seen as collaborators with the "German fascists" and opponents of Soviet power.[51] What the Jews perceived as liberation many Ukrainians saw as reoccupation. The soil of Eastern Galicia was soaked in blood. But who spilled the blood and for what reason has remained for many decades open to interpretation, obfuscation, and distortion.

Very little has been written on the fate of Eastern Galicia's few remaining Jews during these last months of German occupation and early period of Soviet rule in Poland's former eastern territories. While historians have begun to examine the ethnic cleansing of the Poles and the repression of the OUN-UPA by the Red Army and NKVD (Soviet secret police), histories of the Holocaust, including works focused on this region, have not devoted much attention to these crucial months.⁵² The main reason for this seems to be that lack of official documentation and a reluctance to rely on personal testimonies have combined to deter historians from this task: most German documents were destroyed; Soviet records were inaccessible for many decades, are not always easy to come by even today, and are not particularly reliable; and documents and pamphlets by Polish and Ukrainian underground organizations, scattered in numerous archival holdings, provide only fragmented and highly partisan information.

And yet, for the few survivors of the mass murder of the Jews in this region, it was precisely these last months of the occupation that remained seared most deeply in their minds. It determined to a large extent the manner in which they remembered, and the perspective from which they told their Holocaust experience as a whole. These Jewish narratives of murder and survival are not only missing from mainstream Holocaust historiography, but also differ profoundly from those related by Ukrainians and Poles. From this perspective we can say that quite apart from the different manner in which the events were actually experienced by these different protagonists, the divergence in their subsequent telling and historical reconstruction has contributed to the ongoing memory wars, ranging from political rhetoric to scholarly disputes.⁵³

The fact of the matter is that we actually possess numerous eyewitness reports, in diaries, letters, postwar testimonies and written accounts, as well as in judicial records and memoirs. These personal perspectives offer an extraordinarily rich source of information on the entire war, complementing official records and enabling us to sketch a detailed picture of genocide on the local level. Historians have underused these accounts, viewing them as both too subjective and too painful. This has greatly impoverished our understanding of crucial aspects of World War II and the Holocaust. These are reports from hell on earth, where there was little room for pity and forgiveness. Yet they also contain moments of sacrifice, compassion, and humanness by members of the local population as well as, remarkably, some German military and administrative personnel.

In June 1943 the Germans declared Buczacz and the surrounding towns and villages *Judenrein,* or clean of Jews. All Jews not employed on the few remaining agricultural farms and labor camps could be shot on sight. Many hid in peasants' homes, barns, and sheds. "They had to pay a lot of money to the peasants who were hiding them," wrote Eliasz Chalfen, aged seventeen, in a testimony he deposited in the Displaced Persons camp of Leipheim, Germany in November 1947: "Those peasants went to town and shopped as they had never done before … This made things easy for the Ukrainian bandits, who went … straight to the houses that had been pointed out to them as hiding Jews, and easily found their hiding places … [and] would immediately execute them in the yard of the house. Denouncing Jews at that time reached unprecedented levels; the peasants themselves began murdering and chasing them out …"⁵⁴

Ester Grintal, aged eighteen at the time, recalled in 1997 that when "the Ukrainian militia passed through" the forced-labor farm where she worked, she would "hide in the toilet and count the shots knowing by that how many people were killed." Later, "Cossacks and others who had collaborated with the Germans" appeared in the area and "began murdering" the Jews: "They did not have enough guns so they hanged people, or killed them with axes, etc. They came to our camp with some collaborators from the village. They locked [us up] in an empty barn … They began beating us … They shot a line of people with one bullet … but the bullet didn't reach me. Again I was put in a line, and again the bullet didn't kill me. So they began killing people with knives. I was stabbed three times."[55]

The German army doctor who treated Grintal a few days later reportedly said: "What did the Ukrainian swine do to you?"[56] We cannot say precisely who those Ukrainians were. From Grintal's description it appears that in her specific case they belonged to units that had fought alongside the Germans. Many testimonies refer to the Banderowcy or Banderivtsy, the common Polish and Ukrainian designation for the men of OUN-UPA derived from the name of their leader, Bandera. At times this term was confused with the common German description of partisans and resistance fighters as bandits. But in 1943, the OUN, which had previously collaborated with the Germans, was turning against them, even as it saw the approaching Soviets as its real enemy. The ranks of the UPA were filled with men who had previously served as policemen or in Schuma units in German uniforms and had participated in the mass murder of the Jews. Subsequently Ukrainians who had served in the Waffen-SS Division "Galicia," crushed by the Red Army in summer 1944, also joined the UPA. And then there were also real bandits and brutalized peasants who exploited the chaos in the region to loot, rape, extort money, and murder, for whom the Jews were simply the easiest targets.[57]

Pity and empathy were rare, though not entirely extinct, sentiments during those dark times; they stood out precisely because they were no longer expected. More often, cruelty and betrayal dominated the experience of the hunted. Arie Klonicki wrote in his diary in 1943: "The hatred of the immediate surroundings … knows no boundaries. Millions of Jews have been slaughtered and it is not yet satiated!"[58] He and his wife, who were hiding in the fields not far from Buczacz, were denounced and murdered shortly thereafter. Joachim Mincer recorded in his diary that in nearby Tłumacz, a series of "executions took place in the prison yard. The perpetrators," he stressed, "were mainly Ukrainian policemen as well as members of the [German] criminal police," and "the main perpetrator was an individual by the name of Bandrowski," who "liked to shoot Jews on the street." Bandrowski "shot the sister of [Judenrat member] Dr. Szpitzer in her yard." She, in turn, "had been denounced by young Kolewicz, a worker of the electric factory." This same "Kolewicz also shot Friedl Haber, while his friend Sytnik shot the young fourteen-year-old daughter of the Weischler family."[59] Mincer himself was killed in 1943. Yoel Katz, seventeen at the end of the war, vividly recalled many years later how the peasants surrounded his camp, shouting: "All the children out, we are going to kill you!" Some were killed with axes; others put in a row and shot with a single bullet. He stresses: "The Germans who came from the front protected us from the Ukrainians until the Russians arrived."[60]

Conflicting memories of rescue and betrayal reflect the chaos and vagaries of fortune at the time. Edzia Spielberg-Flitman, liberated at the age of fourteen, recalled that in early July 1941 her aunt and cousins were axed to death by a group of Ukrainian villagers, including the children's female teacher, just after the Red Army pulled out and before the Germans arrived. But toward the end of the occupation she was hidden with her mother and brother by a "poor farmer with a wife and four children." The peasant woman said to them, "It doesn't matter how long it takes, we will share our bread and potatoes with you." Yet the peasant who hid Edzia's relatives nearby betrayed them, and they were murdered by Ukrainian policemen. Later Edzia worked as a washerwoman for a German army unit, but was denounced as a Jew by a Ukrainian workmate. Instead of killing them, the German commander escorted Edzia and her family to the Soviet lines, saying: "I hope you all live well." She recalled that "the Ukrainians ... were worse than the Germans," not least because in her estimation, "80 percent" of her family "were killed by the Ukrainians who were our friends."[61]

By that time, spring–summer 1944, most of the Jews of Galicia had already been murdered. But without these personal perspectives, we would have known close to nothing about this period. In 1948 Mojżesz Szpigiel, aged forty-nine, testified that in January 1944 Ukrainian militiamen had murdered most of the surviving 120 Jews on the farm where he worked, including his 14-year-old son: "It is important to state," he emphasized, "that this killing was not a German action, that it was performed by Ukrainian policemen and bandits." Most survivors of that massacre were butchered in yet another bandit attack. "The child orphans," reported Szpigiel, were "stacked up in a pile," while other victims were "lying with open guts." The local German administrator, a certain Vathie, had tried to protect his workers. When he left, "the Jews earnestly cried." But his replacement, a young German army officer, is said by Szpigiel to have promised them: "As long as I am here, nothing will happen to you."[62] We do not know the name of this particular officer; our only source of information about him comes from the Jews he saved. A few hundred survivors converged on the town of Tłusty, near Buczacz, where the officer was stationed, until the Red Army arrived.

Personal testimonies and interviews, many given only recently, and some by surviving elderly Christian eyewitnesses, further add to this picture. In 2003 the ethnic Polish resident of Buczacz, Julija Mykhailivna Trembach, recalled the

German "crimes against the Jews … how they buried them alive … and how those people dug their own graves." She had a front-row view: "From the street where I lived … I could see how the ground was moving over the people who were still not dead."[63] The ethnic Ukrainian Maria Mykhailivna Khvostenko remembered looking out of her classroom window in Buczacz and seeing "a crowd going around the municipal hall toward the bridge," surrounded by "gendarmes with dogs, Gestapo and police with six-pointed stars [i.e., members of the Jewish Ornungdienst]," who were "hurrying it toward the" killing site: "There were women, men, old people and young—our schoolmates and friends." From "the fall of 1942 to the end of 1943," Khvostenko reports, the Germans "conducted roundups" with terrifying regularity. "They would arrive on Thursday evening" and "'work' all night, and the next morning as we hurried to school we could see … corpses of women, men and children lying on the road." The Germans "would throw [infants] from balconies onto the paved road … they were lying in the mud with smashed heads and spattered brains … We could hear machine-gun fire" from the killing site.[64]

For some of those not targeted, genocide proved profitable. The Ukrainian gymnasium teacher Viktor Petrykevych wrote in his unpublished diary in January 1944 that, while most people in Buczacz were experiencing "unprecedented destitution … some people … who before the war were earning very little, make fortunes, gaining more money than they would have ever dreamed of in the past." The source of this new wealth soon became clear: as the Red Army came closer, many "merchants, craftsmen, and so forth, who were living in houses that had formerly belonged to the Jews … began moving out … They anticipate Jewish revenge."[65]

To be sure, there was no Jewish revenge. The few Jews who returned to Buczacz following its recapture by the Soviets left soon thereafter. According to some accounts, they were all living in one building for fear of attacks by their neighbors. This was a violent time: reports of killings of Jews either by OUN-UPA fighters or local bandits continued for months after the liberation. No one cared much about the survivors, let alone the dead.[66] In the area of Buczacz, as in vast tracts of Eastern Europe more generally, much of the population did not perceive the Red Army's return as liberation, and quite often considered the Soviet repression of local nationalists—who had previously collaborated with the German authorities in the hopes of furthering their own particular agendas—as precisely that much-feared Jewish revenge, which Jews may well have hoped for but were in fact in no position to exact. The association between Jews and Communists, labeled in Poland as *żydokomuna,* combined with the much more material worry that returning Jews might claim back their property from the locals who had moved in, both explains the continued anti-Jewish violence and the divergent memory and historiography of the postwar era in Eastern Europe.[67]

And thus, the final phase in the transformation of Buczacz into a homogeneous community came with the return of the Soviets. Thanks to a wealth of hitherto inaccessible documents, it is now possible to reconstruct the liquidation and deportation policies by the Soviet authorities in 1944–49.[68] While large numbers of Ukrainian fighters, along with their families, were sent to Gulags or exiled to Kazakhstan, most of the surviving Poles were sent to Poland in a vast Polish-Ukrainian population exchange. The brutalization of the war years also left its marks. Investigations of the genocide of the Jews often culminated in summary justice. As Jewish survivor Rene Zuroff recalled in 1995 about events in Buczacz:

> There were also hangings of collaborators in the municipality. People, both Jews and Christians, would tell who the collaborators were and these collaborators would be rounded up and hanged in the town square. I was a little girl and we would go for our entertainment to the hangings and we were totally happy to go to our daily hangings of the horrible collaborators—who mutilated their victims. We saw them strung up and urinating and I'd be in heaven. My mother would come and drag me away and I begged to have my daily entertainment. There was none of all these trials with witnesses, one would say, "He did it, string him up!"[69]

The inhabitants of contemporary Buczacz are former Ukrainian residents and their descendants, villagers who moved into town after the war, and ethnic Ukrainians deported from Poland. Most know very little about their town's past. The Communists had subsumed the genocide of the Jews under a general narrative of Soviet martyrdom and heroism.[70] The new Western Ukrainian authorities have resurrected the nationalists of World War II as heroic figures, neglecting to mention their role in the destruction of their Polish and Jewish neighbors. Thus the fate of the Jews has remained outside the official historical narrative.

The survivors and exiles, however, never forgot their hometown: communities of memory around the world preserved their separate narratives and passed them on to their children. A memorial association in Wrocław has published a stream of personal accounts by Polish survivors.[71] Ivan Bobyk, who was the Ukrainian mayor of Buczacz during the German occupation and, for obvious reasons, left the town before the Soviets arrived, put together a memorial book narrating the history of the town and the region from the Ukrainian perspective.[72] Conversely, the Jewish memorial book edited by Yisrael Cohen contains much valuable historical scholarship and personal testimonies but has almost nothing to say about the Christian inhabitants of the town.[73]

Material remains and sites of commemoration similarly reflect these split and often-conflicting memories. On the Fedor Hill in Buczacz, where thousands of Jews were murdered, a large memorial to Ukrainian freedom fighters has been erected.

Figure 6.5. UPA memorial on Fedor Hill, taken in 2006 by Sofia Grachova.

On another hill, next to the famous linden tree, a new statute of Ukrainian nationalist leader Stepan Bandera overlooks the town.

Figure 6.6. Bandera monument in Buczacz, taken in 2008 by Omer Bartov.

There are no memorials to the Polish population, although Buczacz is filled with edifices constructed under Polish (and Habsburg) rule. But the Roman Catholic church was renovated by Father Ludwik Rutyna, who returned from decades of exile in Poland. Before his death in 2010 he had succeeded in making it into a modest new center of Roman Catholicism in a predominantly Greek Catholic region.

Jewish life has not revived in Buczacz, and attempts to commemorate the victims have been largely unsuccessful. A memorial put up by survivors in the Jewish cemetery immediately after the liberation was removed by the Soviet authorities.

Figure 6.7. Jewish cemetery monument, 1944. Yad Vashem Archives, item 10247954, photo 10002/1

A small memorial stone to the victims on the Fedor Hill, which lay broken on the forest floor for decades, was put up again some years ago but remains unmarked and difficult to find, as are the mass graves for some five thousand Jews surrounding it.

A new and unassuming memorial in the Jewish cemetery is hidden from view and already crumbling. No information about the Jews of Buczacz is available in the town, save for a few photos of Agnon in the local museum. A plaque put up next to the author's former house does not mention his Jewish identity.

Thus the history of Buczacz and its demise must be sought elsewhere. Dozens of archives in Russia, Ukraine, Austria, Germany, France, Britain, the United States, and Israel contain vast amounts of information written in nine

Figure 6.8. Fedor Hill 1944 memorial, taken in 2003 by Omer Bartov.

Figure 6.9. New Jewish cemetery memorial, taken in 2007 by Omer Bartov.

languages on this little borderland town. As noted above, German court records provide especially rich materials on the period of the Holocaust, as do the hundreds of written, audiotaped, and videotaped testimonies by survivors, stored in Poland, the United States, and Israel. Finally, interviews with scores of local Ukrainians, exiled Poles, and surviving Jews constitute an especially valuable source for reconstructing the fraught interethnic relations and the daily life of genocide in Buczacz.

In 1995 I interviewed my mother about her hometown. For the first time she spoke about her childhood, and that conversation set me off on this long journey. We had planned to visit Buczacz together; she had not been there since leaving it at the age of eleven in 1935. But not long after the interview she fell ill and passed away in 1998. When I finally reached Buczacz, I was glad that my mother had not seen the erasure of memory so blatantly displayed there. But I am sorry that she, and so many other people with whom I spoke over the years about the town they loved, and who recalled cherished memories of childhood in a prewar world that seemed, from a distance, to have been an era of innocence on the eve of destruction, will no longer be able to read the much-delayed book I am finally completing. I dedicate it to their memory.

Notes

1. This is a central theme of Jewish diaries, testimonies, and memoirs, as well the innumerable *yizkor bicher* (memorial books) produced by survivors of Jewish communities especially in Eastern Europe. The New York Public Library possesses 700 such volumes, of which 650 are accessible online: http://legacy.www.nypl.org/research/chss/jws/yizkorbookonline.cfm (accessed 20 January 2013). Jan T. Gross, *Neighbors: The Destruction of the Jewish Community in Jedwabne, Poland* (Princeton, NJ, 2001) presented for the first time to the wider public a reconstruction of a communal massacre as an inherent component of the Holocaust. See also Joanna B. Michlic and Antony Polonsky, eds., *The Neighbors Respond: The Controversy Over the Jedwabne Massacre in Poland* (Princeton, NJ, 2004) and Andrzej Żbikowski, "Pogroms in Northeastern Poland—Spontaneous Reactions and German Instigations," in *Shared History—Divided Memory: Jews and Others in Soviet-Occupied Poland, 1939-1941,* ed. Elazar Barkan, Elizabeth A. Cole, and Kai Struve (Göttingen, 2007), 315–54. A longer-term and more personal view of interethnic relations is Shimon Redlich, *Together and Apart in Brzeżany: Poles, Jews, and Ukrainians, 1919-1945* (Bloomington, IN, 2002). Recent studies include Barbara Engelking, *Jest taki piękny słoneczny dzień... Losy Żydów szukających ratunku na wsi polskiej 1942-1945* (Warsaw, 2011); Jan Grabowski, *Hunt for the Jews: Betrayal and Murder in German-Occupied Poland* (Bloomington, IN, 2013); and Barbara Engelking, "Murdering and Denouncing Jews in the Polish Countryside, 1942-1945"; Omer Bartov, "Wartime Lies and Other Testimonies: Jewish-Christian Relations in Buczacz, 1939-1944," and Andrzej Żbikowski, "'Night Guard': Holocaust Mechanisms in the Polish Rural Areas, 1942-1945: Preliminary Introduction into Research," all in *East European Politics and Societies* 25, no. 3 (2011): 433–56, 486–511, 512–29.

2. Early German scholarship on Nazism repeatedly referred to this "mechanism." Academic and popular media discussions of the "*Judenvernichtung*" often presented it as a bureaucratic, faceless process: few of the perpetrators had contact with the victims, and the victims had no independent

existence outside of administrative abstractions. Influential works in this genre include Martin Broszat, "Hitler and the Genesis of the 'Final Solution': An Assessment of David Irving's Theses," in *Aspects of the Third Reich,* ed. H.W. Koch (London, 1985), 390–429, and Hans Mommsen, "The Realization of the Unthinkable: The 'Final Solution of the Jewish Question' in the Third Reich," in Mommsen, *From Weimar to Auschwitz* (Princeton, NJ, 1991), 224–53. Such distancing can also be attributed to ideology, as in Daniel Jonah Goldhagen, *Hitler's Willing Executioners: Ordinary Germans and the Holocaust* (New York, 1997); to peer pressure and obedience to authority, as argued in Christopher R. Browning, *Ordinary Men: Reserve Police Battalion 101 and the Final Solution in Poland* (New York, 1992), employing the theories of Philip Zimbardo and Stanley Milgram; or to psychological "doubling," as argued in Robert Jay Lifton, *The Nazi Doctors: Medical Killing and the Psychology of Genocide* (New York, 1986). Franz Stangl, commandant of Sobibór and Treblinka, offers an example of extreme distancing when he speaks of his victims as Lemmings in Gitta Sereny, *Into That Darkness: From Mercy Killing to Mass Murder* (New York, 1974). The notions of "social death," introduced in Orlando Patterson, *Slavery and Social Death: A Comparative Study* (Cambridge, MA, 1982), and of demonization, suggested in Leo Kuper, *Genocide: Its Political Use in the Twentieth Century* (New Haven, CT, 1981), assume a lack of intimacy between killer and killed. For an excellent analysis, see James Waller, *Becoming Evil: How Ordinary People Commit Genocide and Mass Killing* (New York, 2002).

3. Dan Laor, *S.Y. Agnon: A Biography* (Tel Aviv, 1998) [Hebrew], 13–48.

4. Overviews in Dieter Pohl, *Nationalsozialistische Judenverfolgung in Ostgalizien 1941- 1944: Organisation und Durchführung eines staatlichen Massenverbrechens* (Munich, 1996); Thomas Sandkühler, *"Endlösung" in Galizien: Der Judenmord in Ostpolen und die Rettungsinitiativen von Berthold Beitz, 1941-1944* (Bonn, 1996). Buczacz's Ukrainian mayor during the German occupation writes: "In 1941, before retreating, the Bolsheviks destroyed and burnt all the city archives, leaving literally not a shred of paper. The census, taken in a hurry, showed over 8,000 Jews, over 3,600 Ukrainians, and 3,500 Poles." Ivan Bobyk in *The City of Butchach and Its Region: A Historical and Memoiristical Collection,* ed. Mykhailo Ostroverkha et al. (Ukrainian) (London, 1972), 475. Bobyk cites a letter sent by Jewish survivor Isidor Gelbart in 1969 stating that, "in 1939 there were in Buczacz about 8,000 Jews." Under Soviet rule this number fluctuated because of Soviet deportations, Red Army conscription, and masses of refugees from German-occupied Poland. In the early period of Nazi rule, as Gelbart's letter notes, the Jewish population of Buczacz "grew considerably, because at that time Buczacz was called 'Eldorado,' that is 'paradise' for the Jews from all around the region, including L'viv." This was because mass killings began in Buczacz only in fall 1942, months later than in many other communities. But Gelbart ascribes this also to "the City Council of Buczacz," and especially to Mayor Bobyk's "humane attitude and sacrifice," whereby "he helped each and every Jew as much as he could" and "managed to delay for some time efforts by the Gestapo to set up a 'ghetto.'" See Ostroverkha, et al., eds., *The City of Butchach and Its Region,* 475–79. German documentation does not support this last assertion. Gelbart's 1948 testimony in Yad Vashem Archives [hereafter YVA], 033/640, tells a more complex story: "The first Germans arrived around 8 am on July 7, 1941. [Wehrmacht records indicate 5 July; see note 43, below.] On the same day a Ukrainian police force was established and thus right away Jewish women were dragged out of Jewish homes to serve as cleaning women and were mishandled. Whoever had protection from the Ukrainians could still seek help; the Ukrainian Iwan Bobyk was appointed mayor, and fortunately this man was a good and decent human being, unprejudiced, and he tried as much as possible to stand by Jewish people." (For more on early Ukrainian violence, see note 42, below.) Gelbart notes that after the first mass shooting of the "intelligentsia" in August 1941, "the Gestapo did not operate in Buczacz; instead there was a German gendarmerie under the command of a police sergeant ... a man with humane principles who kept good contacts with the Judenrat, so that until November 1941 there was relative calm in the city.... At the end of October 1941 we heard for the first time about an *Aktion*; while in all other cities Jewish *Aktionen* were common, Buczacz was considered to be a paradise, as many Jews who fled to Buczacz from other

cities said." Still, probably because of a personal relationship, in May 1943 Bobyk helped Gelbart and his family find a hiding place where they remained until the liberation.

5. For a definition of a *shtetl* based on percentage of Jews in a town's population, see Yehuda Bauer, *The Death of the Shtetl* (New Haven, CT, 2009), 3–4.

6. In 1870 the 6,077 Jews of Buczacz constituted 67.9 percent of the total population of 8,959. Majer Bałaban, "Buchach (Buczacz)," in *Jewish Encyclopedia,* ed. L. Katznelson and Baron D. G. Ginzburg (St. Petersburg, 1906–13) [Russian], vol. 5, 135. By 1886 the percentage dropped to 62.9 percent, with 6,281 Jews, 1,920 Poles, and 1,761 Ukrainians. *Special Orts-Repertorien der im oesterreichischen Reichsrathe vertretenen Königreiche und Länder,* ed. k.k. statistischen Central-Commission, vol. 12: *Galizien* (Vienna, 1886), 66. In 1914 Buczacz's population was 13,000 inhabitants: 3,500 Poles, 2,000 Ukrainians, and 7,500 (57.7 percent) Jews. Mieczysław Orłowicz and Karol Kwieciński, eds., *Ilustrowany Przewodnik po Galicyi* (Lviv, 1914), 141.

7. In 1890 Eastern Galicia had a population of 3.1 million, 19 percent Roman Catholic, 66 percent Greek Catholic, and almost 14 percent Jewish. Jews comprised 47 percent of the town and city population, but 7.26 percent of the village population. The district of Buczacz had a total population of 113,170—27 percent Roman Catholic, 58 percent Greek Catholic, and 15 percent Jewish. While the urban population of the district, totaling 33,857 people, was made up of 27 percent Roman Catholics, 32 percent Greek Catholics, and 40 percent Jews, the rural population, 79,313, comprised 26 percent Roman Catholics, 55 percent Greek Catholics, and only 4 percent Jews. Galicia as a whole (West and East) in 1910 numbered 3.6 million Poles (45 percent), 3.4 million Ukrainians (43 percent), 872,000 Jews (11 percent), and 65,000 Germans (0.8 percent). The total population had risen by 3 million to nearly 8 million since 1849. But in Eastern Galicia the percentage of Ukrainians had declined from 71 percent to 62 percent because of Ukrainian emigration and Polish colonization. See Paul Robert Magocsi, *A History of Ukraine* (Seattle, 1996), 424; Jit, *Stosunki narodowościowe w Galicyi wschodniej* (Kraków, 1894), 15–16, 38–39, 75–77.

8. Seen clearly in Peter Longerich, *Holocaust: The Nazi Persecution and Murder of the Jews* (New York, 2010).

9. See Omer Bartov, *Erased: Vanishing Traces of Jewish Galicia in Present-Day Ukraine* (Princeton, NJ, 2007); Daniel Mendelsohn, *The Lost: A Search for Six of Six Million* (New York, 2006); Marianne Hirsch and Leo Spitzer, *Ghosts of Home: The Afterlife of Czernowitz in Jewish Memory* (Berkeley, CA, 2010).

10. Rogers Brubaker, "Aftermaths of Empire and the Unmixing of Peoples," in Brubaker, *Nationalism Reframed: Nationhood and the National Question in the New Europe* (New York, 1996), 148–78; Marco Carynnyk, "Foes of our Rebirth: Ukrainian Nationalist Discussions about Jews, 1929-1947," *Nationalities Papers* 39, no. 3 (2011): 315–52; Götz Aly and Susanne Heim, *Architects of Annihilation: Auschwitz and the Logic of Destruction,* trans. A.G. Blunden (Princeton, NJ, 2002).

11. Samantha Power, *"A Problem from Hell": America and the Age of Genocide* (New York, 2002).

12. See, e.g., Larry Wolff, *The Idea of Galicia: History and Fantasy in Habsburg Political Culture* (Stanford, CA, 2010). The exception was the violent peasant response to the Polish uprising of 1846, primarily in Western Galicia where the peasantry was mostly Polish (Roman Catholic). But this had little impact on such Eastern Galician towns as Buczacz where the peasants were mostly Ukrainian and the social conflict with the Polish landlords acquired a national aspect. Piotr S. Wandycz, "The Poles in the Habsburg Monarchy," in *Nationbuilding and the Politics of Nationalism: Essays on Austrian Galicia,* ed. Andrei S. Markovits and Frank E. Sysyn (Cambridge, MA, 1982), 75–81; John-Paul Himka, *Galician Villagers and the Ukrainian National Movement in the Nineteenth Century* (New York, 1988); Keely Stauter-Halsted, *The Nation in the Village: The Genesis of Peasant National Identity in Austrian Poland, 1848-1914* (Ithaca, NY, 2001); Kai Struve, *Bauern und Nation in Galizien: Über Zugehörigkeit und soziale Emanzipation im 19. Jahrhundert* (Göttingen, 2005). On fabricating a cult of the Polish nation see Patrice M. Dabrowski, *Commemorations and the Shaping of Modern Poland* (Bloomington, IN, 2004). On Polish nationalism's dark side, see Brian Porter, *When Nationalism Began to Hate: Imagining Modern Politics in Nineteenth Century Poland* (New York, 2000);

Joanna Beata Michlic, *Poland's Threatening Other: The Image of the Jew from 1880 to the Present* (Lincoln, 2006). The eighteenth-century Cossack and Ukrainian serf rebels against Polish rule, known as the *haidamaks,* were active mostly east of what became Austrian Galicia in 1772. But Ukrainian national poet Taras Shevchenko's 1841 poem "Haidamaki," which celebrated Cossack leader Ivan Gonta's slaughter in 1768 of two thousand Poles and Jews (as well as his own "Polish" children) in Uman, became the rallying cry of Ukrainian nationalism later in the century. Also idealized were the allegedly Robin Hood–like *opryshky,* rebel-bandits of southern Galicia's Carpathian foothills. Magocsi, *A History of Ukraine,* 294–300; *Taras Shevchenko: Selected Works, Poetry and Prose,* trans. J. Weir (Moscow, 1979), 72–117; Krzysztof Lada, "The Ukrainian Topos of Oppression and the Volhynian Slaughter of Poles, 1841-1943/44" (Ph.D. diss., Flinders University, 2012).

13. John-Paul Himka, "The Lviv Pogrom of 1941: The Germans, Ukrainian Nationalists, and the Carnival Crowd," *Canadian Slavonic Papers* 53, no. 2–4 (2011): 209–43; Kai Struve, "Tremors in the Shatterzone of Empires: Eastern Galicia in Summer 1941," in *Shatterzone of Empires: Coexistence and Violence in the German, Habsburg, Russian, and Ottoman Borderlands,* ed. Omer Bartov and Eric D. Weitz (Bloomington, IN, 2013), 463–84.

14. For the final outcome of this undertaking, see Omer Bartov, *The Voice of Your Brother's Blood: Buczacz, Biography of a Town* (New York, forthcoming). Many of the sources mentioned here will be cited below. The town's memorial book is Yisrael Cohen, ed., *The Book of Buczacz* (Tel Aviv, 1956) [Hebrew and Yiddish].

15. Nathan Neta Hanover, *The Book of the Deep Mire* (Tel Aviv, 1944–45) [Hebrew]; published in English as *Abyss of Despair (Yeven Metzulah),* reprint ed., trans. Abraham J. Mesch (New Brunswick, NJ, 1983). See also Joel Raba, *Between Remembrance and Denial: The Fate of the Jews in the Wars of the Polish Commonwealth during the Mid-Seventeenth Century as Shown in Contemporary Writings and Historical Research* (New York, 1995).

16. Silke Kramer, ed., *Das Reisejournal des Ulrich von Werdum (1670-1677)* (Frankfurt, 1990), 210–11.

17. François-Paulin Dalairac, *Les anecdotes de Pologne, ou, Mémoires secrets du règne de Jean Sobieski III. du nom* (Paris, 1699), 230, cited in Sadok Barącz, *Pamiątki Buczackie* (Lviv, 1882), 12.

18. Dalairac, *Les anecdotes,* 228, cited in Barącz, *Pamiątki Buczackie,* 12.

19. "Ów, starosta, baby strzelał po drzewach i Żydów piekł żywcem," *Słownik Biograficzny* 28 (Krakow, 1984–85): 113–14; Czesław Miłosz, *The History of Polish Literature,* 2nd ed. (Berkeley, CA, 1983), 143–47; Stanisław Grodziski, *Wzdłuż Wisły, Dniestru i Zbrucza* (Krakow, 1998), 136–37; Adam Żarnowski, *Kresy Wschodnie II Rzeczypospolitej: Buczacz* (Krakow, 1992), 8. Wolff, *Galicia,* 145, cites Leopold von Sacher-Masoch, *Graf Donski,* 2nd ed. (Schaffenhausen, 1864), 343, whose fictional giant Ruthenian peasant Onufry recalls: "My father told me how the former master, the father of our count, made the peasants climb up into trees and cry 'cuckoo' and then shot them down like forest birds." This story, notes Wolff, derives from Galician accounts of the 1780s about a Polish nobleman who sent a peasant or a Jew up a tree and then shot him down.

20. Barącz, *Pamiątki Buczackie.*

21. Shmuel Yosef Agnon, *The City Whole [Ir U'meloah]* (Tel Aviv, 1973) [Hebrew].

22. See, e.g., Nancy Sinkoff, *Out of the Shtetl: Making Jews Modern in the Polish Borderlands* (Providence, RI, 2004); Marcin Wodziński, *Haskalah and Haṣidism in the Kingdom of Poland: A History of Conflict* (Portland, OR, 2005).

23. For some examples see Cohen, *The Book of Buczacz,* 212–24.

24. Antoni Siewinski, "Diaries from the Buczacz-Jazłowiec region, from the Great War of 1914 to 1920—a family account," Jagiellonian Library (Krakow, Poland), manuscript division: BJ 7367. Siewinski was born on 2 January 1858, in Lviv, and was employed as the principal of the boys' school in Buczacz. The last entry in his diary is dated 14 March 1939.

25. Aba Lev, "The Devastation of Galician Jewry in the Bloody World War," in *Jewish Chronicle,* vol. 3, ed. L. M. Klyachko et al. (Leningrad-Moscow, 1924) [Russian, trans. from Yiddish], 174.

26. S. An-sky, *The Destruction of the Jews in Poland, Galicia, and Bukovina,* trans. Shmuel Leib Zitron, 4 vols. (Berlin-Charlottenburg, 1929; reissued by Stybel in Tel Aviv in the 1930s) [He-

brew], v. 4, 406. Originally written in Yiddish on the basis of Ansky's Russian-language wartime diary: S. An-Ski, *Gezamelte Shriften,* 15 vols. (Warsaw: An-Sky, 1923) [Yiddish], vols. 4–5. On 28 January 1915, Ansky wrote in his diary that reportedly "forty girls were raped in the shtetl of Buczacz." My thanks to Polly Zavadivker for sharing this as yet unpublished translation with me. See also abridged English translation, S. Ansky, *The Enemy at His Pleasure,* trans. and ed. Joachim Neugroschel (New York, 2002), and Gabriella Safran, *Wandering Soul: The Dybbuk's Creator, S. An-Sky* (Cambridge, MA, 2010), 225–57. Note inconsistencies in spelling of the author's penname.

27. See, e.g., situation reports, Austrian-Hungarian (KuK) 36th Infantry Division, on fighting in and around Buczacz: Österreichisches Staatsarchiv (ÖSA) / Kriegsarchiv (KA) / Neue Feldakte (NFA), 36.I.D., op. Nr. 431-460, 1.-30.9.1915, K. 2123; ÖSA/KA/NFA, 36.I.D., op. Nr. 461-491, 1.-31.10.1915, K. 2124. Austrian recruitment of local population in Buczacz and elsewhere to repair war damages: Central Archives of Historical Records, Warsaw (AGAD), zesp. 311 C. K. Ministerstwo dla robot publicznych, jedn. 250: "Heranziehung der Zivilbevölkerung in den wiedereroberten Gebieten Ostgaliziens zum Straßenbau," 16.11.1917, 5.12.1917, 10.11.1917, 12.1.1918; lists of destroyed city buildings in Buczacz, KuK Construction Ministry, June and July 1918, Central State Historical Archives of Ukraine in Lviv [hereafter TsDIAL], fond 146, op. 48, spr. 31–32, totaling 569 houses. For Russian occupation, see, e.g., note by Lieutenant-General Miezentsev, Assistant Head of the Gendarmerie Department of the Provisional Military General Government of Galicia to the head of the Department, 3 January 1915: "According to available information, some positions in town councils and courts in the Ternopil District are still held by Jews … for instance … Mayor Stern of Buczacz. Considering that after the occupation of the country by Russian forces all Jews retain an unfriendly disposition [toward the Russians] and do not cease to hope for a return of Austrian forces, as well their greed and exploitation of the population, I would suggest the necessity of replacing Jews still holding administrative offices by persons of Ruthenian or Polish origin" [in Russian]. Central State Historical Archives of Ukraine in Kiev [hereafter TsDIAK], fond 365, op. 1, spr. 30, 29. See also note by the Governor of Ternopil Czartoryjskii about suspicion of espionage by the Buczacz citizen Munish Hershkov Bauer, 12 March 1917: TsDIAK, fond 361, op. 1, spr. 2110. Russian operational orders and administrative memoranda concerning Buczacz: TsDIAK, fond 363, op. 1, spr. 2, ark. 51; fond 365, op. 1, spr. 254, ark. 6; fond 361, op. 1, t. 3, spr. 2672, ark. 3.

28. For a Ukrainian account about the area of Buczacz, see, e.g., Ivan Krypiakevych and Bohdan Hnatevych, *History of the Ukrainian Army* (L'viv, 1936) [Ukrainian], 502–12. For Polish accounts, see, e.g., Central Military Archives [hereafter CAW] in Warsaw: 334.183.1, 332.46.1, 331.7.1; I.400.2213. See also Witold Hupert, *Zajęcie Małopolski Wschodniej i Wołynia w roku 1919* (Lviv-Warsaw, 1928), 42–43, 96–105; Stefan Wierżyński, *Zarys historii wojennej 14-go Pułku Piechoty* (Warsaw, 1929), 3–13; Władysław Laudyn, *Bój pod Jazłowcem, 11.13.VII 1919* (Warsaw, 1932), 4–8; Ministerstwo Obrony Narodowej / Wojskowy Instytut Historyczny, ed., *Wojskowy Przegląd Historyczny* 39/1–2 (Warsaw, 1994), 160–63, 176–77.

29. See, e.g., testimonies on Ukrainian violence against Polish civilians in Buczacz County, 1918–19: CAW I.400.1554; Parliamentary Commission for the Investigation of Ukrainian Raids against Polish Civilians, testimonies from Buczacz: Central Archive of Modern Records (AAN) in Warsaw—Ministry of the Interior, Eastern Section (MSZ), 5341a, 227, 233–34.

30. See, e.g., reports on the political situation in Eastern Galicia in 1920 by the British embassy in Warsaw: The National Archives (Kew) (TNA), Foreign Office (FO), London, 688/2/3, 229–30; report by Vice-Consul in Lemberg on his journey in Eastern Galicia in March 1920: FO 688/2/3, 295–303; report by British Military Mission to Poland on a trip east of Tarnopol, 5 January 1921: FO 688/9/2/, 553–56; report by British Consul Leeper on his visit to Eastern Galicia in spring 1924: FO 688/15/12, 679–88. See also "L'Ukraine Occidentale," by Ievhen Petrushevych, President of the Supreme Council of the Western Ukrainian Republic, 1921, with references to Buczacz, in German Political Archive of the Foreign Office (PAAA), Collection: Pol. 1, Foreign Policy regarding Galicia, 1921–1939, R 81428; Polish response: "Galicie Orientale en chiffres et en graphiques," Comité de Défense Nationale à Lviv (Warsaw: State publication, 1921), R 81429;

and reports by the German embassy in Warsaw on the situation in Galicia, PAAA, files 42 and 52. See also Stanisław Skrzypek, *The Problem of Eastern Galicia* (London, 1948). On anti-Jewish violence, see William W. Hagen, "The Moral Economy of Popular Violence: The Pogrom in Lviv, November 1918," in *Antisemitism and Its Opponents in Modern Poland,* ed. Robert Blobaum (Ithaca, NY, 2005), 124–47; and a recent Polish perspective, Leszek Kania, *W cieniu Orląt Lwowskich: Polskie sądy wojskowe, kontrwywiad i służby policyjne w bitwie o Lviv 1918-1919* (Zielona Góra, 2008). An overview in Carole Fink, *Defending the Rights of Others: The Great Powers, the Jews, and International Minority Protection, 1978-1938* (New York, 2004).

31. For a Ukrainian perspective, see *Publications of the Ukrainian Scientific Institute,* v. 15, Pavlo Shandruk, ed., *The Ukrainian-Russian War of 1920 in Documents* (Warsaw, 1933) [Ukrainian], 114–17, 120–51, 216–37. On Polish-Ukrainian collaboration against the Red Army with Buczacz as the temporary headquarters of the Ukrainian Army, see Marek Tarczyński, ed., *Bitwa Lwowska 25 VII-18 X 1920: Dokumenty operacyjne,* Part I (Warszawa, 2002), 146–47, 211–13, 314–15, 339–40, 378–79, 412–13, 444–47, 468–70, 514–16, 528–29, 660–63, 747–60, 818–21, 871–73, 896–99, 912–15, 976–79. For the Bolshevik view, see S.M. Koroliskii, N.K. Kolesnik, and I.K. Rybalka, eds., *The Civil War in Ukraine, 1918-1920: A Collection of Documents and Materials* (Kiev, 1967) [Russian], 336–39.

32. For a general history of the OUN, see Franziska Bruder, *"Den ukrainischen Staat erkämpfen oder sterben!" Die Organisation ukrainischer Nationalisten (OUN) 1929-1948* (Berlin, 2007). For historiographical controversies over this organization, see note 50, below.

33. William W. Hagen, "Before the 'Final Solution': Toward a Comparative Analysis of Political Anti-Semitism in Interwar Germany and Poland," *Journal of Modern History* 68, no. 2 (1996): 351–81; Szymon Rudnicki, "Anti-Jewish Legislation in Interwar Poland," in Blobaum, *Antisemitism and Its Opponents,* 148–70; Holger Michael, *Zwischen Davidstern und Roter Fahne: Juden in Polen im XX. Jahrhundert* (Berlin-Brandenburg, 2007), 85–122.

34. Ezra Mendelsohn, *The Jews of East Central Europe between the World Wars* (Bloomington, IN, 1983), 68–83; Moshe Mishkinsky, "The Communist Party of Poland and the Jews," and Abraham Brumberg, "The Bund and the Polish Socialist Party in the late 1930s," both in *The Jews of Poland between the Two World Wars,* ed. Yisrael Gutman et al. (Hanover, NH, 1989), 56–74 and 75–94; Celia S. Heller, *On the Edge of Destruction: Jews of Poland between the Two World Wars* (Detroit, 1994), 249–93. On Polish Marxist intellectuals, many of them Jewish, see Marci Shore, *Caviar and Ashes: A Warsaw Generation's Life and Death in Marxism, 1918-1968* (New Haven, CT, 2006). For pre-1914 Jewish politics, see Joshua Shanes, *Diaspora Nationalism and Jewish Identity in Habsburg Galicia* (New York, 2012).

35. See, e.g., Starosta Buczacki, Nr. B 19: "Ekscesy ukraińskie w Trościańcu," Buczacz, 12 June 1934: State Archives of Lviv Oblast [hereafter DATO], fond 231, op. 1, spr. 2264, 14–16; Starosta Buczacki, Nr. 9/33/Taj. "Żydowskie życie polityczne," Buczacz, 29 January 1933; Posterunek Policji Państwowej w Buczaczu, Nr 304/Taj./35, "K.P.Z.U. w Buczaczu—informacje," Buczacz, 24 June 1935: DATO, fond 231, op. 1, spr. 2325. See also minutes of the local branch of the Ukrainian "Prosvita" (Enlightenment) organization from 1930–39, e.g., TsDIAL, fond 348, op. 1, spr. 1379, and spr. 1385, with references to Polish repression.

36. See, e.g., *Księga Adresowa Małopolski, Rocznik 1935/1936,* 12–13.

37. Tom Segev, *Simon Wiesenthal: The Life and Legends* (New York, 2010), 29–43; Samuel D. Kassow, *Who Will Write Our History? Emanuel Ringelblum, the Warsaw Ghetto, and the Oyneg Shabes Archive* (Bloomington, IN, 2007), 17–26; Cohen, *The Book of Buczacz,* 225–28.

38. S.Y. Agnon, *A Guest for the Night: A Novel,* trans. Misha Louvish (Madison, WI, 1968).

39. See report on activities, acts of terror and sabotage by the OUN in Buczacz area in 1931–32: AAN, Ministry of the Interior (MSW), Nationalities Unit, 1251, 77–78; Ukrainian raids, anti-Jewish and anti-Polish activities in the Buczacz area in 1937, CAW VIII.800.72.1, 24, 95.

40. See, e.g., reports of Polish State Police on OUN activities in villages around Buczacz: State Archive of the Security Service of Ukraine (HDA SBU), Ternopil, spr. 3787-II. See record of Soviet trial (1956–57) of Volodymyr Antonovych Kaznov'sky (Volodymyr Kaznovs'kyi, Ka-

znowski), commander of the Ukrainian police in Buczacz and former public prosecutor, with list of names and records of other police officers, and their prewar political engagement, police interrogations, and court testimonies: HAD SBU, Ternopil, spr. 30466, vols. 1–2; 26874; 14050-P; 736; 3713; 14340; 9859-P; 8540-P; 8973-P; 14320-P. See also Soviet investigation of the murder of Jews and Poles in the area of nearby Potok Złoty by Ukrainian militiamen and German police officers mentioned also in connection to killings in Buczacz: State Archives of the Russian Federation (GARF), fond 7021 (Soviet "Extraordinary State Commission"), op. 75, delo 371, 6–11 / United States Holocaust Memorial Museum Archives [hereafter USHMMA], RG 22-002M, Reel # 17 (Ternopil region). For context, see Gabriel N. Finder and Alexander V. Prusin, "Collaboration in Eastern Galicia: The Ukrainian Police and the Holocaust," *East European Jewish Affairs* 34, n. 2 (2004): 95–118; Marina Sorokina, "People and Procedures: Toward a History of the Investigation of Nazi Crimes in the USSR," *Kritika* 6, n. 4 (Fall 2005): 797–831; Joshua Rubenstein and Ilya Altman, eds., *The Unknown Black Book: The Holocaust in the German-Occupied Soviet Territories*, trans. Christopher Morris and Joshua Rubenstein (Bloomington, IN, 2008).

41. Jan T. Gross, *Revolution from Abroad: The Soviet Conquest of Poland's Western Ukraine and Western Belorussia*, expanded ed. (Princeton, NJ, 2002); Bogdan Musial, "*Konterrevolutionäre Elemente sind zu erschiessen*": *Die Brutalisierung des deutsch-sowjetischen Krieges im Sommer 1941* (Berlin, 2000). Karel C. Berkhoff, *Harvest of Despair: Life and Death in Ukraine under Nazi Rule* (Cambridge, MA, 2004), 14, cites Soviet documents indicating a total of 8,789 Ukrainian, Polish, and Jewish prisoners killed by the NKVD in Ukraine.

42. Rossoliński-Liebe, "Debating, Obfuscating and Disciplining the Holocaust," 203, estimates over thirteen thousand Jewish victims; Dieter Pohl, "Anti-Jewish Pogroms in Western Ukraine," in Barkan, *Shared History*, 306, estimates up to thirty-five thousand killed. See also K. Struve, "The Explosion of Violence: The Pogrom of Summer 1941," in Bartov and Weitz, *Shatterzone of Empires*, 463–84; Frank Golczewski, "Shades of Grey: Reflections on Jewish-Ukrainian and German-Ukrainian Relations in Galicia," in *The Shoah in Ukraine: History, Testimony, Memorialization*, ed. Ray Brandon and Wendy Lower (Bloomington, IN, 2008), 114–55; John-Paul Himka, *Ukrainians, Jews and the Holocaust: Divergent Memories* (Saskatoon, 2009). Timothy Snyder, *Bloodlands: Europe between Hitler and Stalin* (New York, 2010), makes a larger argument about the link between Stalinist and Nazi mass murder. For a critique of this thesis, see Omer Bartov, "Featured Review," *Slavic Review* 70, no. 2 (2011): 424–28.

43. Moshe Wizinger (1947), Yad Vashem Archives (YVA), 03/3799, writes:

> The well known Ukrainian eye doctor Hamerski told the Jewish delegation headed by Dr. Blutreich and Eldenberg that the Ukrainian intelligentsia does not support the murder of the Jews, but they themselves are helpless, because those who are ruling now are the leaders of the hitherto secret Ukrainian bands.... In the meantime, the robbing, rape and murder increased. One night, the Great Synagogue was gutted.... The scrolls of the Torah were taken all the way to the bridge.... unbound ... [with] one end ... attached ... [to] the bridge while the other nearly reached the water. This brought upon a harsh protest from the Ukrainian priests, who turned to the leader of the Ukrainian bands, Dankowicz, with a categorical demand to stop profaning the Holy Places ... The ihumen [abbot] of the Basilian Ukrainian Monastery ... proposed to the Jews to carry the scrolls to the monastery where they would be safe.

George (Gershon) Gross, videotaped testimony, USC Shoah Foundation for Visual History and Education [hereafter USCSF], Deerfield Beach, Florida, 17 June 1996, relates the same story. And see note 4, above, for Isidor Gelbart's testimony on anti-Jewish Ukrainian violence on the first day of the German occupation. The first German army unit entered Buczacz on 5 July 1941. The next day it reported: "A Ukrainian militia took over local police duties until the arrival of German troops." For this and other German army reports see Bundesarchiv-Militärarchiv (Freiburg i.B) (BA-MA) RH20-17/32, 5.7.41, 6.7.41; RH26-101/8, 5.7.41; RH24-52/3, Kriegstagebuch

(KTB), Heft 2, 40-42, 55; RH20-17/38, 6.7.41, 12.7.41; RH20-17/277, 7.7.41; RH26 257/8, KTB Nr. 5, 20.5.41-12.12.41; RH26-257/10, Anlagen z. KTB Nr. 5, Bd.2, 12.7.41, 13.7.41; RH20-17/33, 11.7.41, 12.7.41. The self-proclaimed Buczacz "sich" (militia) soon expanded to over a hundred men initially commanded by Tadei Kramarchuk and Andrii Dan'kovych, and assisted by the local OUN representative Myron Hanushevs'kyi; it was taken over in late July by the 37-year-old Kaznovs'kyi. The "sich" abused, looted, exploited, and murdered Jewish inhabitants of Buczacz; in mid July it participated in the execution of forty politically suspect Jews, Poles, and Ukrainians. On 25 August the militia assisted a German police unit in a mass shooting of 400 to 650 members of the Jewish intelligentsia in Buczacz. See note 40, above, for Kaznovs'kyi's trial records, also containing a 1951 letter by survivor Markus Kleiner detailing crimes committed by the Ukrainian police chief. In fall 1941 the militia came under direct German control as an indigenous local police, or Hilfspolizei, and provided men for such Schuma units as that stationed in Czortków.

44. See, e.g., Alicia Appleman-Jurman, *Alicia: My Story* (New York, 1988), and Mina Rosner, *I am a Witness* (Winnipeg, 1990), both of whom were protected at some point by Poles. Yitzhak Bauer, interviewed by me in 2003, recalled: "We had a teacher in elementary school, a neighbor, an 'endek' [member of the Polish nationalist and antisemitic National Democracy Party]… Whenever he met Grandmother or Mother, he would remove his hat and greet them politely. His son and daughter were often in our home. But when I stood by the blackboard trying to solve some problem … he said to me … 'Żydku ci nie ma pożytku,' meaning, 'Jew-boy, you are of no use to me.' And to this day this phrase haunts me. But during the German occupation he behaved very well. He even greeted me when we met, always with his hat." See also Bruder, *"Den ukrainischen Staat erkämpfen oder sterben!",* 168, citing an OUN-UPA (on UPA see below, and note 51) report on Western Ukraine from March 1943: "The Poles very eagerly help the Jews and hide them, in order to save them from extermination by the Germans, because they view the Jews as their natural allies in the struggle against the Ukrainians." On the changing Jewish perceptions of Poles, see Havi Ben-Sasson, *Are We Jewish Poles? Relations between Jews and Poles during the Holocaust from the Jewish Perspective* (Jerusalem, 2009) [Hebrew].

45. See, e.g., testimony by Zofia Pollak of Buczacz, then sixteen, who survived the last weeks of the German occupation hidden with her father and brother in the barn of a poor peasant who had once been helped by her father. "He said: 'Whatever I have I will share with you …' He covered us with hay.… We were there in one position, we couldn't move and this is how we were liberated on February 23, 1944 …" See also testimony of Edzia Spielberg-Flitman, below, and note 62.

46. George Gross (note 43, above) says about the *Ordnungsdienst* (OD): "The Germans would say they need five hundred people. The [Jewish] police went" to seize them. Of a Judenrat member who had survived, he says that he "had to hide, like Eichmann. If they found him they would kill him." Wizinger (note 43, above) writes: "The countless demands by the Germans or Ukrainians were fulfilled immediately" by the Judenrat, whose officials "were able to lead a very good life and to amass large sums of money," while the OD were "robbing, killing, worse than the Germans." There are many more such accounts.

47. Yitzhak Bauer, in the aforementioned 2003 interview (note 44, above), recalled joining a small Jewish resistance group in the forest. But in 1968 he testified to a West German court that he had joined the OD in November 1941. Numbering some thirty men, the OD "carried out the orders of the *Judenrat,* but during *Aktionen* … we were put at the disposition of … the Gestapo or the local gendarmerie." On 27 November 1942, Bauer "was assigned to participate in the cleanup of the Jewish hospital." Those of the approximately one hundred patients "who could not move were shot right there and then in their beds. The others were taken out to the railroad station … and transported to extermination in Bełżec." Bundesarchiv Berlin (BAB) 162/5182: "Aufklärung von NS-Verbrechen im Kreis Czortków / Distrikt Galizien, 1941–1944, Sammelverfahren gg. Brettschneider u.a.," deposition, 10 January 1968, 6212–14. In an interview I conducted with Buczacz survivor Zeev Anderman in 2002, he related that in April 1943 his brother Janek had shot

a Ukrainian policeman with a pistol during a mass execution, and was then beaten and burned alive in the town square. Yitzhak Shikhor (Szwarc) provides a similar description of the incident in Cohen, *The Book of Buczacz*, 246. But Szwarc's original Polish-language testimony notes that after someone from a group of Jews that was about to be executed "shot a Ukrainian policeman and injured a German," the Germans "found a weapon that probably belonged to the Jewish policeman Janek Anderman," who was then killed. Izaak Szwarc, *Żydowski Instytut Historyczny* (ZIH) 301/327 and USHMMA, RG-15.084 Acc.1997 A.0125 1945, Reel 5.

48. For Jewish testimonies see, e.g., Cohen, *The Book of Buczacz*, 233–302. For a West German court's summary of the events, see the 1962 trial of Heinrich Peckmann, commander of the Czortków Sipo outpost in April to October 1943, and Kurt Köllner, *Judensachbearbeiter* (official in charge of Jewish affairs) in Czortków from July 1942 to early 1944: "Urteil Landgericht (LG) Saarbrücken 6 Ks 2/62 gegen Kurt O. Köllner und P," *Justiz und NS-Verbrechen. Sammlung deutscher Strafurteile wegen nationalsozialistischer Tötungsverbrechen 1945-1966* [hereafter J.u.NS-V], v. XVIII: 658–83.

49. *J.u.NS-V*, LG Saarbrücken 6 Ks 2/62, 657; Bundesarchiv Zwischenarchiv Dahlwitz-Hoppengarten (MfS) ZB 827, Akte 2, and GLA Karlsruhe 309 Zug. 2001_42/881: Eisel Werner (last commander of the Czortków Sipo outpost), R.u.S. (Rasse- und Siedlungshauptamt) Fragebogen, 1 September 1944.

50. See note 32 and John-Paul Himka, "The Ukrainian Insurgent Army and the Holocaust," paper presented at the convention of the American Association for the Advancement of Slavic Studies (AAASS), November 2009, http://www.academia.edu/1071581/The_Ukrainian_Insurgent_Army_UPA_and_the_Holocaust (accessed 16 January 2013); Timothy Snyder, "The Causes of Ukrainian-Polish Ethnic Cleansing 1943," *Past & Present* 179, no. 1 (2003): 198–234; Lucina Kulińska and Adam Roliński, ed., *Kwestia ukraińska i eksterminacja ludności polskiej w Małopolsce Wschodniej w świetle dokumentów Polskiego Państwa Podziemnego 1942-1944* (Krakow, 2004); Lucina Kulińska and Adam Roliński, ed., *Antypolska akcja nacjonalistów ukraińskich w Małopolsce Wschodniej w świetle dokumentów Rady Głównej Opiekuńczej 1943-1944* (Krakow, 2003); Grzegorz Motyka and Dariusz Libionka, *Antypolska akcja OUN-UPA 1943-1944: Fakty i interpretacje—redakcja naukowa* (Warsaw, 2002). For historical controversies over the OUN-UPA, see Per Anders Rudling, "The OUN, the UPA and the Holocaust: A Study in the Manufacturing of Historical Myths," Cark Beck Papers in Russian and East European Studies, No. 2107 (Pittsburgh, 2011); Grzegorz Rossoliński-Liebe, "Debating, Obfuscating and Disciplining the Holocaust: Post-Soviet Historical Discourses on the OUN-UPA and Other Nationalist Movements," *East European Jewish Affairs* 42, no. 3 (2012): 199–241; John-Paul Himka, "Debates in Ukraine over Nationalist Involvement in the Holocaust, 2004-2008," *Nationalities Papers* 39, no. 3 (2011): 353–70.

51. Grzegorz Motyka, *Ukraińska partyzantka 1942-1960: Działalność Organizacji Ukraińskich Nacjonalistów i Ukraińskiej Powstańczej Armii* (Warsaw, 2006); Jeffrey Burds, *The Early Cold War in Soviet West Ukraine, 1944-1948* (Pittsburgh, 2001).

52. See notes 4, 32, 50, and 51, above. Such major monographs on the Holocaust as Longerich, *Holocaust*, and Saul Friedländer, *Nazi Germany and the Jews, 1939-1945: The Years of Extermination* (New York, 2007), have little to say on this region.

53. See notes 9, 32, and 52, above. See also Johan Dietsch, *Making Sense of Suffering: Holocaust and Holodomor in Ukrainian Historical Culture* (Lund, 2006); Wilfried Jilge, "The Competition of Victims," *Krytyka* 10, no. 5 (2006): 14–17 [Ukrainian]; Jilge, "The Politics of History and the Second World War in Post-Communist Ukraine (1986/1991-2004/2005)," in *Divided Historical Cultures? World War II and Historical Memory in Soviet and Post-Soviet Ukraine,* ed. Wilfried Jilge and Stefan Troebst, topical issue of *Jahrbücher für Geschichte Osteuropas* 54, no. 1 (2006): 51–82.

54. Eliasz Chalfen, YVA M1/E 1559 (1947).

55. Ester Grintal (Nachtigal), videotaped testimony, USCSF, Netanyah, Israel, 21 September 1997 [Hebrew].

56. Ibid.

57. See notes 32, 50, and 51. See also Timothy Snyder, *The Reconstruction of Nations: Poland, Ukraine, Lithuania, Belarus, 1569-1999* (New Haven, CT, 2003), 165–78. On the Waffen-SS "Galicia" Division, see Michael James Melnyk, *To Battle: The Formation and History of the 14th Galician Waffen-SS Division* (Solihull, 2002). The book contains no mention of anti-Jewish violence; see, e.g., ibid., 5–6 for the march into Galicia in June–July 1941.

58. Arie Klonicki-Klonymus, *The Diary of Adam's Father* (Jerusalem, 1969) [Hebrew], 47.

59. *Przeżycia i rozporządzenie Joachima Mincere,* probably written in 1943, YVA.

60. Yoel Katz, videotaped testimony, USCSF, Netanyah, Israel, 11 December 1995 [Hebrew].

61. Edzia Spielberg-Flitman, videotaped testimony, USCSF, Skokie, Illinois, 14 March 1995.

62. Mojżesz Szpigiel, USHMMA, reel 37, 301/3492, Łódź, 10 March 1948.

63. Julija Mykhailivna Trembach, written by her daughter, Roma Nestorivna Kryvenchuk, in 2003, collected by Mykola Kozak. Trembach stresses that "our people, Ukrainians and Poles, tried to help" the Jews "however they could. They made dugouts in the ground, and Jews hid there. Secretly people would bring food to those dugouts. And God knows how much food I brought by myself." Married to a Ukrainian man, Trembach refrains from mentioning local complicity in the murder of the Jews. Buczacz, she says, was "populated mostly by Jewish people. They were cultured, wealthy, enterprising and intelligent people. All the so-called 'stone houses' in the center of the town belonged to them. Jewish people constituted the local intelligentsia." References to Jewish wealth in Galician towns were the staple of antisemitic rhetoric in nineteenth-century nationalist literature. See, e.g., polar descriptions of a Galician marketplace in Ivan Franko, *Fateful Crossroads* (1900), trans. Roma Franko, ed. Sonia Morris (Winnipeg, 2006), 178–79, and Agnon, *The City Whole,* 269.

64. Maria Mykhailivna Khvostenko (née Dovhanchuk), interview with Mykola Kozak, 2003. Khvostenko does not mention the Ukrainian auxiliaries and police who were invariably present at such roundups. Her reluctance to mention local complicity does not prevent her from criticizing present attitudes: "On the western slope of Fedir [Fedor] Hill there is a small forest where the Jewish community that was murdered in 1942-1943 by the German fascists is buried. It's time for our city—and not only the city, but also the region and the country—to pay attention to the place where the fascists murdered many Jews and to honor their memory, to put a decent monument or a sculpture. For they were honest citizens of the city and the country, who loved our land and our city, worked for it and suffered guiltlessly.… We should honor and remember them so that it will never happen again." A decade later this has still not been done in Buczacz.

65. Viktor Petrykevych diary, private (courtesy of Bohdan Petrykevych). My thanks to Sofia Grachova for acquiring, transcribing, and translating this diary.

66. Spielberg-Flitman, USCSF/1995, recalled that "the Ukrainians … had pogroms after the war … they were still killing us. They were so brutal." Aliza Rosenwasser (Gripel), liberated at age nine, related that upon returning to Buczacz she found that "they dismantled the floor between the two stories" in her family house: "Perhaps they thought there was money inside the floor." When the few returning Jews searched for the mass grave on the Fedor Hill, "we didn't know how to find it, because there was no trace. Then we came to a clearing in the forest … all around things were growing, but this section of the mass grave was entirely bare … Later they explained" that "the soil was too rich" with corpses to allow any vegetation. YVA 03/10402, VT-1612, 17 July 1997, transcript, 55. Bronia Kahane, fourteen at the time, recalled that when she returned to Buczacz four months after its second liberation she was told: "There are not too many Jews here. There's one building; knock and they'll let you in. We have to be under the key [i.e., locked in] because we're afraid during the night they shouldn't kill us." She adds: "I never went back to my house … because they said don't you dare go back because they're going to kill you." Videotaped testimony, USCSF, South Fallsburg, NY, 8 August 1995.

67. Jan T. Gross, *Fear: Anti-Semitism in Poland after Auschwitz: An Essay in Historical Interpretation* (New York, 2006); Jan Tomasz Gross with Irena Grudzińska Gross, *Golden Harvest: Events at the Periphery of the Holocaust* (New York, 2012); John-Paul Himka and Joanna Beata Michlic,

ed., *Bringing the Dark Past to Light: The Reception of the Holocaust in Postcommunist Europe* (Lincoln, NE, 2013).

68. See, e.g., TsDIAL, fond R-1, op. 1, spr. 101, situation reports of the Regional Committee of the Communist Party in Ternopol (Ternopil), 3 September—3 November 1944, including: report to Nikita Khrushchev on the liberation of Buczacz, 1 August 1944, 103–06; report on Soviet fighting against the OUN-UPA in the region, 130–42. Spr. 284: reports on resettlement of populations in the Ternopol, 23 March—4 November 1945: "evacuation operation," 19 April 1945, 2–3; "settlement" of Ukrainians from Buczacz district, 13–14, 28. Spr. 561: annual report for 1946 on fighting against the OUN-UPA, 150–74. Spr. 871: Communist Party inquiry about the "struggle against the Ukrainian-German Nationalist in 1946," 83–103.

69. Rene Zuroff (Tabak), videotaped testimony, USCSF, Bellmore, NY, 31 August 1995.

70. See, e.g., Igor Duda, *Buczacz: The Guide* (Lviv, 1985) [Ukrainian]: "The treacherous aggression of Fascist Germany interrupted socialist construction. On July 7, 1941 the Hitlerites occupied Buczacz. During the time of the occupation they exterminated about 7,500 civilians from the city and the villages of the district; 1,839 young men and women were seized for forced labor into Germany. 137 buildings were destroyed, as well as a number of industrial enterprises and schools. Nevertheless the population did not submit to the Fascists." No mention of Jewish victims or local collaborators.

71. See "Głos Buczaczan," ed. Władysław Sklarz, (Wrocław: Towarzystwo Miłośników Lwowa i Kresów Południowo-Wschodnich / Klub Buczaczan, 1992–).

72. Ivan Bobyk, *The City of Butchach,* a massive volume, dedicates only a few pages to the Jews, 475–79. See also Dział Rękopisów Biblioteki Zakładu Narodowego im. Ossolińskich (Boss), sygn. 16621/I Dokumentacja Dotycząca zatrudnienie polskich in ukraińskich pracowników w instytucjach działających w Czortkowie i okolicy w latach 1942-1944, v. 1, 24: "Stadtverwaltung Buczacz, Stand 16. Juni 1942," where Bobyk appears under number 1 in city administration. Bobyk's Polish police file describes him as a "presumed member of U.W.O., an unreliable organization hostile to the Polish State." DATO, fond 274, op. 4, spr. 78, p. 13. UWO was the Ukrainian Military Organization, founded in 1920 and headed by Yevhen Konovalets, who then became the first leader of OUN until his assassination by an NKVD agent in 1938.

73. Cohen, *The Book of Buczacz*.

CHAPTER 7

"If He Knows to Make a Child…"
Memories of Birth and Baby-Killing in Deferred Jewish Testimony Narratives

SARA R. HOROWITZ

Belated memory narratives, whether spoken or written, offer an invaluable portal to understanding how the Nazi genocide was perpetrated, experienced, recollected, and narrated. One particular narrative moment opens up the effect of Nazi atrocity on subsequent gendered identity—the ways in which people come to think about themselves as men and as women—in complex and palpable ways. The moment in which otherwise ordinary people come to reveal their participation in infanticide, the killing of babies and children, is often explicitly isolated by the rememberer as a memory of particular horror amid a sea of horrors.

Drawing largely on oral accounts and life writing about the Holocaust from the late 1980s and beyond, this essay looks at the place and significance of such moments in what are often termed "belated" testimonies or memoirs. While many researchers have privileged the much earlier firsthand accounts that were rendered as close to the events as possible, on the assumption that memory was then sharper, more accurate, and less influenced by other accounts, others have noted an essential correlation between earlier and later accounts, even an increased sharpness of memory and deeper understanding of its impact.[1] Moreover, while taped oral accounts introduce layers of mediation that may deflect or distort the flow of testimony, they also provide a context for new information and insight. As Lawrence Langer notes in his study of the videotaped testimonies at the Fortunoff Video Archive for Holocaust Testimonies housed at Yale University, such belated accounts yield reflections and insights

---

Notes for this section begin on page 150.

"captured nowhere else." In these oral accounts, "several currents flow at different depths" as recounters visibly engage with the act of remembering and "touch exposed nerves that the witnesses themselves did not realize."[2] Significantly, it is precisely in later testimonies that we may find people willing to talk about matters that did not often find their way into earlier firsthand accounts, perhaps because these matters were too painful to put to words, or regarded as too shameful to make public.

For this reason, I prefer the term "deferred" testimonies to describe accounts of matters once considered unspeakable, but that finally find their way into some kind of narrative about a traumatic past. Looking at videotaped accounts archived by the Shoah Foundation since the mid 1990s, along with documentary films and outtakes produced decades after the war years, makes clear not only what happened during the war years, but how people struggle to recount and cope with their experiences. For those who recollect and recount their firsthand experiences, the accounting may be postponed through a deliberate decision or through an inability to give voice to such memories, to draw them into a story to be told to others, or even to oneself. Historians have begun to utilize collections of such accounts to produce cumulative microhistories of the destruction of European Jewry, mining individual testimonies for corroborative facts that enable a reconstruction of the past. While such aggregation is important to the construction of history, the individual testimonies also allow a focus on the ways in which personal memory is brought into language, into storytelling. The passage of time may help the rememberer to develop narrative and psychological frames through which the unbearable may, in fact, be borne and transmitted.

While all Jews were targets of the Nazi genocide, the survival of Jewish babies during the Holocaust was particularly precarious. In some ghettos, sexual intercourse and pregnancy were outlawed by the Nazi authorities. Infractions could be harshly punished, sometimes by death. One woman recollects that in a ghetto in Latvia, "You were not allowed to get pregnant … so nobody dared to get pregnant." Whether or not she was correct in her assessment of the effect of the ban on Jewish reproduction, she recollects that, then in her early twenties, these regulations governing the Jewish body affected her sexuality. "[T]hat ended my sex life. I was just too afraid."[3] Others scoffed at the absurdity of attempting to regulate the sexuality of an entire population. In the full range of circumstances in which Jewish women found themselves during the Shoah, women became pregnant, then aborted, miscarried, or carried to term. Crushing physical labor, food scarcity, and rampant epidemics made pregnancies difficult, and yet, many women delivered healthy babies. Families and communities were forced to contend with the increased needs and dangers that babies and small children imposed on an already impossibly stressed set of circumstances. With the constant threat of roundups, the presence of a baby posed an added danger for the mother and for the community. When hiding from Nazi round-ups, whether inside or outside the ghetto walls, the unpredictability of a baby's cries posed a threat to everyone else. In many concentration camps, women who were visibly pregnant or accompanied by small children were selected for immediate killing.

When recounting the events of the Shoah years later, many survivors point to the murder of children as one of the harshest memories—one that remains difficult to speak of or to assimilate into a meaningful narrative of the past. Years later, the memories are visceral; they are identified as moments that the survivor will "never forget," or that he or she cannot describe without breaking down or lapsing into silence. For example, one woman recollects the deportation of children from the Kovno Ghetto: "They took the children away in a bus, and they took them in, and there was music [she cries, wipes eyes with tissue] and the mothers were going to see the children, they put the dogs, the dogs start to bite them, the mothers, and they took the children away and they killed them."[4] Almost sixty years later, she breaks down weeping as she recollects this, something she did not do even when recounting the death of her mother and father. Another woman recalls the live burial of a child born in the barracks of Auschwitz-Birkenau. Then a teenager, decades later, in her sixties, she states that the memory stays vividly with her as her greatest trauma.[5] In a straightforward manner, a man relates overhearing the killing of a newborn in a forest near Lviv where he was hiding as an adolescent with his parents. After telling the story as a man of almost seventy, he pauses for a long time, looking down and to the side, rather than at the interviewer or the camera. The silence is broken only when the interviewer asks where he went after liberated. Deep in memory, he mutters, "Hm?" and she repeats the question.[6]

But it is not the killing of babies by the perpetrators of genocide that I will discuss here, although there are ample and graphic descriptions of this by eyewitnesses, including the helpless and devastated parents. Nor is it the killing of newborns in labor camps by Jewish doctors, midwives, nurses, and others in defiance (rather than in enactment) of genocide. I focus rather on where testimony locates the heart of darkness of the Nazi genocide: parents who killed their own children. Later, many years later, eyewitnesses, and sometimes the parents themselves, put the memory of this act into words.

A substantial number of testimonies acknowledge, either as something witnessed firsthand, or as something widely known at the time, that parents—and particularly mothers—were under tremendous pressure to keep their children absolutely silent when trying to elude detection, whether by German soldiers, local militia, or nosy neighbors. A significant number of third-party accounts mention the accidental or deliberate killing of small children under such circumstances by close relatives, in full view of the mother. In one extended example, a woman from Lublin recollects hiding in an attic with relatives. Among the people secreted with them were two sisters, one with her husband. The other sister, whose husband had been killed months earlier, had a three-month-old baby. The fugitives in the attic remained tensely quiet as German soldiers search the house. The soldiers were about to leave when the baby suddenly cried out. The woman remembers the soldiers shouting, "Alles ausstrecken, Juden ausstrecken," resuming their search of the premises.

> In a moment, that uncle, that other sister's husband, he took a pillow and he choked that child to death, and I saw it, and the mother was tearing her hair out [gestures to her own hair]. She didn't scream, because we would all be killed that time, and I started, I want to scream, and my grandmother she hold my breath [covers her own mouth and nose with her hand] I shouldn't scream, and I was crying, I couldn't believe my eyes, I never saw it in my life, something, a picture like that. And the baby stopped crying and the baby was dead.... Do you know, after that child got quiet, there was such a silence in that place, we only could hear the heartbeats, everybody's heart was beating like a motor.[7]

The reenacted gestures highlight the traumatic nature of the memory.[8] A teenager when the event occurred, and a grandmother by the time she recounts it, the woman's body movements touch on two points of identification in the narrative: with the mother, whose gestures of grief she faintly mimes, and with the baby, whose suffocation she pantomimes. Like the baby, she, too, was physically silenced by someone other than her parents; by this time, her own mother and sister had been killed. Without saying so directly, her telling incorporates her own remembered fear for her life and her survival at the expense of the baby. She is at once the murdered child, the grief-crazed mother, and the survivor complicit in the killing.

Others recollect the mother or father killing the child, either accidentally or deliberately. Often, remembered accounts of such deaths emerge as vignettes or frozen images that come to represent the absolute horror of the Shoah. A woman from Vilna told her interviewer, "Some people killed their children, I didn't want to tell you. But they did. They did. Jewish people would kill their own little girl."[9] Sometimes the parent reluctantly yielded to overwhelming group pressure from others who saw a baby as a clear endangerment of the common welfare. A man who, as a boy, was hidden near Lublin, remembers, "Children started to cry, and the adults were telling the mothers to stifle their children, and if they didn't stifle him, stifle them, then we would all be found out. And there was a woman sitting next to me with a small child, maybe two people away, and that quieted her child by choking it. By smothering the child. And pretty soon we were found out anyway."[10] In descriptions such as this, it is unclear whether the intent is to silence the child—with the killing an accident—or whether the mother understands that she is smothering her child. Sometimes the parents themselves decided that killing their child was the only option available to them, enacting what Lawrence Langer has termed a "choiceless choice."[11] A woman recalls that in the Riga Ghetto, "I saw a mother after the baby was born, she kissed it, and then she choked the baby."[12] A survivor of the Kovno Ghetto recollects hiding in a secret room in a basement: "There was a mother, she had a child, a small baby.... So the mother, we, she, the baby start to cry, so she was afraid the baby's going to give out all the twenty people, so she took a pillow and she choked her—they shouldn't get us, all the people. But they find us anyway."[13]

In some accounts, such actions come to stand for the disintegration of moral and social norms, the breakdown of intimate bonds under tremendous pressure and fear. Sonia Bielski describes the remembered desperation of people in hiding: "This was a war, a terrible war, a war of survival. If you could survive yourself, you didn't give a hoot for nobody else. Mothers and fathers was killing the children … because they were in someplace … and the child was hungry and they were crying so they killed them by themself in order that they should not find out that people was here."[14] A woman who survived under a series of false identities remembers, "A lot of mothers, a lot of women, or men, they choked their mothers if they were very old and they could not go to hide some place. They choked them. They were dead. Mothers choked their babies, because with a baby you couldn't go nowhere.... They knew, like this, they both gonna go.... Because you can't tell the baby, 'don't cry'.... If we would have a baby there it would be, we all would be lost."[15] A woman who, as a child, had hidden in the forest with her parents, remembers seeing a father kill his 2-year-old daughter with his wife looking on, so that the young couple could be taken in by the partisans, unencumbered. "They were shot two weeks later.... And they deserved it. People were cruel, very, very cruel."[16]

Jewish responsa literature dating from the war years attempts to place unthinkable choices within a moral compass. Using classical rabbinic sources to think through the ethics of such killing—that is, if and when a child might be sacrificed to preserve the lives of others—decisors of Jewish law, such as the Lithuanian rabbi Ephraim Oshry and the Warsaw rabbi Shimon Efrati (or Efrusi), were often consulted on matters of Jewish law (*halakha*) and ethics under duress during the Holocaust, and responded to halakhic questions about the accidental or deliberate killing of a baby whose cries threatened to reveal the hiding place of a group of Jews during a roundup.[17] They, and others, framed their difficult deliberations in terms of competing ethical imperatives: to preserve one's own life, to preserve the lives of others, not to be the agent of murder, not to allow a renegade to endanger an entire community. Rather than see in desperate behavior a sign of moral degeneration, they try to provide some modicum of moral clarity and, at the same time, to place extreme actions in the compelling context so as to assuage the resulting feelings of shame and culpability.

In a similar spirit, when recollecting a mother who threw her baby to the ground during a selection so that she herself might live, one woman reminds her listener that no one could be certain they would not do the same thing in her place, as unimaginable as it seems in the normal world. She warns, "C'est difficile de comprendre et certainement pas juger… ça je n'oublierer jamais, et ça je ne jugerer jamais" [It is difficult to understand and certainly not to judge … this I will never forget, and this I will never judge].[18] The intense emotional impact of participating in or witnessing such events is clear from her comment, even when recollected and revealed years later. Often in third-person descriptions of parental infanticide, the speaker stumbles while talking about it, temporarily unable to continue the story. Many note the torment inflicted on the parents. One woman remembers a mother in the Białystok Ghetto who smothered her child during an *Aktion* and "became later crazy. She never got over … it's not that she wanted to save the rest of thirty or something people, but, but she didn't know what she was doing. She got crazy, she never recovered."[19] Some people begin to cry, asserting that the witnessing of a mother smothering her child is something they will never forget, calling it the worst memory of the war years. A woman who recounted seeing a mother smother her baby in the Stryj Ghetto comments, "It had a horrible effect. I mean, to this day, I don't think about it all the time, but I have flashes."[20] Another woman, remembering how a woman in Auschwitz-Birkenau gave birth and then "has to bury her own child, otherwise she will die," adds, "I won't forget that, not even in a thousand years, if I live life a thousand years."[21] As a bitter coda, some conclude their vignette by noting the futility of such fearsome choices: "And pretty soon we were found out anyway."[22] "The baby didn't have to die. We had to go back anyway."[23] Others acknowledge that they owe their own survival to the sacrifice of a child.

Understandably rarer than such third-person accounts are firsthand accounts by parents themselves regarding the killing or abandonment of their own children. In one frequently quoted illustration of the way in which this kind of memory falls outside the boundaries of straightforward narrative, Lawrence Langer quotes at length from the videotaped testimony of Bessie K, who hid her swaddled baby in her coat during a selection in the Kovno Ghetto. When the baby's cries gave it away and a German reached for the child, the mother hands over what from that point onward she refers to as her "bundle."[24] Later, in the Stutthof concentration camp, when asked by an acquaintance about her child, she responded, "What baby? I didn't have a baby. I don't know of any baby." In the 2008 documentary film *Mum,* Canadian director Julia Creet traces how she learned, well after her mother's death, that her Christian Hungarian-born mother was actually a Jewish survivor of Auschwitz. Following a trail of personal and archival clues, Creet eventually learns that her mother had been married before and had a little girl. Four generations of Jewish women were deported together to Auschwitz: Creet's (and the toddler's) mother, grandmother, and great-grandmother, together with the child. Just before the selection at arrival, Creet's mother took her child from the arms of the child's great-grandmother and gave her to the child's grandmother, unwittingly relinquishing both her daughter and her mother to be killed in the gas chamber. Creet had not known of the existence of her murdered sibling. Her mother left behind a body of writing that obliquely outlined the fabric of her life before and after the war, but excised her first motherhood.[25] Here I do not suggest that all parents concealed the existence of a murdered child, but that moments of narrative that touch on the terrible [and unwilling] implication of the parent in the murder are, understandably, rarely fulsome or straightforward.

One extended account is given by Ruth Elias, a Jewish woman from Moravia, who, at the age of nineteen, was taken first to the Theresienstadt Ghetto, and then to a series of labor camps including Auschwitz and Ravensbrück. Elias was interviewed by film maker Claude Lanzmann for his 1985 film *Shoah,* but little of the nearly eight hours of filming made it into the final cut. In the outtakes, Elias describes her pregnancy and childbirth in Auschwitz, under the direct supervision of Josef Mengele.[26] In the summer of 1943 she married and became pregnant in the Theresienstadt Ghetto, and was unable to obtain an abortion. Deported to Auschwitz in December, she understood her pregnancy as a death sentence. Through her own resourcefulness and the help of other women, Elias concealed her condition. For example, when the women in her barracks were forced to walk naked for a selection, Elias insinuated her pregnant body between two rows of young "beautiful" women, hoping that their bodies would distract Mengele from looking too closely at hers. Elias was eventually taken to a labor camp in Hamburg, where the block elder betrayed her secret to the SS overseeing her work detail. She was sent to Ravensbrück and then back to Auschwitz, presumably to be killed. Astonished that he had allowed a pregnant woman slip by undetected, Mengele took a special interest in Elias, placing her in the infirmary, under his supervision. She gave birth under abysmal conditions: "There was no cotton wool, no boiling water. There was nothing, I laid in my own dirt." After the birth, Mengele ordered Elias's breasts bound with cloth, so that she could not nurse her child. He wished to see, Elias explains, just how long an infant could last without food. For days, Elias and the baby lay in their own filth, with the baby crying constantly. Mengele visited daily and took notes. Finally, she remembers, he announced that on the following morning he would come for Elias and her baby; it was understood that they would be taken to the gas chamber. This is how she describes her last night: "And in the evening when the lights went off and it's starting to be night I know it will be my last night and my child she couldn't cry anymore. It's terrible, I can hear the voice, the noise. It was not a voice even. And I started to cry because I've known tomorrow I'm going to die with my child. The lights went off and I started to scream because at night everything is terrible."

Elias then recounts how she survived Auschwitz, although her baby did not. A Jewish woman doctor approached her with a syringe filled with morphine, and instructed her to inject a lethal dose into the baby. Elias recollects, "I told her, how can I give this to my child, how can I be the murderer of my child. She told me, I have made an oath of Hippocrates, and I must save lives. You're young and I must save your life. The child can't live—look at the child how it's looking. But you're young and I must save you. And you will give this to your child because I can't." By then, Elias explains, she had lost the will to live. Resigned to dying with her baby, she refused. Over the course of the night, however, the doctor succeeded in persuading Elias to inject the morphine into the dying baby. When Mengele came for them in the morning, the tiny corpse had already been removed. His plan disrupted by the unexpected absence of the baby, he allowed Elias to join a labor detail. Depressed and apathetic, she managed to remain alive until liberation.

As Elias narrates her experience, she inverts conventional tropes about motherhood and mothers who kill. Mythical figures, such as Medea, who murdered her children and fed them to her husband, horrify the Western imagination, because they pair the sanctified and idealized figure of the mother with the image of the ruthless killer and cannibal. Mothers who kill their own children are emblems of unthinkable evil. At the same time, infanticide was not an unheard of event in Europe. Legal literature is replete with cases of women accused of killing their newborn infants, often by exposure but sometimes by asphyxiation, most frequently out of economic need, but sometimes out of social convenience. Some cultural anthropologists and sociologists have suggested that under certain circumstances, killing one's children may be understood as an empowering act for women. Scholars studying slavery, for example, note that for slave women, infanticide may be a means of sparing their children a life of misery, or a means to destroy the product of a rape by their owner, or the means to subvert their owner's economic welfare by diminishing his property.[27]

For Elias, however, the terms are different. While she benefited directly from her baby's death, one might see the morphine injection not as murder but as a coup de grâce administered to a child who, in some sense, was dead already—doomed, with no chance of reprieve. At the same time, unlike impoverished women who seek economic survival, or slave women who strike a blow at the system that controls them and owns their body, nothing in Elias's narrative suggests that she understands her act as one of subversion or resistance. To the contrary—in describing her own succumbing to the woman doctor's persuasion, she tells Claude Lanzmann, "I didn't wanted to but she started to talk to me, into me. And the more she talked, the less I had ... any *Widerstand*... I didn't have..." she is at a loss, and Lanzmann prompts her, "Resistance." She repeats, "Resistance." One might say that Elias sees her act as consonant at some level with the Nazi genocide, ending the life of a Jewish child. Belatedly, Elias comes to understand her own survival as allowing for a future. After years of struggling with depression and suicidal thoughts, she married and gave birth to two sons. But the circumstances of her first childbirth shape the intimate grammar through which she experiences her subsequent ones years later. For example, when Elias gave birth again after the war, she panicked when the hospital nurse took the child from her. "… the moment I saw she's taking the child away I started to scream. Don't take my child away, you will kill my child. Don't take my child away. I started to cry. The doctors and nurses were looking at me. Nobody has known and nobody cared about people from concentration camps what they went through. They thought I went mad."

Because of gender segregation in camps, the killing of one's child most often fell to the mother as a matter of circumstance. In some situations, however, the fathers of infants performed this act. When the parents of the infant were together—because they were hiding or part of a group of partisans—the father's harsh job often was, as it were, to "take care" of the newborn by killing it and disposing of the body. One man recollects that during a clandestine attempt to cross the Bug River into Ukraine, he saw a father smother his child by covering the child's mouth. The parents buried the child, and the father recited the Mourner's Kaddish over the grave. The memory is tinged with deep sadness, and a bitter acknowledgment of the futility of the parents' suffering, as the group was turned away by the Soviet forces.[28]

Most recollections of such killings depict greater violence toward the baby, in narratives that capture the desperation and chaos of the circumstances, and that deny parents the comfort of ritual mourning. One man remembers that when he was a child hiding in the forest, two women became pregnant after their respective husband and lover returned from a foray into a nearby village "slightly inebriated." Months later, with German planes strafing that area of the forest, one woman was shot and the other went into labor, "two tents away" from where the boy was huddled. Other women attended her to midwife the birth. "And all of a sudden I hear 'Ahhh, aaaah, aaaaah, aaaah,'" he recollects, imitating the sound of a baby crying. "Now the question came, we have a baby, what are we gonna do with the baby? I mean, the Germans are there, I mean, we got a real problem. So the decision was made by the hierarchy that we got to get rid of the baby. The father, I don't know what he did with the baby, but, uh, the baby was not alive in the morning."[29] As this remembered vignette suggests, it was seen as the father's responsibility to kill the child—not only because the mother was too weakened to do so, but because the father was seen as somehow culpable for creating this danger to the common weal. It would be difficult to pinpoint the circumstances under which a couple's intimacy results in pregnancy, but this narrative clearly links the men's drunken state with irresponsibility toward their partners and toward others in the forest. Both irrepressible sexuality and a capacity for violence are bound up in this sense of masculine identity. To be a man is to desire, to impregnate, to kill. There may be a suggestion that the need to kill his child is a form of punishment for an undisciplined desire, as well an acknowledgment that the baby, in some sense, "belongs" to the father who alone has the right to take its life.

Many references to this male responsibility come from accounts by women—often women who have midwifed the birth. Unlike the segregated circumstances of labor camps, where women assisted in the birth and in the killing of the child, in the forests there was frequently a gendered division of labor. Women would attend to the birthing mother, and men would see to the killing. When the father was not present, another man—often a father himself—would assume that harsh charge. One woman recollects having to help with a birth when she was still a teenager. "I didn't know how to deliver a child, she didn't know how to deliver a child.... She had a baby and she wasn't even allowed to say 'whoo' out loud." When the baby began to mewl, it was clear to everyone that the child must be killed. One man picked up a piece of wood to bludgeon the baby, but the sound was unbearable to the mother and the woman who assisted her. "... so I pulled a piece of string, I said in Russian to him, take this and kill it, so he took the string and squeezed, and when it got dark he took the baby's body, wrapped in a sack of potatoes, and just went out and buried it somewhere. And I was left with her." In narrating this story, she makes a point of noting that the man was married with children of his own. This parenthetical remark sets him up as an appropriate surrogate for the baby's absent father, attributing to him other dimensions of masculine identity. At the same time, she blurs the boundaries between male and female responsibilities. While she assisted in bringing life into the world and the unnamed man took a life, she describes her role with greater ambiguity. "I had to deliver a child ... and the kid had to be killed in my presence. I even help how to do it. I'd suggest what to do with this little boy that was born just five minutes before." As her narration makes clear, it was not a simple gendered division of emotional labor—compassion to women, cold assessment to men—but a shared negotiation of an impossible situation that demanded a series of acts. The woman brought to the chain of events a less grisly way of killing the child, but did not dispute the necessity of killing.

Accounts by fathers themselves are rare. One such account is that of Berek, an Orthodox Polish Jew given safe haven with his wife, Lola, on a farm near Kraków, in return for the promise of repayment after the war.[30] The couple was sheltered and fed in a small secret room in a stable. Until she went into labor, Lola did not realize that she was pregnant. Berek delivered the baby, their first. When the 13-year-old son of the farm owner came to the stable with food, Berek instructed the boy to tell his mother that his wife had just given birth. Eventually, the boy returned with a message: "If he knows to make a child, then he knows what to do." Berek and Lola discussed their situation and agreed that the baby must be killed. Even so, they tried to nurture him. Because Lola was unable to nurse, Berek heated up some milk in an empty shoe polish can.

The discordance of nurture and murder jar his narrative. He recollects, "... and I give him two spoons of milk before I kill him, before I kill him." His interviewer asks why he fed him. Berek responds simply, "Because the child was hungry. He was crying." Berek describes how he strangled his newborn son, gesturing with his hands around his own neck. He remembers saying to his wife, "I killed my own son," and they cried together.

But Berek dared not leave the secret room to bury the baby. Because Stephan, the farm owner, was away, Berek placed the tiny body in a small box and covered it with stones. When Stephan returned, the men opened the box to retrieve the body for burial. The baby began to cry. As it turns out, Berek had not killed his son; he only rendered him unconscious. Faced with having to kill him all over again, Berek persuaded Stephan to leave the baby in a basket near the home of a childless couple who might take him in. Returning home one night, the man did not notice the basket immediately, but his dog led him to it. He reasoned that the baby must belong to a partisan who could not care for him. When he brought the child home, his wife suspected that it was his, born out of wedlock to another woman. Once she was persuaded of the circumstances, she agreed to take him in. The couple baptized the baby and raised him as their own.

Berek recounts every detail of the baby's precarious rescue as though he himself stood watch. Then he notes that, since he could not leave the secret room, it was Stephan who stood guard. After the war, the town was occupied by Soviet forces. Hearing Berek's account, a Jewish officer offered to retrieve Berek's son, but Berek refused to take his child by force. Instead, he sought out the priest who had baptized the boy and he identified himself as the father. The priest arranged a meeting between Berek and the man who had taken in his baby. Weeping, the adoptive father pleaded with Berek to leave the boy in their care. He said, "You are young, and we like this child very much. Please give us the child." Berek did not demand the return of his son. Instead, he acknowledged the bond between the boy and the adoptive father. "You are the same father as I am. You have the same rights to him like I am." Over time, the priest persuaded the adoptive couple to give the boy to his birth parents.

Berek's account of the killing, resurrection, abandonment, and recovery of his child is told many years later, decades after Lola's death. In Berek's telling of the night of the baby's deliverance, we see resonance of the story of the biblical Moses, so much so that we may read Berek's account as a midrash on that prototypical Jewish narrative of destruction and redemption.[31] The book of Exodus tells of a Jewish woman who attempts to rescue her son from a genocidal decree by placing him in a basket and floating him down the river, hoping for the kindness of strangers. Hidden among the reeds, the baby's sister keeps watch. The basket is spotted by the daughter of Pharoah, who—against the prevailing edict—fishes the baby out of the reeds and raises him as her own.

In the biblical narrative, the perpetrator, Pharoah, is a man, but all the other critical agents are women.

But in Berek's account, all the key players are men, with women—mothers—relegated to the periphery. His story offers competing definitions of manhood: a man makes babies and kills them. A man rescues the baby, adopts the baby, and loves the baby. A soldier offers to take the baby by force. Berek repudiates certain traditional manly roles involving force, power, violence, and patriarchal ownership, in favor of roles more often associated with women. He, and not his wife, nourishes the newborn. The adoptive father has compassion on a foundling and brings him to his wife. It is Stephan's wife who coolly commands the death of the child. All the life-giving roles are played by men: the man who plots a way to rescue his son, the man who watches, the man who rescues the basket and raises the child as his own, in defiance of the Nazi genocide. Although the episode that begins this story—Berek strangling his newborn son—fits the gendered framework established in many accounts of infanticide, Berek tells it in a way that breaks that framework. Early on he describes his discussion with his wife about the baby's fate: "I said to my wife, 'What can I do? To kill a child!'" His wife responds, "If God's will is like this one, you must kill the child." Although the actual killing falls to Berek, he casts the decision as his wife's.

In fitting his narrative into the tropes of this foundational biblical account, Berek conveys his sense of the miraculousness of survival. Crafting a midrash on the birth and rescue of the biblical Moses frames Berek's experiences as yet another iteration of a mythic pattern of redemption. Placing his story in line with the paradigms of Jewish collective memory, Berek aligns his experiences with Jewish interpretations of catastrophe. It is not surprising that Berek's way of narrating overturns conventional gender roles. The powerlessness of Jewish men in face of the Nazi genocide—powerlessness to protect their families or to prevent their own humiliation—placed them in the position of women, shattered their sense of themselves as men, emasculated them. In a similar way, the radical powerlessness of the Israelite men is highlighted by the unexpected agency of women in Exodus. At the same time, when given the opportunity to exercise force, to reclaim a power that has been associated with the masculine, Berek pointedly rejects the construction of a violent masculinity associated with the SS and the SA in Nazi Germany. Berek recuperates a sense of gendered identity not by adopting a hypermasculinized notion of male power, but by collapsing polarized notions of gender roles, and in so doing, repudiating force and power as the only way to be a "real man."

The voice of the child, of course, remains unheard. Since the dead cannot tell their stories, the victims of murder cannot render their own account. In any event, these victims were killed before acquiring language skills. For many, the only sensory experience of their lives was pain. Only the rare instances of reprieve offer some possibility of their perspective. At the end of Berek's testimony, his grandson, a teenager, appears in the room. The grandson calls his grandfather "a heroic man" whose story proves that "human spirit can conquer" adversity. Berek's son, however, does not appear in the videotaped testimony.

But a very different child resurrection narrative, retold from several perspectives, sheds some light on the aftereffects. The wartime diary of Moshe Maltz describes the predicament of an extended family hiding in a hayloft above the pigsties in a Polish barn. Published posthumously by Maltz's children under the title *Years of Horror—Glimpse of Hope,* the diary gives a sense of the chaos and desperation of Jewish families during the Nazi genocide.[32] When Maltz's 4-year-old niece, Feyge Chashe, cried inconsolably for hours, the woman hiding them, Franciszka Halamajowa, warned that the child would give them away, threatening not only the family and their rescuer, but other Jews hiding on her property. The family agreed to "do something," and after discussion, reached "a terrible decision"—to poison the child with substances that a doctor hiding with them had brought. The doctor tried to feed the child a spoonful of poison as relatives held her down, but she resisted and spat out the liquid. Eventually, they forced sufficient poison into the child. Maltz writes in his diary, "Feyge Chashe ... appears unconscious. She does not seem to be breathing." Later, as the doctor placed the body in a burlap bag for burial, he felt a pulse. The family and their rescuer agreed that the child's miraculous resurrection indicated that her survival "must be God's will." Maltz's diary does not record the effect on the child, either at the time or later, except to note that when she regained consciousness her lip was blistered. From that time on, the family would cover Feyge Chashe's head with blankets to dampen the noise of crying—"not tightly enough to smother her, but enough to muffle the sound."[33]

Several later sources recount the events in Maltz's wartime diary from other perspectives. In 1997, three of the hayloft refugees videotaped accounts of their experiences during and after the war: Maltz's brother, Shmelke;[34] Maltz's son Chaim, now Herbert;[35] and Feyge Chashe, now Frances or Fay Malkin.[36] While there are slight discrepancies in detail between the diary and later accounts, the sources accord in substance. Herbert and Fay, children during the war, recollect the twenty-one months above the pigsty in a fragmented, imagistic manner. Herbert repeatedly states that the events in the hayloft seem "like a dream." Fay describes her memories as "points," "flashes," disjointed "fragments" that present themselves "like pictures" rather than as a continuous narrative. Both observe that their accounts of that time contain both actual memories and stories repeated to them by the adults. From Fay's vivid narrative, years later, of the attempt to kill her during the war, it is clear that she felt assaulted and terrified. She recollects crying inconsolably. The more the adults tried to quiet her, the harder she cried. She remembers being placed lying down on straw, crying as her uncle and the doctor attempted to force a pill into her mouth. "I remember the pill," she says. She didn't know what it was, "but I knew it was bad." The day of the attempt on her life, Fay recollects fighting, refusing to swallow, and pleading, "I'll be good, I'll be good, just take this pill away. I'll be good. I'll stop crying." Afterward, she remembers, the adults kept her sedated and silent by dissolving sleeping pills in her drink. She remembers the subsequent months in the hayloft as alternating between sleeping and eating.

Like Maltz's diary, Shmelke's account captures the chaos and brutality of the time, and the precariousness of Jewish life. While he does not elaborate on the attempt to kill his niece, both the wartime and the deferred accounts describe the dire circumstances in which the killing of children had become, if not routine, then common. Following a roundup, Maltz saw an acquaintance "burying his infant grandson... [whom]...he himself had smothered."[37] This shifted atmosphere and ethos helps explain how a group of adults could not only contemplate but enact the deliberate killing of a niece and daughter. Maltz's diary observes the pervasive reluctance to allow families with children to share a hiding place. He notes the practice of giving children sleeping pills to ensure their silence, adding that "some of the children who take the pills never wake up again."[38] Maltz records his wife's account of being turned away from places of shelter during an *Aktion* because she was with two children. Desperate, she concealed their 5-year-old son in a woodpile, then hid in an attic with their year-old daughter. The girl's crying alerted a German soldier, who ordered a member of the Judenrat into the building to investigate. The Jewish man located them, and persuaded the mother to hand over her child. Later, Maltz found his wife looking "as if she had gone out of her mind."[39]

For Fay, recounting it decades later, this story exemplifies the "philosophy of ghetto.... You save yourself. If you have to give away a child, if you have to give away a mother... you save yourself because you have to survive to bear witness." As she tells it, the sacrifice of the child is not an example of the degeneration of morality—the valuing of one's own life above the life of others—but a painful ethical choice on behalf of the collective: "... the Jewish race has to survive." Fay's understanding of the broad ethos of survival suggests a framework that permitted her to come to provisional peace with the adults who agreed to sacrifice her for their own survival. "They couldn't allow 13 people, plus Mrs. H and her family, to be killed because one five year old child was crying.... And I understand this."

In a 2009 documentary about the family's rescue, *No. 4 Street of Our Lady*,[40] Fay explains that she only came to understand the import of what had happened when, years later, someone asked her mother, "How could you let them kill your daughter?" But the psychological wedge that the episode inserted between mother and daughter lurks just beneath the surface in her 1997 account, as well. Struggling against the men attempting to poison her, she remembers calling out to her aunt for help. "My mother was there… but she wasn't the one I was calling for…" After the war, the family referred to her as their "miracle child." But if her story is miraculous, it is not redemptive. In a 2013 interview, she notes that in later years she felt isolated and rejected, emotionally distanced from her mother and separate from the extended family.[41] She describes an ongoing difficulty coming to terms with the past.

Indeed, the 1997 videotaped accounts of Herbert and Fay, the two child survivors of the hayloft, reveal radically different aftereffects. Herbert describes a trajectory of acclimatization and achievement in postwar America, from not speaking English to becoming a pharmacist. He recollects easy friendships, a loving marriage, strengthening of religious faith, and ultimate triumph over Hitler, who "tried to kill me." He observes, "I've been blessed in every sense of the word." By contrast, Fay remembers a life of loneliness and isolation, with few friends, little professional satisfaction, and troubled family relations. She reflects, "I feel sorry for the little girl that was me. They took my life away by taking all the things that were maybe normalcy that I would have liked." While many things can account for the different narrative moods, including basic temperament and the rupture of Fay's nuclear family during the war, it is difficult to discount Fay's death and resurrection as strong factor in later difficulties.

As a researcher, I find the accounts of infanticide difficult to bring into the compass of scholarly analysis. I fear doing violence to my audience, doing an injustice to the fabric of testimony, or diminishing its import by casting upon it the cool lens of scholarship. The parents, extended families, and those around them were placed in situations not of their own making, and emerged traumatized by the encounter with horror. But deferred narratives bring the memory of these events into the compass of our knowledge of the Holocaust. With the distance of time passed, under the pressure of time running out, stories kept private or untold come to the surface, placed in the public domain by their tellers. These deferred narratives not only recount the past, but add layered meaning to the aftereffects of trauma. Enfolded in these fearsome memories are negotiations of ethical, religious, and psychological means to contend with an unthinkable act that had become commonplace. For many, the killing of children remains the darkest of memories. Some parents, such as Ruth Elias and Berek, eventually evolve ways to integrate their stories into the normalized life that follows. Some accounts, such as Fay Malkin's, resist the attempts of others to mediate the past through redemptive narratives. The descriptions in these deferred accounts are visceral, painful to recount, painful to hear and to read. But the alternative is to leave such accounts outside of our sense of the human, and to leave ourselves unaccountable for the worst that can—and does—happen.

Notes

Much of the research for this study was conducted under the aegis of a fellowship at the Center for Advanced Holocaust Studies at the United States Holocaust Memorial Museum. I gratefully acknowledge the support and assistance provided.

1. See, for example, Yehuda Bauer, *Rethinking the Holocaust* (New Haven, CT, 2001), and Joanna Michlic, "The Aftermath and After: Memories of Child Survivors of the Holocaust," in *Lessons and Legacies X: Back to the Sources: Reexamining Perpetrators, Victims, and Bystanders,* ed. Sara R. Horowitz (Evanston, IL, 2012), 141–89.

2. Lawrence L. Langer, *Holocaust Testimonies: The Ruins of Memory* (New Haven, CT, 1991), ix, 31. See also Geoffrey H. Hartman, "Learning from Survivors," in Hartman, *The Longest Shadow: In the Aftermath of the Holocaust* (Bloomington, IN, 1996), 133–50.

3. Interview 39586, Herta Adler, Visual History Archive, Unversity of Southern California Shoah Foundation [hereafter USCSF].

4. Interview 33142, Luba Feinstein, Visual History Archive, USCSF.

5. Interview 48919, Reneh Ben-Dat, Visual History Archive, USCSF.

6. Interview 11479, Allen Brayer, Visual History Archive, USCSF.

7. Interview 14339, Dora Abend, Visual History Archive. USCSF.

8. For further discussion of the place of gesture in traumatic narrative, see Julia Creet, "On the Sidewalk: Testimony and the Gesture," *Applied Semiotics* 15, http://french.chass.utoronto.ca/as-sa/ASSA-No15/article4en.html (accessed 1 March 2013).

9. Interview 43618, Helene Burt, Visual History Archive. USCSF.

10. Interview 8527, Aaron Elster, Visual History Archive. USCSF.

11. Lawrence L. Langer, *Versions of Survival: The Holocaust and the Human Spirit* (Albany, NY, 1982), 72.

12. Interview 39586, Herta Adler, Visual History Archive, USCSF.

13. Interview 33142, Luba Feinstein, Visual History Archive, USCSF.

14. Interview 23579, Sonia Bielski, Visual History Archive, USCSF.

15. Interview 14681, Jenny Backenroth, Visual History Archive, USCSF.

16. Interview 43618, Helene Burt, Visual History Archive, USCSF.

17. See, for example, Irving J. Rosenbaum, *The Holocaust and Halakhah* (New York, 1976), 31–40; Robert Kirschner, ed., *Rabbinic Responsa of the Holocaust Era* (New York, 1985); Yehezkel Fogel, ed., *I Will be Sanctified: Religious Responses to the Holocaust,* trans. Edward Levin (Northvale, NJ, 1998), 91–93, 117–21, 127–37; Esther Farbstein, *Hidden in Thunder: Perspectives on Faith, Halachah and Leadership during the Holocaust,* trans. Deborah Stern (Jerusalem, 2007).

18. Interview 34594, Paula Borensztein, Visual History Archive, USCSF. My translation.

19. Interview 6832, Mira Becker, Visual History Archive, USCSF.

20. Interview 46571, Rena Goldstein, Visual History Archive, USCSF.

21. Interview 22511, Danka Cyngler, Visual History Archive, USCSF.

22. Interview 8527, Aaron Elster, Visual History Archive, USCSF.

23. Interview 45387, David Englander, Visual History Archive, USCSF.

24. Langer, *Holocaust Testimonies,* 49; Langer, *Admitting the Holocaust: Collected Essays* (New York, 1996), 151–52.

25. Julia Creet, dir. *Mum.* York University, 2008. DVD.

26. Claude Lanzmann, Shoah Collection, United States Holocaust Memorial Museum, Story Number RG-60.5003, tapes 3112-3118. In 1988, Elias published her memoir in German: *Hoffnung erhielt mich am Leben: Mein Weg von Theresienstadt und Auschwitz nach Israel* (Munich, 1988). Ten years later, it was published in English translation as *Triumph of Hope: From Theresienstadt and Auschwitz to Israel,* trans. Margot Dembu (New York, 1998).

27. See, for example, Glenn Hausfater and Sarah Blaffer, ed., *Infanticide: Comparative and Evolutionary Perspectives* (New York, 1984); Lionel Rose, *Massacre of the Innocents: Infanticide in Great*

Britain 1800-1939 (London, 1986); Nancy Schrom Dye and Daniel B. Smith, "Mother Love and Infant Death, 1750–1920," *Journal of American History* 73, no. 2 (September 1986): 329–53.

28. Interview 45387, David Englander, Visual History Archive, USCSF.

29. Interview 11479, Allen Brayer, Visual History Archive, USCSF.

30. Interview 1359, Bernard Feiler, Visual History Archive, USCSF.

31. For further discussion of midrash on the biblical account of the exodus and its relationship to Jewish negotiation with catastrophe generally, and with the Holocaust in particular, see Sara R. Horowitz, "Gender, Genocide, and Jewish Memory," *Prooftexts* 20, no. 1 (January 2000): 158–90.

32. Moshe Maltz, *Years of Horror—Glimpse of Hope: The Diary of a Family in Hiding*, trans. Gertrude Hirschler (New York, 1993).

33. Quotes in Maltz, *Years of Horror*, 98, 99.

34. Interview 27706, Shmelke Samuel Maltz, Visual History Archive, USCSF.

35. Interview 24942, Herbert Maltz, Visual History Archive, USCSF.

36. Interview 25210, Frances Malkin, Visual History Archive, USCSF.

37. Maltz, *Years of Horror*, 60.

38. Maltz, *Years of Horror*, 51.

39. Maltz, *Years of Horror*, 56.

40. *No. 4 Street of Our Lady*, dir. Barbara Bird, Judy Maltz, Richie Sherman, 2009.

41. John T. Ward, "The Day She Should Have Died," *Drew Magazine*, Winter 2013, http://www.drewmagazine.com/2009/01/the-day-she-should-have-died/ (accessed 1 March 2013).

CHAPTER 8

"Why Didn't They Mow Us Down Right Away?"
The Death-March Experience in Survivors' Testimonies and Memoirs

DANIEL BLATMAN

The question in the title sounds provocative. But this question, asked in similar ways that express the same idea, reappears in the testimonies of many death-march survivors from the last few months of World War II. Some survivors phrased it: "Who had any further need for a few hundred Jews who were still alive?"[1] Or: "Why did they haul us through that snow and freezing weather, and not murder us on the spot?"[2] Their bewilderment can be traced to one common denominator: when survivors reconstruct what they felt at the moment they set out on the death march, they recall being in the dark about the purpose of this last act of the Nazi genocide. They were still confused and terrified by the new and unfamiliar rules that the Nazis introduced when they began to evacuate the concentration camps in January 1945. They had had firsthand experience of the extermination apparatus and had survived, for the time being, only thanks to their ability to work. From their standpoint—with the war winding down, their own strength running out, the liberating armies approaching, and the Germans retreating—the evacuation could have only one purpose: their final elimination, somewhere in the near future.

The experience of the evacuation and death marches in the last months of the war was etched in the memories of the survivors differently than was their time in the camps. The circumstances of the evacuation and the overall chaos that reigned during that period required different skills of coping with the ef-

---

Notes for this section begin on page 167.

forts to survive. The concentration camp was characterized by institutionalized terror. With time, however, it became a routine: "The camp was violence and violence was the camp," as Wolfgang Sofsky put it. Its rules were internalized and became part of the murderers' habitus.[3] This was violence that took place in a closed space with known rules. But in the period of the death marches, the violence moved outward, to the open spaces, with new and unfamiliar conditions for the prisoners and their guards and escorts.

The death marches took place in the twilight world between concentration camp and liberation, in the months of the great *Götterdämmerung* of the Third Reich. During these months, new and unfamiliar patterns of murder and violence took shape. They cannot be defined as a direct continuation of the slaughter perpetrated by the Nazis in the concentration and death camps through the end of 1944. Against the reality of the collapse and convergence into the rapidly shrinking territories of the Reich, new motives for murder emerged. In addition, the murderers defined the community of victims differently than they had defined the enemies of the Reich slated for liquidation in previous years. The community of murderers became much more diffuse and broader than just the experts of the SS murder industry, as it had existed until the end of 1944. Some 715,000 concentration camp prisoners, for whom the period of evacuation and death marches began in January 1945, were forced into this new reality, which lasted until the end of the war.[4]

The period of the death marches was relatively brief—only a few months. For many of the prisoners who went through it, it was shorter than their period in the camps, which sometimes went on for a year or even several years. But it was carved into their memories as an event that transcended the bounds of the horror they had known and lived until then. It was an experience that utterly shattered the murderous monotony of concentration camp life and hurled the prisoners into an existential Charybdis for which even the camps could not have prepared them. The term "death marches" was preserved in their memories of Nazi atrocities as an enigmatic concept about which it was almost impossible to speak, a reality that went far beyond the bare facts reported by the survivors in their testimonies or memoirs. It was a monstrous reality, an experience that could in no way be seen as human and that pushed the limits of man's capacity to understand it. This article draws on the accounts and testimonies of death-march survivors and examines what details of those horrifying days stayed imprinted in their memories. It makes no pretense of explaining this historical era in its entirety or of presenting the story of a specific death march. Its purpose is, rather, to take a close look at the elements common to the memories of many death-march survivors. Its assumption is that the new stage of the Nazi terror, transferred from the camp into a new and unknown arena, brought with it different patterns of responses by the victims.

The Enclosed Space of Violence: The Camp and the Liberation

Imre Kertész, a young Jew from Budapest who was deported to Auschwitz in 1944 and liberated in Buchenwald in 1945, returned to his hometown after the war. In the tram, on his way home, he met a stranger who bought him a ticket, because he himself didn't have money for one. The man tried to engage Kertész about his time in the camp, and with marked embarrassment asked if he had undergone harsh experiences of hunger, torture, abuse, and other horrors. To every question, the young man gave the same laconic answer: "Naturally." The stranger finally lost patience: "Why do you keep saying 'naturally' ... when you are referring to things that are not natural at all?" To which the young survivor responded: "In a concentration camp ... they are very natural." The man continued: "But... well, ... the concentration camp itself is not natural." "I didn't even answer him," writes Kertész, "because I began to understand that there are certain subjects you can't discuss, it seems, with strangers, ignorant people...."[5]

Over time, the memory of the camp, which became an existential and natural situation for the survivors after their liberation, dimmed into a vague and infinite blur of a thin, compressed past, with no real depth, as described by Primo Levi: "The hardest thing to capture was precisely the boredom, the total boredom, the monotony, the lack of events, every single day the same. That is what being in prison feels like, and it generates a curious effect by which the days as you live them seem eternal but as soon as they are over they collapse into instants because they have nothing in them. The past is compressed, thinned, it has no depth."[6]

But the routine, like any routine, became boring. Even if it was a routine accompanied by suffering and death, it was, when all is said and done, a fixed system. In the boring routine created by the regularity and repetition of constant horrors, the most salient episodes were imprinted in the prisoners' minds. Some of these memories are terrifying, others positive; they reverberated in, controlled, and shaped prisoners' consciousness, even though, at the time, the events were part of the unraveling fabric of life. It was a monotonous past in which suffering and torture were an everyday reality, taken for granted, the stuff of daily life. The camp became a banal existential space, but one whose real meaning was almost impossible to describe. Even in the heart of "the other planet," in the extermination compound and alongside the crematorium, a sort of apathetic and meaningless routine developed. "Without your noticing it, it became part of the routine; you can get used to everything and everything taking place around you no longer makes any impression—you scream, you watch apathetically, day after day, as tens of thousands of people around you vanish without a trace," wrote the Sonderkommando Nahman Leventhal in his diary.[7]

The moment of liberation was one of the most significant of all those imprinted on the memories of the concentration camp survivors. In contrast to the timeless and grey reality of the camp, which later memoirs and testimonials represented in various ways, it was a miraculous experience. For more than one survivor, the recollection of the moment of liberation was shaped by his or her personal background, political affiliation, or his or her status in the camp. For example, Jorge Semprun, a Communist who had fought in the Spanish Civil War and later joined the French Resistance, began his book about his life in Buchenwald with a description of the final days before his liberation and the encounter with the American soldiers on the actual day. He was afraid that the guards would try to kill all the prisoners at the last moment before the liberating forces arrived, or would send them on a death march. In the end, only some of the Buchenwald prisoners were evacuated in early April 1945. Thanks to a series of circumstances, when the camp was liberated on 11 April there were still twenty-two thousand prisoners who had not been evacuated or sent on death marches.[8] When the American soldiers arrived, Semprun writes, he did not understand why they were looking at him so strangely. Then he burst out in uncontrollable laughter, amused by the fact that he was still alive.[9]

On liberation day, Imre Kertész was lying in one of the barracks in Buchenwald, sick and exhausted. This day was engraved in his memory as an irritating, screeching hallucination, a confused jumble of languages in the background of the dramatic events. In the Tower of Babel of languages spoken in the camp, the underground operatives took over the public address system and, in the final hours before the arrival of the American forces, gave the prisoners instructions as to what they should do during the liberation. It was a situation in which imagination and insanity were intertwined—but in those few hours it was something quite different that instinctively troubled the teenager. These events and the ensuing chaos in the camp interfered with the most important item of all: the routine distribution of the daily soup ration was delayed for several hours and he was afraid it might not come at all. Only after a modicum of order was restored and he learned that the soup was being cooked did he begin to think, for the first time, about freedom.[10] As we will see, for many death-march survivors the moment of liberation came in a different way and was preserved in their memories in a completely different fashion.

Death and horror are an inseparable part of the familiar narrative continuum of the story of life in the camps. Eluding death, survival, and liberation break up this continuum. In the survivors' minds, liberation was etched as an event that transcended nature or reality, as an event with divine or miraculous significance. Some seven thousand ailing prisoners, many of them on the brink of death and unable to join the march when the camp was evacuated on 18 January, stayed in Auschwitz after it was abandoned by the Germans.[11] Those who were strong enough to leave their barracks began to wander around in their tattered uniforms, looking for food in the empty huts and SS quarters. The silence around them seemed unreal; many were convinced that it was another exercise in deception by the Germans, who would come back at any moment and kill them all. Being a prisoner in Auschwitz, when Auschwitz was no longer Auschwitz, was an unknown and unfamiliar psychological state and created a menacing emptiness.[12] The Red Army's arrival at the camp on 27 January 1945 was taken as a sign from God by the sick prisoners who had stayed behind. When he saw the liberators, one of them remembered, "I was certain I was seeing the Divine Presence."[13] Primo Levi, who was among the prisoners who were not evacuated, saw the Germans' departure as an event with elements of biblical deliverance.[14] His having stayed alive was an inconceivable absurdity, an event contrary to every law of nature.

But only a relatively small number of concentration camp survivors had not been evacuated and were consequently liberated in the camps where they were imprisoned. This usually was the result of local or chance circumstances and not because the camp staff had decided not to evacuate it. For most concentration camp prisoners, the Nazi terror did not end in this way. Before liberation, they had to endure another period which, though short, was full of agony and suffering: the period of the evacuations and death marches. Their road to liberation was different than that of the prisoners who stayed in the camp and was dominated by unprecedented pain and torments, even in comparison to their time in the camp. In their testimonies and memoirs, the survivors recounted this ordeal at greater length and in greater detail than the earlier period of their imprisonment in the camps, despite its shorter duration.

Into the Open Space of Violence: Evacuation

On the whole, there was a vague sense that evacuation was impending even before the prisoners set out. In some camps, there had even been incomplete preparations for it. Ultimately, however, it was still a dramatic event. This is especially noticeable among the prisoners who were evacuated from Auschwitz and its satellite camps in the winter of 1945. Many of them testified that the entire operation was carried out suddenly. There had been no preparations and they could not even attempt to make plans for what was in store. Their daily routine was totally shattered. One female survivor of Auschwitz related: "One morning there was suddenly an unusual noise. The SS awakened the dying, sleeping women, exhausted from labor, with unaccustomed sadism. Within minutes we were lined up in ranks of five. Everyone received half a loaf of bread, which the starving women ate immediately.... We wrapped our feet in newspapers before we pushed them into our heavy wooden clogs so that it would be warmer for us on the road, which was covered with a thick, slippery layer of snow. No one knew what we were facing...."[15]

Only a few had the essential skill—especially from the psychological perspective—of quickly assessing what was about to happen: how should they react to the new situation? Henri Graf, a prisoner in Auschwitz, tells how the prisoners began arguing among themselves after the Kapo informed them that they were about to be evacuated because Germany did not want them to fall into the hands of the Bolsheviks, who might kill them. None of them believed in "Germany's generosity" and various questions and conjectures were raised about the meaning and purpose of the evacuation. One of the issues was whether it would be wiser to elude the evacuation and stay in the camp. But the fact that those who were infirm and unable to march were to be left behind raised concern that the stay-behinds were going to be killed.[16]

The ability to make physical preparations for evacuation in a brief time, when possible, was the immediate boundary that marked out those with better chances of surviving the first stage of evacuation. For instance, in the bedlam before the evacuation from Gross-Rosen, when those about to leave were given cans of meat, some prisoners took advantage of the commotion to go back and stuff extra cans into their bags before the evacuation began. Where the prisoners had a little time, even only a few hours, between the announcement of the evacuation and departure, some took advantage of the interval to pack a blanket and hide a bit of sugar, bread, and margarine. In the chaos of the evacuation, other prisoners risked their lives and stole food from the camp kitchen.[17]

The camp, despite all its horrors and its routine of death, had been a stable reality. The ability to survive the daily ordeal depended on many factors. One of them was precisely the routine: waking up, roll call, turbid "coffee," work, soup, roll call, sleeping in the barracks—these elements of life gave prisoners a framework within which they could attempt to stabilize their effort to survive. The unplanned evacuation disrupted this routine and thrust the prisoners into unexpected changes and transitions from one extreme situation to another. As one survivor described it:

> Buna was a dying monster. How I hated and feared that beast when its heart furiously pumped methanol through its snarled network of veins. And now that it was innocuous, I should have felt happy—overjoyed—but I wasn't. Hadn't I dreamed of seeing it like this? Yes, but the slaves had become overacquainted with his taskmaster. I knew what it expected from me and that I could endure its many tortures. What monster was I being herded to now along this icy path? Could I survive its demands, its torments, or would it be the one to finally devour me and spit out my ashes?[18]

The departure from the camp was sometimes accompanied by a sense of fear and sorrow. But this was not only a departure from the familiar routine. For the Jewish prisoners, the departure had an additional dimension. They were leaving their murdered family members behind in Birkenau: "We were leaving behind our beloved ones, the souls of those who had been robbed of light and life forever. There was a great sadness in our hearts and we did not know what our own fate would be."[19] Many of the evacuees were both physically and mentally unable to endure the change. This was the case even before one takes into account their escorts' light trigger fingers. The prisoners' exhaustion, starvation, and poor physical condition, which doomed many of them, were often intensified by the feeling that death was inevitable.

The strongest memory that remained with the prisoners evacuated from the camps in Poland in the winter of 1945 was the endless fields of snow and of slogging through them, which quickly brought them to the realization that this was an obstacle that could not be hurdled. Looking back years later, they had trouble describing the image imprinted in their minds by the march in the snow. To explain what happened, they needed an analogy taken from a different historical period and a reality they thought was perhaps easier for a modern audience to understand: "… and then the march began, and in order to compare it somehow, anyone who has seen the film about the 1812 Russian-French war, and the scenes of the retreat of the French from Moscow, the snow-covered soldiers, the soldiers with crystals of ice on their lips, on their moustaches, soldiers without head coverings and with a layer of snow, and soldiers retreating with torn boots and toes protruding from the torn leather, soldiers who collapsed out of weakness, starvation—it was nothing compared to the hell of the retreat, of the death march …"[20]

The cold wind blew snowflakes into the marchers' faces, piercing their eyes and burning their throats and making it impossible for them to see or breathe.[21] The long line of marchers making its way from Auschwitz to Gleiwitz quickly turned the snow into solid and slippery ice, a surface that could not be walked on without falling down. The fear was that those who fell would have trouble getting back up on their feet and would be shot by one of the guards.[22] After a short while, the camp became an object of nostalgia. As bizarre as it seems, the death march made the prisoners see their time in the camp as "a golden era" in comparison to the conditions they had to endure now. A prisoner from Blechhammer, one of the Auschwitz satellite camps,[23] explained this paradox: "Two weeks had passed since we left Blechhammer, which by now we were referring to as 'golden Blechhammer.' We remarked to each other that it hadn't been so bad there. After all, we had a straw bed to lie down on, with two blankets. Each morning there was a portion of bread and each evening some warm soup. What warm soup would have meant to us now!"[24]

The evacuated prisoners faced circumstances in an arena where the violence was utterly different from what they had known before. For many these produced a sense of defeat, hopelessness, and apathy in their struggle for existence, even without taking the guards' murderous violence into account. It was a sense that no matter what they did or how hard they tried, the conditions made survival impossible now, even after they had managed to survive the camp. One of the survivors described it as follows:

> I was busy with my thought of farewell. I had done my final accounting. I had said goodbye to life, to my loved ones, both alive and dead, to all my memories, to everything that was good and beautiful in my life. My thoughts were all a blur, but I continued to drag myself along, weeping bitterly, with not just tears but blood dripping from my body. I felt that I simply couldn't keep on living. I had done everything, I had fought, I had overcome the torments—but this time I felt it really was the end; not just my hours, but even my minutes, were numbered. I felt like a defeated boxer who had taken the knockout punch in the very last round.[25]

The loss of the desire to continue the fight for survival is a well-known phenomenon in the life stories of concentration camp prisoners. Deterioration into the existential state of a "Muselmann" was a sign that a person had surrendered and reconciled himself to the inevitable death sentence. But unlike the situation in the camps, where there was still a chance that a prisoner might keep fighting for his life with the help of his companions or some sort of improvement in his life, on the death marches the time that elapsed between the mental capitulation and the final sentence was a matter of minutes: "Anyone who can't walk drops out of the line and stands by the side of the road, with an SS man next to him. A few people who can't keep up with the pace also leave the line and stand on the side. We pass by them. When they are already behind us we hear a few single shots … and we know what happened. Their killing spurs all the others to try harder and harder, to the point of total exhaustion."[26]

The other prisoners took note of the death sentences that their exhausted companions accepted with full lucidity, even though it was the guards who carried them out. In the words of Abraham Kimmelmann's testimony (1946):

> That was something that one is not able to tell. A man full of his senses, in whom everything is still functioning, he is feeble and can't run any more, he stands by himself under a tree, his eyes shining like, like reflectors. And he waits for the moment when the whole formation will have passed by till the hindmost guards will arrive with the block leader, also an SS man, who will shoot him. Can you imagine what this is? A man with his full mental abilities, who knows what is going on and he waits for death. And so every three [or] ten meters, one saw somebody standing under a tree, or sitting down, and such a man would be shot and thrown into the ditch.[27]

This situation, of people giving up the fight and waiting by the side of the road for the coup de grâce, caused inconceivable frustration to the friends of those who decided to give up. This was particularly prominent when the incident was played out in a closed and supportive setting, where prisoners who had been together for a long time in the camp constituted a cohesive group whose goal was to make sure that its members reached the day of liberation alive. This was the case for a few members of the French underground in Bad

Gandersheim, one of Buchenwald's satellite camps. Robert Atelme, a member of this group, described the situation as follows:

> Maybe Francis [his friend—D.B.] really can't go on anymore. Paul has no way of knowing, neither does Francis. When he said: "I'm staying here," his body decided to quit too. Maybe his time, too, has come, the time when he refuses to hear any more about any of this.... Francis knows he'll be killed if he decides to stay. And Paul can't do anything about it. By now he doesn't even have the strength to examine the significance of his own powerlessness, or the fatality of Francis's decision. It all takes place in haze, and Paul has barely enough strength to argue with Francis.[28]

This struggle was waged in an arena of violence that was completely different from the violent, closed, and crowded space of the camp. The new arena influenced the behavior of both the guards and the prisoners. The "spatial dynamic" is crucial for shaping the violent patterns of genocide, ethnic cleansing, or mass slaughter. The relationship between the people and the space colors their interaction (as opposed to what had gone on in the camp); the nature of the space affected the behavior of both the murderers and their victims.[29] The murderousness of the guards and the escorts is one of the aspects of the spatial reality that was different here. The harsh conditions of the evacuation, the muddled orders received by those in charge of the convoys, which frequently failed to specify a precise evacuation route and did not provide the means required to implement it, the persistent fear that prisoners would escape, the incessant pressure of the advancing Allied armies, and the fear of being taken captive with the prisoners—all these factors pushed the guards to engage in murderous conduct on a scale never before seen.[30]

The desire to reach another camp or a railroad station so that the prisoners could be loaded onto trains—and the sooner the better—was one of the main threats to the marchers' lives. The longer the march lasted and the more options were closed off, the greater was the danger that the moment would come when those in charge of the convoy would decide to murder the prisoners. One of the facts that the prisoners grasped right away, within a few hours after the evacuation began, was that all the rules that the camp had followed, more or less, about the execution of death sentences were null and void in the new reality. Any guard or escort could pull the trigger without having to account for his actions. Yitzhak Grabowski, a prisoner at the Jaworzno camp, put it this way: "That's how it was. Anyone who took his time and didn't come back quickly got shot. There was a gunshot and another gunshot, real gunshots—they fired the way you would shoot mad dogs. Until then, we'd never seen such a thing. We'd seen hangings and we'd seen all kinds of things for whatever offense that people seemed to have done, but suddenly we saw that people were really worth nothing, no one cared, and they fired right and left, without consideration for anything. Then we saw the blood on the white snow, and we kept on walking."[31]

This different space in which the prisoners interacted with the guards produced strange encounters that could not have been thought possible in the reality of camp life. We must recall that many of the convoy guards and escorts were older men who had been drafted to serve as camp guards only in the final year of the war. Many of them saw this duty as a bother and a burden and had not necessarily adapted to the enormous violence around them. But in the camp, where the rules of daily life were transparent to all, and especially to the SS men in charge, they were forced to adapt to the expected rules of conduct. In the open space of the evacuation, though, other conditions applied. For dozens of kilometers, the prisoners and guards marched side-by-side, sharing the difficult experience of the snow-covered road and freezing cold. The relaxation of the systematic discipline did not result only in greater brutality and unrestrained violence during the death marches. It also produced manifestations of humanity by guards who had apparently refused to accept it in the first place. The survivors recalled such moments as expressions of compassion that often made the difference between their ability to survive and their certain death. Willy Berler recalled a strange meeting of this kind with a guard who hailed from his hometown, Czernowitz, and even knew Yiddish, because he had lived alongside Jewish neighbors for years: "About 20 kilometers from Auschwitz, in a middle of a column of exhausted and frozen prisoners, walking in what history will call the Death March, a strange, almost friendly, dialogue develops between a *Häftling* and an SS man, both from Bukovina. We are not exactly equals, because I use the polite form of address of 'Sir' and '*Sie*,' while he addresses me with the familiar '*Du*.' Even if he does speak Yiddish better than I do, he still belongs to the master race, while I remain a sub-human, whose right to exist has been refused by decree."[32]

Another survivor recalled that during the evacuation from Herzbruck (a satellite camp of Flossenbürg), the prisoners were accompanied by older guards for whom the assignment was beyond their ability as they walked alongside the convoy, breathing heavily and struggling under the weight of their ammunition belts and weapons. They did not have an organized food supply, so the guards went off to requisition food from farmers in the area and gave some of it to the prisoners in exchange for help carrying their personal equipment.[33] In another case, a survivor recalled a conversation with one of the guards, who asked him his age. When he heard that he was nineteen, the guard confessed that he had a son of that age and had no clue what had happened to him, because he had been sent to the Eastern front. The survivor recalled: "No SS man had ever opened up to me or to any of us. He took an egg out of his pocket and gave it to me. This act moved me so much that I still haven't forgotten it today."[34]

But the thing that most perplexed the prisoners, especially the Jewish ones, was why they had been kept alive and why the Nazis were going to the trouble of shuttling them from place to place instead of murdering them all. Obviously, they could not possibly know about the various orders that had been issued about the evacuation, the attempt to keep this vital labor force intact as long as possible, or about Himmler's manipulations during those weeks and his orders to keep the Jews alive as part of his bizarre negotiations with the Allies.[35] This question was especially significant for the Jews evacuated from the East: after all, they knew exactly what had happened to their families and communities; but now, all of a sudden, they were being taken from the camps and transferred to Germany or Austria. When they testified about this after the war, they were often bewildered. As one Auschwitz survivor put it: "… The march lasted days and nights without anyone knowing where we were being taken. If they wanted to mow us down somewhere with a machine gun, why didn't they do it right away? Maybe there were special facilities for this? Maybe they were leading us to some new facility where people were being killed by gas? In fact, the whole thing seemed totally unnecessary, since at least two-thirds of those being led already lay lifeless along the sides of the road. In another few days, we'd have all ended up that way."[36]

The feeling among the prisoners was that the evacuation had several goals; but none of them could have thought that it would end in their liberation by the Allied forces. Some thought that the point of the evacuation was to hide the evidence of what had gone on in the camps from the advancing Russians. Some said that other camps were certainly being prepared for the Jews in Germany, to finish the job begun in the East—the annihilation of all Jews still alive.[37] On this point there was a difference in the thoughts of the Jewish and non-Jewish prisoners. In the columns of evacuees, the differences and distinctions between Jews and non-Jews that had existed in the camps tended to disappear. The circumstances of evacuation made distinctions impossible, as one of the survivors described the situation in a nutshell: "Jews were mixed with non-Jews and the absolute separation that had been maintained so meticulously while [I] was in Kochendorf was not preserved."[38] But unlike the Jews, the non-Jewish prisoners could hope that, despite the conditions of the evacuation and the guards' murderous brutality, if they developed the right survival tactics, helped each other, and had a little luck, they could manage to survive the horrors and make it to liberation day.[39] The Jewish prisoners, however, were certain that there was no way, after the murder of millions of their kinsmen, that the Germans would allow them, of all people, to survive.

This is an important and salient point in the survivors' testimonies. They couldn't believe that the purpose of the evacuation was a genuine wish to keep them alive so that they could continue serving the German war machine. They were convinced that the only reason they had not been murdered before the abandonment of the camp was that the murderers had not had enough time, whether because the enemy armies were too close or for some other technical reason. That belief influenced their calculation of their efforts to survive.

Survival Efforts, Escape, and Liberation

The death marches afforded the prisoners a thin chance for survival. But the prisoners' ability to survive the evacuation was the result of several factors: their condition when the convoy set out, the length of the death march, the food and equipment that the prisoners had managed to obtain, whether the evacuation was on foot or by train, and so forth. Another factor that often determined the prisoners' fate was whether they belonged to an intimate and supportive group during the weeks of the evacuation or had to cope with the protracted nightmare alone. Of course, their social affiliation and membership in a group had been tremendously important in prisoners' ability to survive in the camps. Membership in a political movement, common nationality, and kinship—all these gave an individual a better chance of surviving there. The evacuation, undertaken in a panicky and disordered fashion, often shattered these frameworks. Prisoners who had shared a barracks or a workplace and had formed a supportive social setting found themselves marching alone in an endless column, composed mostly of strangers. In this state of affairs, those who managed to stay with a group of friends had better prospects for survival.[40]

The capacity to improvise was another factor that could make the difference between survival and extinction. On the death march of the Jews from Mauthausen to Gunskirchen, one of the last and most horrific of all, the prisoners were not given any food and the conditions of the evacuation were extraordinarily difficult. A survivor tells: "We trudged without food for two days. The French Jews who had recently arrived at Mauthausen saved our lives. They taught us how to extract snails from their shells and swallow them. I didn't enjoy the sticky taste, but by that point, any food would have been delicious."[41]

The survival techniques demanded a kind of creativity and intuition that the survivors would not fully understand until many years later. Two brothers from Hungary, aged fifteen and sixteen, developed one such technique when they were evacuated from Buchenwald. They separated at the foot of each hill they had to climb and resolved to meet again when the column of marchers reached the top. Then they separated again and agreed to reunite at the bottom of the hill. One of them explained this decision in a fictionalized account of the brothers' wartime ordeal, written by Israeli author Malka Adler:

> Today I know. The decision to part from my brother before every hill gave me strength. We had to analyze the situation. We had to plan, to think about how we would live on. I had a goal. I had a reason to make an effort to climb the hill. I knew my brother was waiting for me up there and it gave me hope on the difficult march. We spoke. We touched each other. We looked at each other and I saw that he cared about me. Thousands were left behind on the roads, done for, and one person, only one, took care of me and I took care of him. We lived for each other like a small torch in the great darkness.[42]

Naturally, it was not possible to create a plan for survival on the death marches. It was not a matter of finding a better job or of a larger ration that one could wangle from the camp kitchen through personal connections. The space in which it was possible to try to survive was small, random, and subject to gross chance: a guard's lapse of attention when civilians threw food to the prisoners passing through their town; the ability to scout out the occasional piece of rotten food that had been thrown out; and, on rare occasion, to receive food distributed by the convoy officers, suitable walking shoes, an extra blanket taken from a prisoner who had died. But it may well be that the strongest survival tool was the hope that this Via Dolorosa would end soon and would necessarily be followed by a different reality, as Giuliana Tedeschi wrote in her memoirs:

> The temperature had fallen, shoulders ached, teeth chattered. I took a shelter by a wall with four other friends. I could feel life gradually slipping away from me and my fear grew. I had the very clear sensation that I was close to the "final solution." After months and months of suffering and every kind of moral and physical torture, it was terrible now to feel that freedom was so near and to be desperately afraid of not having that last ounce of strength still necessary to survive! A profound regret, which went beyond any feeling of affection or family tie, a regret for life itself, filled me with sweet emotion. There was a progressive detachment from existence; it went on step-by-step, without any more traumas now, as my physical strength faded away. And yet the world, emerging purified and new from this gigantic tragedy, would be a better place, must be a better place, must reward our yearning for perfection, our thirst for improvement, so that the martyrdom of so many not be in vain. I want to live because I need this new world—I need to feel myself born again![43]

The moment prisoners were outside the camp fence, situations that facilitated escape and hiding arose naturally. But the decision to try to escape from the convoy was almost always unplanned and a matter of a split second. Prisoners who had set out on death marches and were able-bodied, at least at the start of the evacuation, evidently realized, after several days on the road, that their strength was giving out. Because they were still standing, however, they understood that if they wished to try to escape their inevitable fate—having to sit down by a tree and wait for the hindmost guard to arrive—they would have to do so before that moment. They fixated on this thought before they made up their minds to escape; the decision to go ahead with it usually came about when an appropriate situation presented itself, such as an air raid that targeted their train, causing the prisoners and the SS men to scramble for cover, or a sense that the guards were slacking off and no longer focused on their task. One of the survivors interviewed by David Boder described this situation: "Yes, the SS went along. They were changed many times. Any prisoner who could not continue walking or had stopped for a moment was immediately shot. The road was covered with hundreds of prisoners, of our Jews. One nice day, it was on the 13th of April, I contemplated my chances. I looked upon the death, and

I saw that I have no way out, to live. So I decided, this night I must run away. If they shoot me, then I am out of luck. If not, then perhaps I will succeed in remaining alive. And that evening I ran away."[44] The decision to try to escape was influenced by various other factors as well. For instance, some women prisoners hoped their non-Jewish appearance would make it easier for them to hide among the local population.[45] The proximity of the front led some to believe that they would manage to lie low for the short while until the liberators arrived. A last factor was the ability to speak the local languages and impersonate a Polish or Lithuanian woman.[46]

Escape itself did not assure survival, of course. In most cases, the guards shot at the escapees and sometimes, if they had time, even conducted a hasty search. The regions that the death marches crossed were usually teeming with army units, police and SS forces, Volkssturm companies, and various other units, all of which regarded the escapees as a menace that had to be wiped out ruthlessly as soon as encountered. Prisoners who fled for their lives, especially if they were Jewish, Russian, or Polish, had to manage to stay out of harm's way until the liberation forces arrived—sometimes for days. Not all of them were successful. And it was just now, after they had managed to escape, that they tumbled into a state of apathy, despair, and hopelessness as a result of hunger, poor physical condition, and the sense that they had to hide, like hunted animals, from every civilian or uniformed person. For these reasons, some decided to turn themselves in to a local resident and hope that they would be lucky and not killed at once.[47]

The decision to escape was also a product of various factors other than the proximity of the liberating forces. Foremost among these was the escapee's hope of blending in with the surrounding society. The realities of the death-march period led to different patterns of encounters between general society and victim than in previous years. Earlier, when the murder campaign was in full swing, persecuted Jews who tried to find shelter with the surrounding population had to cope mainly with their unwillingness to help, for reasons ranging from antisemitism to indifference to fear of German punishment. They had one advantage, however: they almost always tried to hide in areas where they had once lived; as such, they were familiar with the town or the countryside. In small localities, they also knew the non-Jews who had been their neighbors. Many were fluent in the vernacular, be it Polish, Ukrainian, Russian, French, or Dutch. Still, none of this assured survival.

During the evacuation period, by contrast, many prisoners found themselves in unfamiliar surroundings and among a population whose language they did not speak. Sometimes they had no idea where they were—in Poland, in Czechoslovakia, or perhaps already in Germany. For many, this proved an insurmountable hurdle. One of the most obvious examples is that of the Greek Jewish prisoners who had been in Gęsiówka, the camp established atop the ruins of the Warsaw Ghetto after its destruction in 1943. Gęsiówka was evacuated in July 1944. The Greek Jews did not even dream of trying to hide in the "Aryan" part of Warsaw during their months of labor in the camp, despite the fact that it was relatively easy to find concealment in the demolished ghetto or among the Poles.[48] One day during the evacuation, when they were allowed to approach the Vistula River to drink, some prisoners jumped into the water and tried to get away. The guards opened fire, but the Greek Jewish prisoners made no attempt to exploit the uproar to run away, even though they could have sought shelter in many nearby localities, and even though the Germans were clearly in total retreat. One of the survivors, Yehiel Daniel, explained this after the war: "Where would you escape to? Do you know where to escape to? What escape? Who thought about escaping? You don't know where you are. You don't know—Poland, not Poland, not Germany. Maybe you're between Poland and Germany.... You don't know the language, you don't know a thing. Also, it's better to be together.... Exactly where would I go?"[49]

The sense that even escape from the convoy offered no hope seems to have been shared by many Jewish prisoners. Even when it would have been possible to get away, when security was lax and the guards showed complete apathy, only a few Jewish prisoners tried to escape: "It was possible to escape but it would have been useless. The transport of 300 young girls was accompanied by only a single guard, but he, like us, knew that escape was pointless."[50]

In addition to feeling that their chances of finding refuge with the local population were slim and that they would probably be handed over to the convoy escorts by any civilians they encountered, the Jewish prisoners lived with a pervasive sense of loss. What was the point of trying to save their lives, what was the purpose of making all that effort? As one of the female survivors recalled: "Where would we go? To whom? Home, parents, family—they were all long gone.... Who would give us shelter? Who would open the door for us? The non-Jews could only hand us back to the Germans—that was always how they helped the Jews. And the Germans, who were panicking and saw their end was nigh, would have no compunctions about killing a few more Jews."[51]

In the end, the survivors' most vivid memory was the sight of the horror. The evacuation and death marches are described in hindsight as a hell that beggars description; nor can they understand how they survived. One survivor, who spent the last part of the murderous evacuation in an open train car en route to Dachau, recalled the moment before liberation as follows:

> I saw that I was lying in a pile of bodies strewn on the bottom of the car. I saw a few of them move, raise and drop an arm or leg. I saw heads moving, I saw eyes opening like mine and quickly shutting so as not to see the horror we were lying in—because most of the bodies weren't moving any more, weren't raising their arms or legs, weren't opening or closing their eyes. They were dead, they had been dead for days, and we were stuck among them. We, too, were taken for dead. And above us all, on top of our dead bodies, were our companions who were still alive,

who could still manage to sit up. The air in this death car was thick. The smell of corpses filled the car, but our companions who were alive smelled exactly like the dead.[52]

It is no wonder that the survivors of the death marches did not greet liberation, when it came, with any particular joy, and certainly did not have the sense of a miraculous revelation described by those released from the camps. The evacuation period left the survivors with their senses dulled and with the insight that there was no line between life and death. In the words of one survivor: "We felt no joy or festiveness. There was no room in our hearts to give thanks for the 'miracle' that had befallen us. The Americans may have liberated us, but it would not be easy for us to be liberated from the numbness of our emotions. If we had survived, it was only because we had kept the feeble wick of our lives burning weakly through the cautious and diluted use of our emotional forces."[53] To sum up, one must remember that unlike any other period during the years of the Nazi genocide, the death-march era is badly lacking in contemporary documentation. We can count on the fingers of one hand the official orders and instructions relating to the evacuations and how they were to be performed. Obviously the victims kept no diaries. Everything else—a huge quantity of material—belongs to the category of postwar testimony and memoirs. An accurate analysis of this documentation can give us a broader picture of that unique and horrible human experience, as well as enable us to understand better the nature of the final phase of Nazi genocide.

Notes

1. Testimony of Abraham Shupungin, United States Holocaust Memorial Museum Archives [hereafter USHMMA], RG 50.120 #148.
2. Henri Graf, *Ne pas mourir, Auschwitz A5184,* ed. François Fouquet (Rouen, 2007), 132.
3. Wolfgang Sofsky, *The Order of Terror: The Concentration Camp* (Princeton, NJ, 1997), 225.
4. On the death-march period and its significance, see Daniel Blatman, *The Death Marches: The Final Phase of Nazi Genocide* (Cambridge, MA, 2011), especially 1–18, 407–32.
5. Imre Kertész, *Fateless* (Evanston, IL, 1992), 180.
6. Primo Levi, *The Voice of Memory, Interview 1961–1987,* ed. Marco Belpoliti and Robert Gordon (New York, 2001), 251.
7. Ber Mark, *Megilos Auschwitz* (Tel Aviv, 1977), 391.
8. Daniel Blatman, "The Death Marches, January–May 1945: Who Was Responsible for What?" *Yad Vashem Studies* 28 (2000): 185–90; Katrin Greiser, *Die Todesmärsche von Buchenwald. Räumung, Befreiung und Spuren der Erinnerung* (Göttingen, 2008), 64–76.
9. Jorge Semprun, *Literature or Life* (New York, 1997), 8–10.
10. Kertész, *Fateless,* 171–72.
11. Andzej Strzelecki, *Endphase des KL Auschwitz: Evakuierung, Liquidierung und Befreiung des Lagers* (Oświęcim, 1995), 255–56.
12. Ewa Schlus, *Yaldut akheret. Masa ha-hayyim shel Ewa* (Jerusalem, 2001), 130–31.
13. Jean Oppenheimer, *Journal de route 14 mars—9 mai 1945.* Collection Témoignages de la Shoah (Paris, 2006), 64.

14. Primo Levi, *If This is a Man* (New York, 1959), 187.

15. Memoirs of Katherine (Bloch) Feuer, USHMMA, RG-02.209, 3.

16. Graf, *Ne pas mourir,* 129–30; Testimony by Yaacov Kravcik, Yad Vashem Archives [hereafter YVA], O-3/4118.

17. Shmuel Leitner, *Be-mahanot Germania 1941–1945* (self-published, n.d.), 89; Aurelia Pollak, *Three Years of Deportations* (Ra'anana, 1991), 104; Yechiel Shefer, *Dappey-Ed, Zikhronot hahayyim shel Yechiel Shefer* (self-published, 2004), 75.

18. Pierre Berg (with Brian Brock), *Scheisshaus Luck: Surviving the Unspeakable in Auschwitz and Dora* (New York, 2008), 167–68.

19. Pollak, *Three Years,* 104–5.

20. Testimony of Yitzhak Peri, YVA, O-3/9952.

21. Berg, *Scheisshaus Luck,* 168.

22. Willy Berler, *Journey through Darkness: Monowitz, Auschwitz, Gross-Rosen, Buchenwald* (London, 2004), 127.

23. On the evacuation of Blechhammer, see Blatman, *The Death Marches,* 92–94.

24. John Ranz, *Inhumanity: Death March to Buchenwald and the Last Jews of Bendzin* (Bloomington, IN, 2007), 39.

25. Moshe Hoch, *Hazarah me-ha-tophet* (Hadera, self-published, 1988), 123.

26. Testimony of Zvi Bar-Lev (Blecher), Moreshet Archive, Givat Haviva [hereafter MA], A.860.

27. Testimony of Abraham Kimmelmann, David Boder Collection, Voices of the Holocaust Archive [hereafter Boder Collection] http://voices.iit.edu/interviewee?doc=kimmelmannA (accessed 17 September 2012).

28. Robert Antelme, *The Human Race* (Marlboro, VT, 1992), 243.

29. Shannon O'Lear and Stephen L. Egbert, "Introduction: Geographies of Genocide," *Space and Polity* 13, no. 1 (2009): 1–8.

30. Blatman, *The Death Marches,* 368–82.

31. Testimony of Yitzhak Grabowski, YVA, O-3/7001.

32. Berler, *Journey through Darkness,* 129.

33. Leitner, *Be-mahanot Germania,* 100.

34. Israel Koren, *Hissaredut, September 1, 1939 ad May 7, 1945* (self-published, 2001), 79–80.

35. See Ian Kershaw, *The End: Hitler's Germany, 1944–45* (London, 2011), 329–31; Yehuda Bauer, *Jews for Sale? Nazi-Jewish Negotiations, 1933–1945* (New Haven, CT, 1994), 246–50.

36. Beny Wirtzberg, *Mi-gey ha-harigah le-sha'ar ha-gay* (Ramat Gan, 1967), 72–73.

37. Berler, *Journey through Darkness,* 126; Susan Cernyak-Spatz, *Protective Custody: Prisoner 34042* (Cortland, NY, 2005), 219–20.

38. Eliezer Schwartz, *Avdut ve-Avadon* (n.d.), 116; on some aspects of the fate of Jews and non-Jews during the death marches, see Blatman, *The Death Marches,* 192–96, 424–27.

39. See John Wiernicki, *War in the Shadow of Auschwitz: Memoirs of a Polish Resistance Fighter and Survivor of the Death Camps* (Syracuse, NY, 2001). Wiernicki, a member of the Polish underground, was sent from Auschwitz to Buchenwald in December 1944 and then to Ohrdruf. He was among the prisoners who were evacuated from the camp in a terrible death march in April 1945.

40. Testimony of Yisrael Gutman, YVA, TR-3/1650.

41. Avraham Kafitza, *Na'ar tzair mesiakh im ha-mavet* (Tel Aviv, 1999), 55.

42. Malka Adler, *Itchko ve-Bernard* (Tel Aviv, 2004), 137–38.

43. Giuliana Tedeschi, *There is a Place on Earth: A Woman in Birkenau* (New York, 1992), 212–13.

44. Testimony of Bernard Warsager, Boder Collection, http://voices.iit.edu/interviewee?doc=warsagerB (accessed 17 September 2012).

45. Marsha Casper Cook (as told by Sala Lewis), *Sala: More than a Survivor* (New York, 2001), 32.

46. Testimony of Rivka Politanski, YVA, O-3/12210.

47. Testimony of Bernard Warsager, Boder Collection, http://voices.iit.edu/interviewee?doc=warsagerB (accessed 17 September 2012).
48. Testimony of Yaakov Sides, YVA, O-3/6209.
49. Testimony of Yehiel Daniel, YVA, O-3/9991.
50. Testimony of Tova Bienert, MA, A.232.
51. Khanka Schlezinger-Virnik, *Ha-dappim sheli* (Ra'anana, 2004), 142.
52. Schwartz, *Avdut ve-Avadon,* 133.
53. Kafitza, *Na'ar tzair,* 56.

Part IV

RETHINKING SELF-HELP AND RESISTANCE

CHAPTER 9

Documenting Catastrophe
The Ringelblum Archive and the Warsaw Ghetto

SAMUEL KASSOW

In the summer of 1943, in the Maidanek concentration camp, the noted Jewish historian Yitzhak Schiper told a fellow inmate that

> Everything depends on who transmits our testament to future generations, on who writes the history of this period. History is usually written by the victor. What we know about murdered peoples is only what their murderers vaingloriously cared to say about them. Should our murderers be victorious, should *they* write the history of this war, our destruction will be presented as one of the most beautiful pages of world history, and future generations will pay tribute to them as dauntless crusaders. Their every word will be taken as gospel. Or they may wipe out our memory altogether, as if we had never existed, as if there had never been a Polish Jewry, a ghetto in Warsaw, a Maidanek. Not even a dog will howl for us.
> But if *we* write the history of this period of blood and tears—and I firmly believe we will—who will believe us? Nobody will *want* to believe us, because our disaster is the disaster of the entire civilized world.... We'll have the thankless job of proving to a reluctant world that we are Abel, the murdered brother.[1]

Unlike Schiper, Emanuel Ringelblum had no doubt that the world would indeed believe what had happened—as long as it had the proper evidence. Through the secret Oyneg Shabes archive that he organized in the Warsaw Ghetto in November 1940 he set out to leave a mass of evidence whose thoroughness, objectivity, and sheer scope would force those "future generations" to look the truth in the face.

The Germans thought that they would not only kill the Jews but also write their history and determine how posterity would remember them. Jews in the Warsaw Ghetto were all too aware of the Nazi film crews who roamed

---

Notes for this section begin on page 189.

the ghetto to depict Jews as filthy degenerates. All over Europe the Nazis were showing the film *The Eternal Jew* (1940) that compared Jews to rats.

Through diaries, ghetto archives, and secret chronicles, Jews underscored their determination to write their own history. One could indeed resist with pen and paper as well as guns; buried time capsules might thwart Nazi hopes to erase the memory of their Jewish victims. Through the written word, Jews did all they could to ensure that future generations would write about them on the basis of Jewish rather than Nazi sources.

In March 1944, shortly before his capture by the Gestapo, Emanuel Ringelblum and his close associate Adolf Berman sent a letter to the Yiddish Scientific Institute in New York in which they described how the Jews in the Warsaw Ghetto doggedly resisted Nazi attempts to dehumanize them. The letter told an incredible story of cultural resistance and of a tough struggle that the Jews waged for their human dignity and national honor. Berman and Ringelblum mentioned the names of writers, poets, actors, intellectuals, and fighters and they recounted the determination of ordinary Jews not to let the Germans grind them down.[2]

But even as Ringelblum was composing this important message, he could not hide his fear that his greatest achievement—the underground archive he organized in the Warsaw Ghetto—might be lost forever. In a private letter to Berman, also written in March 1944, he worried that neither of them would survive the war. And then what would happen to the "OS"—the all-important archive? If there were no survivors, who would be able to find it?[3]

Ringelblum indeed had good reason to worry. Of the sixty or so collaborators whom he mobilized in this incredible project of documentation, study, and cultural resistance, only three survived the war—Hersh Wasser, his wife Bluma, and the journalist Rachel Auerbach. They pressured and cajoled Jewish leaders in newly liberated Poland to start searching for the buried documents under the ruins of what had been a school at Nowolipki 68. It was a very difficult process to find them underneath the heaps of rubble of what used to be the Warsaw Ghetto.[4]

Finally in September 1946, searchers uncovered ten tin boxes, the first cache of the archive, which was buried in August 1942. The second cache, buried in February 1943, was found in December 1950 and the third, buried in April 1943, was never recovered.[5] Many documents and photographs, especially in the first cache, were lost to water seepage and mold, and it is probable that parts of the first cache vanished forever. Nonetheless about twenty-five to thirty thousand usable documents have survived.[6] A catalogue and reader's guide recently published by the U.S. Holocaust Memorial Museum and Indiana University Press runs to more than five hundred pages. The value of the archive for the study of the Warsaw Ghetto becomes even greater when one remembers that Warsaw suffered enormous damage during the Jewish and

Polish uprisings and thus, when compared with other cities, fewer archives and wartime materials survived.

Thanks to the materials of the Oyneg Shabes archive we have a deeper understanding of the social and cultural history of the Warsaw Ghetto, which was, like most ghettos, not just an antechamber to the death camps but, in Gustavo Corni's words, a "unique social structure in which elements of the traditional pre-war Jewish society continued to exist."[7] The lives of ghetto inhabitants did not begin in 1939 or 1941, and any serious research on ghettos must frame questions that recognize not only rupture but also continuities—exactly the approach that Ringelblum and his archive took.

Indeed Ringelblum's determination to start the underground archive reflects critical continuities between his prewar activity and his wartime role in the Warsaw Ghetto. Before the war Ringelblum played three major roles: political activist, community organizer, and historian. These three roles were all intertwined. The kind of historian Ringelblum chose to be was shaped by his political involvement and his activities as a community organizer. The first major commitment that Ringelblum made was to radical, Marxist politics. He was part of a generation of Jewish youth that came of age in a time of dislocation, war, economic upheaval, and growing antisemitism. In theory they were equal citizens of the Polish Republic but in practice most felt like second-class citizens.

Ringelblum was born in 1900 in Buczacz, then in Habsburg Galicia; in 1914 his family fled to Nowy Sącz in Western Galicia to escape the advancing Russian armies. The very week that he turned seventeen, in November 1917, two major events took place that would have an enormous impact on his life. The first was the announcement of the Balfour Declaration, a promise by the British government to help establish a Jewish national home in Palestine. The second was the Bolshevik overthrow of the Russian provisional government and the establishment of a Soviet state that promised world revolution and equality for all oppressed peoples, including Jews. In interwar Poland many young Jews sought salvation through Zionism while others looked to Moscow. Ringelblum, however, embraced a movement that was convinced that Zionism and a Soviet-inspired world revolution were perfectly compatible. As a teenager in Nowy Sącz, he joined the Poalei Tsiyon Party, a movement founded and shaped by Ber Borochov, who died in 1917. Borochov had called for Jews to fight for both a territorial base in Palestine and Socialist revolution in the Diaspora.[8] It was in the party group in Nowy Sącz that Ringelblum would make two close friends, Raphael Mahler and Artur Eisenbach, who would also become renowned historians of Eastern European Jewry. When the party split in 1920 into a right wing and a Yiddishist pro-Soviet left wing faction, Ringelblum joined the latter, a move that would have an enormous impact on his subsequent development as a historian.[9]

The Poalei Tsiyon, and above all the intellectual legacy of Borochov, affected Ringelblum in many important ways. Inspired by Borochov's teachings about the ongoing economic marginalization of Diaspora Jewry, the party stressed the study of Jewish economic and social history. Borochov was also a keen Yiddishist, one of the pioneers of modern Yiddish studies; his teachings made Ringelblum a passionate supporter of modern Yiddish culture. At an early age Ringelblum threw himself into the party's educational activities, which were directed at poor Jewish workers who had been forced to leave school at an early age. The party imbued Ringelblum with a devotion to the plight of the Jewish masses and this dedication to the struggle for the welfare of the Jewish poor inspired him both before the war and in the Warsaw Ghetto.

In 1930 Ringelblum began to work for the most important Jewish relief organization in interwar Poland, the American-based Joint Distribution Committee (JDC), as an editor of its monthly journal *Folkshilf*, and later as a community organizer. His activities focused on the network of almost nine hundred free loan societies—the so-called *gmiles khesed kasses*—that the JDC had organized in Poland by 1939.[10] Ringelblum was convinced that the "microcredit" extended by these societies to needy Jews in small towns had an impact far out of proportion to the actual amounts of money disbursed.[11] For beleaguered small-town Jews fighting boycotts and anti-Jewish violence in the 1930s, the *kasses* were a vital source of moral support and a reminder that they were not alone.

Ringelblum noted the critical difference between traditional charity and the ethos of self-help that the Joint was trying to develop.[12] The JDC expected local Jewish communities to provide half of the capital of the *kasses* eventually, a provision aimed at fostering healthy partnership rather than a destructive dynamic of handouts and charity. *Folkshilf* stressed that Jews had to fight back against Polish attempts to marginalize them economically. Vocational training, courses to teach Jews new skills and occupations, stood at the center of its message. The Joint also insisted that local Jews overcome political differences and work together. Political wrangling could not stand in the way of working for the common good. This was another lesson that Ringelblum took with him into the Warsaw Ghetto when he emerged to help lead the ghetto's most important relief organization, the Aleynhilf.

When Nazi Germany expelled seventeen thousand Polish Jews in October 1938, the JDC director Yitzhak Giterman sent Ringelblum to the border town of Zbąszyń to organize relief activities for the desperate refugees. Ringelblum showed himself to be a superb organizer, and his success in Zbąszyń led to greater responsibilities in the JDC.[13] His relationship with Giterman grew closer. Indeed Giterman would play a major role in the leadership of the Oyneg Shabes archive.

In addition to his political activism and to his growing stature as a community organizer, Ringelblum was also becoming an accomplished historian of Polish Jewry. In 1919, Ringelblum left Nowy Sącz and enrolled in the history faculty of Warsaw University. His historical training proceeded under the guidance of two key mentors: Professor Marceli Handelsman of Warsaw University and Dr. Yitzhak Schiper, a well-known historian of Polish Jewry (who was not on the university faculty). Handelsman and Schiper were not only historians; they were prominent, politically engaged public intellectuals, and clear role models for Ringelblum. From the very beginning of his career as a historian, Ringelblum saw the writing of history as a personal and national mission. Historians were not just scholars. They were also fighters in a battle that Polish Jewry was waging for national dignity and equality. Even studies of the distant past were used to support or refute antisemitic accusations that Polish Jews were aliens who had weakened the country and who had stymied the development of a Polish middle class.

Jewish historians like Ringelblum felt a pressing obligation to show that Jews lived in Poland by right and not on sufferance. Their toil and sweat had helped build the country and they had fought for its welfare and independence. Ringelblum was a Marxist who rejected the idea of eternal and inevitable Polish antisemitism. Hatred of Jews, he believed, was largely the result of the manipulative capitalist system and of ignorance, and thus Jewish historians could build vital bridges between the two communities. Much of Ringelblum's historical research on various topics between 1450 and 1800 focused on Polish-Jewish relations: the deep links that bound Jews to the Polish land, and Jewish participation in Poland's battles for freedom.[14] This concern with Polish-Jewish relations would also play a major role in the secret ghetto archive, as Ringelblum went out of his way to collect material on Jewish participation in the war against the Germans in 1939 as well as Polish-Jewish economic collaboration such as smuggling.

In 1923 Ringelblum and Rafael Mahler, his close friend and party comrade, founded the "Young Historians Circle" (Der Yunger Historiker Krayz), which would hold monthly meetings until 1939. After 1925 the Circle played a major role in the Historical Section of the YIVO, the Yiddish Scientific Institute, which was founded in Vilna in that year.[15] Ringelblum, like the other historians of the Circle, embraced the unofficial motto "history for the people and by the people." History was not a monopoly reserved for scholars and specialists; indeed Jewish scholars needed ordinary Jews—dedicated amateurs—to collaborate in a effort to gather documents, record local folklore, and to photograph and study local cemeteries and synagogues.[16] Ringelblum was one of the founders of the Jewish *landkentnish* (know the land) society. This society encouraged Jews to hike the Polish countryside, kayak along its rivers, and ski in its mountains, thus asserting their own ties to the country. "Engaged tourism" was a response to the fact that Polish guidebooks largely omitted Jews and Jewish sites from their purview.[17]

Ringelblum and other YIVO scholars hoped that the very process of historical research and "engaged tourism" would bolster a new secular Jewish sensibility and Yiddish secular culture.[18] "*Zamling*"—the collection of documents and folklore—would also ensure that future generations would not have to rely on gentile sources and unfriendly official documents to study Jews; it signaled the determination of a stateless people to protect their identity and their national dignity. Indeed, the secret Oyneg Shabes archive that Ringelblum organized in the Warsaw Ghetto was a direct continuation of this YIVO imperative of engaged scholarship.

Jewish historians, Ringelblum argued, also had to change the way Jews saw themselves and their own past. Jewish history was more than a story of rabbis, scholars, and businessmen. The Jewish past was not an idyllic fable of Jews, rich and poor, walking together to pray. Jewish historians had to write about ordinary Jews, the poor, women, apprentices, and beggars. They had to show that the Jewish past also saw class struggles and the battles waged by the poor for social justice. These poor Jews had been forgotten and the Jewish historian had an obligation to protect their memory and thus give them posthumous honor and recognition. One example was Ringelblum's tribute to some obscure eighteenth-century Warsaw Jewish jesters. "These jesters," Ringelblum wrote, "can be seen as the ancestors of Jewish actors, who in hard times did what they could to amuse the Jewish masses. At the same time they enriched and disseminated popular culture [*folksshafung*]. Therefore let us mention their names so that they will be remembered [*l'zikhroyn oylem*]"…[19] (When Ringelblum wrote these words he did not know that a few years later he would be doing the same for the Warsaw Yiddishist intelligentsia and the Polish Jewish masses.)

In a 1955 essay, a former member of the Circle, Meir Korzen, noted that before the war, Ringelblum was known more as an organizer than as an original thinker and historian.[20] Korzen was not entirely wrong, but he ignored the sociocultural context of interwar Polish-Jewish historiography. Without university or government support Jewish historians needed good organizers. Less concerned with academic fame than with encouraging the writing of Polish Jewish history, Ringelblum saw himself as a facilitator as well as a scholar. It is well that he did so. A Meyer Balaban or a Schiper, the most famous and accomplished Jewish historians in prewar Poland, would not have organized a collective undertaking like the Oyneg Shabes. Ringelblum did. He also believed that one of the major priorities of the Oyneg Shabes archive was to make it easier for future historians to do research. To that end, when the archive began in November 1940, he wanted to cast a wide net and to collect as large a variety of material as possible. There was no way of knowing at that moment, he told

Hersh Wasser, what was "important" and what was not. That was an issue for future historians to decide.[21]

To be sure, Korzen underestimated Ringelblum, who compiled a respectable record as a historian, all the more remarkable for the fact that his many jobs left him little time to work in archives. He published the first academic history of early Warsaw Jewry; landmark articles on Polish-Jewish relations in the eighteenth century; an important monograph on the Jewish role in the Kosciuszko Uprising; a splendid investigation of the Jewish book trade; many articles on the history of Jewish medicine in Poland; and an excellent study of discussions of the economic restructuring of Polish Jews in the eighteenth century. He did so with practically no financial help and little time. And after all, he was not yet thirty-nine when the war broke out.

While the Circle was not linked to the Left Poalei Tsiyon per se, Ringelblum himself was deeply convinced of a clear link between the party's ideology and the serious study of Jewish history.[22] He wanted the Historiker Krayz to "impart a new spirit to the writing of Jewish history. [We want] to liberate Jewish historiography from the influence of religious and nationalist attitudes. This is a pioneering circle since almost all of its members are trying to solve the problems of Jewish history from the standpoint of historical materialism."[23]

Thus Ringelblum could never escape a certain tension between his political engagement and his scholarly principles. But he was committed to objective scholarship, and he stubbornly resisted calls by party radicals in the 1930s to boycott the YIVO because of its alleged devotion to its alleged fetish of "bourgeois science" and "ivory tower scholarship."[24] In the Oyneg Shabes he strove to include collaborators from different political groups. The research guidelines that he prepared for the Oyneg Shabes are rigorous and comprehensive. But it would also be a mistake to discount entirely the impact of the party's ideology on his historical writings and his work in the Oyneg Shabes. The late Nachman Blumenthal went too far when he praised Ringelblum for completely transcending party biases.[25] In a January 1944 letter Ringelblum reiterated just how much the party's ideology meant to him.[26]

One does not have to look hard to see the impact of Ringelblum's political views in his wartime writings. Although he tried to involve all groups in the archive, he could not entirely mask his ingrained aversion to the Bund, his party's major nemesis in interwar Poland.[27] His prewar antipathy to the "Jewish bourgeoisie" emerged as a constant theme in his ghetto diary; he compared the Warsaw Judenrat to the hated kahal in Tsarist Russia that protected the interests of rich Jews by catching poor children for service in the Russian army.[28] He was not completely fair in his treatment of Adam Czerniaków, the head of the Warsaw Judenrat. He bitterly resented the alleged favoritism shown by Czerniaków to prominent converts in the ghetto. Ringelblum had little sympathy with the counterargument made by Czerniaków and Judenrat member

Abraham Gepner that to boycott converts like Professor Herszfeld and Józef Szeryński would be a demonstration of disloyalty to Poland in a time of national emergency. Indeed Gepner reacted angrily to Ringelblum's attacks on the Judenrat's reception of converts and accused him of lacking Polish patriotism.[29]

Ringelblum was pro-Soviet, but like the rest of his party, support of the Soviet Union did not blind him to unpleasant realities. He was well aware of Stalinist terror and of the ongoing decline of Yiddish culture there.[30] On the other hand, as the war progressed, Ringelblum believed more than ever that the Soviet Union, with all its faults, represented the Jews' only hope in the postwar era.

Ringelblum came into his own when the war began. Before the war he had worked in the shadows of others, people whose mentorship he willingly accepted. But one by one, those whom he most respected and looked up to either left or were killed.[31] The time had come to fulfill an enormous national and human responsibility, to gather eyewitness accounts and documents of Jewish society in wartime. What Ringelblum realized was that this was a collective, not an individual enterprise. With the Oyneg Shabes archive he won his place in history.

In September 1939, Ringelblum had just returned to Warsaw from Switzerland, where he had been a Left Poalei Tsiyon delegate to the twenty-first Zionist Congress in August. Polish defenses crumbled within days, and many key Jewish leaders fled the Polish capital. Artur Eisenbach, Ringelblum's brother-in-law, begged Ringelblum to leave but he refused. Somebody had to stay, he insisted, to organize relief and to lead. As Ringelblum told the journalist Rachel Auerbach, who was planning to flee to her native Galicia, not everybody had the right to run.[32] He discovered during the siege of Warsaw, as did many other ordinary Warsaw citizens, that he was capable of physical courage. He stood his civil defense watches under heavy fire and carried a wounded woman to a hospital in the middle of an air raid. And every day, Ringelblum made the long journey to his office in the headquarters of the Joint Distribution Committee where he helped organize emergency relief and refugee aid.[33]

Two major strands of Ringelblum's prewar activity, history and social welfare, now came together. He became a major leader of the major Jewish mutual aid organization in Warsaw, the Aleynhilf, and helped coordinate aid to refugees and soup kitchens. He also helped organize an extensive network of more than one thousand house committees and tried to make them into the social base of the Aleynhilf. He and others consciously used the Aleynhilf to create posts for the Jewish intelligentsia—teachers, writers, scholars, and others who might otherwise be doomed to starvation in the ghetto. As time went on, Ringelblum began to see the Aleynhilf as a counterpoint to the Judenrat, a symbol of a "democratic" as opposed to a "bureaucratic" Jewish institution. In turn, this consciousness of representing the *real* community permeated the self-perception of the Oyneg Shabes collective. It was largely through the Aleynhilf, as well as through his contacts in the YIVO, the Joint, and the Left Poalei Tsiyon that he recruited many of the key members of the Oyneg Shabes Archive, which he organized as a formal group in November 1940.³⁴

Through a process of trial and error, Ringelblum and his key collaborators established an effective organizational structure for the Oyneg Shabes. At the center of the archive was an executive committee that met on Saturday afternoons. The committee raised money, made decisions about strategy and research agendas, and also decided on the recruitment of personnel. The Oyneg Shabes also included writers and contributors. Some contributed only a few articles or essays while others wrote on an ongoing and frequent basis. The Oyneg Shabes also needed interviewers and information gatherers, especially to find out what was going on in the refugee centers. This was very dangerous work, since the risk of contracting typhus was high. The archive also tried to make two or three handwritten copies of each document. One of the most critical groups in the archive was the "technical staff" led by the teacher Israel Lichtenstein. Only this staff had physical possession of the materials as they flowed into the archive and only they, plus Ringelblum and a few others, actually knew the archive's location.

Ringelblum brought together a close cadre of about sixty collaborators that included religious Jews and Communists, Bundists and Zionists, well-known prewar leaders, and obscure refugees. It would go too far to say that the Oyneg Shabes worked in complete harmony or that party differences entirely disappeared. But the Oyneg Shabes collective was imbued with a common mission—to document Jewish life under the Nazi occupation and to ensure that future historians would write on the basis of Jewish, and not just Nazi, materials. To assure secrecy, the archive mostly operated on a "need to know basis" with careful screening and tight compartmentalization. This caution exacted a price, both in terms of valuable people whom the archive chose not to involve (Yitzhak Schiper and Meyer Balaban) and materials that the archive chose not to collect. But the Gestapo never tracked down the archive. Indeed the Oyneg Shabes, as Rachel Auerbach pointed out, had more luck saving documents than people.³⁵

Unlike the Łódź Ghetto archive, which was, one might say "semi-official," or the Białystok archive, where Judenrat leader Efraim Barash provided Mordecai Tenenbaum with some financial support and a room, or Herman Kruk's documentation efforts in the Vilna Ghetto, where ghetto commandant Jacob Gens would occasionally drop by to unburden himself, the Oyneg Shabes tried to keep a firewall between itself and the Judenrat.³⁶ Even more, it saw itself as part of an alternative community (to borrow a term from Lucy Dawidowicz) that supposedly represented the "real voice" of Warsaw Jewry, as opposed to the "official" and "corrupt" Judenrat. Such a stance affected the collection priorities of the archive, at least until the beginning of the Great Deportation in July 1942. Over time the Oyneg Shabes pursued changing and overlapping agendas. The first, begun in 1940 was *zamling* (collecting)—the collection of testimonies, diaries, candy wrappers, tram tickets, restaurant menus, official decrees—anything that could give future historians insights into the life of the ghetto including material culture. This remained a priority of the archive right until the end.

But in 1941 the Oyneg Shabes adopted a new project: the Two and a Half Years Project, an ambitious plan to compile a sixteen-hundred-page study of Jewish life under the Nazi occupation based on questionnaires, interviews, and defined topics that included eighty different subjects, such as women, children, corruption in the ghetto, the ghetto street, religious life, Polish-Jewish relations, German-Jewish relations, and much more.[37] As was the case with *zamling,* this project also reflected how not only Ringelblum but most of the other members of the Oyneg Shabes executive committee had been active in the prewar YIVO, with its emphasis on social history, its populism, its concern for the collection of Jewish documents, and its encouragement of Yiddish as a scholarly language. The YIVO also stressed interdisciplinary approaches, the collaboration of scholars and ordinary Jews, the use of questionnaires and surveys to encourage the writing of "history by the people and for the people." We also see here the keen prewar interest of Ringelblum in material culture and what later came to be called *Alltagsgeschichte.*

Each topic within the project had a team leader. Some Oyneg Shabbes members supervised multiple topics. Ringelblum stressed the importance of securing multiple perspectives, for example, the views of religious and secular Jews, of young people, and so on.[38] Special mention should be made of the studies of Jewish women by Celia Slapakowa, the essay on children by Aaron Koninski, the reportages of Rachel Auerbach and Peretz Opoczynski, and the more than four hundred shtetl monographs that Ringelblum called the crown jewel of the Oyneg Shabes. The Oyneg Shabes tried hard to begin serious study of the economics of the Warsaw Ghetto: exports, the search for niche markets, the balance of trade, prices, the dollar-złoty exchange rate, and Polish-Jewish economic relations. Ringelblum believed that the OS enjoyed only limited success in this field, but in hindsight, he underestimated the achievements of the archive, especially in harnessing the gifted economist Jerzy Winkler to write a penetrating study of trade with the Aryan side.

This ambitious attempt to study wartime Jewish society also reflected, it might be said, the key role that Warsaw played in prewar Jewish Poland as a nodal point of contestation. More than Jewry in any other city, with the possible exception of Łódź, Warsaw Jewry was a mosaic of different groups and tribes: Hasidism, Bundists, a large working class, Litvak migrants, Galician intellectuals, a large Polish-speaking component that included much of the middle class and professional intelligentsia, as well as the Yiddish-speaking masses. Warsaw exemplified the ongoing tensions and clashes of interwar Polish Jewry, tensions and clashes that assumed a new relevance in the Warsaw Ghetto. Warsaw was also the center of political parties and welfare organizations, it boasted the highest concentration of the Jewish professional intelligentsia, and it reflected in concentrated form the rapid cultural transformations that were changing Jewish Poland.

In an essay on the Oyneg Shabes written in late 1942 or early 1943, Ringelblum amplified some of the principles that underlay the work of the archive.[39] He stressed the importance of casting as wide a net as possible and writing down impressions and information immediately. Memory, Ringelblum insisted, was tricky, especially in the ghetto where changes occurred so quickly, and where those changes were usually for the worse. The war had turned days into weeks and weeks into years. By December 1939, the tough prewar days seemed like a picnic. A year later, the Jews were locked up in a ghetto and the prewar days seemed wonderful—certainly not worth writing about. And when the Great Deportation to Treblinka began in July 1942, even the terrible ghetto hell of 1941 seemed like an elusive paradise. What seemed important and significant today might be totally forgotten tomorrow. And if one put off writing today, what guarantee was there that the writer would be alive tomorrow?

Ringelblum the historian had an implicit intuition of the important difference between contemporaneous testimony and survivor memory. Had survivors written long after the war, their memoirs would have been skewed by the knowledge of the terrible disaster that engulfed everybody. It is probable that all the sketches about the microcosms of ghetto life between 1940 and 1942 would have been forgotten. Who would have cared about Peretz Opoczynski's sketches of house committees and the post office? Who would have bothered with Janos Turkow's essay on theaters in the ghetto? In one of Cecilia Slapakowa's interviews with ghetto women, we read that, "in the tragic destructive chaos of our present day life we can nonetheless observe flashes of creative activity, the slow development and birth of forces that are building a base for the future."[40] Could this have appeared after the war? Survivor identity would have overwhelmed who the Jew had been. The before would have been erased by the after. But like many others, even Ringelblum, for a long time, refused to believe the worst.

The massive study project was in full swing when the Great Deportation began. In the last week of July 1942 a hurriedly convened emergency meeting of the Oyneg Shabes ordered the immediate collection and burial of all documents, photographs, and artifacts.[41] Team leaders gave up their raw data, interview records, and questionnaires, and this unfinished material became one of the most important parts of the first cache of the archive buried in August 1942. It is important to remind ourselves that this study project began before the Oyneg Shabes leaders learned about the full dimensions of the Final Solution. In the true tradition of the prewar YIVO, they were striving to produce engaged scholarship that somehow straddled the built-in tension—in the best Dubnovian tradition—between the quest for scholarly objectivity and nation building. It is not farfetched to infer that Ringelblum himself hoped that the Two and a Half Year project could help build what we now call a "usable past" for postwar Polish Jewry. He hoped that these lessons would include more interest in Yiddish and more cultural pride.[42] He wanted to discredit the Jewish bourgeoisie and expose those elites who failed to meet the test of wartime leadership, to document the resilience and resourcefulness of the Jewish masses, and to demonstrate that in a moment of trial the Jews had once again proven their loyalty to Poland.

One of the key factors that made the extraordinary work of the Oyneg Shabes possible—and especially the Two and a Half Years Project—was the fact that, compared to some of the other large ghettos, the Warsaw Ghetto had a relatively large degree of what I would call "social space." Compared say to Łódź, the Warsaw Ghetto was less isolated and its economy, if we can call it that, was less regimented. In 1940 and 1941 the Warsaw Ghetto had developed, as has been seen, a strong "alternative community" based on more than one thousand house committees, a parliament of the house committees chaired by Ringelblum, and the critically important Aleynhilf—a prime example of what Yehuda Bauer has called an "intermediate organization" in the ghetto, those standing between the Judenrat and the underground organizations.[43]

The Oyneg Shabes and the Aleynhilf existed in a symbiotic relationship. Most Oyneg Shabes leaders, including Ringelblum, Joint Director Yitzhak Giterman, Hersh Wasser, and Menakhem Cohen, also occupied leading positions in the Aleynhilf. The Oyneg Shabes folded most of its operating expenses into the budget of the Aleynhilf, which provided employment to most of the Oyneg Shabes staff. Just as important, it was through the Aleynhilf that the Oyneg Shabes was able to collect information and documents while at the same time preserving secrecy. Interviews with refugees, information gathering in soup kitchens and schools, essay-writing contests targeted at specific subgroups such as young people, and study projects of social problems in the ghetto could all be labeled as Aleynhilf projects. Directors of soup kitchens or schools could alert the Oyneg Shabes to interesting sources of information or individuals to be interviewed. Needless to say, until the entry of the United States into the war, the Aleynhilf benefited from its association with the JDC, and was thus treated by the Germans with a relative degree of moderation.

A careful reading of Oyneg Shabes materials affords some valuable insight into the escalating dilemmas faced by the Aleynhilf. Over time initial optimism gave way to growing anxiety about the ability of Warsaw Jewry to hold out and about the ability of Aleynhilf to counter dwindling resources and falling morale.

By May 1942 Ringelblum was asking in his diary: what should the Aleynhilf do? Should it try to distribute its resources equally, thus saving nobody in the end, or should it help a chosen few, an elite?[44]

By the same token, as we see from the writings of Rachel Auerbach and others, working for the Aleynhilf was morally fraught. It was well and good to tell oneself, as Ringelblum, Auerbach, and the others did, that they were working on behalf of the real community, that they worked for organizations that truly represented the Jewish masses. But those very masses, starving and desperate, often saw people like Ringelblum as arbiters of life or death, who had access to jobs and food and who protected a favored few, well-connected friends and party comrades. It is to Ringelblum's credit that, for the most part, there is little evidence of censorship in the Oyneg Shabes, and that there is a lot of material criticizing the "alternative community" that he so fervently supported.

With the onset of mass murder of Warsaw Jewry, the Oyneg Shabes was decimated. The documents reflect the inhuman strain on the dwindling group of members. Per Ringelblum's own admonitions, there is an instructive difference between Oyneg Shabes materials and postwar memoirs. Oyneg Shabes materials show an incredible degree of anger directed against other Jews—who are mentioned much more than the Germans. Even close friends and co-workers turned against each other, if only temporarily.[45]

One might assume that once the group understood that few Polish Jews would survive the war, they would throw up their hands in despair. Incredibly, however, the work continued, now with new agendas. One was to send four detailed reports to London via the Polish Underground.[46] These reports included eyewitness accounts of escapees from Chełmno and Treblinka, as well as reports of eyewitnesses from other towns. Especially noteworthy was the 100-plus-page interview that Rachel Auerbach conducted with Avrom Krzepicki, an escapee from Treblinka and the eyewitness account of Chełmno by "Szlamek."[47]

In September 1942 Ringelblum asked the left-wing Polish Jewish writer Gustawa Jarecka to write a report of the Great Deportation that had just sent over three hundred thousand Jews to Treblinka. Jarecka only managed to finish the introduction before the Germans deported her and her two children. In December 1950, the introduction surfaced in two milk cans discovered by Polish construction workers:

> The record must be hurled like a stone under history's wheel in order to stop it.... One can lose all hopes except the one—that the suffering and destruction of this war will make sense when they are looked at from a distant, historical perspective. From sufferings, unparalleled in history, from bloody tears and bloody sweat, a chronicle of days of hell is being composed, in order that one may understand the historical reasons that shaped the human mind in this fashion and created government systems which made possible the events in our time through which we passed.[48]

In her introduction, Jarecka set down many reasons to write in the face of death. Through the written word one could confront the terrible present with dignity of the past and recapture the themes and symbols of prewar culture. In the face of horror, language could simultaneously frustrate and console. To write was to assert precious individuality even on the brink of death. To write was to resist, if only to bring the killers to justice. To write was to complete the defeat of the killers by ensuring that future historians would use the victims' cries to change the world.

Like Jarecka, Ringelblum also wanted to cast a "stone under history's wheel." He was absolutely convinced that the story of Jewish suffering, no matter how terrible, was a universal story, not just a Jewish one.[49] And evil, no matter how great, could not be placed outside of history. However terrible their sufferings, the Jews were still part of universal history, not outside it. The archive could still become a weapon in the struggle for a better future. Even though he now knew that most Polish Jews would not survive, he still continued the Oyneg Shabes with new agendas. The Oyneg Shabes now collected all official documents and placards that recorded the mass murder; eyewitness accounts of Treblinka; studies of the rump ghetto and shops; reports to be sent abroad. In retrospect these sources, part of the second cache unearthed in milk cans in 1950, provide valuable insights into how Warsaw Jewry came to support the idea of armed resistance, a degree of mass support that was missing in Vilna and Białystok.

One of Ringelblum's most important goals was to explain for future historians the behavior of the "Jewish masses" during the war, to shield them against future charges of cowardice and fecklessness.[50] Before the war he had often complained that historians of Jewish society should not have to depend on gentile sources. In the face of the greatest catastrophe in European Jewish history, it became doubly important to leave markers and guideposts for future generations. During the deportation, Ringelblum kept returning to the theme of Jewish behavior, and one can see that he was anticipating the question that would merge after the war: why did they allegedly "go like sheep to the slaughter"? He was more anxious than ever to point out what he called "dos shtile heldntum funm yidishn masnmensh"—the quiet heroism of the ordinary Jew. These ordinary Jews had no money, no contacts on the Aryan side, not a chance of survival. Ringelblum wanted future historians to remember that there was much more to the ghetto than demoralization and corruption—which the archive faithfully documented. There were hundreds of thousands of ordinary Jews who worked in the house committees, struggled to support their families, helped their neighbors, looked after each other's children, and who went to their deaths without anyone to record their name or remember them. They too resisted.

When the Warsaw Ghetto uprising broke out in April 1943, Ringelblum was trapped in the fighting ghetto, caught by the Germans and sent to the labor camp of Trawniki. There he and others in a camp resistance organization managed to establish clandestine contact with the underground Jewish National Committee. In August 1943, his party comrade Adolf Berman sent two intrepid couriers, Tadeusz Pajewski and Emilka Kossover, to Trawniki to rescue Ringelblum and bring him back to Warsaw, where he rejoined his wife Judyta and his 14-year-old son Uri in a crowded underground bunker on Grojecka 81.[51]

In those last months of his life, in terrible conditions, Ringelblum sat and wrote. In a kind of *apologia pro vita sua,* Ringelblum memorialized the progressive Jewish intelligentsia, and especially the murdered leaders who had done the most to shape him as a historian and as a public figure: Yitzhak Schiper, Shakhne Zagan, Yitzhak Giterman, and many others. Ringelblum rarely wrote about himself, but in these essays, he came closest to leaving his final testament. In his essay on Mordecai Anielewicz, Ringelblum paid a poignant tribute to the young commander of the Jewish Fighting Organization, who was killed in May 1943.

One of Ringelblum's last works was indeed his masterpiece on Polish Jewish relations in World War II.[52] As Ringelblum himself wrote, the picture that emerged, at least until the onset of the Great Deportation, was far from one-sided. There was evidence of Polish help as well as many documents showing the opposite. But the archive supports the conclusions reached by Havi Ben-Sasson and others that the real turning point in the way Jews viewed Poles came with the beginning of mass murder in 1942. Ringelblum was torn between his emotional involvement as a victim and his sense of duty, as one of the last Jewish historians left alive in Poland, to evaluate a complicated and fraught topic intelligently and objectively. Little wonder that this radical Marxist in his introduction compared himself to a *soyfer,* a scribe about to write a Torah scroll. He should purify himself in a ritual bath and he should remember that the slightest mistake would render the entire manuscript impure.

The Ringelblum study was thus a unique synthesis of the immediacy of contemporaneous testimony with the analytic perspective of retrospective historical analysis. It reflected the tension between the imperative of historical objectivity and shock of the enormous crimes that he witnessed not as a bystander but as a direct victim. Detached historians could make necessary distinctions between perpetrators and bystanders, between Polish and German antisemitism, between active complicity and indifference. For a member of a victimized people, to do so required a major effort of intellectual discipline. Ringelblum rejected blanket accusations that all Poles rejoiced in the murder of the Jews. After all, Poles had and were risking their lives to help him. He emphasized that the mass killing was instigated by the Germans, not the Poles. Furthermore the Germans were so determined to kill every last Jew that even had Poles extended more help, that would not have saved the majority of Polish Jews, only a few more individuals.

But Ringelblum also made some damning judgments. Although Jews were Polish citizens, they were abandoned by the Polish Underground and by the Underground government. They were seen as aliens, and their fate was of little concern. Why was it, Ringelblum asked, that when Germans pursued a fleeing Polish fighter through a crowded street, all they had to yell was "Catch the Jew" for someone to hand him over? Why was it that so often the last sight Jews saw from the cracks of the cattle cars were the smirks of their Polish fellow citizens? Poland, Ringelblum concluded, had failed the elemental moral test of solidarity with its Jewish population. His final verdict was harsh: "Polish Fascism and its ally, anti-Semitism have conquered the majority of the Polish people. It is they whom we blame for the fact that Poland has not taken an equal place alongside the Western European countries in rescuing Jews."[53] To the very last, as this essay showed, Ringelblum remained an engaged historian, convinced that scholarship could also serve important national and political agendas. Even in the face of death, Ringelblum hoped that his *Polish-Jewish Relations* might contribute to a better Poland after the war, and improve Polish-Jewish relations in the future.

On 7 March 1944 a Polish informer betrayed Ringelblum's hideout to the Gestapo. The Germans took all the Jews there to the Pawiak prison. Ringelblum and his son Uri sat in a separate cell with the other men. The late Yekhiel Hirschaut was a prisoner in Pawiak and wrote in his memoirs that as soon as the other Jewish prisoners learned that Ringelblum was in the death cell, they looked for ways to rescue him. They hatched a plan to attach Ringelblum to a work detail in the prison. Hirschaut sought out Ringelblum. Ringelblum told him how the Gestapo had just tried to torture information out of him. He was covered in black and blue marks, his son Uri sitting on his lap. Hirschaut outlined his plan: we can try to get you out of here. "And what about my wife and child?" Ringelblum asked. There was a long silence: Ringelblum understood and said that he could not leave his family. And he pointed to his son: "Vos iz er shuldik, der kleyner-tsulib im veytigt mir shtark dos harts" [why is the little one guilty? My heart is breaking because of him.] Hirschaut never saw Ringelblum again.[54] The Germans shot all the Jews they caught in the bunker as well as two of the Poles who helped them.

When searchers opened the first tin boxes of the archive that were retrieved in 1946, they found a testament written by Israel Lichtenstein, who had supervised the burial of the boxes in 1942. Lichtenstein concluded his stirring testimony with the following words: "We are the redeeming sacrifice for the Jewish People. I believe that the nation will survive. We the Jews of Eastern Europe are the redeemers of the People of Israel…"[55] At the very end of his life, he reaffirmed his belief in the future of the Jewish people. He did not see them as faceless victims but as a people, part of a living and resilient nation. This is an important legacy of the Oyneg Shabes archive.

If any one group of historians inherited Ringelblum's mantle and put wartime Jewish sources and archives at the front and center of their research it was what Dan Michman has called the "Israel School" of Holocaust historiography (in turn influenced by the Jerusalem School), strikingly similar to Ringelblum's approach.[56] This Israel school showed much more interest in studying the victims rather than the perpetrators, in researching ghettos rather than weighing in on the intentionalist-functionalist debate. Israeli historians continued where Jewish historians in postwar Poland left off, and their work included pioneering studies of individual ghettos, beginning with Yisrael Gutman on Warsaw and continuing over time with Michal Unger on Łódź, Sara Bender on Białystok, Yael Peled on Kraków, and others.[57] All of these studies remind us the critical importance of the wartime Jewish archives. It is doubtful that Yisrael Gutman could have written his book on the Warsaw Ghetto, for example, without the resources of the Oyneg Shabes archive. Dan Michman also reminds us that these historians saw "Jewish society as a living and active collective that must be studied with an eye on its social, economic and cultural aspects." Ringelblum would have put it exactly the same way.

Notes

1. Alexander Donat, *The Holocaust Kingdom* (New York, 1965), 211, quoted in Alvin Rosenfeld, *A Double Dying: Reflections on Holocaust Literature* (Bloomington, IN, 1980), 37–38.

2. The text of the letter can be found in Jacob Shatzky, ed., Emanuel Ringelblum, *Kapitlen geshikhte fun amolikn yidishn lebn in Poyln* (Buenos Aires, 1953), 545.

3. Adolf Berman Collection, Archive of Kibbutz Lohamei Ha'getaot, File 358, Letter of Emanuel Ringelblum to Adolf Berman, 1 March 1944. At the height of the Great Deportation from the Warsaw Ghetto, the Oyneg Shabes discussed the possibility that the archive might find its way to the YIVO after the war. See Abraham Lewin, *A Cup of Tears: A Diary of the Warsaw Ghetto* (New York, 1988), 141, entry of 29 July 1942.

4. Rachel Auerbach, "Vi azoy iz oysgegrobn gevorn der Ringelblum Arkhiv," *Arbeter Vort*, 27 June 1947.

5. The second cache was buried in aluminum milk cans, which preserved the documents much more effectively than the tin boxes of the first cache. It was only by accident that Polish construction workers happened upon the milk cans in December 1950 and handed them over to the Jewish Historical Institute in Warsaw. The third cache was buried under the premises of the brushmakers' shop on Swietojerska 34 shortly before the outbreak of the Ghetto Uprising. Later it became the site of the Chinese embassy in Poland. That cache was never found.

6. According to Tadeusz Epstein, who has prepared the most comprehensive catalogue of the archive, cache I contained 25,540 pages of material, cache II 9,829 pages. Cache II covered the period from August 1942 until February 1943. See Robert Moses Shapiro and Tadeusz Espstein, eds., *The Warsaw Ghetto Oyneg Shabbes-Ringelblum Archive: Catalogue and Guide* (Bloomington, IN, 2010).

7. Gustavo Corni, *Hitler's Ghettos: Voice from a Beleaguered Society, 1939-1944* (London, 2003).

8. For an excellent discussion of Borochov, whose intellectual legacy was in fact much more complicated that the Left Poalei Tsiyon believed, see Matityahu Mintz, *Naye tsaytn, naye lider* (Tel Aviv, 1993).

9. The definitive study of the Left Poalei Tsiyon in Poland is Bina Garncarska-Kadri, *Bihipusei derekh: Poalei Tsiyon Smol b'Polin ad milhemet ha'olam ha'shniya* (Tel Aviv, 1995).

10. For more on the *kasses* see Samuel D. Kassow, "Community and Identity in the Interwar Shtetl," in *The Jews of Poland between the Two World Wars*, ed. Yisrael Gutman, Ezra Mendelsohn, Jehuda Reinharz, and Chone Shmeruk (Hanover, NH, 1989), 216; also Yitzhak Giterman, "Gmiles khesed kasses in der itstiger shverer tsayt," *Folkshilf*, April 1936.

11. Sometime in late 1943 or early 1944 he wrote an essay on Yitzhak Giterman, who had been shot by the Germans in January 1943. In this essay Ringelblum devoted a great deal of attention to the *kasses* and to their significance. See Emanuel Ringelblum's journal, *Ksovim fun Geto* (Tel Aviv, 1985), vol. 2, 127.

12. Ibid.

13. Emanuel Ringelblum, "Zbanszyn," reprinted in Ringelblum, *Kapitlen geshikhte*, 500–501.

14. Indeed some scholars, such as Jacob Shatzky, believed that Ringelblum at times crossed the line that divided objective historical research from apologetics that tried too hard to score political points. For example Shatzky believed that Ringelblum exaggerated the pro-Polish stance of the Jewish masses in the Kosciuszko Uprising. See Jacob Shatzky, "Menakhem Ben Faivish Ringelblum," in Ringelblum, *Kapitlen Geshikhte*, xxxi.

15. On this circle, organized by Ringelblum in 1923, see Raphael Mahler, "Der krayz 'Yunger Historiker' in Varshe," in Mahler, *Historiker un Vegvayzer* (Tel Aviv, 1967), 303.

16. Lucjan Dobroszycki, "YIVO in Interwar Poland: Work in the Historical Sciences," in Gutman et al., *The Jews of Poland between the Two World Wars*, 496–97.

17. See Samuel Kassow, "The Jewish Landkentenish Society in Interwar Poland," in *Jewish Topographies: Visions of Space, Traditions of Place*, ed. Anna Lipphardt, Alexandra Nocke, and Julia Brauch (London, 2008).

18. See Raphael Mahler's introductory remarks to *Bleter far geshikhte* (1931); see also Ringelblum, "Fun der reaktsiye," *Landkentnish*, no. 1 (1933).

19. Emanuel Ringelblum, "Dos ineveynikste lebn fun varshever yidn fun der farkerter zayt," in *Kapitlen geshikhte*, 101

20. Meir Korzen, "Emanuel Ringelblum lifnei ha-milkhama u'biyameha harishonim," *Yediot Yad Va-shem*, n. 21–22 (1959).

21. Hersh Wasser, "The Ghetto Archives: The Enterprise of Doctor Emanuel Ringelblum," in *A Commemorative Symposium in Honor of Dr. Emanuel Ringelblum and his Oneg Shabbat Underground Archives* (Jerusalem, 1983), 35–43.

22. See for example Emanuel Ringelblum, "Dr. Y. Shiper un di virtshaftsgeshikhte fun di yidn in Poyln," *Vilner Tog*, n. 295 (1926). Here he points out that Borochov's analysis of the Jewish condition encouraged and required serious research into Jewish economic history. He also stressed the interrelationship of Jewish and non-Jewish history. One could not study Jews in isolation; one could not understand Jewish history unless one understood the general historical context in which they lived.

23. Emanuel Ringelblum, "Bleter far geshikhte," *Arbeter Tsaytung*, no. 45 (1934).

24. Emanuel Ringelblum, "Der YIVO un di yidishe arbetershaft," *Arbeter Tsaytung* (August 1931).

25. Dr. Nakhman Blumental, "Der historiker-tsu der ferter yortsayt," *Arbeter Tsaytung*, n. 3 (1948).

26. Letter of Emanuel Ringelblum to Adolf Berman, 24 January 1944, Adolf Berman Collection, Archive of Kibbutz Lohamei Ha'getaot.

27. Hersh Wasser asserted in 1954 that Ringelblum invited the Bund to participate in the Oyneg Shabes but met with a refusal. Nonetheless, Wasser continued, several Bundists worked in the archive as individuals. See Hersh Wasser, "Vi iz es geven?" *Unzer Veg*, March 1954. It is interesting to note that after the war, Bundists treated Ringelblum with hostility. In 1953 a harsh attack on Ringelblum appeared in the Bundist journal *Unzer Tsayt*. The writer, Y. Hart [Sholom Hertz] lambasted Ringelblum for being a "dictator" who abused his authority in the

disbursement of relief funds. See Y. Hart, "Vegn Ringelblum's notisn fun Varshever geto," *Unzer Tsayt,* no. 7-8 (1953); "Nisht di khronik fun di tragishe Varshever yidn," *Unzer Tsayt,* no. 9 (1953). One important member of the Oyneg Shabes archive was David Cholodenko, who was also a Bundist. His obituary, which appeared in *Doyres Bundistn,* totally ignored his collaboration with Ringelblum.

28. Emanuel Ringelblum, *Ksovim fun geto,* vol. 1, 335.
29. Ringelblum, *Ksovim fun geto,* vol. 1, 232.
30. Natan Ek, "Mit Emanuel Ringelblum in Varshever Geto," *Di Goldene Keyt,* no. 24 (1956).
31. Two of Ringelblum's most important mentors were Left Poalei Tsiyon leader Shakhne Zagan and Joint Director Yitzhak Giterman. Zagan was deported to Treblinka in 1942 and Giterman was shot in 1943.
32. Rachel Auerbach, *Varshever Tsvoes: bagegenish, akivtetn, goyroles, 1933-1943* (Tel Aviv, 1974), 63. Ringelblum also told her that "a decision had been made to employ as many of the Jewish intelligentsia as possible in the institutions of the (Aleynhilf)—to save the cadres."
33. Auerbach, *Vershever Tsvoes,* 42–52.
34. See Hirsh Vasser, "*A Vort vegn Ringelblum Arkhiv,*" 3, YIVO Institute for Jewish Research Archives [hereafter YIVO Archives].
35. Rachel Auerbach, *Varshever Tsvoes,* 9.
36. Emanuel Ringelblum, *Ksovim fun Geto,* vol. 2, 88.
37. Ringelblum, *Ksovim fun geto,* vol. 2, 83.
38. Ringelblum, *Ksovim fun geto,* vol. 2, 84.
39. Ringelblum, *Ksovim fun geto,* vol. 2, 76–102.
40. Archiwum Ringelbluma, Jewish Historical Institute Warsaw, [hereafter AR I], 49, 3 [I follow the system used by the Jewish Historical Institute. AR I refers to the first part of the archive found in 1946 and AR II refers to the second part. The file number is 49, followed by the page number].
41. Lewin, *A Cup of Tears,* 141, entry of 29 July 1942.
42. For example, in a diary entry of 23 March 1941 Ringelblum noted with approval an increase of interest in Yiddish in the ghetto.
43. See Yehuda Bauer, "Jewish Leadership Reactions to Nazi Policies," in *The Holocaust as Historical Experience,* ed. Yehuda Bauer and Nathan Rotenstreich (New York, 1981), 173–89.
44. Ringelblum, *Ksovim fun Geto,* vol. 1, 365, entry of 26 May 1942.
45. See for example Israel Lichtenstein's outburst against Ringelblum at the end of July 1942 in AR I, Pt. 1, n. 1190.
46. See Ruta Sakowska, "Archiwum Ringelbluma-Ogniwem Konspiracji Warszawskiego Ghetta," *Biuletyn Żydowskiego Instytutu Historycznego* [hereafter *BZIH*], n. 152 (1989), n. 153 (1990), n. 155–156 (1990): 189–219; "Two Forms of Resistance in the Warsaw Ghetto—Two Functions of the Ringelblum Archives," *Yad Vashem Studies,* 21 (1991); Walter Laqueur, *The Terrible Secret: Suppression of the Truth About Hitler's "Final Solution"* (Boston, 1980).
47. AR II, 299, "A mensh iz antlofn fun Treblinke." This is Krzepicki's account as written down by Auerbach. On "Szlamek," the escapee from Chełmno, see Ruta Sakowska, "Szlamek-ucieknier z osrodka zaglady w Chełmnie nad Nerem," in *BZIH,* n. 131–132 (1984).
48. As translated in Joseph Kermish, ed., *To Live with Honor and Die with Honor: Selected Documents from the Warsaw Ghetto Underground Archives "O.S.",* (Jerusalem, 1986), 704.
49. Hersh Wasser recalled that Ringelblum once said that, "I do not regard the archive as a separate project, as a matter only of Jews, for Jews and by Jews. My whole being revolts against that concept. As a Jew, as a historian and as a socialist, I can't agree with such an approach. In the whole complexity of social processes, where everything is interdependent, it is impossible to shut ourselves off in our narrow world. Jewish pain and Jewish liberation is part of a [wider story]." See Hersh Wasser, "A Vort vegn Ringelblum Arkhiv," 15–16, YIVO Archives.
50. At the end of 1942 Ringelblum noted that one of the first questions that Poles asked fleeing Jews on the Aryan side was why they did not resist. Ringelblum, *Ksovim fun geto,* vol. 2, 401.

51. Basia Berman, "Rydzewski: Ringelblum oyf der Arisher Zayt," in *Linke Poalei Tsiyon*, 19 April 1948.

52. See Emanuel Ringelblum, *Polish-Jewish Relations during the Second World War*, ed. Joseph Kermish and Shmuel Krakowski (New York, 1974).

53. Ringelblum, *Polish-Jewish Relations*, 247. As we have seen, Ringelblum had a tendency to label as "fascist" anyone whom he saw as an opponent of the progressive left. In 1934, he also called the Jewish bourgeoisie "fascist."

54. Yekhiel Hirschaut, *Finstere nekht in Paviak* (Buenos Aires, 1948), 199.

55. AR, I, 1190.

56. Dan Michman, "Is there an 'Israeli School' of Holocaust Research?" in *Holocaust Historiography in Context: Emergence, Challenges. Polemics and Achievements*, ed. David Bankier and Dan Michman (Jerusalem, 2008), 37–67.

57. Michal Unger, *Lodz: The Last Ghetto in Poland* [Hebrew] (Jerusalem, 2005); Sara Bender, *The Jews of Białystok during World War Two and the Holocaust* (Hanover, NH, 2008); Yael Peled, *Jewish Krakow, 1939-193: Resistance, Underground, Struggle* [Hebrew] (Lohamei Hagetta'ot, 1993).

CHAPTER 10

Integrating Self-Help into the History of Jewish Survival in Western Europe

Bob Moore

The role of Jewish self-help in countering Nazi persecution has generally been marginalized in accounts of righteous (gentile) rescue attempts, or treated in isolation as part of the "Jewish" resistance to Nazism. These two disparate strands of analysis and interpretation of Jewish survival, at least in Western Europe, fail to acknowledge the importance of the relationships and connections between Jewish and non-Jewish actors in this process.[1] By looking at specific case studies taken from Belgium and France, this chapter will seek to demonstrate how pre-existing contact between Jewish and non-Jewish individuals and organizations, and their continued cooperation during the occupation period, served to play a positive and possibly crucial role in Jewish survival when compared with countries like the Netherlands where this cooperation was far less evident or entirely nonexistent. Although by no means an exclusive categorization, these contacts can perhaps best be examined within a series of general headings: community, organizational, religious, and underworld.

Community Connections

Making any objective assessment of the position of Jews within specific local communities is fraught with difficulties and makes national or even civic generalizations impossible. Objective conditions could vary between neighborhoods and even between streets. Moreover, the chances of reconstructing these relationships through historical sociology have probably been lost. Nev-

Notes for this section begin on page 206.

ertheless, it is possible to demonstrate trends in particular neighborhoods that were unusual and served to help Jews resident there during the occupation. These factors might include communities where (working-)class solidarity was more important than religious or racial differences, or where patterns of social intercourse also had little to do with those divisions. Perhaps more contentious is the thought that the very layout and structure of the housing involved would affect the ways in which people would interact with each other—the closer the contact, the more approachable neighbors would become in times of crisis.

In examining organized Jewish self-help, it is important not to lose sight of the actions of individuals in attempting to safeguard themselves and their families. In both France and Belgium, many Jews who attempted to hide themselves started by making individual personal arrangements with gentiles. Such arrangements were to a degree dependent on previous relationships between Jews and non-Jews in particular neighborhoods, workplaces, or in schools. Perhaps inevitably, these are the most difficult to quantify, and conclusions about integration and assimilation in particular locations can only be of a generalized nature. Nevertheless, one could point to the contrasts between Brussels and Antwerp, where there were ostensibly closer relationships between Jews and non-Jews in certain districts of the former that facilitated requests for help when the deportations began. Likewise the eleventh arrondissement in Paris seems to have been a community where pre-existing connections and working-class solidarity facilitated gentile help for Jews under threat.

A different form of self-help can be seen in the behavior of the Parisian middle classes. During the exodus of June 1940 in France, many Jewish families fled Paris with their children. Substantial numbers returned after the signing of the armistice but there were many that chose, and had the resources, to stay away; either in what became the Vichy zone or even in the countryside of the German-occupied zones. Even at this point, some parents who had returned to Paris thought about making some more permanent provisions for their offspring. There were strong traditions of children being sent into the countryside during the summer holidays and it was only natural to adapt these prewar arrangements to provide a sanctuary for them at a time of crisis. The same patterns can be seen in Belgium where, for example, Beatrice Meschman recalls her father taking the family to stay in rural Ottignes for the summer holidays, and then converting the arrangement into a permanent one for his children.[2] There were also examples of entire families moving from their city addresses and establishing themselves in rural communities or in hotels where they were left in peace by the local authorities for the duration of the occupation. As French Jews were never sought by the authorities in the same way as their foreign counterparts, many were ostensibly able to disappear and thus to survive the occupation in relative safety. While such private arrangements were only really available to the middle classes, people in the poorer districts could sometimes benefit as well. Charities operating in the cities ran "vacation colonies" where children could spend time in the fresh air of the countryside, and these arrangements sometimes led to children being removed for extended periods.

Political affiliations could also merge with communal relationships, especially in working-class districts. Jews could be found as adherents to a wide range of nonconfessional political parties from the nineteenth century onward. While liberalism allowed them to retain allegiance to their faith, those who espoused social democracy, anarchism, or later communism generally rejected religion in favor of a secularist ideology. Party affiliations provided a potential source of contacts for those under threat, but it was the Communist and far-left groups that had the greatest experience of clandestine activity before the outbreak of war and which therefore had the biggest advantages, but also ran much higher risks of discovery—by both the indigenous authorities and later by the occupying Germans. Secrecy and cell organization had been integral to the work of the Communist International Red Help and other left-wing welfare organizations from the 1920s onward. All were involved in helping comrades from Nazi Germany and Fascist Italy who had fled abroad to escape persecution, but also used their economic power to make sure that they continued to work for the cause—whether in Spain or later against the Nazis closer to home. These organizations therefore provided a defensive cloak against the attentions of the local police and security services, but also formed the basis for later active and armed resistance in both France and Belgium. While this tendency was supposedly atheistic and unaffected by religious or racial distinctions, the fact that identifiable (and exclusively) Jewish resistance groups emerged during the occupation suggests that these divisions continued to play some role even in left-wing circles.

Organizational Connections

Perhaps the best example of Jewish and non-Jewish groups working together across a broad political spectrum can be seen in the Belgian Comité de Défense des Juifs (CDJ). Established in September 1942 as a national organization to help Jews threatened by Nazi policies and to oppose the collaboration of the Association des Juifs de Belgique (AJB), created by Germans in 1941, the CDJ originated among members of the Independence Front (FI).[3] The FI was a broadly based resistance movement founded on 15 March 1941 by the journalist Fernand Demany, who brought together leaders from a broad spectrum of political and welfare organizations.[4] These included the Communist Main d'Oeuvre Étrangère (MOE), a long-standing immigrant welfare organization, and Solidarité Juive, which had been created in 1939 specifically to help Jewish political refugees from Poland.[5] Their involvement was crucial given that 95 percent of the Jews in Belgium were relatively recent immigrants from Eastern Europe who had not become Belgian citizens. Although branches of the CDJ seem to have emerged more or less simultaneously in five major cities when the first deportations began in July 1942, its leadership was centered in Brussels.[6] Yet even before this, both the FI and the Belgian Communist Party had been instrumental in warning the Jewish population about the potential dangers they faced.[7]

The CDJ leaders ultimately represented a broad cross-section of the Jewish community and political opinions—and also demonstrated a degree of cooperation with non-Jewish groups and individuals. Pre-eminent was Hertz (Joseph/Ghert) Jospa, a Communist activist of Romanian/Bessarabian origins whose wife, Yvonne, also played a key role in the organization. He was joined in Brussels by the left-wing Catholic Emile Hambresin who had been editor of the periodical *L'Avant Garde* and president of the Comité Belge contre le Racisme. Both were engineers by profession and had come into contact in the 1930s as members of the Ligue pour combattre l'Antisémitisme.[8] Other leaders included Abusz Werber of Poale Zion and Israël Mandelbaum of Solidarité Juive. To bring bourgeois middle-class Jewish elements into the organization, Chaïm Perelman, professor in the faculty of philosophy and letters at the Free University in Brussels, was coopted, and some of the first meetings were held at his house.[9] There were also other representatives from "legal" Jewry; the industrialist Benjamin (Benno) Nykerk and the secretary of the Brussels Jewish community, Edouard Rotkel,[10] both of whom were associated with mainstream Zionism, and Eugene Hellendael, another rich industrialist, who was invited to join in his capacity as a member of the Brussels branch of the AJB.[11] Although bourgeois representatives in the CDJ did express some qualms about working with Communists like Jospa, they seemed prepared to stifle these reservations in order to create an organization that would benefit the community as a whole.[12]

As the CDJ established itself, it developed four subsections: propaganda, finance, false papers, and material aid.[13] Its propaganda initiatives were mainly directed against the AJB, advising Jews to ignore its directives and to resist German measures. These efforts included a thriving underground press comprising illegal newspapers in French, Flemish, and Yiddish with print runs of between one thousand and five thousand copies.[14] They also included individual contacts between Jews and non-Jews in various professions and through links with the FI.[15] The degree of cooperation between organizations is remarkable when compared with circumstances elsewhere in Western Europe. The fact that the CDJ became directly involved in helping 12,000 adults and a further 3,000 children (of whom 2,443 were supported financially), and instrumental in indirectly assisting perhaps another 15,000 people, testifies to the sheer scale of its operations. The CDJ used at least 138 separate secular or religious institutions and at least 700 individual families to hide the children, the vast majority in Brussels or Wallonia.[16]

Operations on this scale required huge amounts of resources and money—not least in providing monthly subventions to families and institutions to feed and clothe the children. Food parcels came from the Red Cross and even from the German-inspired Secours d'Hiver (Winter Help). The latter was expedited by Roger van Praag, a Jewish civil servant who had returned from military service and been offered a job working for the Secours d'Hiver as an alternative to working directly with the Germans. Van Praag had managed to hide his Jewish origin, avoid registration, and also to falsify an "Aryan" background for his family.[17] Practical help also came from groups across the political spectrum, including the general Sociétés de Secours Mutuels and the Secours Populaire, as well as the Jewish Secours Sioniste and the aforementioned Solidarité Juive. This cooperation was aided by pre-existing links and the personal contacts between welfare workers and administrators working for these agencies. One very good example of this can be seen in the section of the CDJ devoted to helping children. Created and run by Maurice Heiber (Héber), it benefited from close cooperation with the Oeuvre Nationale de l'Enfance (ONE), led by Yvonne Nèvejean, which had direct links with institutions run by the Catholic Church.[18]

Finding the money to finance the CDJ was inevitably difficult, but here again, the links to non-Jewish organizations undoubtedly aided its cause. Although it began fundraising by appealing to rich Jews for donations and by making richer Jews pay double for CDJ services in order to subsidize the rescue of poorer Jews, the CDJ could not meet all of its financial obligations and had to raise funds outside the community. Some money came from welfare agencies such as ONE, but the expansion of CDJ activities in sheltering those underground needed ever-larger infusions of capital. To solve this potentially intractable problem, Benno Nykerk was able to persuade the Banque de Bruxelles to provide a *prêt d'honneur* (unsecured loan) for the sum of BFr 3 million in installments of BFr 250,000, and in May 1943 he traveled illegally to Switzerland for the first time to meet Saly Mayer, the American Jewish Joint Distribution Committee (JDC) representative for Europe in Switzerland. Mayer guaranteed a monthly subvention of SFr 20,000, raised progressively to SFr 100,000 per month, which was then smuggled into Belgium. The Save the Children Fund provided two subventions of BFr 500,000.[19] Individuals were known to have contributed by offering letters of credit, but BFr 5,000,000 came directly from the Société Belge de Banque and BFr 1,100,000 from the Société Générale.[20] These were huge sums, but had to be set against the scale of CDJ operations where the total expenditure during the occupation was estimated to have reached BFr 48 million.[21] This whole process seems to have been expedited by the contacts between the well-known Jewish businessmen within the CDJ and the wider business and finance community.

As a result of its cosmopolitan origins, the CDJ was able to cooperate with non-Jewish organizations to find addresses and hiding places for around twelve thousand adults, amounting to almost a quarter of the entire Jewish population. Catholic institutions and welfare organizations had been used extensively for the placement of children, but this was not possible when it came to adult Jews. Placing more than one or two fugitives in convents or cloisters was seen as dangerous. If one group was discovered by Gestapo raids, all other similar institutions would then immediately become suspect, thus jeopardizing others, including many children.[22] Hiding could also be expedited through the use of false papers made out with addresses where the individual was not known and had not previously been registered as a Jew. To expedite this, the CDJ was able to call on help from the FI and sympathetic local officials who incorporated these false identities into existing population records.[23]

Indeed, the integration of a broad-based Jewish self-help organization with wider resistance movements and elements within the civil service and the Catholic Church may provide the explanation as to how so many adult Jews survived in Belgium. While some were in hiding "underground," many others managed to survive by living false lives more or less in the open, while at the same time limiting their movements to reduce the risk of scrutiny of their identity documents. In total, the CDJ may have helped as many as thirty thousand individuals, encompassing not only the Jews in Belgium, but also those passing through the country and several thousand labor draft evaders. While its work did include finding hiding places through its contacts with other institutions and organizations across the country, it is clear that in many cases, "rescue" did not involve non-Jewish rescuers at all, but depended on Jews hiding independently behind false identities.

The example of the CDJ, while unique in some respects, demonstrates the importance of the role of independent immigrant welfare organizations and their connections with the (left-wing) political world in providing the basis for an organized response to Nazi persecution after the occupation began. These pre-existing welfare and political links also formed the basis for practical cooperation between Jewish and non-Jewish agencies at the point when the deportations commenced. Thus Jewish social workers already had close contacts with their non-Jewish compatriots, and there were also existing links through these networks to Catholic charities and institutions. Although set up in opposition, some CDJ leaders continued their roles at the AJB as a means of gaining information, cloaking their own activities and subverting the latter's operations. This allowed the CDJ to act as an alternative focus and source of help and information for endangered Jews in ways that were not replicated elsewhere in Western Europe.

While not having all the same attributes as the CDJ, its French equivalent, the Rue Amelot Committee in Paris also benefited from its connections with non-Jewish individuals and organizations. Its origins were entirely Jewish and its leaders were drawn primarily from the ranks of the Russian and Polish immigrant community and its welfare agencies. Its three most prominent leaders had all been politically active long before they arrived in France. Maître Léo Glaeser had fled from Russia after the 1905 revolution; Yéhuda Jacoubovitch was a Bundist from Poland who had been jailed for his opposition to Tsarism and who arrived in France in 1913; and David Rapoport had been involved in both the 1905 and 1917 uprisings before coming to France in 1920.[24] Their reformist left-wing backgrounds did not automatically make them amenable to cooperation with the Communists, and there were inevitable objections from both the Bundists and the right wing of Poale Zion. Moreover, there was also a strong feeling that working with the Communists would merely make the Amelot Committee more susceptible to greater surveillance by the security services. In this respect at least, there were differences to the construction and organization of the CDJ.

More comparable with Belgium was the relationship between the Amelot Committee and the officially sanctioned representative Jewish organizations. The Union Générale des Israélites de France (UGIF) had been created at the behest of the German and Vichy authorities in November 1941 as a national organization to represent the Jews in their dealings with state and occupation institutions. Many French Jews were reassured by its existence—and especially if they themselves enjoyed its protection from internment or deportation.[25] By contrast, most non-French Jews had already drawn their own conclusions about the UGIF, even if they continued to rely on it for welfare, and the Zionists and the Éclaireurs Israélites de France, a Jewish Scout Movement also expressed their disquiet at UGIF policies.[26] Despite this widespread distrust, the very existence of the UGIF did provide some benefits in shielding the activities of Amelot workers who had some protection through association with UGIF-Nord, which worked in the German-occupied zone. Thus after the introduction of the yellow star and the beginnings of the roundups in July 1942, the Amelot Committee was able to identify and rescue Jewish children left abandoned by the arrest of their parents, and its leadership benefited from having the identity cards issued to UGIF personnel that protected them from arrest.

Important here is that open and clandestine Jewish organizations, while suspicious of each other, were even more suspicious of both the Vichy authorities and the Germans, and acted as an essential counterweight to collaborationist agenda forced on the UGIF. Equally important were the links that these groups had to international Jewish charities, primarily the JDC, and to other Christian groups such as the Quakers, YMCA, and the Comité Inter-Mouvements Auprès d'Evacués (CIMADE), links that had been forged in welfare work for evacuees and foreign Jews in the camps in the southern zone.²⁷ Some of these activities had originated in relief work for refugees from the Spanish Civil War, but had come to include large numbers of Jews when the French state chose to intern enemy aliens after the outbreak of a European war in September 1939. While internment was undoubtedly detrimental to the Jewish refugees in the short term, the collaborative relief work begun in this period was to provide well-established contacts with non-Jewish welfare networks even before the fall of France and the beginnings of the deportations.

The Rue Amelot Committee moved toward illegality only slowly, and its relations with the Jewish Communist organization Main-d'Oeuvre Immigrée (MOI) and its Solidarité organization remained fraught, but all were all heavily involved in welfare relief for a Jewish population that was being increasingly subject to economic and social marginalization. When the UGIF was given advance warning of the planned deportations in July 1942, its leaders saw no reason to spread panic by disseminating the information and only belatedly warned the Amelot Committee on 13 July.²⁸ In response, the Committee, with no time and no legitimate means of publishing, used word-of-mouth to spread the word while Solidarité managed to issue a single tract that reached sections of the immigrant community. Until the summer of 1942, Solidarité and the Amelot Committee had assumed that anti-Jewish actions were only of concern to the Jews themselves, but after the major raids in Paris on 16 and 17 July, they began to look for more outside help. The Communist-oriented Mouvement Nationale Contre le Racisme (MNCR) reacted to the first deportations by identifying two hundred Catholic and Protestant institutions likely to hide Jews, and the Amelot Committee began widening its contacts with non-Jewish welfare organizations.²⁹

The Amelot Committee thus became an integral part of the underground communal response to the plight of the immigrant and refugee Jews in France, although it remained a legal organization and attempted to tread a path that involved cooperation both with the Jewish Consistory and UGIF on the one hand and the Communists on the other. Its primary problem had always been to obtain the funds necessary to maintain its welfare work. Once the initial shock of the German invasion had subsided, the return of some Jewish businessmen to Paris meant that some funds were forthcoming. In addition, the, Comité de Bienfaisance offered some support, and the Oeuvre des Secours aux Enfants (OSE) began to receive funds from the Vichy zone.³⁰ However, with costs continuing to rise, an envoy was sent to the unoccupied zone where the JDC representative in Marseilles, Herbert Katzki, provided a monthly subvention and the Quakers were used as intermediaries to convey the funds to Paris.³¹ In this way, the Amelot Committee functioned in a kind of semi-legality, merely ignoring most Vichy anti-Jewish legislation, and by the autumn of 1940, it was regularly supporting at least 1,125 families, a number that continued to increase as "Aryanization" closed down businesses and forced many Jews into unemployment.[32] It remained under constant German and French surveillance until 1 June 1943 when its dynamic leader, David Rapoport, was arrested and the whole organization dissolved by the authorities soon afterward.[33]

Responsibility for those previously looked after by the Amelot Committee fell to the UGIF, which soon saw the advantages of reconstituting many of the committee's legal activities, albeit under new leadership. Thus the illegal work of placing and supporting children in hiding had a means to continue. Instead of using the Rue Amelot clinic as a coordination point, parents were put in touch with social workers who expedited hiding places in the city and its suburbs with the finances provided by sympathetic local government officials. Placements outside the city had been taken over by non-Jewish organizations after the Committee had been dissolved, but its payment of foster parents and the work of finding material aid for families underground had to be rebuilt, using non-Jewish helpers as go-betweens.[34]

Although not as striking as the Belgian example, the history of the Rue Amelot Committee further demonstrates the importance of the linkages between Jewish and non-Jewish groups as a part of the contacts and cooperation between medical and welfare groups in Paris. Thus when the deportations began, the Jewish organizations had partners whom they could trust to engage in the work of sheltering and supporting Jews—and especially Jewish children—in hiding. Moreover, their profile in particular parts of the city also provided important contacts with the local authorities and individual civil servants who could be trusted to help with material aid when the time came.

A different form of organizational contact can be seen in the work done by non-Jewish groups that specialized in migrant and refugee relief. For example, the Service Social International d'Aide aux Emigrants (SSAE) had sent social workers into French internment camps to help the refugee families from 1939 onward, and had worked to effect releases whenever possible. Its finances came from rich individuals and from large companies, and it also benefited from contacts in the United States that remained able to send funds to France until the end of 1941.[35] As an organization officially recognized by the state, the SSAE had to tread carefully, but it was able to use its formal status as a useful cloak for the clandestine elements of its activities. This was embodied in the l'Entraide Temporaire. Established to aid refugees at the outset of the war, it was reactivated in February 1941 by one of its founders, Denise Milhaud, in response to the application of antisemitic laws to foreign Jews whom she knew.[36] She and her co-workers concentrated on helping Jewish artists and workers who had lost their nationality as a result of their countries' being removed from the map, such as Czechs and Poles. But their work also included non-Jews. The organization was ostensibly part of the Red Cross, but this was merely a camouflage. In 1942, both Denise Milhaud and her doctor husband Fred became employees of the

UGIF, which gave them access to the UGIF children's homes and clinics in the occupied zone.[37] In these cases, the Jewish and other beneficiaries seem to have been no more than passive recipients of aid, but there seems little doubt that the cooperation between welfare organizations in this period meant that both had links to Jewish organizations operating in the same areas. Of critical importance here is the existence of independent organizations devoted to migrant and refugee relief, which could continue and adapt their work once the occupation began.

Religious Connections

Although often mistrusted by the Jewish community, Catholic missions that proselytized to Jews nonetheless formed a gateway to harnessing the wider institutional power of the church, both spiritual and temporal.[38] For example, the Couvent des Péres de Notre-Dame de Sion, led by Théomir Devaux, had been a center for ecumenical discussion.[39] Devaux's reputation made it a target for the Gestapo but in spite of this he became ever more involved in helping both Jewish adults and children. As early as 1941, he was finding false papers and hiding places for those in danger.[40] As a churchman of repute, he was able to use his contacts within the church to place children in religious institutions across the country or with peasant families.

Devaux and other clerics motivated to help often had clear anti-Nazi credentials or had a history of ecumenical contact with the Jewish community and/or with other Christian and welfare groups. They were able to harness Catholic religious and secular institutions to help in the work of sheltering and supporting Jewish fugitives, both in the capital and in the provinces. Their mobilization in many cases predated the major roundups of July 1942 and shows how the early raids in Paris acted merely as a catalyst for further and more concerted action. Later, certain Catholic institutions in France became involved primarily at the prompting of ecclesiastical superiors such as Cardinal Archbishop Pierre-Marie Gerlier of Lyon, but it was these pre-existing and autonomous contacts that had the most immediate impact during the summer of 1942.

Perhaps the best example of all these factors working in tandem comes from Belgium. It seems that Catholic priests in those Brussels districts that had higher than average Jewish populations, such as Schaerbeek and Anderlecht, responded to direct requests for help or were recruited by members of the CDJ to help in the work of rescue. Some had been involved in missions to convert the Jews before the war while others were approached simply because of their leading position within the local community. Their influence could also help in recruiting the assistance of sympathetic local civil servants who could acquire papers and falsify records. Away from Brussels, there were other centers of activity: in Namur, led by Father Joseph André, and in Leuven where Father Bruno Reynders was instrumental in hiding many Jewish children. In all these cases, it seems that the actions taken were done with the tacit approval of their ecclesiastical superiors, including Cardinal Archbishop Jozef Ernst van Roey of Mechelin. Most pertinent in this context is the organization of rescue in Liège. Here, it was the personal contact and friendship between the Catholic bishop, Monsignor Louis-Joseph Kerkhofs, and Rabbi Joseph Lepkifker that led to the latter being sheltered in the bishop's palace under an assumed identity. His wife and son were sheltered in a Catholic institution run by the bishop's niece. Kerkhofs seems to have had no compunction in harnessing other Catholic institutions to help hide Jews and was recorded as encouraging his subordinates to share in the work. One recalled a meeting where the bishop "desired that his priests should know how much pride he had in those who risked their life to save the lives of others."[41]

Kerkhofs was also able to recruit secular helpers who had good resistance credentials. Thus he approached the practical, devout, and committed Catholic local lawyer, Albert van den Berg, and the two were instrumental in creating a network that would ultimately save several hundred Jewish children as well as some adults. His choice of van den Berg also highlights another important factor, namely, the pre-existing traditions of resistance—in this case not to state authority, which might have been a motivating force for others—but specifically against the idea of German rule. Van den Berg himself had served in World War I as a soldier, but many members of his immediate family had been involved in resistance, including in Walthère Dewé's famous network, La Dame Blanche. Thus it was no surprise to find that van den Berg became associated at some level with Dewé's World War II network, Clarence, at an early stage. Van den Berg was perhaps uniquely placed to be the secular head of a rescue network. He had contacts with the business community throughout the city and also sat on the governing boards of many local institutions and welfare organizations.[42] The fact that the local rabbi had placed his trust—and the lives of his wife and son—in the hands of the local bishop undoubtedly made it easier for other Jews in the city to do likewise.

Making sense of the precise roles in creating and running such rescue networks creates a problem for the historian because of the diffuse and sometimes incomplete nature of the sources. Disaggregating the role of individual Jews and their various community organizations from the part played by secular gentile groups and the Christian churches is fraught with difficulties. Testimonies to support claims for Yad Vashem's "Righteous among the Nations" tend to accentuate the roles of the non-Jews—as do many of the texts that focus on the work of the churches in aiding Jews in hiding, where the latter tend to be portrayed as passive recipients of help. Conversely, the few institutional records and histories of Jewish organizations tend to highlight the instances of self-help, something that is also true of the summary descriptions of the work of the CDJ. Thus identifying the prime movers in asking for, or volunteering, rescue opportunities depends to some extent on the source being used. However, this methodological problem should not detract from the overall conclusion that the propinquity of Jews and non-Jews in particular localities directly affected their abilities to work together at an early stage in the occupation and to mount a more effective collective response when the deportations began.

Before leaving the links between the Christian churches and the Jews, it is worth reflecting on the apparently disproportionate role in rescue played by the Protestant minorities in these overwhelmingly Catholic countries. The nonconformists in Brussels were involved in providing baptismal and confirmation certificates as well as hiding places for Jewish children, but this seems to have been largely at the behest of the CDJ.[43] In France, there appears to have been a mixture of responses. Pastor Henri Roser in Aubervilliers had a number of Jewish friends whom he helped shelter with food and false papers. Pastor Paul Vergara ran a center for nonviolent resistance in Paris and mobilized his parishioners to help find false papers. Likewise his more famous counterpart, André Trocmé from Le Chambon-sur-Lignon, went out of his way to offer help via the Quakers, an offer that led to the mobilization of his entire community. These latter examples also highlight another feature of "religious" rescue in Western Europe, namely, the crucial role of church leaders in motivating much larger numbers of believers.

Underworld Connections

In attempting to escape from the Nazis, many upright and law-abiding Jews were forced to seek out contacts in the underworld that could provide false papers, ration cards, or addresses—indeed anything that might help survival underground. Those trying to escape to neutral territory were also more than likely to need the services of professional *passeurs* to cross the well-guarded frontiers. Those who were caught were often brought before the courts and then identified as Jews. They would then be sentenced, but in most cases sent directly to transit camps as punishment cases. However, it is also important to recognize that not all the Jews were upstanding members of the community and that some could also be found among the criminal classes. Their healthy aversion to the police and the legal system in general could hold some advantages when the persecution began in earnest.

For example, Daniel Meyerson was a Dutch Catholic convert from Amsterdam resident in Brussels with his Jewish wife who was arrested in November 1940 for stealing military supplies and foodstuffs (with the assistance of some

German soldiers). His judicial record shows that he had no previous convictions but he was given a five-year sentence. His wife was given a two-year sentence and had returned to Brussels by May 1944 when she was informed of her husband's death in custody in an ordinary German jail. Ostensibly, their Jewish origins had not been discovered by their jailers and they had both remained in civil prisons throughout.[44] Even cases brought to the German military courts in Brussels could involve groups of defendants, some of whom were ostensibly Jewish, but who were nonetheless sentenced to civil detention and not handed over to the Gestapo or SS.

An even more colorful and remarkable story was that of Israel Steinberg, whose criminal record as a pickpocket began in 1930 when he was arrested by the Viennese police. He was subsequently prosecuted in Kraków, Halle, Brunn, and finally Brussels in 1937—all for the same type of crime. Expelled from Belgium, he was again apprehended by the Viennese police in 1938 and by the Brussels police in 1939. He was subsequently escorted to the border for a second time, but reappeared almost immediately in Liège where he was again apprehended committing a crime. As an archetypal undesirable alien, he should have been deported, but because war had now broken out he was instead sentenced to ten months in prison.

Steinberg's sentence was unfinished when Belgium was occupied, but, classed as an enemy alien, he was moved to an internment camp. At some later stage, the Sicherheitsdienst (SD) must have identified him as a Jew because he was moved to KZ Breendonk and then in February 1943 to the Dossin Barracks in Mechelen where he was included on the twentieth transport to the East on 19 April 1943. As is well known, this transport was halted by the Belgian resistance and Steinberg was one of those who managed to escape and make his way back to Brussels.[45] Living under the alias of Alberto Ferrari, he nevertheless found it impossible to give up his chosen "profession" and he was again arrested for pickpocketing by the Belgian authorities in June and November 1943. He was then sentenced to six months in jail for various offenses and in this way survived to the liberation without ever leaving Belgium.[46]

However, this unlikely survivor failed to mend his ways. Released in 1946 and supposedly repatriated to Vilna where he had claimed to have left a wife and five children, he continued to attract the attention of the Belgian police and was convicted by Belgian courts again in 1954 and 1956, after which he disappeared from the judicial records altogether. By this stage he was reputedly seventy-six years old. From the myriad stories of rescue it is evident that many Jews who survived and escaped the clutches of the Nazis owed their survival in part or in full to the activities of the criminal classes. However, it is also the case that some Jews were themselves long-standing members of those classes and, thanks to the strange workings of the judicial system, could perversely find that their arrest and convictions saved them from deportation.

As suggested in the introduction, this is by no means an exhaustive or even a comprehensive survey of all the interrelationships between Jewish and non-Jewish individuals and agencies during the Nazi occupation of Western Europe. What it does seek to highlight is where particular types of contact and attitudes made a positive contribution to the possibilities of hiding and rescue. The question of neighborhood relations is by far the most nebulous and difficult to portray, yet some localities were clearly more conducive to the provision of aid to their Jewish residents than others. In organizational terms, the existence of Jewish migrant welfare groups from the prewar period that could continue their activities after the occupation began was a crucial benefit in countering the influence of the AJB and UGIF. As their work had always involved collaboration with other state and private welfare agencies, it proved to be of enormous value when more concerted action was required. Likewise these contacts also extended to religious organizations engaged in welfare activities and included the harnessing, but not necessarily approval, of church missions to proselytize to Jews. As both the French and especially the Belgian examples demonstrate, the links between leading churchmen and rabbis could and did prompt extensive rescue operations in specific localities. Thus to give the most accurate picture of how Jewish survival was expedited, these examples of cooperation between Jewish self-help and non-Jewish rescue activities need to be built back into the wider history of rescue in the Holocaust period.

Notes

1. This point has been stressed most recently by Renée Poznanski, "Rescue of Jews and the Resistance in France: From History to Historiography," *French Politics, Culture and Society* 30, n. 2 (2012): 8–32.

2. Beatrice Meschman, *Never To Be Forgotten: A Young Girl's Holocaust Memoir* (Hoboken, NJ, 1997), 69, 78.

3. Front de l'Independence (French); Onafhankelijkheidsfront (Flemish).

4. Centre d'Etudes et de Documentation Guerres et Sociétés Contemporaines, Brussels, (hereafter CEGES-SOMA), AB2167 René De Lathower, *Comité de Defense des Juifs*, Introduction. He records that many of the records of CDJ activities remained in private hands or had been lost in the postwar era. Lucien Steinberg, *Le Comité de Défense des Juifs en Belgique, 1942-1944* (Brussels, 1973), 36.

5. CEGES-SOMA Directie-Generaal Oorlogslachtoffers (DGO) R123 232.159 *8 Ans au Service du Peuple,* 4; Maxime Steinberg, *L'Étoile et le Fusil. Part II: 1942, Les cent jours de la déportation des Juifs de Belgique* (Brussels, 1984), 60–61.

6. Steinberg, *Le Comité de Défense des Juifs,* 39; CEGES-SOMA AB2167 De Lathower, *Comité de Defense des Juifs,* 2; Lieven Saerens, "Die Hilfe für Juden in Belgien," in *Solidarität und Hilfe für Juden während der NS-Zeit,* ed. Wolfgang Benz and Juliane Wetzel, vol. 2 (Berlin, 1998), 250.

7. José Gotovitch, "Resistance Movements and the 'Jewish Question,'" in *Belgium and the Holocaust: Jews Belgians Germans,* ed. Dan Michman (Jerusalem, 1998), 281–82. Communist views on Jews were equivocal with the "poor deported Jews" being contrasted with the "spared Israelite capitalists."

8. Maxime Steinberg, *L'Etiole et le Fusil. Part III: La Traque des Juifs,* 2 vols. (Brussels, 1987), vol. 1, 66; Lieven Saerens, *Vreemdelingen in een Wereldstad: Een geschiedenis van Antwerpen en zijn joodse bevolking (1880-1940)* (Tielt, 2000), 695–96.

9. CEGES-SOMA AB2167 De Lathower, *Comité de Defense des Juifs,* 17, Testimony by Ghert Jospa; Steinberg, *Le Comité de Défense des Juifs,* 31, 69. Perelman just refused to cooperate with German ordinances and was supposedly dismissed by the University of Brussels, but he continued to work there unofficially until the liberation. Saerens, "Die Hilfe für Juden," 251.

10. His name is also given as Rotgel and Rotkehl in various books and contemporary reports.

11. CEGES-SOMA AB2167 De Lathower, *Comité de Defense des Juifs,* 22–23; Lucien Steinberg, "Jewish Rescue Activities in Belgium and France," 603–4; http://www1.yadvashem.org/yv/en/righteous/pdf/resources/lucien_steinberg.pdf (accessed 25 March 2014); Steinberg, *La Traque des Juifs,* vol. 1, 67–69; Betty Garfinkels, *Les Belges face à la persécution raciale 1940-1944* (Brussels, 1965), 88–89.

12. Steinberg, *Le Comité de Défense des Juifs,* 68.

13. Steinberg, *Le Comité de Défense des Juifs,* 74–75; CEGES-SOMA AB2167 De Lathower, *Comité de Defense des Juifs,* 2.

14. CEGES-SOMA AA1915, Heiber: Dossier 13 CDJ. Ofipresse no. 23, 12 October 1945; CEGES-SOMA AB2167 De Lathower, *Comité de Defense des Juifs,* 9, 19; CEGES-SOMA DGO R123 232.159 *8 Ans au Service du Peuple,* 10; Steinberg, *Le Comité de Défense des Juifs,* 77–82.

15. Saerens, *Vreemdelingen,* 703. CEGES-SOMA AB2167 De Lathower, *Comité de Defense des Juifs,* 19.

16. CEGES-SOMA AA1915, Heiber. Roger van Praag to M. Denis, Premier Commissaire d'Etat, 12 August 1952.

17. Steinberg, *Le Comité de Défense des Juifs,* 29–30.

18. Saerens, *Vreemdelingen,* 695–96.

19. CEGES-SOMA AB2167 De Lathower, *Comité de Defense des Juifs,* 41; Garfinkels, *Les Belges,* 89–90, also records subventions from the Belgian banks, from the Ministries of Justice and Finance, and diversions of funds by Blum and Vandenberg from AJB funds; Steinberg, *Le Comité de Défense des Juifs,* 114–15.

20. Saerens, "Die Hilfe für Juden," 254; Steinberg, *Le Comité de Défense des Juifs,* 115.

21. CEGES-SOMA AB2167 De Lathower, *Comité de Defense des Juifs,* 10, 29; CEGES-SOMA AA1915 Heiber: Dossier 13 CDJ. Ofipresse No. 23, 12 October 1945; Steinberg, *Le Comité de Défense des Juifs,* 116.

22. Steinberg, *Le Comité de Défense des Juifs,* 110.

23. CEGES-SOMA AB2167 Comité de Defense des Juifs: Temoignages et Documents, 15.

24. Béatrice Le Douairon, "Le Comité 'Rue Amelot' 1940-1944 à Paris: Assistance aux Juifs et Sauvetage des Enfants" (master's thesis, Paris Sorbonne, 1994), 10, 25.

25. For a detailed history of the UGIF, see Jacques Adler, *The Jews of Paris and the Final Solution: Communal Response and Internal Conflicts, 1940-1944* (New York, 1987), 81–161.

26. Adam Rayski, *The Choice of the Jews under Vichy: Between Submission and Resistance* (Notre Dame, IN, 2005), 58–59.

27. Asher Cohen, "Rescuing Jews: Jews and Christians in Vichy France," *British Journal of Holocaust Education* 3, n. 1 (1994): 8–9.

28. Adler, *The Jews of Paris,* 123.

29. Adler, *The Jews of Paris,* 193.

30. Adler, *The Jews of Paris,* 168. Originally founded in St. Petersburg in 1912, the OSE grew into an international Jewish children's charity with its Paris branch opening in the early 1930s.

31. This was done on the orders of Joseph Schwartz, the JDC's European director. See Lucien Lazare, *Rescue as Resistance: How Jewish Organizations Fought the Holocaust in France* (New York, 1996), 48, 259.

32. Le Douairon, "Le Comité 'Rue Amelot'," 15–16.

33. Jacqueline Baldran and Claude Bochurberg, *David Rapoport* (Paris, 1994), 192–93, 213–17. The precise nature of the denunciation and arrest remain unclear, not least since the Paris police prefecture destroyed much of its archives on Jewish affairs in 1948–49. Le Douairon, "Le Comité 'Rue Amelot,'" 77.

34. Baldran and Bochurberg, *David Rapoport,* 200–201; Le Douairon, "Le Comité 'Rue Amelot,'" 81–82. This was expedited by Juliette Stern (WIZO) at the rue Bienfaisance, which had escaped the attentions of Gestapo and CGQJ agents.

35. Fred Milhaud and Denise Milhaud, *L'Entraide Temporaire. Sauvetage d'Enfants Juifs sous l'Occupation* (Paris, 1984), 3; Camille Ménager, *Le Sauvetage des Juifs à Paris: Histoire et Mémoire* (Paris, 2005), 168.

36. Ménager, *Le Sauvetage des Juifs à Paris,* 166; Limore Yagil, *Chrétiens et Juifs sous Vichy (1940-1944) Sauvetage et Désobéissance Civile* (Paris, 2005), 531–32.

37. Milhaud and Milhaud, *L'Entraide Temporaire,* 4.

38. An organization in Paris set up to help prisoners of war was easily adapted to help Jews and was able to call on the help of Catholic secular organizations such as the Jeunesse Ouvrière Chrétienne (JOC) for support, as well as on religious foundations such as the Sisters of St. Vincent de Paul and the Sisters of the Visitation, Yagil, *Chrétiens et Juifs,* 518–21; Michèle Cointet, *L'Eglise sous Vichy, 1940-1945* (Paris, 1995), 293–98.

39. Madeleine Comte, *Sauvetages et baptêmes. Les religieuses de Notre-Dame de Sion face à la persecutions des juifs en France (1940-1944)* (Paris, 2001), 87.

40. Yad Vashem Archives [hereafter YVA], M31/ 7245 (Devaux).

41. Florence Matteazzi, "L'attitude du clergé face à la Shoah dans le diocese de Liège," in *Entre la peste et le cholera: Vie et attitude des catholiques belges sous l'occupation,* ed. Fabrice Maerten et al. (Gerpinnes, 1999), 182, Deposition of Abbé Louis Célis.

42. Léon Papelux, "Un Liègeois qui sauva des centaines de Juifs (1940-1944)," *La Vie Wallonie* 54 (1980): 282; Papelux, "Le Réseau van den Berg," *La Vie Wallonie* 55 (1981): 139–41; YVA, M31/1361, Emile Bouflette; Matteazzi, "L'attitude du clergé," 187.

43. Sylvain Brachfeld, *Ze hebben het overleefd* (Brussels, 1997), 88–89; Schlomo Kless, "The Rescue of Jewish Children in Belgium during the Holocaust," *Holocaust and Genocide Studies* 3, no. 3 (1988): 284–85.

44. United State Holocaust Memorial Museum Archives, RG 65.001M, Roll 272, No. 7335, Zuchthaus Rheinbach: Personal Akten Daniel Meyerson 355/41.

45. See Marion Schreiber, *The Twentieth Train: The Remarkable Story of the Only Successful Ambush on the Journey to Auschwitz* (London, 2003), 244.

46. Rapport par M.Dumonceau, 11–14 October 1976: Israel Steinberg, CEGES-SOMA MVDO 497.266.018. Schreiber, *The Twentieth Train,* 299 lists an Israel Steinberg as deportee No. 1210 on the twentieth transport. His occupation is given as a tailor and birthplace Vilna. His birthday is given as 14 July 1890, presenting a discrepancy between this and his police record.

CHAPTER 11

Jewish Communists in France During World War II
Resistance and Identity

Renée Poznanski

In the first months after World War II, France soothed its wounds with dual memorial narratives, one Communist and one Gaullist. Some commemorated the seventy-five thousand French who had been shot. Others emphasized the heroic role of Free France and its leader, General de Gaulle, as the embodiment of the real France, which a handful of Vichy usurpers had tried to steal. The Jews of both French and foreign nationality who had been victimized by antisemitic legislation on French soil and had then been hunted down—including the seventy-six thousand deported to the death camps—were totally hidden from public view. As victims, they were diluted in the more vast pool of the victims of war and occupation. As resistance fighters, they were of interest to no one, except the Jewish organizations that, in order to find a place in the dominant discourse, used their publications to recount the exploits of the Jewish Resistance and congratulated themselves on their contribution to the liberation of the homeland.

In the 1980s, after a turn—one might even call it a revolution—that affected both historiography and memory, the Jews finally made their collective and loud entrance into the narrative of France during the Occupation. A series of challenges to the accepted wisdom ensued in these years, igniting passionate debates. Most of these challenges were linked to the nature of the Vichy regime; quite a few revolved around the fate of the Jews of France. Two of them directly addressed the role of the Jewish Communists in the Resistance.

Notes for this section begin on page 222.

The first of these two debates targeted the French Communist Party. It had taken credit for some spectacular resistance operations that had in fact been conducted by foreigners—especially Jews—under Party supervision and control. Postwar Communist Party writing omitted the important Jewish contribution. Fighters' names were even deliberately Gallicized. Worse still, the Communist Party during the war neglected the security of the Jewish and/or foreign organizations and sacrificed them so it could credit itself with additional heroic deeds. In the historical revision, the Jews and/or foreigners who had fought in Communist organizations regained their place of honor in the saga of the Resistance.

In the second of these controversies, however, it was the Jewish Communists who found themselves in the dock. They had surely been heroic but they had followed the Party's orders and their actions had had no connection to the specific destiny of the Jews in France. At most, they had exploited the Jews' situation for propaganda ends and to recruit more Jews for the Party. Consequently, it was wrong to record their operations under the heading of a Jewish resistance that focused, by definition, on rescue operations. Historians and survivors argued passionately about these two issues, which undermined essential elements of the identities of both Jews and Communists.

Many years have since passed. The last Jewish Communists who fiercely defended their image and who increasingly underscored the Jewish dimension of their wartime and resistance activities are no longer among us. Moreover, following the collapse of the Communist bloc in 1989, the Communist threat no longer seems to be so urgent to their opponents, who devoted such ardor to depicting them as Stalinists who then changed their tune after the revelations of crimes committed by Communist regimes. An age of concord seems to have arrived and, with it, an era of historical reflection unburdened by the ideological passions that had distorted it only a few years earlier. Yet the question remains. Communist Jews or Jewish Communists played a leading role in the Resistance in France. Were they Jewish resistance fighters or were they Communist resistance fighters? Although this question is less politically explosive today, it is essential in gaining a more precise view of those years' specifics and of the complex reference identities that the Jews in France adopted.

Who Were the Communist Jews?

Between the wars, Communist influence in France grew among immigrant Jews, to the point that its prestige surpassed that of Jewish Socialists of the Bund before World War I.[1] In the fall of 1925, Jewish Communists held a majority of the seats on the board of the Kultur-Lige, a cultural institution founded three years earlier. The Communists employed a dense network of social, cultural, and sports' organizations, rather than labor unions, to exercise sway over immigrant Jews. This was possible because a majority of the Jewish immigrants were artisans and petty merchants, not amenable to the union model. Jewish immigrants thus traveled a double path when they joined an organization controlled by Communists: these organizations' ideology and objectives steered the immigrants toward integration into the French political community, while their modus operandi focused on community-based operations.

At its Fifth Congress, held in Lille in June 1926, the leadership of the French Communist Party pushed the development of Communist influence by deciding to establish a department to work among foreigners (the Main d'Oeuvre Étrangère or MOE) and organized by language subsections. The objective of the MOE was to disseminate the Party's ideas and politics among immigrants. According to a French police report, a working group of Jewish Communists held its founding session on 1 July 1927.

In 1932, the MOE changed its name to Main d'Oeuvre Immigrée (MOI), because the word "immigrant" had fewer political connotations than "foreigner," which had come under attack by the radical Right. Despite growing anti-Communist repression, the twelve different language groups that were formed grew in size and strength, especially at the time of the Popular Front in 1936.[2] The Italian and Jewish groups were the most active. The importance of the latter can be measured by the fact that its secretary was ex officio one of the five members of the collective leadership of the MOI, which oversaw all of the language groups. The only Yiddish-language Jewish Communist daily in Europe, the *Naie Presse,* founded in January 1934, had ten thousand readers and was financed entirely by donations and subscriptions. Its vitality was cited as an example to be emulated by the other language groups of the MOI.

Many immigrant Jews found the organizations created by the Communist Party to be a route for their collective integration into French political society, alongside the individual integration supported by the emancipation model that the Republic had made available to French Jews. But the format of this political activism—within the language groups of the MOI—preserved a Jewish microsociety. Moreover, this integration also took place through social and cultural organizations—such as the Farband, which served as an umbrella organization for hometown societies from eastern Europe (*Landsmannschaftn*). The latter reinforced the community frameworks of the immigrant Jews' social life and created an identity model that was foreign to French political culture and that the Party, too, considered to be temporary.

In the growing xenophobia of the 1930s, when French intellectuals, previously seduced by Soviet radicalism, grew disenchanted after the Moscow trials, the Communists' success in immigrant Jewish circles necessarily interfered with communism's spread among the Jewish bourgeoisie, whose members had already been French for several generations. The exceptions to this rule were some intellectuals; it was the anti-fascism of the Communist Party that attracted them, including Pierre Villon, otherwise Pierre Ginsburger, from an Alsatian Jewish family and the son of a rabbi, who joined the Communist Party in 1932;[3] Maurice Kriegel-Valrimont;[4] and a number of writers and journalists, including André Wurmser, Pierre Abraham, and his brother Jean Richard Bloch.

By contrast, Jews who were recently naturalized French citizens, who were members of the second immigrant generation, or who arrived in the country while still children were receptive to the Party's liberation rhetoric. In this category were Georges Politzer, born in Hungary in 1903, and Jacques Solomon, born in 1908 to a Romanian father. Another key figure was Henri Krasucki, who after the war became the head of the largest Communist labor union, the Confédération Générale du Travail or CGT. For Politzer and Solomon, it was a personal commitment; for Krasucki, it was what he called a "community engagement in Communism." Carried along by a family tradition of activism, Krasucki found himself attracted to the Jewish youth section of the MOI. Referring to the 1930s he recalled sixty years later what it had been like: "I felt even more at ease because they were young people like me, they were French, they were not immigrants, but the children of immigrants! ... In our minds we were all French, but we knew that we were the children of immigrants."[5] By creating the MOI and its affiliated organizations, the Communist Party had provided Krasucki with a road for collective integration, achieved in two steps, into the French community, by means of political activism.

The Many Facets of the Jewish Communists' Resistance Activities

During the war, the three categories of Jewish Communist activists—immigrants, the children of immigrants, and native-born French Jews—were affiliated with two different types of underground organizations: the language groups of the Communist Party, under the authority of the MOI, and the several levels of the apparatus of the Party's French organizations. The second type of underground organization includes many nameless Jewish resistance fighters, anonymous in the mass of those who took part in the various Communist Party operations. But Communist organizations also included senior cadres of the underground party apparatus. Joë Nordmann, for example, founded the National Lawyers' Front in April 1941 to serve as an organization for the forces of judicial resistance and served as editor of its underground paper, *Le Palais libre*. Maurice Kriegel-Valrimont played a leading role in the Paris uprising. Pierre Villon was the Party treasurer and, with Kriegel-Valrimont, one of the three heads of the Military Action Committee (COMAC) set up by the National Resistance Council (CNR). Finally, there were Georges Politzer and Jacques

Solomon, who edited the underground periodical *L'Université libre,* an activity that led to their arrest and execution at Mont Valérien on 23 May 1942. It is easiest to track the careers of Communist Jews of the first category, the first- or second-generation immigrants who belonged to the language groups—mainly the Jewish group, but also the Hungarian, Romanian, German, Polish, and others. Their activities fall into three categories, which I can review only briefly.

First, as a result of the dual systems of antisemitic legislation (German and French laws) that battered the Jews of Paris, where the vast majority of the Jews in France were living at the start of the occupation, the main route of recruitment involved assistance to Jews who had been pauperized. The first underground Communist organization created in the Jewish street took the name Solidarité. But welfare activity later became of secondary importance. It was taken over by a new organization, the National Movement against Racism (le Mouvement National Contre le Racisme or MNCR), founded after the mass roundups of the summer of 1942, when the anti-Jewish persecution switched into high gear; but it focused it energies on helping underground operatives and their families.

Second, and of far greater importance, were Communist propaganda activities, thanks to the emergence of an extremely diverse underground press. Some of these publications were in Yiddish (*Unzer Wort*) and others in French. They appealed to Jews or the French population at large. They were supported by organizations that explicitly represented themselves as Jewish (such as the Union des Juifs pour la Résistance ou l'Entraide or UJRE) or by one (the MNCR) that claimed to represent all anti-racists in the country. Underground publications appeared both in the occupied and Vichy zones. They included newspapers specifically for the Jewish youth and others for women as well as countless pamphlets, with articles that kept a close eye on the evolution of the hunt for and persecution of the Jews.

Above all, though, they did everything they could starting in the fall of 1942 to disseminate all available information about the fate of the Jews deported to the East, at a time when the general underground press remained mute on this subject. They called on the French people to save the children. This too was a notable exception in the underground press as a whole, Communist or otherwise. Yet they also loyally parroted the slogans of Communist propaganda. Pride of place was given to solidarity with the Soviet Union, praise for the victories of the Red Army and the heroism of its soldiers, the necessity to open a second front in Europe, and denunciation of the Germans as responsible for the massacre in the Katyn forest; to the struggle against the departure (or "deportation") of French workers to Germany; and to attacks on the wait-and-see attitude of the other movements. Solidarity between the French people and the persecuted Jews was one of the central themes of these texts, which called on the Jews to join the Communist organizations in order to strengthen the Jewish resistance and thereby win their right to full integration in postliberation France.

The third category of activity was military. Young Jews rapidly found their place in the operations of the Special Organization of the underground Communist Party, before expressly military Communist units, the Francs-Tireurs et Partisans de la Main d'Oeuvre Immigrée (FTP-MOI), were established in the spring of 1942.[6] Of the four FTP-MOI units set up, Jews constituted some 90 percent of the members of the first unit, composed of Romanians and Hungarians, and all of the second, or "Jewish" unit. After the Party's only armed group in Paris was paralyzed by the arrest of one of its leaders in October 1942, and then by the capture of the entire general staff of the Paris-region FTP in January 1943,[7] young Jews were the spearhead of its military operations in the capital. Of the 162 operations claimed by the MOI between July 1942 and July 1943, the Jewish unit, which at the time had around forty members, took credit for fifty-nine; the Romanian-Hungarian unit carried out thirty-eight other operations.[8] Operations peaked in the first half of 1943, before the Jewish organization was dissolved in July in the wake of a string of arrests. To this should be added thirty-nine operations carried out by the railroad-sabotage unit, in which Jewish partisans constituted an overwhelming majority, before November 1943.[9]

It was the German occupation of the Vichy zone south of the demarcation line in November 1942 that spurred guerrilla operations. The FTP-MOI groups were responsible for most of the attacks in Grenoble between September 1943 and March 1944 (the Carmagnole group) and for those in Lyons after May 1944 (the Liberty Group). In and around Toulouse, until the spring of 1944, the Marcel Langer group, named for one of its founders (who was guillotined by the Vichy authorities on 23 July 1943 after having being arrested in possession of a suitcase full of explosives),[10] was the major instigator of armed operations. But the situation was different from that in Paris. Although the Jews were strongly represented—sometimes even dominant, as in the original Carmagnole-Liberté organization—and often set up their own squads within each of these organizations, they never organized in an identifiable Jewish unit. In Lyons, as well as Grenoble and Toulouse, they fought side by side with Italians, Spaniards, Poles, anti-Nazi Germans, and others.

As liberation approached, bolstered by the record of resistance activities they could show, the Jewish Communist leaders tried to win themselves a dominant position in the French Jewish community. In emulation of the National Front model, with the French Communists at its head, a single organization, the Union des Juifs pour la Résistance et l'Entraide or UJRE, which combined all of the illegal Jewish Communist organizations, was founded in Paris in late April 1943.[11] The first step was the establishment of an umbrella organization for all of the immigrant Jewish organizations affiliated with the Jewish resistance, as part of a General Defense Committee, in Grenoble, at the end of July. This marked a strategic turn to attract French Jews. The Communists had realized that they had "to expand their influence among French Jews" in order to "realize the total unity of the Jewish population of France,"[12] as stated in an internal report dated December 1943. It was the first stage of a political strategy that sought to install Jewish Communists at the head of the representative organization of French Jewry. The second stage was the establishment, in January 1944, of the Conseil représentatif des Israélites de France (CRIF), whose charter was signed in May 1944,[13] and which provided the avenue by which the Communists made their official entrance into the organized Jewish community.

This brief and somewhat cursory tour of the Jewish Communist resistance during the war helps clarify the complexity of their identity. They were Jews and they were Communists; but they were also French, or dreamed of being integrated into France and finding their place in its prewar emancipation model. Each of these ingredients might wax or wane in various proportions, depending on the particular category of Jew; but all of them were always constantly relevant.

French-Communist Jews

The anomalous place of the French Jews in Communist narratives is particularly well illustrated by the case of Joë Nordmann. Born in 1910 into a well-to-do Jewish family in Mulhouse in Upper Alsace (which transferred to France from Germany in 1919), Nordmann joined the French Communist Party with the rise of Hitler in 1933. As a lawyer who defended Communist causes in the interwar period, he was disbarred by Vichy's Statut des Juifs of October 1940. In 1942 in Paris he founded the underground journal *Le Palais libre,* which aimed its articles at the legal profession.

Early in 1943, Nordmann drafted a lengthy article about the Jews of France, which was never published, even in *Le Palais libre.*[14] The article focused on the foreign Jews.[15] After referring to the thousands of Jewish volunteers who fell in 1916 singing the *Marseillaise* even though they could not speak French, Nordmann explained that twenty years later it was antisemitism that made their children affiliate with separate Jewish organizations. His mention of sacrifices on the battlefield was not original; the justification for the behavior of the second generation was. We must suppose that it was intended to answer a reproach frequently hurled at the second generation of Jewish immigrants.

Nordmann followed with his experienced lawyer's analysis of French laws and German orders that had rained down on the heads of the Jews in France: "Such are the texts," he summed up, before asking: "Ruined, branded, isolated from the world, confined at home, will the Jew henceforth live in his serene mediocrity? Will the [Jewish] army veteran, protected by the French law, continue to practice in the law courts or treat patients?" He answered these questions negatively, pointing to "our collaborators' bureaucratic practices." Thus, departing from the general rule in Communist publications, he emphasized not the blameless attitude of the French population but the relentlessness of French collaborators.

In the lines that followed, Nordmann described the roundups while noting clearly that French police, not the Germans, arrested Jews. He described the regime of horror in the Drancy camp, which had become a reservoir of hostages. He reviewed the history of the Vel d'Hiv roundup. Yes, he wrote, there had been policemen who warned the Jews of the impending peril; but there had also been militiamen who had "executed the orders they received with redoubled savagery." Indeed, the relative mildness of Vichy's early years vanished in the subsequent waves of arrests. "Of the deportees," he noted ominously, "there was almost no individual news. Sometimes witnesses reported the inhuman treatment they were receiving in the pernicious climate of central Europe; people jammed for days in the same cattle car; people who died while doing forced labor; all of these children who would never find their parents again ... and even the little boys who are said to have been sterilized." Now, added Nordmann, arrests were continuing.

His next paragraph seems to be a response to the earlier articles published in the Communist press as well as to the sworn antisemites:

> Thousands of Jews have fled the Occupied Zone, their zone of terror, with false papers, guided by smugglers.... When they return, they will no longer find their relatives or their possessions. Of course the newspapers recount the "orgies" on the Côte d'Azur and the Germans recognize or appoint "honorary Aryans." But should we forget the immense physical and spiritual misery of the masses on account of a few naughty rich people or "dissidents"? Should we forget that this mass includes not only the poor (for there are in fact many such Jews), but also many scholars, like Prosper Weill, artists and men of letters (Julien Caïn), people who have enriched our national heritage; as did their ancestors, for generations past, and as their children will do in a regenerated France, despite everything.

A kind of pleading brief followed, an astonishing brief, far from Communist and general French orthodoxy, that attests to Nordmann's need to respond once and for all to the charges being flung around in his circle. At the same time, he distanced himself by means of the first-person plural in which he included himself among the French people in contrast to the Jews:

> In the past, before 1939–1940, the French antisemite, rational and moderate, held it against the Jews that they were setting up a state within a state, supporting one another, marrying among themselves: this partiality, the privilege of every religious group, was in fact disappearing. If the Jews are sticking together today, it is because the legal and bureaucratic persecution forces them to do so. Because our attention is being drawn—so strongly!—to them, let us study them: there are not only intellectuals and merchants among them, but also many tailors, jewelers, and

craftsmen. Not all capitalists are Jews: look rather at the cartels that are established under the cover of being organizing committees ... for the black market! When it is a question of the cultivation of Palestine, the Jews have shown that they know how to be manual laborers.

If their character has some peculiarities, if they have certain "elective affinities" among themselves, that is appropriate for a community of origin. Why should it be more astonishing among them than in our provinces where people speak the local dialect, practice the same religion, and are famous for their obstinacy or miserliness? ... The Jews have taken over a dominant role in our public affairs because we have allowed them to do so, by showing ourselves less enterprising, less active than they are. Wasn't Paris colonized a few years ago by a series of provincial officials, including a prefect of police? No one considered them to be foreigners. French like us, mixing with us, the Jews of France are a sort of moral province, without territory. We write "the Jews" with a capital J[16] as we would write, for example, the Celts with a capital C. They constitute an important element of the "national" economy whose laws currently exclude them. The government of Marshal Pétain has rephrased the Catholic formula, "God, Family, Fatherland," as "Work, Fatherland, Family"; many Jews know precisely this threefold concern.

After the war it would be a mistake to enact a new "statute" for them, even if it is advantageous. A differential regime creates gaps. No more than it would be appropriate to have, in the future, a "France of the interior" as opposed to "Alsace-Lorraine," should we contemplate "Jews" and "others".... Extending our hand today to our unfortunate brothers, in the small measure to which individual initiative can compensate for deliberate cruelty, we will ask them, equal in rights with [piece torn off] to help us, tomorrow, rebuild the France to which we aspire.

In this text, Nordmann clearly deviated from the current orthodoxy, whether French or Communist: the emphatic use of the capital letter to designate the Jews as a nationality rather than a religion; their identification as a "moral province without territory," the reference to the Jewish manual laborers in Palestine: all bear the mark of the lawyer.

After the war, in an unpublished document he intended for his family, he wrote of an attachment to his "family history."

In this regard, I feel simultaneously rejection and dependence, affection and repudiation. Affection, because I am leaving to my descendents this narrative, written for them. Repudiation of the ancestral religious faith. Not without contradiction, since I am an atheist, I claim the spiritual heritage of Rabbi Moses.... I can say that I maintain the notion of Jewish survival to which my birth attaches me. And I can say, on the other hand, that I do not feel the close bond of a community with those who share a common origin with me.... I recognize myself in the continuity of the same historical phenomenon. I do not belong, though, to the same people.[17]

This statement explains the idiosyncratic emphases of the unpublished 1943 article. But we must also explain why it never appeared in print. If the author consulted other Party cadres, the text's departure from Communist orthodoxy would have sufficed to leave it unpublished. But Nordmann was responsible for the content of *Le Palais libre* and the article's nonpublication surely disturbed him. In a piece on the statistics of the persecutions, written several months later,

Nordmann made sure to include the number of Jews being interned in France or in Germany, which he estimated at one hundred fifty thousand as of 1 July 1943.[18] But though Nordmann was cognizant of the persecution of the Jews, it is not reflected in the columns of *Le Palais libre,* where we can find only two short references to it. "In issue number 2, dated July 1943, there was mention, in connection with the suicide of Jacques Frank after his release from Drancy, of the fact that he had 'committed the crime of being born' and had been forced to expiate it; in issue number 6, dated March 1944, there was a mention of the 'deportees from Poland and Silesia, many of whom will not return.'"[19]

The key to this relative silence may be provided by Nordmann himself in the last paragraph of his long draft about the Jews of France. In this article, intended for publication in a Resistance periodical, Nordmann felt the need to call for a return after liberation to the status quo ante and to note his opposition to any new Jewish statute, however flexible it might be. One would think that this would go without saying. It was as if Nordmann was answering those who were not truly persuaded. And his fears extended far beyond the ranks of the French legal profession, which had not shed tears over the disbarment of their Jewish colleague.[20] Nordmann's concerns here offer a more comprehensive explanation of the silence of the Communist press in general, save for a minority of periodicals intended for intellectuals, and of the Jewish Communist press itself.

In Nordmann we see a convergence of multiple identities that bear the imprint of diverse influences: the French republican culture that did not recognize community affiliations; the Jewish sensitivity that kept Nordmann from looking in another direction at a time when Jews were being persecuted; and his loyalty to Communism, which imposed its rule on him when he had to decide what to publish in the paper he edited.

Foreign-Communist Jews

A similar complexity appears when we turn to the activities of the immigrant Jews affiliated with the MOI—with a difference, however, because their adhesion to the republican model was more of an aspiration for the future. Here too we must be satisfied with a single example. It concerns the contradictions inherent in the underground papers' coverage of the fate of the Jews who were deported.

In all of the underground articles on this subject, we find the same underlying idea that the Jews and the French were suffering—or were going to suffer—the same martyrdom. Jews and patriots, and Jews and those who evaded the Service du travail obligatoire or STO (the German conscript labor apparatus) were always mentioned in the same breath. This was perfectly in accord with the line pursued by the BBC, which rarely failed to note that the fate of one group (Jews) presaged the fate of the other group (the French nation as a whole). It also fit with the overall theme of Communist propaganda, when the Party Central Committee referred, in the spring of 1944, to the "plans for the extermination of the French people ... devised by the German general staff."[21] This made it possible for the Central Committee to avoid putting itself in an awkward position vis-à-vis the general underground press, which was always so discreet about the persecution of the Jews.

In March 1943, the law concerning the STO brought this confusion to its zenith. "Days of mourning and of shame, when entire trainloads carry off young Frenchmen, torn away from their families, from their fatherland, to die in the service of the Germans.... The sinister slave traders of Vichy are in a hurry to deliver our youth to serve as canon fodder," proclaimed *En avant,* the organ of the Jewish young Communists. The next article referred to the fate of the elderly people arrested during the roundup of February 1943 in Paris: "They will perish en masse during the journey, of thirst, of hunger, of disease, of exhaustion. They will fall, shot, or asphyxiated, like the two million Jews of Poland." The conjunction of these two events allowed the following conclusion: "Today, when the same blows strike foreigners and the French, Jews and non-Jews; today, when the people of France, doomed by Hitler to annihilation, see no way out other than armed struggle: Jewish youth, inaction has become more than cowardice; it is a crime."[22] "French youth are in danger of extermination," added the very next issue.[23]

The same refrain could be found in publications intended for adults. *Notre voix* reminded readers of its earlier warnings: "The racist persecutions and the deportations of the Jews paved the way for and preceded a mass deportation of the entire working population of the country." It went on to draw conclusions more relevant to the present: a war to the death was now being waged against the people of France, and there was no longer any distinction between Jews and non-Jews.[24]

The publications of the MNCR were not to be left behind:

> Throughout France, young people are being picked up for deportation.... Hitler is inexorably pursuing his plan in *Mein Kampf,* the annihilation of the French people. After the tumbrels of Jews sent to be massacred in Poland, there will be trains of our young people sent to labor camps in Germany, waiting to be conscripted into a Nazi uniform.... Hitler attacked Jews and non-Jews the same time and for the same reasons.... To replace the millions of soldiers who have been killed and the German laborers he has drafted and sent to the front, Hitler needs workers from our country. To shatter the resistance of the oppressed peoples, a resistance that grows with each Allied victory, only one method remains to Hitler, re-intensification of the terror.... At the same time that he is thereby trying to diminish our country's capacity for resistance, Hitler is pursuing his goal: the physical destruction of France.[25]

Two months later, the same paper found the nuances that distinguished the several categories of "Nazi atrocities": "From the children doomed to tuberculosis by malnutrition, to the workers deported to serve on the Eastern Front and the Jewish families sent to Poland and burned alive in the lime kilns."[26] However, the deportation of French workers continued to be depicted as one of the manifestations of a "barbarous racism."[27] Younger readers were told that one of the objectives of "the struggle against deportation" was to frustrate the "plan to exterminate the French people."[28]

The horrors of the persecution of the Jews had "activated" the term "deportation," which was now applied to the French workers; the transfer to the French people of the blueprint for extermination followed logically. As for "barbarous racism," the expansion of its field of application should not astonish us. When the MNCR decided to focus its attention on racism and leave "antisemitism" out of its name, the intention was to suggest that Jews were not the only victims. The very first issue of *Fraternité* (1–31 January 1943), which came out shortly before the special issue on the extermination of the Jews of Poland, presented its list of the "victims of racism" in the following order: "Hundreds of French people have been imprisoned. Tens of thousands have been deported. ... Hundreds of the children of deportees have been left without sustenance. Jewish children have been abandoned to their fate.... Intellectuals have been sacked from their posts and imprisoned. Clerics and members of religious orders are persecuted. Jews are constantly being arrested and deported. We must show them our effective solidarity."[29] The Jews were carefully submerged in a list that left no one out: all were presented as "victims of racism."

This was a strategic choice. In March 1944, a report intended to guide the MNCR's work with French youth was explicit about this strategy, from which the organization never varied:

> One must not forget that French youth aged 16 to 20 do not know that there is a Jewish question in politics. The persecution of the Jews touches them, quite clearly, but they see no difference between that and the assaults on the French people as a whole. For them, it is a question of chronological order, nothing more. Only after they join the MNCR can we enlighten them about the true meaning of antisemitism. It is also appropriate to touch them on the sensitive point, which is currently their own situation. This is why, while not neglecting the question of the Jews in any way, the young people's publications and actions never take it for their banner.[30]

This task was even more delicate because the MNCR was the only organization that had set itself the task of making the French people, young and old alike, aware of the results of the antisemitic persecution.

In many cases, the layout of the articles undercut this confusion. Although *J'accuse* wrote in June 1943 that, "they set upon the Jews, and it is France that has to pay," the main headlines of that issue referred to the Warsaw Ghetto

Uprising and the "total extermination of four million Jews in Poland."³¹ What is more, many articles took the risk of turning a discreet focus on the Jews: "Murdered in its soul, amputated in its flesh, mourning its sons who have fallen under the blows of the enemy, on the ruins of its cultural monuments that have been destroyed by savage hands, France resists and feverishly prepares for the great day when the oppressed will turn against the tyrants," one could read in *Droit et Liberté* of February 1944. But, that publication continued, "our suffering [as Jews] is only one part of the suffering experienced by the entire [French] nation but our share is out of proportion to the size of the Jewish community in national life.... A ruthless war is raging between the enemies and ourselves. It has been declared against all, without exception. It is waged against us not because we are plutocrats or Marxists, Freemasons or Judeo-Bolshevists, but only because we are Jews."³²

The manner in which the persecutions were presented, commented on, and interpreted depended, no doubt, on the function assigned to these reports in the realization of the political objectives pursued by the editors of the Jewish section of the MOI. But these objectives clearly included the desire to shatter the silence that blanketed the persecution, to shake the French population out of their apathy, to make them sensitive to the fate of the Jews. The writers were well aware that trying to establish a shared destiny between Jews and non-Jews, without betraying the unique fate of the former, was tantamount to squaring the circle. The Jewish Communist publications were riddled with contradictions precisely because they made the attempt to do so.

Conclusion

The story of the Communist Jews during the war constitutes its own chapter in the history of the Resistance. At a time when silence reigned supreme, the underground publications of the Jewish Communists never stopped publishing reports about the fate of the Jews who had been deported and were doomed to extermination. Their story also constitutes a chapter in the wartime history of the Communists. The especially cruel destiny reserved for Jewish families sparked the courage of the young Jews who were the spearhead of the military operations that the Party's underground organizations conducted against the occupier on French territory.

Yet their story also constitutes a chapter in the history of the Jews of France, whose diversity is reflected by the organizations that took part in the struggle as well as by the types of activities they engaged in, locating their operations in the Jewish street and claiming their role in the organized Jewish community immediately after the war. Thus the saga of the Jewish Communists during the war is situated at the intersection of these three histories, which expands far beyond what I have been able to show here.

Notes

1. Paula Hyman, *From Dreyfus to Vichy: The Remaking of French Jewry, 1906–1939* (New York, 1979).

2. Stéphane Courtois, Denis Peschanski, and Adam Rayski, *Le Sang de L'étranger: Les immigrés de la MOI dans la Résistance* (Paris, 1989), 29ff. At the time, the MOI had twelve subsections: Italian, Polish, Spanish, Jewish, Armenian, Ukrainian, Hungarian, Yugoslav, Czech, Romanian, Russian, and Bulgarian. See Archives of the Russian Center for the Preservation and Study of Documents of Contemporary History [RCPSDCH], Moscow, 517, I, 1523, "Rapport d'organisation sur la MOI en France," 1933. These reports also refer to Greek and Albanian immigrants.

3. Pierre Villon, *Résistant de la première heure* (Paris, 1983).

4. Maurice Kriegel-Valrimont, *Mémoires rebelles* (Paris, 1999), 15ff.

5. Jérôme Pelisse, *Légitimation et disqualification du personnel politique ouvrier: Une socio-biographie de Henri Krasucki* (M.A. thesis, Université de Paris X–Nanterre, 1996–97), 89–90.

6. Courtois, Peschanski, and Rayski, *Le sang de l'étranger*, 145ff.

7. Courtois, Peschanski, and Rayski, *Le sang de l'étranger*, 164–65.

8. See the communiqués and the "Bilan des actions jusqu'à la grande chute de novembre, par détachement et par période," in Boris Holban, *Testament* (Paris, 1989), 296ff. For the operations carried out by the second (Jewish) detachment between March 1942 and April 1943, see Archives of the Musée de la Résistance Nationale (Champigny-sur-Marne) [hereafter MRD de Champigny], Fonds DD. Some of these were confirmed by Intelligence Reports of the Paris region Police Prefecture, for June 1942 to August 1944, Centre de documentation juive contemporaine (Paris) [hereafter CDJC] Fonds Urman.

9. Holban, *Testament*, 283–95, "État des effectifs des FTP-MOI parisiens, juin 1942–août 1944."

10. Claude Lévy, *Les parias de la résistance* (Paris, 1970).

11. David Diamant, *Les Juifs dans la résistance française* (Paris, 1971), 174–75; Jacques Adler, *The Jews of Paris and the Final Solution: Communal Response and Internal Conflicts, 1940–1944* (New York, 1987), 200ff.

12. CDJC, CDLXXIII-93, December 1943, internal report edited by Adam Rayski.

13. On the establishment of CRIF, see Adler, *The Jews of Paris*, and the testimony of Adam Rayski, "La Fondation du Conseil représentatif des Juifs de France," *Le Monde Juif*, 51, no. 24 (1968): 32–37.

14. I learned of the existence of the unpublished draft from Liora Israël, *Robes noires, années sombres. La résistance dans les milieux judiciaires. Sociologie historique d'une mobilisation politique* (Ph.D. diss., Ecole Normale Supérieure de Cachan, 2003). See the book based on this dissertation: Liora Israël, *Robes noires, années sombres. Avocats et magistrats en résistance pendant la Seconde Guerre mondiale* (Paris, 2005), 293–95.

15. "Les Juifs de France," a draft by Joë Nordmann for *Le Palais libre*, MRD de Champigny, Fonds Joë Nordmann, carton n°2, dossier FN, sous-dossier occupation. I would like to thank Guy Krivopissko for sending me a copy of this text.

16. That is—in keeping with standard French orthographical rules—he considers the Jews to be a nationality rather than a religion.

17. Joë Nordmann, "Une histoire de famille" (1999), unpublished typescript. Rabbi Moïse Nordmann, an engraving of whom he kept on the wall of his office, was his great-grandfather's

brother (Nordmann, "Une histoire," 20). I would like to thank Liora Israël for providing me with a copy of this document.

18. Report to Pierre Villon, 15 November 1943, in Israël, *Robes noires, années sombres,* 294–95.

19. Israël, *Robes noires, années sombres,* 294.

20. Robert Badinter, *Un antisémitisme ordinaire. Vichy et les avocats juifs (1940–1944)* (Paris, 1997), 104ff.

21. "La préparation de l'insurrection nationale. Les plans de l'ennemi et les tâches de l'heure," May 1944, Communist Party Central Committee, 4 pages, CDJC, XXII-12.

22. "À bas le STO" and "Jeunes de France! De Paris nous parviennent des détails sur les dernières rafles," *En avant*! 3 (March 1943), MRD de Champigny, Fonds DD.

23. "Vive le 1er mai," *En avant*! 5 (1 May 1943), MRD de Champigny, Fonds DD, CDJC, XXII-4; also in Centre de Documentation de l'Union des Juifs pour la Résistance et l'Entraide, *La Presse antiraciste sous l'occupation hitlérienne. Recueil de journaux, tracts, appels, proclamations et brochures édités par les organisations juives de la Résistance et divers autres mouvements pendant l'occupation de la France, de 1940 à 1944* (Paris, 1950), 85–86.

24. *Notre voix,* 15 March 1943, Bibliothèque Nationale de France, Rés. G. 1470 (711).

25. *Fraternité,* March 1943, CDJC, XXII-5.

26. *Fraternité,* May 1943, CDJC, XXII-5; also in *La Presse antiraciste,* 309–10.

27. "Relève, travail obligatoire? Non! Anéantissement de la France," *Fraternité* (July 1943), MRD de Champigny, Fonds DD.

28. "La lutte contre la déportation," *Jeune combat* 4 (15 August 1943), CDJC, CDLXXI-42 (first page only. For both pages of the issue see *La Presse antiraciste,* 109–10).

29. *Fraternité* 1 (1 January–31 January 1943), Archives Municipales, Ivry, Fonds DD.

30. Report for March 1944, MNCR, CDJC, Fonds DD.

31. *J'accuse* 14 (June 1943), MRD de Champigny, Fonds DD; also in *La Presse antiraciste,* 311–12.

32. *Droit et Liberté* 1 (February 1944), Archives Municipales, Ivry, Fonds DD.

CHAPTER 12

Freedom and Death
The Jews and the Greek Andartiko

STEVEN BOWMAN

Does the title of this volume mean rehearsing, albeit in a new vein, the expert specializations of the contributors? Or does it call for new approaches to rewriting the history of the Holocaust? Scholarship in all disciplines has probed nearly every facet of Nazi thought, its antecedents, its mythical sources, its diplomacy, its aggression, and its murderous policy toward the Jews and other *Untermenschen*. Myriads have also left memoirs, from diplomats to survivors, from Sonderkommando personnel to children, from doctors and other professionals, and of course warriors, many of whom did not survive the final battle. Libraries, and now even the internet, are filled with encyclopedias, monographs, journals, manuscripts, of all sorts in broad areas and narrower subareas depending on interests and discipline.[1]

And of course there are novelists and poets in dozens of languages, many translated into both Hebrew and English. As Menachem Brinker reminds us, historians are restricted by the facts; novelists are not.[2] Literature can fantasize the emotions and passions of the Holocaust period and for many that is sufficient. What shall we do with all that material, historical and fictional, in the postsurvivor generations? Will survivor videos and audios suffice, or will they bore the public we wish to teach? The literature will survive, although culled by time; the scholarship and court records will still answer Holocaust deniers and other antisemites, but what medium will talk to the masses who will need to incorporate this tragedy into their cultural heritage and Jewish memory?

Jews have five major occurrences and memories of national disaster, augmented by a continuous series of local persecutions differently commemorated.

Notes for this section begin on page 235.

As Yosef Yerushalmi has shown, many of these disasters have been entered into the religious calendar as solemn days of public memory. Four hundred (actually 215) years of slavery in Egypt and a redemptive freedom, for example, are the theme of Pesach (Passover). Tisha BeAv recalls the two temples in Jerusalem destroyed by Nebuchadnezzar and Titus. But not all Jewish tragedies and catastrophes are so commemorated. The Crusader massacres of the eleventh century and the seventeenth-century Ukrainian deluge under Bohdan Khmelnytsky have no general commemoration, nor does the thirteenth-century blood libel of St. Hugh of Lincoln (d. 1255).[3] Indeed the blood libels of medieval and modern times were the bane of subsequent European diatribes and have been successfully imported into the Islamic world since 1840.[4] The dissolution of Iberian Jewry in 1492 and subsequent years is subsumed, if even recalled, in Tisha BeAv. Lurianic Qabbalah, in Gershom Scholem's view, was one contemporary attempt to incorporate that epic disaster into his cosmologic mythology.[5] It was more recently suggested by Menahem Begin (in 1977) to move Yom HaShoah to Tisha BeAv in order to concentrate all the major national tragedies.[6] Is it then the fate of the Holocaust to be reduced to a religious/nationalist holy day in the cycle of the Jewish calendar?

Can there be an accompanying text that will capture the emotions and intellect of future generations of Jews? Histories of Jewish resistance during World War II are divided between partisans on the one hand, and spiritual responses on the other. The first was a military response that more often than not resulted in death; the second was geared to survival whether as a spiritual model or physical continuity. Jewish presence in European resistance movements in Europe (and in the Allied armies) was out of proportion to the Jewish demographic percentage in host societies.[7] Jews had an obvious antipathy to Nazism but they were also caught up in the nationalisms of the Allies that welcomed their fighting and other skills even if their identity as Jews irritated some of their fellow citizens and brethren in arms.

Greece, the subject of this chapter, was no exception to these trends, though here, unlike elsewhere, the political and military leadership fully supported Jewish citizenship and extolled Jewish service. After its surrender to invading German forces in April 1941, Greece was divided into occupation zones: Bulgaria acquired Thrace and eastern Macedonia (as well as western Macedonia from Yugoslavia), thus fulfilling its irredentist dream of an exit to the Mediterranean. Germany retained strategic areas such as the former Greek border with now-neutral Turkey, Salonika with its huge port, and eastern Crete. Italy received the vast bulk of Greece and the Greek islands, fulfilling Benito Mussolini's Fascist dream of recreating a *mare nostrum* in imitation of ancient Rome and her empire.

The Shoah in Greece, which I have treated in detail elsewhere,[8] proceeded efficiently and quietly in two stages: the Jews of the Bulgarian and German zones were deported in spring 1943. The Germans deported the Jews in the Italian zone, after the September 1943 withdrawal of the Italians from the war, in spring and summer 1944. Nearly 87 percent of Greek Jewry disappeared during the three and a half years of the occupation. Official community records estimate that nearly thirteen thousand Greek Jews participated in the Italo-Greek war of 1940–41. My own estimate of the number of Greek Jews in the subsequent *andartiko,* as the partisan movement is known locally, is about one thousand men and women, if not actually larger.

Why a greater number is not recorded is a subject for another essay.[9] But Jewish resistance existed throughout Greece and in the various camps to which Greek Jews were transported. It involved intelligence efforts and military action both by Jewish men and women.[10] Yet the motivating factors provide the heart of our subject. The national Greek responses of Jews and gentiles alike were influenced by ancestral memories inherited by the inhabitants of Greece. These memories emphasized the heroic notion of freedom and death. Thus there remains an unanswered question seventy years later. Can a new text emerge from these experiences, not to replace what has been and will continue to appear as documentation and interpretation, but rather to provide a usable literary memory that can be integrated into the millennial history of the Jews?

I will explore three tales of what may be termed "collective suicide," among Hellenized or Greek Jews during the past two millennia. In all three cases the Jews faced imminent death, and in all three they chose to die rather than surrender. While the war they fought in each case was ultimately motivated by religious zeal, the description of their collective deaths was penned by historians in national, so-called "secular" terms. The three episodes I will discuss are Flavius Josephus's eloquent panegyric of the collective suicide of the Zealots at Masada in 73 C.E.; the Hebrew rewriting of this very same event—the *Sepher Yosippon*—by a tenth-century medieval Jewish scholar that introduces a phenomenal change in the inherited textual tradition; and the third episode, anticipated by the second, in which collective death replaces suicide by the Greek Jews of the Sonderkommando of Auschwitz-Birkenau, who rebelled in October 1944, and even by Jews who fought in the more general Greek resistance.

Important throughout is the symbiosis of Greek and Jewish traditions. A martyr, by definition, is a witness to his or her deity or ideology, whose sacrificial death is recorded as an example of proper and praiseworthy action.[11] The tradition of monotheistic martyrdom shares a common source in the teaching of Matityahu, the patriarch of the Hasmonean family that initiated the Jewish revolt against Hellenistic rule and its religious challenges. What is more difficult to show is the extent to which Matityahu's teaching was influenced by ancient Greek ideas of heroic or noble death. I suspect, however, that it is part of the Hellenization process that permeated Jewish life during the encounter between Greeks and Jews.[12]

Josephus, *Bellum Iudaicum*

Josephus, the Jewish priest and commander, wrote his works as a client of the imperial Flavian house—the emperors who conquered his people, destroyed their capital, and obliterated the physical symbol of their religious unity. His *Bellum Iudaicum* (The Jewish War) was the response of a man caught between two worlds: that of the Jews who had just suffered the worst holocaust of their millennial history and that of conquest by the Romans, a brutal civilization replete with violence, venality, and slavery, but also the civil law that was perhaps its greatest legacy. Josephus walked a fine line between history and apology. The emperors were his first critics and also eyewitnesses to many of the events. In his tendentious way Josephus records the stages of the revolt within Jewish society. Given the odds of success, the revolt was suicidal. While recreating its final stage, Josephus nowhere indicates in his text that he was at Masada. He summarizes the ideology of the Zealots in an elegant rhetorical speech by their leader Eleazer ben Yair, namely (to paraphrase), that "the sovereignty of heaven supersedes the rule of man.... And now that we are about to be killed, let us die free under God and so avoid the ignominy and shame of defeat, rape, slavery, and slaughter."

We should compare Josephus's scene at Masada with his personal parallel episode: his defense of Yodfat or Jodpata and its fall to the Romans in 67 C.E., and especially his betrayal of his fellow officers. They argued for suicidal death with honor rather than capture, mockery, and execution in a Roman triumph for those who survived the savage gladiatorial combats that entertained the troops on their return to Rome. Having taken refuge from the burning city and Roman soldiers in a cave with his commanders, Josephus tricks the officers into killing each other through drawing lots. The die is cast, one officer kills another until only Josephus and one other survives, whereupon Josephus convinces the other to live and not die like the rest of his officers. This is not a case of either martyrdom or sacrifice, but rather the collective suicide of a defeated officer corps. It is how Josephus survived. Later he repeats and expands this personal apology to embrace the collective suicide of the 960 Zealot fighters and their families on Masada, the final victory of the defeated Jews against the might of Rome, extolling the sovereignty of God over the rule of man.

Perhaps the collective suicide at Masada happened as Josephus says it did. There were many eyewitnesses. But none left any surviving record, thus allowing Justus of Tiberius's critique that Josephus was tendentious in various matters. Hence one cannot be too suspicious that a fake scene entered contemporary history in Rome itself. The Greeks did it all the time, a rhetorical device that calls into question Josephus's emphasis in his final sentence to his *Bellum* that everything he wrote was true.[13]

At about the same time, the authors of the Gospels penned their own apologies for the new Christian faith; the first dated to just after the destruction of the Temple in Jerusalem. Noteworthy in their argument of a Christian victory over Rome, of the self-sacrifice of God through his incarnation and crucifixion, the two terms, "sovereignty of God" and the "kingdom of heaven" are alternative translations of the Hebrew idiom *malkhut shamayim*. Indeed, scholars disagree as to which is the proper interpretation for the first generation of Christian writers. Was Jesus a political or a religious revolutionary? Or were there two stages to the Jesus movement: the first, revolutionary, that failed to enthrone the messiah Jesus, and the second, spiritual, that eschewed this world for a kingdom in heaven?[14]

The first century thus presents two kinds of self-induced death: one individual [Jesus] and the other collective [Masada], both religious in their call for death to gain, according to the Gospels and Josephus, a martyr's status. The heroic suicide to avoid the shame of capture is part of an ancient military code that was occasionally enforced by religious/mythic sanction in many cultures. Later such death, specifically by noncombatants, e.g., old men and women, would come to be labeled martyrdom as in Maccabees 2 and 4 and paralleled, if not merged, with the more ancient tradition of heroic death.

Sepher Yosippon

In the tenth century in southern Italy, a learned Jew, fluent in Hebrew and Latin, a historian who knew to read, critique, and compare ancient sources in both languages, wrote a history of the Second Temple period. The book of this anonymous scholar is called the *Sepher Yosippon,* the name deriving from the Greek Iosephos.[15] In its many translations, the book has been a major influence on general and Jewish thought for the past millennium, although in recent centuries, most scholars have treated it more skeptically. But though Yosippon has been disparaged by most Jewish historians, the author shows critical historical judgment that anticipated many of his modern successors in the study of this period who read the same sources.[16]

Yosippon's treatment of Masada relies on Josephus's *Bellum* and his *Antiquities* and more directly Pseudo-Hegesippus's *De excidio urbis hierosolymitanae,* usually dated from the latter part of the fourth century of unknown provenance and authorship. Pseudo-Hegesippus expanded on Josephus by adding a theological argument that Christianizes the Jewish story.[17] However, the author of the *Sepher Yosippon* de-Christianized Pseudo-Hegesippus's treatise, while following the latter's summary of Josephus's *Bellum*. He introduced nationalist pride, consequently bringing ancient Jewish history to the forefront of Hellenistic and Roman history rather than treating it as a sideshow of Roman imperialism. His retelling of Masada culminates in the heroic actions of Jewish warriors. Rather than committing suicide as his sources report, Yosippon has them first slaughter their families and then sortie to fight to the last man.

This is a unique reversal of his sources. According to Josephus, Eleazar ben Yair gave an inspired speech that emphasized freedom over slavery, religious liberty to be gained through a voluntary death, a belated victory over the Romans who would have no glory, and no booty in their conquest. To Eleazar this would be a true holocaust, a whole burnt offering of human and material resources to God. By contrast, Yosippon's final scene at Masada is extant in the more elegant prose of two extant variant manuscript sources.

The first is a short version:

> When the morning came, they took their wives and their sons and their daughters and slaughtered them on the ground, and put them in the cisterns, and threw soil upon them. After that the men went forth from the city and engaged in fighting with the Roman camp, and they killed many of them without number. So the Jews fought until all of them were finished in the battle, and they died for God and His Sanctuary.[18]

The longer version reads as follows:

> When the morning came, they took their wives and their sons and their daughters to slaughter them on the ground that they be considered as burnt offerings acceptable before God, because for His Name they went, lest they be killed before the Roman idols.
>
> And they did just as Elazar ben Anani the priest had told them: each man belted on [girt] his fighting weapons, and each man gathered his wife and children to the square of Masada, and each kissed the members of his household and embraced them, and they wept upon each other in great lamenting. Then the priests and the elders called out and said to the women and children as follows: "It is good for you to weep and die here rather than die amidst the idols of the Romans." Then the men drew their weapons, and slew their wives, and their sons and their daughters, and they cast them into the cisterns in Masada, and they closed them up and filled them with soil. And the army moaned throughout that night in weeping, and lamenting, and great grieving, and with much mourning.
>
> They rose early in the morning and all of them went out together as one man from the city in savage fury and fought against the Roman horde, and they killed many of them without number until all of them were finished in the fighting.[19]

It is difficult to discern which of the two is the original ending, or if the short version was augmented by subsequent copyists. The short version better fits Yosippon's terse style. The important point is that the two versions offer two different attitudes to the collective death of the Zealots. The shorter version denotes the *slaughter* of the victims, and the *martyrdom* of the warriors—it is they, not their family members, who "die for God." The longer version spells out the *sacrifice* of the slaughtered victims (who are considered "burnt offerings acceptable before God"), whereas the warriors die a *heroic death* with no hint of martyrdom. In either case it was the memory of this passage and others that

Yosippon immortalized for medieval and modern religious Jews, namely, glory in death as a sacrifice to God. Such dramatic passages guided and supplied a vindication for medieval Jews of the crusading period and subsequent crises in the face of the Christian polemic, forced disputations and persecutions.[20]

Jews have read for a millennium the *Sepher Yosippon* during Tisha BeAv.[21] But the *Sepher Yosippon* is more than a guide to the Second Temple period. It had a modern, secular impact on Zionism, influencing Isaac Lamdan's epic poem "Masada" (1923–24).[22] There is also a novel that must be recalled in the interwar context of the *Sepher Yossipon,* namely, *The Forty Days of Musa Dagh* (1933), written by the Jewish Austrian writer Franz Werfel as a paean to the heroic Armenian resistance during the Ottoman slaughter during World War I. By examining the handful of Armenians on Musa Dagh, Werfel also had considerable influence on the Palestinian Yishuv. The Hebrew translation was widely read during the incident-filled 1930s and the ongoing threats and actions of both Muslim and Nazi devastation thereafter.[23]

The Greek Sonderkommando

The various modes of coping and survival by Jews during the Holocaust have been amply debated during the past half century. But the particular story of the Greek Jews' response to the hopelessness of Auschwitz-Birkenau is still not well known. Of the sixty-five thousand Greek Jews sent to Auschwitz only some two thousand returned to Greece. A small group of those who did not survive included the Greek Sonderkommando members who revolted in Birkenau in October 1944.

The story is complicated and still not clear from the fragmentary sources.[24] A general camp revolt planned by the camp underground for the Christian feast day of 15 August 1944, when the guards would be either inebriated or otherwise unprepared, was postponed, and then postposed indefinitely. Those Poles and others who anticipated their own survival at this late date in the war chose not to sacrifice themselves. Without a general revolt by the camp underground, the Jewish resistance was too weak to initiate its own revolt. Some Greeks expressed a different opinion.[25] Leon Cohen, one of the enslaved Greek Jews, wrote: "We all agreed that even if only one man managed to escape, it was worth undertaking. If you are to die may it be with dignity, holding a gun in your hand rather than shamefully being dragged to the gas chamber like an animal to the slaughter-house."[26]

By October 1944, the camp administration began the reduction of the Sonderkommando—which had been expanded for the murder of over four hundred thousand Hungarian Jews—in stages. On Saturday, 7 October, the numbers of the Greek Jews in the Sonderkommando assigned to crematoria

III and IV were selected for labor elsewhere, the principle being that the last to enter Sonderkommando details would be the first to be removed. Thus far, prior Sonderkommandos had been culled with no resistance. Every three months the newest members were murdered, a few veterans left to initiate and orientate replacements. So it was easy every three months to eliminate the disoriented, disorganized, and depressed youth who did the heavy work in the crematoria.

But on that day the slaves refused to go to their deaths. Joseph Varouh (usually pronounced Baroukh), a regular Greek infantry officer and veteran of the wars against the Italian and German invaders of his homeland and one of the planners of the revolt, shouted the order to charge. In true Hellenic fashion, the Greek Jews charged and overcame the armed SS guards. One guard escaped to raise the alarm. The SS quickly arrived, sealed off the area, and surrounded crematoria III and IV, where the Greeks had barricaded themselves. When the Greek Jews in crematoria III and IV recognized the hopelessness of their situation, they sang the Greek national anthem and the Zionist hymn *Hatikvah*. Then they blew up the crematoria with the dynamite that had been smuggled from the Union Munitions Works by female slaves. The SS executed those who survived the blast on the spot.

In Cohen's final encomium:

> This, then, is the account of the heroic battle of the Greek Jews who worked in the Birkenau Sonderkommando and who fell in battle. Was it madness or courage? At least, they died fighting, showing the free world that Jews, also, could choose to die like free men. By turning themselves into living torches, they had aroused the admiration of their murderers and everyone in their small world, which was Birkenau, respected them. Even those who had been temporarily reprieved envied them ... To sum up, we, the Birkenau survivors, must always remember the extraordinary bravery of a handful of our fellow citizens. In the annals of the extermination camps, heroism of that order was exceptional. As a rule all deportees allowed themselves to be slaughtered like cattle. May the memory of our friends stay with us, forever.[27]

How to read the actions of the Greeks who blew themselves up in the crematorium revolt? Was it a case of martyrdom, of self-sacrifice, or of a collective suicide of fighting men who chose to die free? We can omit a primarily religious explanation for the mass suicide, although many of the Greeks were religious and likely died with *Shma Yisrael,* the traditional doxology affirming allegiance to the national God of Israel, on their lips. For some observers, this defined their act as one of martyrdom. But can one compare their suicides to those of soldiers who sacrifice themselves on the battlefield? The comparison is not as facetious as it may sound. The Greek Jews did not have the option of battlefield surrender as dictated by modern rules of war. But upon their arrival in Auschwitz in 1944, Greek Jewish males noted on their registration forms their military service in 1940 and 1941.[28] They were, furthermore, acculturated to Greek nationalist tradition as a result of the interwar Hellenization imposed by the government on Jewish schools, primarily in Salonika.

Greek had become for most their first or second language. They had learned of the Greek struggles of the nineteenth and early twentieth centuries to "liberate" southern Greece and later Macedonia from the Ottoman Turks. A major result was the nationalization of religious martyrdom as military self-sacrifice. Greek nationalists hearkened back to the century-old Greek uprising in Macedonia in 1821. A well-known painting by Peter von Hess, the founder of genre painting in Munich, captures the moment that marks the end of this struggle, when Georgakis Olympios blew up the Sikou Monastery to avoid surrendering or being slaughtered by the Turks. The painting both summarizes the fighters' heroism and provides romantic inspiration to the youth of the new nation as an icon of the secular Megali Idea—the notion of all Greek lands liberated and united. Dominating the picture is the traditionally clad Olympios, his sword sheathed, one hand bandaged and placed over his heart, the other holding a torch above the powder kegs. However, his face is set, eyes clearly turned heavenward as if in prayer.

Nationalist teachers in Greece regaled Jewish pupils with tales of the glorious deaths of ancient and nineteenth-century Greek heroes. The heroic Greek atmosphere in the final decade of the Megali Idea had been intensified by the Venezelist revolution, which nearly doubled the size of Greece through the addition of parts of Macedonia and Thrace in the Balkan Wars of 1912–13.[29] Cretan writers Nikos Kazantzakis and Pandelis Prevelakis captured the Greek ethic of "Freedom or Death" in their various novels. Romantic paintings of the nineteenth century commemorated warriors touching the torch to the remaining barrels of powder rather than surrendering to the Turks. All of these stimuli in the twenty years following the Balkan Wars provided the background for the new secular national view of life.

Most importantly, however, was that the Greek heroic tradition was Judaized and taught by their Hebrew-school teachers via the Judeo-Spanish translation of *Sepher Yosippon*.[30] These stories also extolled the choice of heroic death rather than submission to the enemy. Another central text to be recalled here is also the Book of Maccabees, resurrected by Jews in the Zionist nationalization of Hanukkah and the impetus for Germanos Metropolitan of Patras to bless the flag of rebellion against the Ottomans in 1821. Here was a conscious imitation of Matityahu the Hasmonean priest, who had initiated the Maccabaean Revolt. The ancient Greek tradition is that of the polis that demanded of its citizens to fight to the death of their families, their city, and themselves rather than to suffer defeat and slavery. The medieval Jewish tradition of the fight to the death is derived from the popular Book of *Yosippon,* which rewrites Josephus's panegyric of Masada as noble death or mass suicide as a warrior's death in battle, his ultimate sacrifice for personal and national honor. The singing of the Greek and Zionist hymns in Auschwitz-Birkenau emphasizes this hybrid nationalism among the Greek Jews.

In sum, if a contemporary painting or tale were to be made of the last moments of the Sonderkommando, then von Hess's romantic creation and subsequent stories could well serve as models, if not inspiration. In essence these, alongside the oral and literary traditions of heroic death in both Greek and Hebrew such as the tales of the *Yosippon* heroes, provided the inspiration for the Greek Jews who took part in the revolt. Theirs was an actualization of the fate of all Greek heroes, that is, to die in honor of self, of God, or of country. Such antecedents sustained Greek Jews in the guerrilla warfare throughout the Greek mountains, in the ruins of the Warsaw Ghetto, and in the crematoria of Birkenau.

The *Andartiko*

Against this dual background of ancient and modern noble death and the religious parallel of martyrdom—the former sacrifice to the state or personal honor and the latter sacrifice to God—we may list several facets of the participation of Jews in the *andartiko*. These include veterans of the Italo-Greek war from October 1940 through the German invasion of April 1941, who refused to surrender and went to the mountains. Later they were joined by other veterans who chose to fight or otherwise aid the resistance rather than be deported. Some of these were killed in the war, as was Colonel Mordecai Frizis, the hero of the Greek counterattack that drove the Italians back to defeat in Albania.

Several Jewish members of the Communist Party became mid-level leaders in the fighting forces; one notable example is Kapitan Kitsos, the nom de guerre of Yitzhak Moshe who was a successful *politikos* and military leader of a small nuclear band in the region of Naousa. When he called for volunteers for a mission, there was no lack of support, for he had the reputation of bringing his men back alive, contrary to many regular Greek army officers who sacrificed men like sheep led to the slaughter in the tradition of World War I. The bravery of the Greeks set a new standard for a bayonet charge against machine gun emplacements and one charge in Crete routed German paratroopers who did not know that the Greeks had no ammunition for their rifles.

Many of the teenage boys and girls who went to the mountains of Free Greece were imbued with socialism that competed with Zionism, especially in Salonika. Daisy Karasso, who married Yitzhak Moshe after the war and moved to Israel, was guided to safety where she joined the Panhellenic Organization of Youth (EPON), a branch of the Greek Peoples' Liberation Army (ELAS), and became an active youth leader. Her younger brother, who escaped from prison, eventually was selected for officer training in the new ELAS army and was an aggressive second lieutenant who was killed attacking a German troop train. Another young woman, Sara Yeshurun, niece of Colonel Frizis, and known as Sarika, was helped by friends to escape with her mother to the hills of Euboea where she began to teach the local girls. Soon she demanded to have her own band, which became an important diversionary group. Her reputation grew when she killed the collaborator who tortured another Jewish teacher whom he mistook for her. By the end of the war she led a company of special troops who impressed greatly the American reporter who came to report on the Greek resistance. And the children: both Christian and Jew were recruited by EPON and engaged in various activities beginning with painting anti-occupation slogans and graduating to sabotage.

Jews could be found in the ranks of numerous units where they adopted Greek aliases, whether Greek Orthodox or noms de guerre drawn from Greek history and mythology. Many had wartime experience as fighters, as supply officers, as translators, as guides to the British liaison officers and later the American military mission, and as recruiters to the resistance army. Most important were those who volunteered for the dangerous job of procuring grain and guns. More appreciated were the doctors and nurses who were honored after the war for their service in the mountains and in the concentration camps where a number were sent, whether deported or incarcerated after capture in the mountains.

Jews were especially useful in the guerrilla-filled mountains for their urban, educated, middle-class skills which they used to fill the gap between the professional officers and the Communist elite and the illiterate or semi-literate brave peasants who served on land and sea in the fight for their *patrida*. Their education served them well in the cities, especially Athens, which was the professional headquarters of the National Liberation Front (EAM), a congeries of anti-fascist prewar parties. They were an integral part of the national resistance to occupation based on ancestral ideals and commitment to freedom or death.[31]

In the historiography of Jewish resistance during World War II the contributions of Greek Jews have been generally neglected. True, there is a small literature in Hebrew and a number of memoirs in various languages. However, the unique character of the Greek experience has not been sufficiently analyzed, if at all noticed. My argument posits two major influences on the Greek Jewish story, aside from the choice to survive or die. The first was the Jewish traditions of *Sepher Yosippon,* an ancient and well-known retelling of the period of the Maccabees and the Jewish revolt against Rome. This medieval classic and the resurrection of 1 Maccabees by the young Zionist movement, which had a strong support in Greece, produced a number of Jewish heroes for the young Jews of Greece. The second was the resurrection of ancient Greek traditions of noble death by the recent rise of Greek nationalism following independence from Ottoman rule in 1830 and the conquest or liberation of Salonika on the eve of World War I. Both influences were taught in the Jewish school system. It is difficult to judge which of the two was more influential given the paucity of source material, but it is perhaps safe to say that Jewish nationalism flourished alongside the Greek nationalism to which the youth were exposed. And to a certain extent both ancient traditions of national resistance and noble death—whether for polis or temple—mutually influenced each other at the dawn of modern nationalism among Greek Jews.

Notes

1. An older but still useful guide is Robert Rozett's bibiographic essay in *The Holocaust Encyclopedia,* ed. Walter Laqueur (New Haven, CT, 2001), 721–35.

2. Menachem Brinker, "Literature and History: Minor Comments on a Major Issue," in *Sifrut vehistoria* (Literature and History), ed. Ra'ya Cohen and Yossi Mali (Jerusalem, 1999), 33–43.

3. The 1992–93 issues of *Zion* were devoted to extensive examinations of the Hebrew Crusader chronicles.

4. See for the latter Bernard Lewis, *Semites and Anti-Semites: An Inquiry into Conflict and Prejudice* (New York, 1986).

5. The Gershom Scholem classic, *Major Trends in Jewish Mysticism* (New York, 1995).

6. See http://cms.education.gov.il/EducationCMS/Units/Moe/Hurban/Mashmaut/ (re Av 1977) or http://www.nrg.co.il/online/1/ART2/133/685.html (re 17 betevet).

7. See Dina Porat, *The Fall of a Sparrow: The Life and Times of Abba Kovner* (Stanford, CA, 2000), ch. 9; Abba Kovner, *On The Narrow Bridge: Essays* (Tel Aviv, 1981) [Hebrew], 41. Most of the combatants of the heroic 16th Lithuanian Division were Jewish and it was a completely Jewish company led by a Jewish commander that broke through the German defense. "... there was hardly a forest in Lithuania, White Russia, Ukraine, and Poland, where the founders of the Soviet partisan movement, pioneers in the forest fighting, were not Jews." See more detailed figures in Ruzhka Korchak-Marla and Yehudah Tubin, eds., *Abba Kovner—Seventy Years 14.3.1918-14.3.1988* (Tel Aviv, 1988), 18–19.

8. Steven Bowman, *The Agony of Greek Jews, 1940-1945* (Stanford, CA, 2009).

9. See Michael Matsas, *The Illusion of Safety: The Story of the Greek Jews During World War II* (New York, 1997).

10. Outlined in Steven Bowman, *Jewish Resistance in Wartime Greece* (London, 2006).

11. One should beware of attributing a martyr's status to every victim as has been done indiscriminately to every Jew who died or was killed in the Shoah. This is not to detract from their tragic deaths as victims, but to distinguish between those indiscriminately murdered and those Jews and gentiles who sacrificed themselves in various ways for some higher purpose, whether religious or ideological.

12. See inter alia Jan Willem van Henten and Frederich Avemarie, *Martyrdom and Noble Death: Selected Texts from Graeco-Roman, Jewish and Christian Antiquity* (London, 2002).

13. In G.A. Williamson's translation of *The Jewish War,* revised by E. Mary Smallwood (New York, 1989), see Smallwood's comments, 18–24: "...its literary merits must be left to the judgment of the readers: as to its truth, I should not hesitate to declare without fear of contradiction that from the first word to the last I have aimed at nothing else."

14. Though a digression, this paragraph recalls the only other sources we have for first-century Judaea as preserved in the New Testament. The two works of John Dominic Crossan, *The Historical Jesus* (New York, 1991) and *The Birth of Christianity* (New York, 1998), inter alia, are useful and informative reads.

15. In the accusative case as was Byzantine grammatical custom.

16. The book was edited by David Flusser from medieval manuscripts in 1978 (2nd ed. Revised in 1981) and a volume of commentary and notes in 1980 as *The Josippon [Josephus Gorionides]* and published by The Bialik Institute in Jerusalem.

17. See Albert A. Bell, Jr., "Josephus and Pseudo-Hegesippus," in *Josephus, Judaism, and Christianity*, ed. Louis H. Feldman and Gohei Hata (Detroit, 1987), 349–61, who argues that it is a new treatise that reflects his own viewpoint and prejudices.

18. Flusser, ed., *The Jossipon*, vol. I, 430.

19. Flusser, ed., *The Josippon*, vol. I, 430–31.

20. See my "'Yosippon' and Jewish Nationalism," *Proceedings of the American Academy for Jewish Research* 61 (1995): 23–51. Dina Porat emphasizes the tensions within Abba Kovner regarding the Shoah and the Resistance. See Porat, *Fall of a Sparrow*, ch. 14.

21. And not every Sabbath as advised in S.Y. Agnon, *Only Yesterday*, trans. Barbara Harshav (Princeton, NJ, 2000).

22. See perceptive analysis in Yael Feldman, *Glory and Agony. Isaac's Sacrifice and National Narrative* (Stanford, CA, 2010), 118–24. See also "'Yosippon' and Jewish Nationalism," and the essay by Yael Feldman and this author "Let Us Not Die as Sheep led to the Slaughter," in *Haaretz*, Literary Supplement, December 7, 2007 [Hebrew and English versions].

23. See the essay by Liel Leibovitz concerning new revised and expanded edition of *The Forty Days* in *Tablet Magazine*, 5 July 2012. "His new novel, [Werfel] informed his audiences [in Vienna], wasn't historical fiction. It was an attempt to come to terms with the fact that 'one of the oldest and most venerable peoples of the world has been destroyed, murdered, almost exterminated,' murdered, worst of all, not by 'warlike enemies but by their own countrymen.' The reference was hardly lost on his listeners."

24. The major treatments of the Sonderkommando revolt rely on the "last messages" prepared on the eve of the proposed and aborted 15 August uprising and buried outside the crematoria, where they were found after the war. Most of the content of this archive was written by Ashkenazim, which influenced later historians. See Reuben Ainsztein, *Jewish Resistance in Nazi-Occupied Eastern Europe* (New York, 1974). For several Ashkenazi diaries see Nathan Cohen, "Diaries of the Sonderkommando" in *Anatomy of the Auschwitz Death Camp*, ed. Yisrael Gutman and Michael Berenbaum (Bloomington, IN, 1998), 522–34. Only the Greek memoirs mention the contribution of the Greek Jews in the uprising of October 1944, which they tend to date to September. One of the letters from August 1943 was found after the war; the author survived and wrote a longer memoir. See Marcel Nazari, *Xroniko 1941-1945* (Thessaloniki, 1991) [Greek].

25. See Hermann Langbein, "The Auschwitz Underground," in Gutman and Berenbaum, *Anatomy of the Auschwitz Death Camp*, pp. 485–502; also his comprehensive survey of resistance in the camps *Against All Hope: Resistance in the Nazi Concentration Camps*, trans. Harry Zohn (New York, 1994).

26. Leon Cohen, *From Greece to Birkenau: The Crematoria Worker's Uprising*, trans. Jose-Maurice Gormezano (Tel Aviv, 1996), 59. Other printed excerpts from Leon's French manuscript appeared in Hebrew in various publications.

27. Cohen, *Greece to Birkenau*, 88–89. The Hebrew version uses "and not to be led like sheep to death" instead of "cattle." The French manuscript is not available. I have adjusted the story based on other sources. See my "The Greeks in Auschwitz" in Rebecca Fromer, *The Holocaust Odyssey of Daniel Bennahmias, Sonderkommando* (Tuscaloosa, AL, 1992), xi–xxv.

28. YIVO Institute for Jewish Research Archives S-2 87 partially lists thirty Greek Jews who filled out forms stating their military experience and other personal particulars, a unique and special corpus of data on the Sonderkommando. See Bowman, *Jewish Resistance in Wartime Greece*, Appendix II.

29. "The Great Idea" characterizes the policy of expansion initiated by the new Kingdom of Greece that lasted until the disastrous invasion of Turkey that ended with the expulsion of the Greeks and Armenians of Smyrna (Izmir) in 1922.

30. Translated by Abraham Asa, Constantinople in 1743-44 and republished in a critical edition of the Ladino version of 1753 by Moshe Lazar (Lancaster, CA, 2000).

31. Further information on these and other individuals is available in Bowman, *Jewish Resistance in Wartime Greece*. Other examples are available in the initial presentation of the Greek Jewish resistance by Joseph Matsas, "The Participation of the Greek Jews in the National Resistance, 1940-1941," *Journal of the Hellenic Diaspora* 17, no. 1 (1991): 55–68, and in Michael Matsas, *The Illusion of Safety*.

Part V

AFTERMATH
Politics, Aesthetics, and Memory

CHAPTER 13

Contested Memory
A Story of a Kapo *in Auschwitz—*
History, Memory, and Politics

TUVIA FRILING

This chapter attempts to unravel the historical, political, and psychological issues that underlay the tragedy of a young Polish Jew, Eliezer Gruenbaum (1908–48), who was denounced after the war as a *Kapo* at Auschwitz-Birkenau. Eliezer Gruenbaum adopted the nom de guerre "Leon Berger" while fighting in the Spanish Civil War.[1] He was the Communist son of Yitzhak Gruenbaum, the most prominent secular leader of interwar Polish Jewry, who later became the chairman of the Jewish Agency Rescue Committee during the Holocaust, and later the state of Israel's first minister of the interior.

Eliezer Gruenbaum's life story encompasses the tensions and tragedies of modern Jewish history—a Jewish community torn between communism, Bundist socialism, Zionism, and ultra-Orthodoxy—while deeply battered by the deliberate Nazi attempt to eradicate it. The course of locating Eliezer Gruenbaum's biography within the varied cultural and political contexts in which he operated brings to life the heart-wrenching debates that have rested in the Jewish community in Europe and Israel from the 1930s until this day. It re-creates not only the horrible dilemmas he confronted, but the Rashomon-like struggle over his memory, with radically different accounts by his loving family, the Communist movement that disowned him, the ultra-Orthodox community that despised him, and the Zionist establishment that struggled to find a place for the wayward son of one of its leading politicians at a time when heroes and heroines were needed for the nation- and state-building processes.[2]

Notes for this section begin on page 248.

Eliezer was the second son of Yitzhak and Miriam Gruenbaum. His father was the leading Zionist politician in interwar Poland, which had the largest, most culturally vibrant, and most politically fragmented Jewish community in the world.[3] Yitzhak was a champion of a secular, nationalist conception of Jewishness, whose major opponents included the Communists—who sought to overcome Jewish particularity through universalist revolution—and the ultra-Orthodox, who condemned the Zionists as heretics for their attempt to establish a Jewish state.[4] The latter struggled to understand how, while so much of Polish Jewry observed the religious commandments, they were being dragged under the leadership of supposedly radical and belligerent Zionists who refused to appease the feudal lord and thus provoked the gentile world to no good end.

As is often the case, these political and cultural tensions ran within families, including the Gruenbaums. Eliezer, like his elder brother Binyamin-Bengio, initially joined the Socialist pioneer Zionist youth movement HaShomer HaTzair.[5] But he left soon afterward for the Communist movement and in 1929, at age twenty-one, Eliezer was arrested by the Polish secret police owing to his clandestine activity in the Polish Communist Party.[6] After Eliezer's trial, conviction and incarceration in the prison of Łęczyca, Eliezer's mother, who refused to wait for her son's prison term to end, used the family's status and connections to effect his release. After he had served about two and a half years of his sentence, he was freed.[7]

Loyal to its revolutionary principals, France continued to open its doors to migrant workers and political fugitives looking for asylum. The city had been a "little Poland" since the first wave of Eastern European immigrants settled in Paris in the late nineteenth century, and it remained a safe haven for Jewish runaways in the 1920s. Young Gruenbaum was one of the asylum seekers. He became an activist in the Polish cell of the French Communist Party and a journalist for its press. As a Communist, Eliezer in 1936 enlisted in the Naftali Botwin Company, one of the International Brigades for service the Spanish Civil War, where he met, among others, Emanuel Mink, the famous commander of the Botwin Jewish Company, who was later one of his comrades in Birkenau.[8]

After the International Brigades were disbanded (in September 1938) Eliezer returned to France. Along with other foreigners, he was confined to the detention camp at Saint-Cyprien. Once again, his mother struggled to use her connections to legalize his status in France, now standing at the precipice of war with Germany. When Eliezer returned to Paris he tried to volunteer for the French Army. This act would have meant shattering all of Eliezer's Communist ideals—he continued to comment on party doctrine. Yet with the defeat of French armies in 1940, Eliezer had larger problems, namely, the German occupation of Paris and the advent of the right-wing Vichy regime.

Eliezer's continued involvement in the French underground Communist Party led to his arrest in Paris by French authorities in April 1941. He was subsequently interned in the Beaune-la-Rolande internment camp near Paris, where he became one of the inmate leaders.[9] In the second half of June 1942, as the Germans began mass deportations to Auschwitz with the help of the Vichy authorities, most of Beaune-la-Rolande's detainees were also deported. Eliezer, along with the rest of the foreign Jewish prisoners, was deported to Auschwitz-Birkenau.[10] As in other cases, the "organized" groups within the camp tried to place their own members in privileged positions in the inmate hierarchy. Gruenbaum became *Blockälteste* (block elder) in Birkenau, earning him the epithet of *Kapo*.[11]

Eliezer Gruenbaum's subsequent role in Birkenau became a matter of bitter contention. Sometimes, he acted with brutality toward the inmates, but whether his deeds were born of cruelty or, as he later argued, a strategic necessity under the morally intolerable conditions of the camp, remained a matter of dispute. During the post-1942 period, as far as we can learn from the documentation that we have, he was a central figure in the Communist underground cell in Birkenau.[12]

In February 1944, as a part of the Nazis decision to remove Jews from *Kapo* positions, Gruenbaum ended his *Kapo* role at Birkenau. He was transferred to the Auschwitz III camp at Buna-Monowitz, where he stayed for a few days until he was sent to the coal-mining camp of Jawischowitz, another subcamp of Auschwitz. There, already feeling the cold shoulder of the underground members, rumors reached Eliezer about a first investigation against him, conducted *in absentia* by his Communist comrades from the camp. Majcher Langman, one of Eliezer's associates, told him that the investigation evolved based on the way Eliezer functioned as a *Blockälteste,* particularly with regard to the depth of his connections with the Nazis. Aggressive expressions were made on his behalf, all actually ex officio. Later he found out that he was being exonerated.[13]

As Soviet forces approached in January 1945, Gruenbaum and his fellow inmates were forced marched to Buchenwald in one of the infamous death marches. Immediately after the liberation, Gruenbaum was put on trial twice at Buchenwald by a tribunal of inmates for his role in the Auschwitz camps. The first investigation was conducted by three members of the Communist party underground cell in Buchenwald, named Kisiel, Stefaniak, and Goldberg. The charges included beating inmates for no reason; giving preferential treatment to Polish inmates while abusing Czech inmates; stealing food portions; and participating in the extortion of money from the Czechs. The second investigation was conducted by a group of reactionary Poles, based on political and ideological differences. In both cases Eliezer was acquitted on the ground of inconclusive evidence.[14]

Under the orders of the Polish Communist Party, he returned to postwar Paris as its representative. While he was there, a judicial inquiry by the Polish Communist Party—held at the same time both in Warsaw and in Paris—found him guilty of having been a brutal *Kapo* at Birkenau and a Communist apostate. He was expelled from the party. Subsequently, he was investigated by a French examining magistrate for the same charges based on a French criminal statute concerning collaboration with the enemy. His friends and his father (by now a prominent official in the Jewish Agency Executive in Palestine) struggled to ensure that investigators would hear Eliezer's side of the story. The charges—during this fourth or fifth investigation—were dismissed for insufficient evidence.[15] An impartial eye notes significant differences between the testimonies of the Communist cell members in Birkenau during the Communist-led investigation in Buchenwald and at the French state investigation.[16]

Still, Eliezer Gruenbaum, now a man without a party, was soon also a man with no country. The French government ordered his expulsion as an undesirable alien. The ruling Communist-dominated government of Poland, embarrassed by its association with a man increasingly stigmatized as a Nazi collaborator, refused Eliezer's request to return there. Thus Gruenbaum, who had rejected Zionism throughout his adult life, was forced to seek refuge in the only place that would have him. Accompanied by his father, Eliezer arrived in Palestine, ironically on May Day—1 May 1946.[17]

In the Yishuv (the Jewish community in Palestine) Eliezer made repeated attempts to explain his role at Auschwitz-Birkenau to the skeptical officials of the Jewish Agency Executive. Still a devoted Communist, Eliezer sought once more to return to Poland, but in November 1947 he was again denied entry—both to the Communist party and to the state—by senior party members, now holding key positions within the new Polish government. While in Jerusalem, isolated and lonely, he met Stefa (Stefania) Rosenzweig, a childhood friend and fellow survivor of the Holocaust.[18]

When the fledgling state of Israel came under attack in May 1948, Eliezer, perhaps under paternal or family pressure, volunteered to join the Haganah—the Jewish army soon known as the Israeli Defense Forces. But rumors of his role as a *Kapo* in Auschwitz-Birkenau led the Haganah—in a very unusual decision in those days—to reject him. Once again his father, now a member of the Provisional Government of Israel—intervened. Eliezer was permitted to enlist and join in the defense of Jerusalem, which was under attack by the Arab Legion of Transjordan's King Abdullah. On 22 May 1948, eight days after Israel's declaration of independence, Eliezer fell in the battle on the outskirts of the city during the defense of Kibbutz Ramat Rachel.[19] By that very evening, rumors circulated that Eliezer was not killed in action as a combat soldier, but that he was executed by his comrades in revenge for his role in Auschwitz. The source of these rumors was ultra-Orthodox extremists in Jerusalem. On learning of his death that same evening, Stefa committed suicide.

The Gruenbaum family thereafter grappled with the rumors about Eliezer's execution and struggled to rehabilitate his reputation. Eliezer's "life after death" in Israeli discourse continued for decades. Indeed the public memory of Eliezer Gruenbaum became a recurrent point of tension in Israeli political culture. His father, Yitzhak, expended much of his political capital to have Eliezer included in *Scrolls of Fire,* the prestigious memorial volume devoted to the fallen heroes of the War of Independence.[20] The perceived pressure exerted by Yitzhak Gruenbaum on the volume's editors ultimately damaged his own reputation, but Eliezer was officially recorded as an independence fighter in 1952.

Nine years later, Eliezer's memory resurfaced in entirely different context. He served as the model for the fictional character Früchtenbaum in one of the most famous early Israeli Holocaust memoirs, *Piepel* (1961, translated into English as *Atrocity*) by the author Ka-Tzetnik, who himself had survived Auschwitz-Birkenau.[21] Früchtenbaum was represented as a loathsome *Kapo* and as a persecutor of Orthodox Jews. Yet the name Früchtenbaum (fruit tree) is also a game of words, and a clear reference to Gruenbaum. In this case the fruit—the son—the Communist Kapo that persecuted Orthodox Jews in Auschwitz, comes from the tree—the father—the ultra-secular Zionist and the chairman of Rescue Committee of the Jewish Agency in Palestine, who did not rescue Orthodox Jews. The fruit, Ka-Tzetnik suggests, did not fall far from the tree. Like father, like son.

Right-wing groups in Israel joined the chorus in attacking the son and father together. Isaac Rembah was the chief editor of *Herut,* the leading newspaper of the Zionist right. In the early 1960s, not long after Ka-Tzetnik's book appeared, Rembah published two articles. The first listed many leaders, authors and intellectuals—Jewish and non-Jewish—who were ashamed of their adult children. The article included Theodor Herzl, Winston Churchill, Franklin D. Roosevelt, Mendele Mocher Sforim, and others. This unfortunate phenomenon, said Rembah, was not limited to the fate of Yitzhak Gruenbaum—the dedicated and important Zionist leader. "If that were the case, I would not have written this article at all," wrote Rembah, "and I would have not mentioned poor Gruenbaum's story."[22] However, in the next article, Rembah promised, he would tell readers why he had an "open and a bitter account" with Yitzhak Gruenbaum.

And so he did. He urged the readers to read Ka-Tzetnik's book. "This book," he said, "is an illustration of what REALLY happened during the Holocaust. In the book you will find the despicable character of Früchtenbaum." Nevertheless, wrote Rembah, "I would not have written my article, just to remind you that there are Jews like Früchtenbaum, who was a Communist, but also that [they] have murdered Jews during the Holocaust ... I wrote this article," he continued, "because the father of this despicable murderer dared to exploit his political power to include this filth into the 'Scrolls of Fire'—our holy of holies, of our hero children. What to an idol in our Temple?" asked Rembah. Moreover, continued Rembah, "at the same time the father exploited his status to convince the corrupted Mapai [David Ben-Gurion's Labor Party] members to include his *Kapo* son in Israel's Bravery Hall of Fame, they rejected our sons, the Lehi [Lohemai Herut Israel] and IZL [Irgun Zvai Leumi] heroes that sacrificed their lives to resurrect our homeland, and refused to include them in this Pantheon. Our brave sons were left out—but Gruenbaum the Kapo was included."[23]

The story of young Gruenbaum and his activities spans at least four decades—from the mid 1920s until the mid 1960s—as well as many countries: from Poland, to France, to Spain, to Germany, and ultimately Israel. The documents reveal different aspects of Eliezer Gruenbaum's character, highlighting his participation in the underground resistance in the death camp rather than his alleged ill-treatment of Orthodox Jews while serving as a *Kapo*. The documentation records his sometimes courageous activity to save his Communist comrades and other inmates in the camp; it allows us to present a Rashomon-like account of four main narratives—the Communist, the ultra-Orthodox, the Zionist (left and right wings), and the familial—and their battle for hegemony. The tale however, was sequestered from him and from his family and was transformed into a symbol ultimately served four narratives—all of which had axes to grind.

The first was a Communist narrative stemming from the fear within the French and Polish Communist parties, including Polish Communist exiles in Paris. They worried that the personality of Eliezer and his like would threaten their ascending political power and thus their chance of coming to power in the immediate postwar world. Eliezer's story threatened to pull them into the depths of collaborationist narratives that had thoroughly discredited the political right. This threat was of such intensity that the Communist leadership in Poland and France simply erased Eliezer Gruenbaum not only from the account of the recent past of Communists in concentration camps but also from his role as a courageous resistance fighter in France and even from their shared history in the International Brigades during the Spanish Civil War.

The second was an ultra-Orthodox narrative, ensuing from the need to create a connection between the father and his son. It was an argumentative smoke screen that enabled an "easy" escape from weighty theological questions. Within the ultra-Orthodox group were those who saw the Zionist state as the mother of all sins, who did not recognize the state or its army, soldiers, and commanders, but who oddly enough were alarmed by the very notion that the "*Frucht*," the rotten fruit, would be included in the state's secular pantheon. They and the vast majority of their sons devoted themselves almost exclusively to studying Torah. Still, they not only thought it inappropriate that Eliezer had fought for the country—which they neither wanted nor recognized—they did everything in their power to deprive him of the honor reserved for those who fell in battle in the state's defense. The cultural swings of the Gruenbaum family came full circle when a younger Eliezer Gruenbaum, Yitzhak's grandson and the son of Eliezer's brother (named in memory of his uncle), came under the influence of the ultra-Orthodox and rabidly anti-Zionist rabbi and publicist Menachem Gerlik, one of Yitzhak's most implacable foes.[24] The defection of the scion of the Gruenbaum family to its ideological adversaries was trumpeted by the ultra-Orthodox press.

A third, Zionist, narrative was that of an embryonic, nascent society that underwent complex processes of nation and society building as well as a bloody war for independence. It needed role models from the Yishuv such as Joseph Trumpeldor, HaShomer, and Hannah Szenes; from the Warsaw Ghetto such as Antek [Yitzhak Zuckerman], Zivia Lubetkin, and Mordechai Anielewicz; as well as "Alik who came from the sea," Uri, and Ayala, "the young and handsome" that had helped immigrants disembark in the dark of nights and "carried their people on their shoulders." A society building its foundations needed its own heroes and symbols that were utterly different from those embodied in a bald, Communist Polish lawyer who had never wanted to be a part of the Zionist state, and who, on top of everything else, had been a controversial block commander in Birkenau, and then in death became a part of the state of Israel's pantheon by accident of his father's position.

And there was also a personal and a family narrative, of the few relatives who believed his story and still believe in his innocence despite his role as his family's black sheep. The narratives all show why Eliezer's story provided such fertile ground for abuse and manipulation, a symbol to be exploited by all. But the tragic story of Eliezer Gruenbaum's life and death also poses unanswerable questions on its own. Was he a villain who at the same time was a hero? Did he succumb to the temptations of his privileged position in Auschwitz, or was he an honorable member of the resistance? Was his chief motivation as blockelder—a role his friends had asked him to assume—simple self-interest, or did he act out of concern for his fellow inmates? Was there a sinister aspect to his character that coexisted with his native charm and charisma? Was he right in claiming he had been unjustly stripped of his heroic deeds, leaving him only with the stain of his collaboration? Where lies the truth and where the fabrication in Eliezer's and his friends' version of their past? Was there an unbridgeable gap of experience between him and his accusers in postwar Poland, France, and Israel, the latter of whom were unable to imagine the moral ambiguities of his position in Auschwitz? To what extent is the discussion burdened and impacted by the fundamental question of what, after all, was the percentage of the "privileged" of different kinds among the survivors? Was there ever a chance—in the various circles of his life—that his voice would be heard? And might his fate have been different—given what he had done—if his name had not been Gruenbaum?

Thus, who, really, are you—Eliezer Gruenbaum/Leon Berger?

Notes

1. See the letter from the Union of Volunteers in Republican Spain, Polish section, 14 December 1945 (79 Beaumarché Boulevard) to attorney André Ballot, Paris and Mr. Marchesseaux, Governmental Commissar, Paris, 20 January 1946, reference no. 13.735. Private Collection of Attorney André Ballot, Paris [hereafter André Ballot, Private Collection]. Ballot was Eliezer Gruenbaum's attorney in the legal proceeding conducted in Paris from September 1945 to 20 March 1946 by the French authorities. Ballot's files are located in a private collection in Paris to which I had special access.

2. The documents on Eliezer Gruenbaum are stored in public and private collections in Israel, Poland, and France. They include Eliezer Gruenbaum's personal diary—written after the war—in which he described his time in Auschwitz and prepared himself for the Polish Communist Party investigation and the French state judicial inquiry. It also includes letters and other documentary sources from his father, Yitzhak Gruenbaum, covering the time he stayed in Paris searching for supporting documents and testimonies on behalf of his son; the varied documents of the Polish Communist tribunal, which were located, after extensive efforts, in the Central Archives of Modern Records, Poland; and records of the French state judicial inquiry—all novel materials published for the first time. It is also based on the diverse records of the ultra-Orthodox community and on Israeli records encompassing the first decades of the fledgling state of Israel, which helped me to analyze and evaluate Eliezer's postmortem story and the political struggle over its definition.

3. See for example, remarks by his direct disciple, Moshe Sneh (Kleinbaum), in Emanuel Meltzer, ed., *Moshe Sneh—Writings* (Tel Aviv, 1995) [Hebrew], vols. 1, 3, and Roman Frister, *Without Compromise* (Tel Aviv, 1987) [Hebrew].

4. On Zionist politics in Poland, see Israel Bartal and Yisrael Gutman, eds., *Broken Chain: Polish Jewry through the Ages* (Jerusalem, 1997) [Hebrew]; Alexander Guterman, *Warsaw Jewish Community between the Two World Wars: National Autonomy Enchained by Law and Reality 1917–1939* (Tel Aviv, 1997) [Hebrew]. On Gruenbaum's role in it, see Frister, *Without Compromise*; Yitzhak Gruenbaum, *Speeches in the Polish Sejm,* ed. Mordechai Halamish (Jerusalem, 1963) [Hebrew].

5. Founded in 1913 in Galicia in Austria-Hungary. For more details see Eli Tsur, *Before Darkness Fell: HaShomer HaTzair in Poland and Galicia 1930-1940* (Sde Boqer, 2006) [Hebrew]; Moshe Zertal, *Den of Youth: Chapters on HaShomer HaTzair in Warsaw 1913–1943* (Tel Aviv, 1980) [Hebrew]; David Zait, *Shomer Dreams of Utopia: HaShomer HaTzair in Poland, 1921–1931* (Be'er Sheeva, 2002) [Hebrew].

6. The Communist Party in Poland was banned after the May 1926 coup by Jozef Piłsudski. The legal issue is discussed in J. Gutner et al., 1929, No. 105/1454, Duracz Archives, situated in the Archive of the Institute of Party History of the United Polish Workers' Party, at the Archiwum Akt Nowych (Central Archives of Modern Records, Warsaw) [hereafter AAN-PPR]

7. Frister, *Without Compromise,* 267–77; Yonatan Gruenbaum, unpublished manuscript, chapter on Eliezer Gruenbaum. Yonatan Gruenbaum's unpublished manuscript has no title. A portion is in the possession of the author. Other portions are quoted by other writers, as noted. The section *HaTragedia shel Eliezer Gruenbaum* was kindly shown to me by Matti Regev.

8. The number of Jews in the International Brigades was disproportionately high. See Sigmund Stein, *Der birger-krig in Shpanye Zikhroynes fun a militsioner* (Paris, 1961); Gerben Zaagsma, *Jewish Volunteers in the Spanish Civil War: A Case Study of the Botwin Company* (master's thesis, University of London, 2001).

9. Gruenbaum testimony, Gruenbaum file no. 15087, AAN-PPR; Gruenbaum testimony in front of Kowalski and Eisner, 13 August 1945, 29 November 1945, André Ballot, Private Collection; Jean Jerome, *Les clandestins (1940-1944): souvenirs d'un temoin* (Paris, 1986), 50–52.

10. It was part of a larger deportation from the unoccupied zone of eleven thousand to thirteen thousand foreign Jews agreed between Vichy Premier Pierre Laval and Theodore Dannecker, Eichmann's representative in France.

11. André Ballot argument, 29 November 1945, André Ballot, Private Collection; Gruenbaum Diary, 13 August 1945 (located in the possession of his heirs). A portion of Gruenbaum's diary was published in Reuven Avinoam, ed., *Gevilei Esh,* vol. 1 (Tel Aviv, 1962). See also Bernard Mark, *Megilat Oshvits* [The Scrolls of Auschwitz] (Tel Aviv, 1978) [Hebrew], 54–55; "The Truth about Gruenbaum," Charles Pepernik, Massuah Archives, Kibbutz Tel Yitzhak, no date.

12. Issac Ochshorn affidavit, documents of the legal proceeding, André Ballot, Private Collection; Yonatan Gruenbaum, unpublished manuscript, chapter on Eliezer Gruenbaum, 18–19; Testimonies from the hearing, Paris 1945–46, Ochshorn testimony, 17 February 1946, Levana Frenk Private Collection in Israel. Another testimony of Ochshorn can be found in Yad Vashem Archives, Jerusalem. See also Bernard Mark, *The Scrolls of Auschwitz* (Tel Aviv, 1985).

13. Gruenbaum testimony, 13 August 1945, AAN-PPR, Gruenbaum file no. 15087; see also Victor Majzlik testimony, 18 July 1945, in the same file.

14. Gruenbaum's testimony, 13 August 1945, Gruenbaum file no. 15087, AAN-PPR. It is not clear from Gruenbaum's words whether two proceedings were held in Buchenwald or only one. However, we can determine from his testimony that the accusations were unfounded, and that he did not act differently from the camp custom. See also André Ballot summation, 110–34 in the file, André Ballot, Private Collection.

15. Document from Ministry of Justice, Directorate for War Crime Investigations Service, Paris, 20 March 1946, André Ballot, Private Collection. Letter from the director to the Legal Assistant of Commissaire de Gouvernement, 11 rue Boissy d'Anglas, Paris, reference no. 2805-ac-jm-52-334, office of Mr. Marchessaux, André Ballot, Private Collection.

16. See Daniel Finkelkraut testimony, October 1945, André Ballot, Private Collection, and compare with his testimony, file no. 15087, 9 August 1945, AAN-PPR.

17. Yonatan Gruenbaum, unpublished manuscript, chapter on Eliezer Gruenbaum, 19; Frister, *Without Compromise,* 299.

18. Uriel Ben-Hanan, "A Grandson from the War," *Hotam* (weekly supplement of *Al HaMishmar* magazine), 12 May 1989, 4–7; Galia Glasner-Heled interview with Rivka Gruenbaum, Eliezer's sister in-law, private collections in Israel held by Glasner-Heled and Eran Turbiner; Frister, *Without Compromise,* 300–301.

19. Uriel Ben-Hanan, "A Grandson from the War"; Frister, *Without Compromise,* 302; Galia Glasner-Heled and Dan Bar-On, "Eliezer Gruenbaum: The Structuring of a Kapo's Story within the Framework of the Collective Memory of the Holocaust," *Alpayim* 27 (2004): 111–46.

20. Nahum Barnea, "King of the Jews and His Sons," *Koteret Rashit,* 3 December 1986, 24–31; Yitzhak Gruenbaum, The former Minister of Interior (as appears on the letterhead), 8 Dizengoff Street, Tel Aviv to IDF Immortalization Department at the Ministry of Defense, 6 August 1952, courtesy of Doron Avi-Ad, IDF and Defense Establishment Archives, Tel Aviv.

21. Ka-Tzetnik is the pen name of Yehiel De-Nur (1909–2001), an Orthodox Jewish writer and Holocaust survivor. De-Nur, one of few who met Eichmann at Auschwitz and survived, testified at Eichmann's trial in June 1961, fainted, and was subsequently unable to resume his testimony. Among his books: *Salamandra* (1946); *House of Dolls* (1953); *Atrocity* (1961); and *Stars of Ashes* (1966)—all deal with his Auschwitz experience.

22. Isaac Rembah, "When Not Fathers but Sons Eat Sour," [Banim achlu boser אכלו בוסר בנים] *Herut,* 10 September 1961.

23. Isaac Rembah, "What of Früchtenbaum and the *Scrolls of Fire?*" [Ma leFrüchtenbaum ve le'Gville Haesh'?—?'מה לפרוכטנבוים ול'גווילי האש], *Herut,* 24 September 1961. Lehi and IZL forces were irregular paramilitary groups connected with the right-wing movements in pre-state Israel. Menachem Begin was the commander of IZL and Yitzhak Shamir was the commander of Lehi.

24. Galia Glasner-Heled and Dan Bar-On, "Eliezer Gruenbaum: The Structuring of a Kapo's Story within the Framework of the Collective Memory of the Holocaust"; Galia Glasner-Heled interview with Rivka Gruenbaum, Eliezer's sister in-law, Glasner-Heled collection; H. Copper "Who Will Laugh Last" cited Eliezer from an interview he gave to the journalist Bezalel Kahan; Menachem Gerlik comment to Eran Turbiner, Turbiner collection.

CHAPTER 14

Pressure Groups versus the American and British Administrations during and after World War II

Arieh J. Kochavi

In the conclusion to his book, *British Jewry and the Holocaust,* Richard Bolchover writes, "...whether British Jews could have succeeded in pushing the British government into meaningful action relating to the Jews of Europe is a matter which must be left to historians of British politics, rather than those of British Jews."[1] In fact Jewish organizations' efforts during World War II to push the British and American governments to aid European Jews should also be examined within the broader context of the effectiveness of non-Jewish pressure groups.

The strategic demands of war in general, and total war in particular, greatly affected policy makers' priorities, and often marginalized humanitarian and moral considerations. During World War II, many pressure groups found it difficult, if not impossible, to influence Anglo-American policies when their demands clashed with military interests. After the war, although geostrategic considerations continued to dominate the two Western powers' priorities, political and electoral considerations now helped pressure groups to induce decision makers, particularly in the United States, to consider their demands favorably as long as these did not clash with the wishes of the majority of the American people.

This chapter will examine case studies of pressure groups, both Jewish and non-Jewish, that tried to spur the American and British administrations to meet their requests during World War II, when the ultimate goal was defeating Nazi Germany. I shall draw parallels to postwar case studies wherein pressure groups,

Notes for this section begin on page 262.

namely, American Jews and the Polish-American Congress (PAC), achieved partial success in influencing the White House position regarding their European brethren in displaced persons (DP) camps in Germany and Austria.

The Governments-in-Exile in Wartime

In early 1940, the Polish government-in-exile appealed to the British government to condemn Nazi crimes in Poland, and to impart clearly to the Germans that they would have to answer for their violations of international law. This idea was met with firm opposition in the British Foreign Office. Sir Orme Sargent, deputy undersecretary of state in the Foreign Office, maintained that any such declaration would be regarded as mere propaganda.[2] Frank Roberts of the Foreign Office even doubted the accuracy of the atrocity reports, which came mainly from Polish and Czech sources. Britain, Roberts thought, was in no position to issue absolutely reliable official statements. Nevertheless, the need to buttress the endurance of both the Polish people and its government-in-exile led the Foreign Office to modify its stand, so that by mid February 1940, London agreed in principle to the publication of a joint Anglo-French-Polish declaration.[3]

Eight weeks passed, however, before the statement was actually published. In part, the delay was caused by differences over the phraseology of the declaration. The British Foreign Office rejected the Polish draft, whereby the signatories of the declaration reserved "the right to pursue and punish according to the full force of the law persons of German nationality guilty of having committed acts in flagrant contradiction of the laws and customs of war."[4] Foreign Office officials further rejected a revised, less controversial draft that stated that the three signatories "desire to make a formal and public protest to the conscience of the world against the action of the German Government, whom they must hold responsible for these crimes which cannot remain unpunished."[5] The Poles were forced to give way in the face of London's determination not to issue a forthright statement. The declaration eventually published in mid April 1940 accused the German government of opening the war against Poland "by brutal attacks upon the civilian population of Poland," and stated that Germany's acts "clearly reveal a policy deliberately aiming at the destruction of the Polish nation."[6] The concluding sentence, however, refrained from threatening with any punishment those responsible for the crimes, either the political leaders or the actual perpetrators. It thus diluted the declaration's message and nullified whatever deterrent value it might have had.

Two years later in April 1942, following the execution in Warsaw of a hundred hostages in retaliation for the killing of two German policemen, London was requested by the Polish government-in-exile to declare that its bombardments of central and western Germany were reprisals for the killing of Polish hostages. The Foreign Office rejected the idea out of hand, stating that military considerations alone determined selection of targets for aerial raids.[7] The Poles also failed to convince the United States government, which was pulled into the war the previous December, to apply stringent measures against the U.S. property of German nationals, and drastic measures against German citizens residing in territory under Allied control. President Franklin D. Roosevelt wrote to General Władisław Sikorski, the Polish prime minster in London, that although the American people were deeply incensed at the barbaric treatment meted out by the Nazis, "they are as yet not prepared to resort to such measures as the indiscriminate bombing of the civilian population of enemy countries, or to the meting out of such treatment to innocent enemy aliens in the United States."[8]

British Prime Minister Winston Churchill's visit to the United States, in June 1942, was regarded by Sikorski as a chance to urge the two Western leaders to consider ways to deter the Germans from continuing their crimes. In a letter to Churchill, the Polish prime minister stressed that the Germans' principal aim was "the extermination of the Polish nation." The Polish prime minister refrained from noting that most of the victims were Polish Jews. Sikorski expected Churchill and Roosevelt to agree on the need for reprisal bombing. Large-scale bombing of nonmilitary objectives in Germany, according to Sikorski, "would undoubtedly restrain the Germans from pursuing their present policy of terrorism." He further argued that the Germans had always interpreted the Allies' strict adherence to the rules of international law as a sign of weakness. Sikorski's requests went unanswered.[9]

In reprisal for the assassination of Reinhard Heydrich, the Reichsprotektor of Bohemia and Moravia, the Germans destroyed the village of Lidice on 10 June 1942. The assassins were Czech resistance fighters who had parachuted earlier into Czechoslovakia from Britain. The Czech government-in-exile, in cooperation with the British Special Operations Executive, had planned and directed the successful attempt on Heydrich's life. A total of 192 men and 71 women of the village were shot to death. Of the 198 women deported to Ravensbrück, 143 returned after the war while of the 98 children that were dispersed, only 16 survived.[10] Several days after the massacre, the Czech government-in-exile asked the British to announce that for every village treated in the manner of Lidice, the Royal Air Force would raze to the ground a small village or town in Germany. Hubert Ripka, the Czech foreign minister, described the massacre in Lidice as "an atrocity which is without parallel in the history of modern warfare." He was certain that such a declaration would not only have enormous impact on the inhabitants of the occupied countries, but would also help the German people to recognize "the kind of calamity in which they will ultimately become involved as a result of the fiendish deeds of the Nazis."[11]

In London, most Foreign Office officials opposed the Czech proposal. Roberts argued that if an announcement were made that air raids constituted reprisals for specific German brutalities, the Germans could abandon these particular crimes and that then, "we should be in a rather difficult position as regards continuing our raids."[12] Dennis Allen, of the Central Department in the Foreign Office, argued against the Czech claim that the suggested declaration would augment the morale of civilians in occupied Europe. He further contended that these people hoped for active measures, not mere declarations. Allen quoted Royal Air Force Marshal Charles F.A. Portal's evaluation, that there was nothing the Germans would like more than the diversion of the British bombing effort from their built-up industrial areas to their villages. He did not rule out the possibility that the Germans might even increase their atrocities, in the hope of diverting Allied bombing to German villages. Allen also raised the possibility of the reprisal policy leading to German counter-reprisals.[13]

Orme Sargent, deputy undersecretary of state in the Foreign Office, took a different approach. He suggested that after the next big raid, Britain would announce the raid had been intended as an act of reprisal for specific atrocities committed by the Germans. Referring to Roberts's apprehension, Sargent remarked, "There is such a large accumulation of German atrocities to work off that I do not think we need be worried by the prospect of not being able to justify our raids because the Germans suddenly stop their atrocities."[14] Sargent failed to convince his colleagues, however, and Whitehall firmly adhered to its rejection of the Czech request, making it clear that the bombing program was carefully designed to systematically destroy Germany's war potential, and that the Air Staff would refuse any suggestion to divert bombers to what they considered to be unessential targets. Whitehall's stand was influenced by Britain's difficult position in the battlefield.[15]

Jewish Organizations in Wartime

Several British and U.S. officials who dealt with the Polish and Czech governments' appeals also dealt with Jewish organizations' pleas. British government officials tended to doubt the information. In particular, they questioned reports from Jewish sources and considered them of little substance. News of the mass killings of Jews first reached the West toward the end of 1941. For example, in November the British Minister in Bern, D.V. Kelly, reported that about 1.5 million Jews who were living in eastern Poland had disappeared. Kelly also learned from the Netherlands' minister in Bern that 50 percent of the Dutch Jews who had been sent to German concentration camps were now dead. About that time, the *Jewish Chronicle* reported that one-third of all the Jews in Bessarabia had been killed, and that thousands had died in pogroms in the Ukraine. In mid

March 1942, the Hungarian representative to the American Jewish Joint Distribution Committee (JDC) reported that two hundred and forty thousand Jews had been murdered by the Gestapo in the Ukraine, and in early April the Dutch government-in-exile reported that ten thousand Dutch Jews had been killed in poison gas experiments at Mauthausen. In the beginning of June, the BBC also reported the physical extermination of the Jewish population on Polish soil.[16]

Nevertheless, in public statements made by British and American officials during the first year after the German invasion of the Soviet Union denouncing Germany's terror and massacres, no reference had been made to the Jews. Even Jewish leaders in Britain and the United States failed to grasp the enormity of what was happening and did not realize at the start of these killings that their European brethren were the object of a methodical extermination campaign. In her book, *Buried by the Times*, Laurel Leff writes that for the first half of 1942 the World Jewish Congress (WJC), which served as an umbrella organization for Jewish organizations worldwide, "tried to confirm that the worst was true; during the second half, the organization struggled to get the world to believe it."[17]

Indeed, on 29 June 1942, the WJC held a press conference in London. They presented a report received from the Jewish Socialist Party in Poland, the Bund, according to which between June 1941 and April 1942 some seven hundred thousand Polish Jews had been killed in German-occupied Poland. The WJC estimated that the Nazis had already murdered more than a million Jews, mostly in Poland, Lithuania, Russia, and Romania. Following this press conference, American Jewish organizations called several mass meetings in various big cities in the United States, the most important of which took place in New York's Madison Square Garden on 21 July. British and American newspapers, including *The Times* of London and *The New York Times*, told their readers of the charges of the massacre of a million Jews, but did so in an inconspicuous, understated manner.[18] Referring to *The New York Times* coverage of the Holocaust, Leff writes, "No American newspaper was better positioned to highlight the Holocaust than the *Times*, and no American newspaper so influenced public discourse by its failure to do so. The first [tendency] makes the *Times'* failure more puzzling, the second more devastating."[19]

British and American officials continued to treat the reports on the systematic killing of the Jews with skepticism, and even disbelief. A characteristic example was the handling of the report, in August 1942, by Dr. Gerhardt Riegner, the Geneva representative of the WJC, of the existence of a German plan for the systematic extermination of Europe's Jews. Rabbi Stephen S. Wise, president of the American Jewish Congress, followed the State Department advice to withhold the news from the press until the Department confirmed the information. It was only on 24 November that Wise informed reporters that 2 million Jews had been murdered, that a mere one hundred thousand of the five hundred thousand Jews formerly in Warsaw were still there, and that the Germans were moving Jews from all over Europe to Poland for mass killing.[20]

Nevertheless, in the beginning of December 1942 Roberts of the British Foreign Office argued that although atrocities were undoubtedly taking place, there was no reliable evidence of a plan to exterminate the Jews. He warned that the time was not suitable "to breathe fire and fury against the Germans in connection with their treatment of the Jews, since Hitler now has in his power our former friends in France and in particular M. [Paul] Reynaud, M. [Georges] Mandel, M. [Edouard] Daladier and M. [Léon] Blum." Roberts further observed that Hitler was in a very difficult mood on the POWs issue, and therefore it seemed better not to irritate the Führer "more than is necessary, [in] particular on a Jewish issue."[21] At the same time, Hitler was angered by the British refusal to desist from shackling captured German soldiers, and in response the Germans manacled thousands of British POWs.[22]

In Washington, the State Department's specialist on refugee issues, Robert Borden Reams, doubted "the desirability or advisability of issuing a statement of this nature." He expressed skepticism about the accuracy of the information that had come from Riegner and others in Switzerland, and warned that a statement from Washington would be regarded as official confirmation that in turn could lead to "further pressure from interested groups for action which might affect the war effort." Reams also feared that should the Germans decide to release Jews living under their control, the burden of caring for them would fall upon the United States and Britain.[23]

About this time, Jewish leaders in the United States were stunned to learn that both London and Washington made a distinction between atrocities committed against Allied nationals and those directed against Axis citizens, including German, Romanian, Slovakian, and Hungarian Jews. International law during World War II did not consider offenses committed by an enemy nation against either its own nationals, or those of other Axis countries, as war crimes. Such acts were deemed part of the domestic policy of a sovereign state. Nevertheless, the WJC called London's attention to the fact that the Jews "form a special class of victims," as the crimes against them were being committed only by reason of their connection with the Jewish race and faith. In light of the special character of the crimes being committed against the Jews, the WJC asked to collaborate in the work of the proposed United Nations War Crimes Commission (UNWCC). The British government declined.[24] Roger Allen of the Foreign Office maintained that crimes committed against Axis nationals were not war crimes, and that considering them as such would involve extending the scope of the proposed commission. The issue, he argued, was political, not legal, and should be dealt with as such.[25]

Allen's remark reflected a tendency among some Foreign Office officials to consider the plight of European Jews within the wider context of the Zionist struggle over Palestine. Allen seemed to be concerned about the possible political ramifications of recognizing Zionist-affiliated organizations as legitimate representatives of the Jewish people. His position should be considered against the backdrop of Whitehall's decision, on the eve of the war in Europe, to rescind its support of the proposal to partition of Palestine into separate Arab and Jewish states. The new policy was part of Whitehall's effort to appease the Arabs, and was manifested in the White Paper of May 1939, which envisioned the establishment, within ten years, of an independent Palestinian state with an Arab majority within all of Palestine. It provided for the immigration of seventy-five thousand Jews for a period of five years (any further immigration would be conditioned on Arab consent), and limited the sale of land by Arabs to Jews. The Zionists tried to undermine the White Paper restrictions by fostering illegal immigration of Jews from Europe, among other means.[26]

Despite the opposition of some British and American officials, on 17 December 1942 British Foreign Minister Anthony Eden issued a statement in Parliament, in the name of eleven Allied governments, to the effect that the German authorities "are now carrying into effect Hitler's oft-repeated intention to exterminate the Jewish people in Europe." Eden concluded by stating that those responsible for these crimes would not escape retribution.[27] The statement caused great excitement in Parliament, but led to no practical results. The Foreign Office continued to oppose attempts to include the murder of Jewish residents of the Axis countries in the category of war crimes.[28] Furthermore, two weeks after he had issued the declaration, Eden chaired a Cabinet Committee on the Reception and Accommodation of Jewish Refugees, which decided that Britain could not admit more than one to two thousand refugees. Not only did opposition to granting asylum to Jewish refugees prevail; officials in both Britain and the United States continued to express doubts regarding the veracity of reports on the extermination of the Jews. The gap between public declarations and the policy actually taken remained as wide as ever.[29]

By the summer of 1943, Jewish organizations had failed both to influence London and Washington to publish another statement denouncing the barbaric atrocities committed by the enemy, and to convince the Foreign Office to support Jewish collaboration in the work of the United Nations War Crimes Commission. Allen dismissed the argument that the Jews were a special class of victims, and warned against accepting the claim that all crimes committed by the Nazis against Jews "are to be classed as war crimes." He further maintained that the Jewish organizations "have long been angling for separate representation not only in connection with war crimes but also with regard to the peace settlement generally. It is, I think, agreed that we should resist such proposals."[30] Here again, the Foreign Office official was mainly concerned with geopolitical considerations—the struggle over Palestine's future in the aftermath of the war. Several weeks earlier, on 19 April 1943, British and American teams met in

Bermuda to examine ways to rescue Jews. The ten-day conference was a fiasco that produced no practical results.[31]

American and British POWs in Wartime

Official British and American policies toward the safety of Allied POWs in Nazi Germany provides another perspective in analyzing the wartime priorities of Allied policy makers. In contrast to the previous cases, when decisions regarded non-British or U.S. citizens, the fate of British and American soldiers was now at stake. The murder of forty-seven British POWs who had escaped Stalag Luft III on the night of 24–25 March 1944 raised concern, both in London and Washington, but no serious attention was given to the issue.[32] The Allied invasion of Normandy on 6 June 1944 augmented fears of possible German reprisals. Broadly speaking, intelligence projections held that, unlike the SS, the Wehrmacht in general adhered to the provisions of the Geneva Convention of 1929, and that German military commanders would not allow action to be taken against Allied POWs. Intelligence analysts thought it possible that Nazi die-hards would resist to the bitter end and that, fully armed, utterly ruthless, and totally indifferent to the consequences to either their country or themselves, they might try to avenge the defeat of their Führer and the Nazi cause, even at "five minutes past twelve." Their victims would be both British and American prisoners of war and enslaved workers.[33] Still, there was no similarity between German policy toward British and American POWs and that toward Soviet prisoners. All in all, about three and a quarter million Soviet POWs perished in German captivity, approximately two million of them during the second half of 1941.[34]

The exchange of seriously ill and wounded British and German POWs in September 1944 provided both the Americans and the British with an opportunity to learn about an impending change in German attitudes toward the POWs. In a memorandum circulated among the British War Cabinet in October 1944, James Grigg, the secretary of state for war, reported that interrogation of repatriated POWs revealed an apprehension in the camps concerning the attitude that SS and Gestapo personnel would adopt toward POWs. In some camps, German staff had hinted to the prisoners that there was a chance they would be used as hostages or even killed outright.[35]

British and U.S. officials both worried that Hitler and his associates might threaten to murder some or all of the prisoners unless the Allies agreed to come to terms.[36] In early November 1944, U.S. officials concluded that recent military developments indicated a high probability of large-scale mistreatment of American POWs in Germany, particularly U.S. Army Air Force personnel, upon cessation of hostilities in Europe.[37] These fears were also based on Hitler's order of 1 October 1944, which transferred supervision of all POWs and internees to Heinrich Himmler, who delegated actual control of POW affairs to his right-hand man, SS Lieutenant General Gottlob Berger.[38] In January 1945, U.S. Secretary of War Henry Stimson wrote in his diary, "We are now afraid that there will be mass murders as the Russian troops and our troops converge on the present camps in Germany where our prisoners are being held."[39] Five weeks earlier, in 17 December 1944, during the Battle of Bulge, eighty-four American prisoners were murdered by their German captors in what became known as the Malmédy massacre.[40]

The possibility that the Germans might begin to kill British and U.S. POWs without inhibition led the vice-chief of the Imperial General Staff, Lieutenant General Archibald E. Nye, to present the War Cabinet with three alternatives for assisting the POWs, or even providing them with some kind of protection. Two of the alternatives were categorized as direct assistance, namely, the use of airborne troops and the dropping of arms to prison camps. The third was to issue grave warnings, backed up, if necessary, by counter-threats.[41] The Americans accepted the British proposal to use troops and aircraft to assist POWs only when it would not interfere with battlefield operations, as in any case the basic premise for action was "upon the cessation of organized German resistance or of hostilities."[42]

This order of priorities had been manifested toward the end of February 1945, when General Dwight D. Eisenhower, supreme commander of the Allied Expeditionary Force (SCAEF), and General Harold R.L.G. Alexander, supreme allied commander in the Mediterranean (SACMED), were asked to prepare a plan "to dispatch troops by land or air in order to provide for the maximum initial security of such prisoners [U.S. and British POWs] in the European Theater and for [the] earliest possible evacuation of such prisoners using aircraft for this purpose wherever practicable." It was made clear, though, that protective troops and aircraft were to be deployed only "where their use does not conflict with gaining victory in the battle."[43] Though aware of the threat of German retaliation, both commanders believed that the best way to ensure the prisoners' safety was to allow military operations to unfold as planned. The defeat of the enemy came first.

That the overwhelming majority of Allied POWs would survive Nazi captivity, however, was ultimately far from self-evident, especially after D-Day. Still, when discussing options, both London and Washington ruled out diverting troops from the overall war effort. Even when Berlin replaced the Wehrmacht soldiers in charge of the camps with SS troops and later forced tens of thousands of British Commonwealth and American POWs to march into the German heartland, there was no change in Allied priorities.[44] Furthermore, the two powers continued devastating air raids on German cities, aimed to demoralize ordinary German civilians, despite the fear of reprisal acts against the POWs.[45]

The Allied military victory indeed saved the lives of British and American POWs. But it is hard to escape the conclusion that Allied leaders took a calculated risk. The anxiety of POWs' families played no role in the decision-making process. When, for example, it was suggested in February 1945 to ask the Germans to allow POW camps to be overrun by the advancing Red Army instead of evacuating Allied prisoners, Foreign Office officials rejected the idea. In the words of Deputy Undersecretary Sargent, "It would most certainly create in the minds of the Germans an impression of weakness at the very moment when it is so vital to drive home the overwhelming superiority of the Allies."[46]

The Postwar Period: Polish DPs

After World War II, Polish DPs formed the largest national group in the American and British occupation zones in Germany and Austria, and constituted the main problem for the American and British occupation authorities. Unlike the 2 million Soviet DPs, forcibly repatriated after the war ended as part of an arrangement with Moscow, Polish DPs could decide whether they wanted to return to Poland or not. Though eager to solve the DP problem as quickly as possible, both the Americans and the British were opposed to forcible repatriation of Polish DPs, most of whom were anti-Communists. The policy was to grant the DPs time and opportunity to decide their own future.[47] In the fall of 1945, Polish DPs in the British occupation zone of Germany were estimated at about 510,000, while the American zone had about 255,000 Polish DPs. By that time, both the British and American military authorities came to realize that the DPs preferred to remain in the camps rather than return to the inevitable hardship that would befall them in their homeland.[48]

In addition to the above, there were also large groups of Jewish DPs of Polish origin. When the war was over, less than sixty thousand Jewish survivors of the Holocaust from several European countries remained in Germany. During the next two years, tens of thousands of Jews fled Eastern Europe and the Balkans, so that by the end of 1947 the number of Jewish DPs in the western zones had increased to approximately 230,000, the overwhelming majority of whom were Polish Jews.[49] Concerned over the plight of their brethren DPs, Polish and Jewish organizations in the United States tried to influence their government's policy on this issue. After the war, the American political leadership proved to be more responsive to pressure groups.

In mid December 1945, Field Marshall Bernard L. Montgomery, the military governor of the British zone, recommended 1 April 1946 as a cutoff date after which "any displaced person who, without reasonable cause, refuses to return to his country would be taken out of his camp and set to work as a civilian in Germany living on German rations and under conditions parallel to Germans."⁵⁰ Most Polish officers working with the DPs in the British zone were affiliated with the former Polish government-in-exile, and the Foreign Office, under pressure by former members of that government, rejected Montgomery's proposal as an effective forced repatriation to a postwar Polish state that was increasingly falling to Communist rule. In fact, between 1946 and 1948 the British admitted tens of thousands of Polish DPs into Britain. But they refused to open the gates to Jewish DPs, and even considered ways of ridding Britain of Jewish refugees who had entered before the war.⁵¹

Like their British colleagues, U.S. military officers in Germany and Austria also wanted to reduce the number of DPs under their care. In mid April 1946, Secretary of State James F. Byrnes informed President Harry S. Truman that the Departments of State and War had decided to close the DP camps by August 1946. Stressing their high cost, Byrnes asserted that, "there is no reason to believe they can be closed with less difficulty next year than now."⁵² Truman ruled out the decision. He feared negative reaction by American Catholics, and some 6 million Americans of Polish descent. Since war's end, the Polish-American Congress (PAC), representing various Polish-American organizations, demanded that the military cease pressure on the Polish DPs to return to "Russian-dominated Poland, where slavery instead of freedom awaits them."⁵³ Truman needed to retain the traditionally Democratic support of Polish Americans in the forthcoming midterm elections of November 1946. Consequently, on 22 April, Byrnes announced the delay in the closure of the camps.⁵⁴

The deteriorating situation in the American occupation zones led the military authorities in Germany to induce Polish DPs to return to Poland. The urgency stemmed from the enormous problems created by the mass influx of ethnic Germans (*Volksdeutsche*) forced from Eastern Europe and by the scarcity of food, fuel, and adequate housing in Germany and Austria.⁵⁵ The PAC complained to the White House about the discrepancy between Byrnes's official policy and actual practice. Hinting at the electoral potential of Polish Americans, Charles Rozmarek, the PAC's president, demanded that Polish DPs be treated like the Jewish DPs, namely, as non-repatriable. Following Democratic defeats in the November elections, Rozmarek stressed that "the unfair discrimination causes tremendous anxiety among millions of Americans of Polish descent, many of whom have relatives in the American Zone of Occupation in Europe [sic]."⁵⁶

Rozmarek was in fact following the steps taken by Jewish organizations in the United States, who had succeeded in gaining the president's ear. Truman's recognition of the Jewish DPs as a distinct national group entitled to separate Jewish camps; his designation of Palestine as the main destination of the Jewish DPs and his appeal to the British to allow entry of one hundred thousand Jewish DPs into Palestine—all had decisive repercussions for the outcome of the Zionist struggle. All helped the Zionist claim that Jewish DPs were part of a single and distinct people, the Jewish nation, for whom Zionism sought a state in Palestine.[57]

The success of both Polish and Jewish organizations in the United States was due mainly to Truman's electoral considerations. Still, White House concessions to both groups were not as significant as they might have been. When non-Zionist Jewish organizations in the United States mounted an intensive, well-financed campaign to permit an expanded, four-year annual immigration quota for refugees coming to the United States, Truman, conscious of the strong congressional and popular opposition, refrained from supporting this initiative. Instead he supported the immigration of one hundred thousand Jewish DPs to Palestine, confronting his wartime ally at the height of the growing joint struggle against the Soviet Union over the shape of the postwar world.[58]

When Congress finally passed the Displaced Persons Act on 25 June 1948, allowing two hundred thousand DPs into the United States over a period of two years, the law included restrictions that minimized the number of Jewish DPs eligible to enter. Preference was given to DPs from the former Baltic States and the eastern regions of interwar Poland now annexed by the Soviet Union. In effect, many former Nazi collaborators from these regions received preference over Holocaust survivors. Truman, though signing the Act, condemned its discriminatory clauses, which prevented over 90 percent of Jewish DPs from entering the United States. Only in June 1950 was new legislation passed to abolish the 1948 restrictions. By then, most Jewish DPs in Europe had already left for the state of Israel, which was established in May 1948.[59]

Official British and American attitudes toward Jewish appeals during World War II corresponded with their reaction to pleas by other powerless pressure groups. Government officials in London and Washington easily neutralized pressures by stressing war priorities and the ultimate goal of defeating Nazi Germany. The reaction of the American and British administrations to the desperate calls of the Polish and Czech governments-in-exile and especially their decision to take a calculated risk with the fate of their own POWs demonstrated the Western powers' order of priorities during total war. When political and military interests clashed with humanitarian considerations, the latter were set aside.

But the two governments found it especially easy to push the pleas of Jewish organizations aside. British and American Jews enjoyed little support among the non-Jewish population and had hardly any leverage with their respective governments. The presidential elections in November 1944 gave the American Jewish community some leverage, as the Zionists succeeded in turning American Jewry into a political force by initiating a competition between the Democratic and Republican parties for the Jewish vote.[60] Nevertheless, for the overwhelming majority of the Jews of Europe it was already too late.[61]

Although postwar success by American Jewish organizations regarding Jewish DPs in Europe was impressive, it was due to unusual circumstances that were themselves limited. Truman, a non-elected president, enjoyed little popularity among the American public and needed the Jewish community's financial assistance and electoral support, especially in the important state of New York (forty-seven electoral votes), but also in Pennsylvania, Illinois, and Ohio. Moreover, the Jewish vote could determine results in a close election.[62] American Jewish demands regarding Jewish DPs and Palestine, furthermore, did not clash with U.S. interests at large; supporting these appeals were in fact a humane gesture which enjoyed broad American support.

Jewish organizations were less successful in appealing for unpopular policies, such as opening U.S. gates to Jewish refugees. When, on 22 December 1945, Truman set out U.S. policy on the absorption of DPs and refugees from war-ravaged Europe, he categorically stated that his country's contribution was limited to the scope of immigration provided for by current legislation, that unused immigration quotas did not accumulate, and that he would not ask Congress to change the law.[63] In short, America's contribution toward a solution for the DP problem would not go beyond allowing DPs entry within the existing immigration quotas. Jewish DPs, most of whom were Polish citizens, had little reason for optimism, since the annual immigration quota for Poland was 6,524.

British Foreign Secretary Ernest Bevin's statement at the Labour Party conference at Bournemouth, on 12 June 1946, that the propaganda in the United States, especially in New York, urging Britain to transfer one hundred thousand Jewish DPs to Palestine, had been motivated by the fact that "they did not want too many Jews in New York," had not been far from the truth.[64] The Displaced Persons Act of 1948 only confirmed Bevin's blunt, undiplomatic statement. In many respects, the attitude that typified the British and American policy toward European Jews before and during the war also persisted during the crucial years afterwards.

Notes

1. Richard Bolchover, *British Jewry and the Holocaust* (New York, 1993), 156.
2. Minute by Sargent, 5 February 1940, The National Archives (Kew), [hereafter TNA], FO 371/24422/C2026. See also Priscillia D. Jones, "British Policy towards German Crimes against the Jews, 1939-1945," *Leo Baeck Institute Yearbook* 36 (1991), 344–45; Bernard Wasserstein, *Britain and the Jews of Europe 1939-1945* (New York, 1979), 163–64.
3. Minute by Roberts, 5 February 1940, TNA, FO 371/24422/C2026.
4. Edward Raczyński (Polish ambassador to Britain) to Halifax, 31 January 1940, TNA, FO 371/24422/C2544.
5. Paris to Roberts, 26 February 1940, TNA, FO 371/24422/C3040.
6. Press notice, 17 April 1940, TNA, FO 371/24423/C5591.

7. Memorandum by W. Dennis Allen, 18 August 1942, TNA, FO 371/30992/C11241.

8. Memorandum of conversation, 25 March 1942, US Department of State, *Foreign Relations of the United States: Diplomatic Papers* (Washington, DC, 1961), [hereafter *FRUS*], 1942, vol. 3, 130–31.

9. Sikorski to Churchill, 22 June 1942, TNA, PREM 4/100/13. See also David Engel, *In the Shadow of Auschwitz: The Polish Government-in-Exile and the Jews, 1939-1942* (Chapel Hill, NC, 1987), 173–85.

10. On the assault on Heydrich, see Callum MacDonald, *The Killing of SS Obergruppenführer Reinhard Heydrich* (New York, 1989), 186–87.

11. Ripka to Anthony Eden, 18 June 1942, TNA, FO 371/30916/C6334.

12. Minute by Roberts, 18 June 1942, TNA, FO 371/30916/C6108.

13. Minute by Allen, 18 August 1942, TNA, FO 371/30922/C11241; Minute by Allen, 20 August 1942, TNA, FO 371/30917/C7870.

14. Minute by Sargent, 19 June 1942, TNA, FO 371/30916/C6108.

15. Nichols to R.M. Makins, 13 June 1942, TNA, FO 371/30916/C5976.

16. Wasserstein, *Britain and the Jews of Europe 1939-1945,* 163–68; Monty Noam Penkower, *The Jews Were Expendable: Free World Diplomacy and the Holocaust* (Urbana, IL, 1983), 59–61; Deborah E. Lipstadt, *Beyond Belief: The American Press and the Coming of the Holocaust 1933-1945* (New York, 1986), 149–58; Richard Breitman, *Official Secrets: What The Nazis Planned, What the British and the Americans Knew* (New York, 1998), 99–109.

17. Laurel Leff, *Buried by the Times: The Holocaust and America's Most Important Newspaper* (New York, 2005), 135.

18. Wasserstein, *Britain and the Jews of Europe 1939-1945,* 135–36, 167–68; David S. Wyman, *The Abandonment of the Jews: America and the Holocaust 1941-1945* (New York, 1984), 19–26; Dina Porat, *The Blue and Yellow Stars of David: The Zionist Leadership in Palestine and the Holocaust, 1939-1945* (Cambridge, MA, 1990), chs. 3–4; David Cesarani, *The Jewish Chronicle and Anglo-Jewry* (New York, 1994), 173–79; Martin Gilbert, *Auschwitz and the Allies: How the Allies Responded to the News of Hitler's Final Solution* (London, 1994), ch. 4; see also WJC to Eden, 18 February 1942, TNA, FO 371/30914/C2000.

19. Leff, *Buried by the Times,* 9.

20. Wyman, *The Abandonment of the Jews,* 42–55; Leff, *Buried by the Times,* 149–57; Lipstadt, *Beyond Belief,* 162–92.

21. Minute by Roberts, 1 December 1942, TNA, FO 371/30923/C11923.

22. Arieh J. Kochavi, *Confronting Captivity: Britain and the United States and their POWs in Nazi Germany* (Chapel Hill, NC, 2005), 40–53.

23. Memorandum by Reams, 9 December 1942, and memorandum, 10 December 1942, National Archives and Records Administration, College Park, MD [hereafter NARA], RG 59, 740.00116EW1939/694; Wyman, *The Abandonment of the Jews,* 73–75, 99, 112–13, 180.

24. A.L. Easterman to Viscount Simon, (Lord Chancellor), 27 October 1942, and Simon to Easterman, 16 November 1942, TNA, FO 371/34368/C8282. For the establishment of the United Nations War Crimes Commission, see Arieh J. Kochavi, "Britain and the Establishment of the United Nations War Crimes Commission," *The English Historical Review* 107, no. 423 (1992): 323–49.

25. Quoted in Jones, "British Policy Towards German Crimes," 349.

26. For the British campaign against Zionist efforts to undermine London's restrictive immigration policy in Palestine during World War II, see Dalia Ofer, *Escaping the Holocaust: Illegal Immigration to the Land of Israel, 1939-1944* (New York, 1990), chs. 7–9, 14; Ronald W. Zweig, *Britain and Palestine During the Second World War* (Woodbridge, 1996), chs. 3, 5.

27. German Policy of Extermination of the Jewish Race, 17 December 1942, NARA, RG 107, Assistant Secretary of War [hereafter ASW] John J. McCloy, 000.51, War Crimes Working File.

28. Arieh J. Kochavi, *Prelude to Nuremberg: Allied War Crimes Policy and the Question of Punishment* (Chapel Hill, NC, 1998), 151–64.

29. Wasserstein, *Britain and the Jews of Europe 1939-1945,* 170–82; Tony Kushner, *The Holocaust and the Liberal Imagination: A Social and Cultural History* (Cambridge, MA, 1994), 173–87; Louise London, *Whitehall and the Jews, 1933-1948* (New York, 2000), 204–23.

30. Minute by Allen, 30 July 1943, and G.W. Harriman to A.L. Easterman, World Jewish Congress, 3 August 1943, TNA, FO 371/34368/C8282.

31. Richard Breitman and Alan Kraut, *American Refugee Policy and European Jewry, 1933-1945* (Bloomington, IN, 1987), 139–42, 178–80; Wyman, *The Abandonment of the Jews,* 104–23.

32. *Hansard, House of Commons,* 23 June 1944, vol. 401, cols. 477–82; Arthur A. Durand, *Stalag Luft III: The Secret Story* (Baton Rouge, LA, 1988), 282–325.

33. Report by the JISC, JIC (44) 322, 29 July 1944, TNA, FO 916/894; see also JSM, Washington to AMSSO, no. 236, 1 September 1944, TNA, PREM 3/364/11.

34. Omer Bartov, *The Eastern Front, 1941-45, German Troops and the Barbarization of Warfare* (London, 1985), 106–41.

35. Memorandum on "Position of Imperial and American Ps/W on Collapse of Germany," 8 January 1945, TNA, AIR 40/280.

36. British Embassy, Washington, to Department of State, 19 October 1944, TNA, CAB 122/684.

37. Top Secret "American-British-Canadian," [hereafter ABC] 383.6. (16 June 1943), Sec. 1-A, note by the Secretaries, American Joint Planning Staff [hereafter JPS], 554, 6 November 1944, appendixes D & E, NARA, RG 165, Records of War Department General and Special Staffs [hereafter RWDGSS], Office of the Director of Plans and Operations [hereafter ODPO].

38. Headquarters Seventh Army, 8 January 1945, Chief of the Party Chancery, Circular Letter 288/44, Subject: "Reorganization of the Control of Prisoners of War," 30 September 1944, TNA, WO 193/345; see also, *Trials of War Criminals Before the Nürnberg Military Tribunals Under Control Council Law No. 10, Nürnberg October 1946-April 1949* (Washington, 1952), vol. 13, 32–34; David F. Foy, *For You the War is Over: American Prisoners of War* (New York, 1984), 20–30.

39. Henry L. Stimson Diaries, entry of 25 January 1945, Reel 9, frame 74, Yale University Library, Manuscripts and Archives, Henry Lewis Stimson Papers, New Haven, CT.

40. Gerhard L. Weinberg, *A World At Arms: A Global History of World War II* (New York, 1994), 766–67.

41. Report by the Vice Chiefs of Staff, WP(44) 512, 9 September 1944, TNA, PREM 3/364/11; Report by JPS, JP (44)234 (Final), 8 September 1944, NARA, RG 165, RWDGSS, ODPO, Top Secret "American-British-Canadian," ABC 383.6. (16 June 1943), Sec. 1-A.

42. Report by the JPS, JCS 1168/1, 28 December 1944, and memorandum by the USCOS, CCS 472/6, 3 January 1945, NARA, RG 218, Records of the U.S. Joint Chiefs of Staff [hereafter JCS] Combined Chiefs of Staff [hereafter CCS] 383.6 (1-15-44), Sec. 2; British Joint Staff Mission [hereafter JSM], Washington to AMSSO, no. 487, 5 January 1945, TNA, PREM 3/364/7.

43. CCS to Eisenhower and Alexander, no. 43767, 26 February 1945, NARA, RG 218, Records of the U.S. JCS CCS 383.6 (1-15-44), Sec. 2; Note by the Secretaries, Combined Chiefs of Staff, CCS 472/8, 27 February 1944, NARA, RG 165, RWDGSS, ODPO, Top Secret "American-British-Canadian," ABC 383.6. (16 June 1943), Sec. 2. See also Memorandum for Field Marshal Wilson, 21 February 1945, TNA, CAB 122/666.

44. For the POWs marches, see John Nichol and Tonny Rennell, *The Last Escape: The Untold Story of Allied Prisoners of War in Germany 1944-1945* (New York, 2002); Kochavi, *Confronting Captivity,* 203–54.

45. Weinberg, *A World At Arms,* 810–19.

46. Minute by Roberts, 22 February 1945, TNA, FO 916/1179; Sargent to Major General L.C. Hollis, War Cabinet Offices, February 1945, TNA, FO 916/1180.

47. For the forced repatriation of Soviet citizens, see Mark R. Elliott, *Pawns of Yalta: Soviet Refugees and America's Role in Their Repatriation* (Urbana, IL, 1982); Nicholas Bethell, *The Last Secret: The Delivery to Stalin of Over Two Million Russians by Britain and the United States* (London, 1974); Nikolai Tolstoy, *The Secret Betrayal* (New York, 1977).

48. Murphy to Byrnes, no.1199, 26 October 1945, NARA, RG 59, 800.4016 DP/10-145—800.4016 DP/10-3145; Malcolm J. Proudfoot, *European Refugees, 1939-1945* (Evanston, IL, 1956), 238–39.

49. Arieh J. Kochavi, *Post-Holocaust Politics: Britain, the United States and Jewish Refugees, 1945-1948* (Chapel Hill, 2001), 161–70, 174–82, 217–19.

50. Lieutenant General B.H. Robertson, chief of staff British zone, to the permanent undersecretary of state, Control Office for Germany and Austria, 8 December 1945, TNA, FO 371/51128/WR3682.

51. Political Division, Control Commission, "Displaced Persons Assembly Centers—Discipline," 31 July 1945, TNA, FO 1032/311; London, *Whitehall and the Jews*, 255–57. For the political arena in Poland, see John Coutouvidis and Jaime Reynolds, *Poland 1939-1947* (Leicester, 1986), 198–310; Stanislaw Mikolajczyk, *The Rape of Poland: Pattern of Soviet Aggression* (Westport, CT, 1972).

52. Memorandum for the president by Byrnes, 12 April 1946, Harry S. Truman Library, Independence, MO [hereafter TL], White House Official File [hereafter WHOF]: Official File [hereafter OF] 127.

53. Memorandum for the president by Byrnes, 12 April 1946, TL, WHOF: OF 127.

54. Note for the Press, no. 268, 22 April 1946, NARA, RG 107, ASW, Formerly Security-Classified Correspondence [hereafter FSCC] of Howard C. Peterson, December 1945–August 1947, ASW 383.7, Refugees and DPs; Byrnes to Robert Patterson, 23 April 1946, *FRUS*, 1946, vol. 5, 155; Truman to Cardinal Samuel Stritch, Archbishop of Chicago, 25 April 1946, TL, WHOF: OF 127.

55. Patterson to Byrnes, 29 November 1945, and Kenneth C. Royall to Dean Acheson, 19 January 1945, NARA, RG 59, 800.4016 DP/11-1745—800.4016 DP/11-3145.

56. Rozmarek to Truman, 31 December 1946, NARA, RG 59, 800.4016 DP/12-1246—800.4016 DP/1-1547; Rozmarek to Truman, 21 March 1947, NARA, RG 59, 800.4016 DP/3-1647—4-3047.

57. Michael J. Cohen, *Truman and Israel* (Berkeley, CA, 1990), 109–21; Arieh J. Kochavi, *Post-Holocaust Politics,* 89–97.

58. Leonard Dinnerstein, *America and the Survivors of the Holocaust* (New York, 1982), 115–61.

59. Dinnerstein, *America and the Survivors of the Holocaust,* 217–53: Hagit Lavsky, *New Beginnings: Holocaust Survivors in Bergen-Belsen and the British Zone in Germany, 1945-1950* (Detroit, 2002), 204–10; Zeev W. Mankowitz, *Life between Memory and Hope: Holocaust Survivors in Occupied Germany* (New York, 2010).

60. Zvi Ganin, *Truman, American Jewry, and Israel, 1945-1948* (New York, 1979), 8–15.

61. Executive Order, "Establishing a War Refugee Board," 22 January 1944, NARA, RG 107, Formerly Top Secret Correspondence of Secretary of War Henry Stimson ("State File"), War Refugee Board; see also Wyman, *The Abandonment of the Jews,* 193–211, 285–87; Ariel Hurewitz, "The Struggle over the Creation of the War Refugee Board," *Holocaust and Genocide Studies* 6, no. 1 (1991): 17–31; Penkower, *The Jews were Expendable,* 129–143; Breitman and Kraut, *American Refugee Policy,* 182–83, 190–204.

62. Cohen, *Truman and Israel,* 59–75.

63. *Public Papers of the Presidents of the United States, Harry S. Truman, 1945* (Washington, DC, 1961), no. 225; Acting commissioner of immigration and naturalization, to Truman, 7 August 1946, TL, WHOF: OF 127.

64. FO to Washington, no. 5827, 14 June 1946, TNA, FO 371/52529/E5546; Lord Inverchapel, British ambassador to the U.S., to FO, no. 3900, 13 June 1946, TNA, FO 800/485.

CHAPTER 15

Traveling to Germany and Poland
Toward a Textual Montage of Jewish Emotions after the Holocaust

MICHAEL MENG

"What is it?" asked *New York Times* editor A.M. Rosenthal in 1965. "It was the ghetto," an anonymous Polish writer replied, as they stood on the rubble of Jewish Warsaw, now buried underneath streets and apartment buildings. "The emptiness and the realization of what lay beneath the buildings," Rosenthal wrote, "made us cold and clammy, though it was July, and my wife wept, and, of course, so did I."[1] A little over a decade later, historian Fritz Stern voiced different emotions about returning to his hometown of Breslau, now Wrocław, writing about "curiosity" and a "stubborn loyalty to the integrity of the past."[2] Amid unfamiliar streets and new Socialist buildings, he stumbled upon traces of the past—his old streetcar route, the stone staircase in his gymnasium, the gooseberries in his grandmother's garden. This pastiche of old and new incited a sense of ease with the memories of his childhood places. Three decades after Stern, literary scholar Marianne Hirsch reflected on traveling to her "hometown." Although she had never been to Czernowitz before in her life, the sounds, sights, and tastes of this place—passed down by her parents who survived the Holocaust—vicariously made it her lost home. Her return provoked "pleasure and affection layered with bitterness, anger, and aversion."[3] In 2008, Maya Escobar, a 28-year-old performance artist from Chicago, blogged about how her friends reacted to her upcoming trip to Berlin: "Germany, how can you go there as a Jew? There are Jews in Germany?" These negative feelings became the "filter" through which Escobar encountered Berlin. She decided

---

Notes for this section begin on page 278.

to create a conceptual project called "Berlin's Eruv" to address "the assumed non-presence of Jews in Germany."[4]

This mélange of Jewish emotions about Central Europe across generations and time reveals this chapter's focus, intervention, and methodology. This essay is about travel, emotions, and space. Broadly traversing the postwar period and three generations of Jewish feelings, it follows three Jewish travelers to explore their emotions about Germany and Poland as expressed in their written or filmic texts.[5] I build from their experiences a montage-like portrait of Jewish encounters with Central Europe to reveal, first, the ambivalent nature of Jewish emotions about the region and, second, to suggest the intense emotional presence of post-Holocaust Germany and Poland among some North American and Israeli Jews.[6]

In so doing, I intervene in several scholarly discussions about Jewish memories of Europe as well as about the continent's importance to post-1945 Jewish history. A sizeable literature now exists on Jewish memories of Europe as a "vanished world" made up of little else than ruins and commemorative plaques.[7] As one scholar has put it, North American and Israeli Jews construe Europe as a "ruined shrine."[8] To be sure, ruination and sorrow are dominant images and emotions among Jews who live outside Europe, but they interact with many others. I show how Jewish emotions about Central Europe are quite complex and multivalent. Relatedly, I argue that postwar Germany and Poland have remained after the Holocaust significant transnational geographies of Jewishness, insofar as both countries have stimulated intense emotions and encounters over the past seventy years from Jews residing far beyond their borders. Even as Israel and the United States emerged after 1945 as central spaces of Jewish life, Germany and Poland have attracted profound, if highly ambivalent, emotional investment from Jews.[9]

To develop and narrate these arguments, I create something akin to a textual montage of multiple, juxtaposed emotions, which I glean from the works of three different intermediaries—travelers Jacob Pat (1890–1966), Amos Elon (1926–2009), and Yael Bartana (1970–).[10] Born in Białystok, Pat traveled to Poland from the United States in 1946 to mourn the country's ruination of Jewish life but also to witness its fragile rebuilding. In the early 1960s, Israeli journalist and writer Elon journeyed across Germany to observe its schizophrenic movement between forgetting and remembering the Nazi past. From 2006 to 2011, Bartana visited post-Communist Poland and reunited Germany as a video artist originally from Israel to probe memories of Holocaust ruination and to invite fantasies of Jewish rebirth in Central Europe. In bringing these three very different travelers together here, I have not selected them as putative representatives of seemingly holistic emotions, ones ordered, say, under the rubrics of generation, politics, or nationality. Rather, I am drawn to Bartana,

Elon, and Pat as travelers whose different experiences I assemble into clusters of emotions to begin forming a montage of Jewish feelings about Central Europe. This nascent composite image, if hardly complete, may capture at least some of the diversity of Jewish emotions about Germany and Poland.

In keeping with my montage-like approach, I forgo trying to write a totalizing linear narrative across the postwar period. Although I provide some diachronic contextualization when necessary, especially for Bartana's multitemporal project, I mostly take synchronic snapshots of key temporal moments—the immediate postwar years of the 1940s, the reconstruction years of the 1960s, and the post-Communist years of the 2000s. This approach also gestures at a rough temporal hypothesis: Jewish emotions about Germany and Poland—their type, intensity, style, and expression—have remained similarly *multiple* and *complex* across time and generations.[11]

Fear, Sadness, Anger

Jacob Pat, a well-known Yiddish writer and labor activist in Poland, went to the United States in 1938 on a business trip and stayed with the outbreak of World War II. As the executive secretary of the Jewish Labor Committee, he traveled to Poland in December 1945 on a sixty-day trip to evaluate the conditions of Jews in the country. He arrived in a Poland ravaged by war, occupation, genocide, postwar violence, and political transformation. Cities, industries, roads, and bridges lay in ruins; some five million Polish citizens had been killed; and the country's prewar ethnic minorities, once making up one-third of Poland's population, were almost entirely gone after the Nazi genocide of Polish Jewry and the postwar forced removal of Germans, Ukrainians, Lemkos, Belorussians, and Lithuanians. Meanwhile, the great powers shifted Poland's border nearly 125 miles to the west, and Polish Communists were consolidating political power between the years 1944–47. Amid this political and demographic upheaval, Jews attempted to rebuild some semblance of everyday life in Poland. In June 1946, the Jewish population totaled about 240,000, after tens of thousands of Polish Jews returned from the Soviet Union.[12] By 1949, the number had dropped to around 98,000, after a surge of anti-Jewish violence, which left somewhere between 500 and 1,500 Jews dead.[13]

Upon his return to the United States in 1946, Pat wrote his travelogue, *Ashes and Fire,* which appeared first in Yiddish in 1946 and then in English translation in 1947. Over ten chapters organized mostly by the cities he visited, it recounts the ruination of Polish Jewry and the hardships of rebuilding Jewish life in Poland based on conversations with survivors, interviews with Polish state officials, and his own observations. While Pat claims to have written objective reportage, his account is as mediated as any text is. Inasmuch as it documents the ruined landscape of Poland, mourns the dead, retells survivor stories, and preserves their memory, it writes Jewish history and bears witness to Jewish disaster, replicating archetypal experiences, memories, tropes, and paradigms of narrating Jewish catastrophes.[14] *Ashes and Fire* is also—and this is my mode of reading it here—an account of emotions expressed by an involved eyewitness, who lost family members in the Holocaust and likely would have died himself had he not traveled to the United States at a fortuitous moment.

Sadness is one of the most dominant emotions Pat evinces. Walking through Warsaw, a city he lived in for nearly twenty years, he barely can distinguish its streets amid all the fragments and detritus that now comprise the postwar urban landscape. He sees "traces of houses, charred covers of prayer books, a bill marked 'Paid,' a broken fork, a rusted spoon, a housewife's earthen pot, a ragged belt, the sole of a shoe."[15] Rather than aestheticizing these ruins, as some postwar observers of urban rubble were apt to do, Pat imbues them with emotive power. He does so on at least two levels. First, he turns to traditional Jewish commands to remember past suffering and to commemorate the dead, embracing the archetypal and emotionally demanding task of memory and mourning: "'Great like the sea is thy breach; who can bring healing to thee?' The ancient, everlasting words of Jeremiah's *Lamentations* ring in my ears. Once again the sea of Jewish suffering runs high. The waves roar, they rise and fall, carrying me with them."[16] Second, he produces some of his most emotive prose, complete with somatic motifs, when he writes about ruins. Shattered stones make Pat tremble, shiver, numb, shake, and cry.[17] As he writes: "and my father's house has left nothing behind—no balcony, no door, no threshold. Only a small, snow-covered pile of rubble, swept by a cold wind. I stood there in the hollow silence of my father's house, facing its nothingness. I cried."[18]

Along with such moments of deep sadness, Pat also expresses fear about being in Poland. On a basic level, this fear concerns his physical safety and the well-being of survivors living in the country, who tell him about how their bodies "begin to shake with fear" once the sun goes down.[19] On a deeper level, Pat voices fear and discomfort about witnessing death, emotions that peak when he visits Auschwitz. "It is night over Oswieczem," Pat writes. "A dark uncanny fear makes our limbs shake. A sudden panic wafts over to us from the ruined crematoriums, the barbed wires, the crumbling gas chambers, the dank torture dungeons, the bones and ashes at our feet."[20] As one gigantic corpse, Auschwitz seemingly laid bare for Pat the fragility of life, making him physically and psychically tremble at sites of human finitude.

To this possible ontological encounter with death, Pat experiences a different, more everyday level of disturbance: he witnesses an aberrant social reaction to death. As he prepares to leave Auschwitz, he notices "fast flitting shapes" moving across the open fields: "Could it be there are people here, running away from us, hiding behind trees? I strain my eyes. Who are these people? Why are they fleeing us? Are they the ghosts of murdered Jews? No—they are the gold-diggers of postwar Oswieczem—man-shaped vultures from the Polish countryside."[21] He explains what is going on: "'There's gold in Oswieczem,' people say, and come in droves to prospect among these Jewish bones. They come with spades and shovels and buckets and pickaxes. They delve with their bare hands elbow-deep in human ashes. They work after sunset and flee at the sight of men."[22] For a short second, Pat may have thought he was watching people harvest food to nourish the body before he realized he was watching humans harvest gold from ashes.[23] Seeing this uncanny practice must have been all the more unsettling, not least because Jews—as all humans do—invest tremendous energy into handling the dead.[24] In early postwar Poland, Jewish survivors excavated dead bodies of friends and family members to give them proper burial in cemeteries.[25]

Pat tells of other distressing moments about the dead, but he also discusses the rebuilding of Jewish life in Poland. Images of ruination coexist with ones of Jewish life: a portrait of a Jewish wedding immediately follows a description of the Warsaw Ghetto. Such juxtaposing images may reflect Pat's conflicted emotions about the prospects of Jewish life in Poland. On the one hand, he appears moved by the "stubborn determination" of Jews to rebuild their lives there. He is also in near awe of the memory work of the Central Jewish Historical Commission, which was established in 1944 to document Nazi crimes.[26] On the other hand, he pities Jews in postwar Poland and seems doubtful about their future life there. Touring a Jewish hospital in Tarnów, he writes of a "melancholy sight"—"old rags, tattered straw sacks, whimpering children, ailing women, war invalids, restless, haggard faces; the pitiful dregs of Poland's Jewry."[27] He concludes that Jews in Poland have "emigration fever," in no small part because "the Polish people as such is rotten with antisemitism."[28] In the end, anger, frustration, and disappointment toward Poland overcome his narrative.

Such negative emotions toward Poland have a deep history. Jews have long felt and still to this day feel anger toward Poland, an emotional response rooted in the traumas of Polish-Jewish relations since the late nineteenth century and above all during the war when Poles colluded in mass murder in multiple ways which historians are just now reconstructing.[29] However, in Pat's case, these negative emotions may also stem from the provenance and genre of his account. His book is based on firsthand experiences of Poland right after the Holocaust, an emotionally burdened space of ruination and death. Physical spaces powerfully shape human emotions; they trigger specific feelings and, crucially, they foreclose others from being expressed. In Pat's text, empathy is a key "lost emotion."[30] After sixty days of traveling across Poland, he barely mentions the country's general devastation, its scarcity of material goods, its population "transfers," its changed geographic borders, and its emerging transformation into a Communist state. The relationship between this absent emotion and the presence of others may be reciprocal. Pat's anger may foreclose the possibility of empathy, and the lack of empathy may only heighten his anger. The genre of Pat's text would only seem to intensify these negative feelings. Although Pat's eyewitness account does not take on exclusively the demands of memorialization, it mourns the death of Polish Jewry somewhat akin to memorial books (*yizker bikher*).[31]

Bewilderment, Discomfort, Empathy

"At Crematorium Number 3 people are speaking German again. '*Vorsicht, Herr Kollege, the mud is slippery. Give me your hand a second.*' '*Danke schön! Bitte schön!*' How odd it sounds in this icy, bleak landscape!" Amos Elon is at Auschwitz with a delegation of defense attorneys and court officers from Frankfurt during a three-day visit of the camp in December 1964.[32] "'*Herr Lanz, please measure the distance to the platform.*' … It is 125 yards from the wash barracks of the Women's Camp to the railroad platform, and 220 yards further from the platform along the wet dirt road to the gas chambers and crematoria." Elon explains what is happening: "The Frankfurt Court has sent them here to measure an outrage with a yard-stick. They have brought their tape-measures and cameras, like policeman to a traffic accident."[33] So begins Elon's account about his travels across West Germany.[34] Elon went to this "haunted land" in pursuit of ghosts. Although not a survivor of the Holocaust—Elon and his family left Vienna for Palestine in 1933—he arrived in West Germany with "resentment."[35] His travelogue moves through a range of conflicting emotions about West Germany, a place that deeply confuses him: Elon reacts sardonically to a country that calculates its crimes with a tape measure; yet he also reacts empathetically to one willing to measure its crimes. He wrote his travelogue in German to "sense in my bones what it means to be a German with this past in the background."[36]

Elon explores two interrelated questions about West Germany's postwar transformation, questions that have long animated and still do observers, scholars, journalists, and commentators both within and outside the country. How have Germans confronted their past? What kind of democracy has emerged in West Germany? Elon's answers to these questions are perhaps less known than those given by his contemporaries, such as Hannah Arendt, Theodor Adorno, Alexander Mitscherlich, Margarete Mitscherlich, and Günter Grass, who all emphasized, albeit in different ways, the presence of numbed emotions, repressed memories, and/or lingering Fascist tendencies in West Germany. Elon shares these views, but he also holds them at some distance, unwilling to follow entirely arguments, as Arendt posited, that Germans have "a genuine inability to feel."[37] Or, as Grass memorably put it, that Germans have to peel onions to shed a round, human tear.[38]

Elon articulates, rather, feelings of confusion, surprise, and unease. He is disturbed by Germany's discordant newness, prosperity, monotony, and tranquility. Its bland neon lights and twisting Mercedes stars point to new beginnings seemingly forgetful of the past. If Poland's ruined landscape saddens Pat, the absence of ruins in West Germany unsettles Elon. As he writes, "the resurrected cities—brand new, clean, sober, infinitely monotonous—stand on the former ruins."[39] The dialectic of urban modernization—the clearing away of the past for the building of something new—has eerily left behind few traces of the Third Reich. Yet, Elon does not read such urban erasure as a symptom of widespread societal repression of the past, an argument the Mitscherlichs made a year after his book came out. Instead, Elon sees how the Nazi past protrudes through Germany's new surfaces in the most contorted and disturbing of ways. Passing through the industrial city of Essen, once the "Armorer of the Third Reich," he finds nearly all traces of its past gone except one. Essen's massive and majestic synagogue stands amid rows of modernist buildings in this new "shopping city." In 1961, city officials transformed the synagogue into the House of Industrial Design to hold an exhibition of mixers, washing machines, and other wonders of the West German economic miracle. This reappropriation of the synagogue may have repressed certain layers of time—the building's history as a sacred space and its violent desecration during the Nazi period—but not the past writ large: the synagogue stood there as a conspicuous embodiment of the past. Germans could not repress the Nazi past altogether; too many of its markers remained to remind them of it.

Indeed, Elon discusses writers and intellectuals who carry "the past as a stone around the neck that becomes heavier rather than lighter with time."[40] Böll, Enzensberger, Grass, Hochhuth, Kluge, and Richter, among others, emerge as heroes in his account for their searing reflections on the Nazi past. Such efforts, combined with German attempts to forget and start anew, lead him to conclude that a kind of "moral schizophrenia" ails West Germany. Germany is like "a double-exposed negative: a pretty modern technicolor photo superimposed on the black-grey shadows of a massacre."[41]

This simile points to Elon's overall confusion about Germany's postwar transformation. Although he seems impressed with Germany's "phenomenal democratic development," he remains concerned about how deeply democracy has penetrated German "minds, emotions, and speech."[42] Some of his worries reproduce hackneyed arguments about putative German authoritarianism, illiberalism, and servility, but others are more incisive. Two concerns stand out in particular. First, Elon asks: "Are [Germans] more tolerant now than they were in the past?" He seems doubtful. Observing relations between labor migrants and West Germans, he emphasizes continuities in previous and current forms of xenophobia: "Guest workers 'smell,' as the Jews used to; they are supposed to be dirty."[43] Second, Elon doubts whether remembrance can produce progressive change in German society and politics. Returning to the Frankfurt Auschwitz Trial of 1963–65, he suggests that German efforts to confront the Nazi past—however halting and circumlocutory they may be—may serve cathartic ends rather than didactic ones. As he explains at length, memory may purge Germans of their emotions:

> What then do these trials achieve? Certainly they give satisfaction to the rest of the world because they 'prove' that the Germans are making an effort to 'overcome' their past. They also satisfy a sense of justice in Germany, a strongly developed sense even under the Nazis. The answer of a prominent West German, Fritz Bauer, Attorney General of Hessen, who is better informed on this subject than most others, is pessimistic.... 'The educational effect of these trials—if they have one at all—is minimal,' says Herr Bauer. 'Some positive effects would be a willingness to practice self-criticism, tolerance, humanitarianism, *Zivilcourage,* to make personal sacrifices when sacrifice can prevent evil or to revolt against unjust orders of authorities.' Has anything basically changed? Herr Bauer does not believe so.[44]

Such pessimism may disturb Elon the most about his travels to West Germany. For what is the alternative? No trials? No discussions? Forgetting the past? Such questions continued to confuse and haunt Elon long after he first traveled to early postwar Germany. Over the following four decades until his death in 2009, he continued to write about Germany's moral schizophrenia as the country changed in multiple ways, yet still struggled to wrestle with its past. He did so in the *New York Times* in 1997, when he appeared sardonically puzzled by Germany's vim for Daniel J. Goldhagen: "I was browsing through the shelves of a large Berlin bookstore recently when an elegantly dressed woman rushed in and asked for four copies ('gift-wrapped, please') of *Hitler's Willing Executioners.*"[45] He did so again, although more critically, when Germany unveiled the Berlin Jewish Museum in 2001. He found the "opening gala" solipsistic, the exhibition ostentatious, and the building didactically tyrannical. The whole thing led him to infer that "with so much hyperbole, so many undoubtedly sincere expressions of guilt and regret, and of admiration for all things Jewish, one could not help feeling that fifty years after the Holocaust, the new republic was, in effect, beatifying the German Jews."[46] Germany continued to bewilder him some four decades later.

And yet, despite his doubts, Elon claimed, in the end, that Germany had undergone a remarkable transformation. Reflecting perhaps his own emotional schizophrenia, he remarked in 2004: "the moral regeneration of Germany in the postwar period is one of the outstanding occurrences of our time."[47] Elon even overcame his earlier pessimism about the didactic effects of memory, as he came to believe in its capacity to alter human emotions and mentalities. In the early 2000s, he introduced his last book, *The Pity of It All: A History of Jews in Germany,* as an elegy to tolerance but also as a call for its enduring relevance.

"This book is the story of a minority at a moment in time that still bears urgently, I think, on our own," he said to an audience in Washington, DC. "Tolerance is the theme; it remains the essential ennobling project of modernity."[48]

Disappointment, Longing, Hope

Elon hardly stands alone in his perplexity about Central Europe. Another commanding figure who shares his hopes and frustrations—our last traveler here—is Israeli artist Yael Bartana, whose work intervenes in German, Polish, and Jewish memories of the Holocaust to critique nationalism and to imagine a kind of cosmopolitan existence of human beings. Stimulated by an "emotional deep disappointment" with, in part, the Israeli-Palestinian conflict, Bartana established in 2010 what she calls the Jewish Renaissance Movement in Poland (JRMiP), a magical realist movement that has called on 3.3 million Jews to return to Poland.[49] JRMiP has a website, a manifesto, and held a conference in Berlin in May 2012, but it mostly exists in Bartana's trilogy of short films shot in Warsaw from 2007 to 2011. *Mary—Koszmary* (Nightmares, 2007) features the movement's leader, performed by Polish leftist activist Sławomir Sierakowski, pleading for Jews to come to Poland; *Mur i Wieża* (Wall and Tower, 2009) depicts the building of a kibbutz on the ruins of Muranów, Warsaw's prewar Jewish district and site of the Nazi ghetto; *Zamach* (Assassination, 2011) ends with the leader's body laying in wake in the Stalinist Palace of Culture and Science, the return of a Jewish ghost named Rifke, and the movement's expansion after the assassination of its leader.

Bartana's idea for the project originated during an emotionally jarring visit to Poland in 2006. At first, she thoroughly disliked Poland. "I found the prejudice against Jews to be very strong there," she said. "It was anti-Semitism at its finest as well as anti-gay, anti-everything that I am."[50] But over time she grew attracted to parts of Poland: "Earnestly, what's even more strange and interesting is that Poland is the only European country in which I felt a strong connection to the place without even understanding why."[51] As she explained further, her connection may not have been to Poland per se than to the memory of prewar Jewish life in Poland, an absence she strongly experienced during a trip to small Jewish towns.

Her trip to Poland inspired Bartana to imagine a project that would critique nationalist politics of all kinds. Stylized as a propaganda film, her trilogy forms a bricolage of images, styles, and motifs from the past—Zionist iconography of strong Jews, Leni Riefenstahl's camera work, Stalinist architecture, archetypal Holocaust images of barbed wire—all channeled toward rejecting political utopianism in the form of nationalism and embracing it in the form of cosmopolitanism. What exactly this cosmopolitan utopianism entails in a world of nation-states is a question for another essay; here I limit myself to discussing the emotions about Central Europe with which Bartana's trilogy engages, especially her first film, which is the one most directly about German-Polish-Jewish relations.

Bartana's project disrupts the dominant ways that Germans, Poles, and Jews have long felt about and recalled the past. It comes after decades of cultural, political, communicative, family, and generational memories of the Holocaust, and makes a series of transnational interventions into these entrenched, emotive memories. Thus, to situate her interventions, we first need to sketch briefly some historical context since the 1960s, where our previous traveler—Elon—left us off. Let us begin with Germany. The dialectical forces of forgetting and remembering have continued to define Germany's relationship to its past in the decades after Elon wrote, with one significant and recent change. Over the 2000s, Germany's contorted encounters with its Nazi past have come to a kind of resting point. Few mainstream German politicians, intellectuals, and journalists today would contest the prominence of the Holocaust in German public life. The intense debates about memory over the 1980s, 1990s, and 2000s have dissipated and a culture of contrition has generally become accepted in public life.[52] To be sure, memories of victimization, resistance, and ignorance remain strong among segments of German society.[53] But remembrance has generally triumphed in the contemporary German public sphere.

What kind of memory stands victorious, however? A cathartic one, as Elon suggested in the early part of his career? Some leftist critics of Germany's current memory culture appear to think so. They believe—to put a phrase on it—that Germany has *memory without emotion*. Vapid speeches, debates, monuments, and memorials, they say, are all that comprise Germany's glossy *Vergangenheitsbewältigung*. For example, German actress Susanne Sachsse, who stars as Rifke, remarked about her involvement in Bartana's project: "It was scary for me and necessary and interesting because in Germany we are so liberal; we think—liberal in a bad way—we think we deal with [the] Holocaust. We did it, everything. We work on it. We have monuments. But it is not true."[54] As she intimated later on, a more genuine working through the past for her would involve more emotion and more political critique than Germany's current memory regime allows.

Somewhat similar concerns about memory have emerged in Poland. Although Holocaust remembrance today has not nearly reached the nonpartisan consensus in Poland as it has in Germany, Poland has nevertheless experienced since the 1970s searing discussions about Polish-Jewish relations, and segments of Polish society have become deeply interested in Jewish culture.[55] Poland is now experiencing a memory boom, a surfeit of remembrance that has unleashed new challenges for Poles committed to Jewish memory initiatives. Polish memory activists now face the same questions their German counterparts do, namely, what all this memory should mean for contemporary society and politics. They seemingly want something more than just markers of remembrance; some memory activists want a more "authentic" memory—however that may be conceived—amid the ubiquity and reproducibility of the Jewish past in post-Communist Poland. Bartana's protagonist, Sierakowski, epitomizes this desire. Founder of the leftist magazine/milieu *Krytyka Polityczna* (Political Critique), he aspires for nostalgia to motivate political change by stimulating more inclusive imaginations of Poland.

Finally, Bartana's project engages with Jewish emotions and memories about Poland. Jewish feelings are confused, to say the least, about a country where modern Europe's largest Jewish community flourished and where the Nazis carried out mass murder against Jews with involvement from Poles. Broadly speaking, two clusters of emotions dominate Jewish feelings about Poland: fear, anxiety, and anger; longing, desire, and attraction. North American and Israeli Jews tend to see Poland as a blighted land of pogroms, antisemitism, exclusion, and death. Over the past twenty years, these negative sentiments have been reinforced by certain modes of travel, above all mass pilgrimages, such as the March of the Living, in which Poland becomes, as anthropologist Jack Kugelmass puts it, "a theater prop in a Jewish pageant about national catastrophe and redemption."[56] These trips reprise Zionist rejections of diaspora, perform Jewish identities of suffering, cast Poland as a pitiful land, and are forcefully emotive. As one pamphlet for the March wrote: "Everywhere we will be surrounded by the local Polish people, and our feelings toward them will be ambivalent. We will hate them for their involvement in the atrocities, but we will pity them for their miserable life in the present. Let us not be carried away by negative emotions."[57] If German memories about the past might be too phlegmatic, Jewish ones might be too adrenalized.

At the same time, Poland also evokes positive longings for the "vanished world" of the *shtetl*, which is often imagined as a wholesome, hermetic space of traditional Jewish life. This nostalgia has taproots stretching back to the mid nineteenth century, but it has intensified since the 1970s amid cultural and political changes among North American and Israeli Jews. Beginning in the 1970s, some Jews became interested in tracing their heritage roots back to Europe. This genealogical turn was inspired in no small part by Alex Haley's Pulitzer Prize–winning *Roots,* a rich tale about an "American family" that moved from West Africa to Virginia. Jews also grew interested in Europe as ties to Zionism and Israel weakened over the 1980s and 1990s; they turned to other geographies, imaginations, and expressions of Jewishness—*klezmer* music, Yiddish language, Sephardic history, Mizrachi culture, diasporism, and travels to the old country (wherever that might be in Europe, North Africa, or the Middle East).

This plurality of Jewish identities has been debated by a number of Jewish scholars, artists, and writers. Philip Roth is the most apposite interlocutor for this essay's themes. In *Operation Shylock: A Confession* (1993), Roth encounters his Doppelgänger propagating the idea of resettling Jews back to their ancestral home in Poland because "Zionism has tragically ruined its own health."[58] On the telephone from Jerusalem, the fictional Roth explains to the "real" one: "You know what will happen in Warsaw, at the railway station, when the first trainload of Jews returns? There will be crowds to welcome them. People will be jubilant. People will be in tears. They will be shouting, 'Our Jews are back!'"[59] In the year 2000, the fictional Roth explains further, Berlin will hold a "pan-European celebration of the reintegrated Jew." The real Roth quips: "Oh, that's the best idea yet.... The Germans particularly will be delighted to usher in the third millennium of Christianity with a couple of million Jews holding a welcome-home party at the Brandenburg Gate."[60]

Now enter the year 2012, Bartana, and the first congress of the JRMiP in Berlin. "We want to return! Not to Uganda, not to Argentina or to Madagascar, not even to Palestine," its manifesto reads. "It is Poland that we long for, the land of our fathers and forefathers."[61] Although some people have interpreted this call seriously, Bartana seeks to inspire new possibilities, imaginations, and emotions through fantasies of return. She is an artist looking to provoke. Her first film plays with multiple memories and emotions about Poland. It opens with Sierakowski, dressed in a black leather trench coat, white shirt, and red tie, walking through a tunnel, down a running track, onto a grassy field, and up the stairs of a small black wooden pedestal.[62] The setting, the film announces, is Warsaw's "Olympic stadium." Built in 1955 by the Communist state, the stadium is now an archetypal ruin—vegetation covers its weathered stones. Sierakowski reaches his lectern, and he proclaims in Polish:

> Jews! Fellow countrymen! People! Peeeeople! You think the old woman who still sleeps under Rifke's quilt doesn't want to see you? Has forgotten about you? You're wrong. She dreams about you every night. Dreams and trembles with fear. Since the night you were gone and her mother reached for your quilt, she has had nightmares. Bad dreams. Only you can chase them away. Let the three million Jews that Poland has missed stand by her bed and finally chase away the demons. Return to Poland, to your/our country! … This is a call, not to the dead but to the living. We want three million Jews to return to Poland, we want you to live with us again. We need you![63]

Sierakowski goes on to critique antisemitism and ethnocultural nationalism before returning to his argument that Poland needs Jews to redeem its sins. As he speaks, a group of young votaries—clad in Communist-style scout uniforms—write on the field the following phrase: "3,300,000 Jews can change the life of 40,000,000 Poles." Shortly afterward, Bartana cuts to an aerial shot of stone pillars in what remains of the stadium's bleachers; the camera stays on this image for about seven seconds. With the screen darkened and somewhat blurred, the pillars look like tombstones. The film creates juxtaposing images of ruination and rebirth.

In so doing, it reprises many of the conflicting emotions that this essay has disclosed: unease, discomfort, fear, sadness, eeriness, longing. But it also unsettles these dominant emotions through Sierakowski's evocative longing for Jews. What he says collides with decades of negative, painful emotions about post-Holocaust Poland as a space of Jewish death. Sierakowski's character—a melodramatic version of himself—unsettles the archetypal "Pole" portrayed in such films as Claude Lanzmann's *Shoah*: a peasant who harbors much antisemitism and little remorse for wartime collusion in the Holocaust. Confident, erudite, and cosmopolitan, Sierakowski appears to be confronting antisemitism, ethnocultural nationalism, and wartime guilt. Who is this Pole? What is this Poland of life and death, antisemitism and nostalgia, forgetting and remembrance? Such confusing ideas and images, as Bartana explained, could only but provoke emotions:

> Last year, at the International Holocaust Memorial Day, we screened 'Mary Kozmary' to an audience of diplomats and Holocaust survivors, and I felt awkward in front of Holocaust survivors and Poles who were deported from Poland. But it was amazing; they were so moved by the thought that Poles would actually invite them to return to Poland, in Polish. They approached Slawomir with emotion, surrounded him, and started speaking old Polish to him. They said that there was no way that they would ever return to Poland, that the Poles were Anti-Semites. But it was their home. Can you imagine being thrown out of Israel and seventy years later being asked to return? It's emotionally overwhelming.[64]

That her project triggers such intense emotions is because Central Europe—as a space and topic—has long been a highly charged site, a landscape of sites, sounds, smells, and tastes, which have elicited a multitude of ambivalent feelings among Jews over the past seventy years.

Notes

1. A.M. Rosenthal, "Forgive them Not, For They Knew What They Did," *New York Times*, 24 October 1965.
2. Fritz Stern, *Five Germanys I Have Known* (New York, 2006), 6.
3. Marianne Hirsch and Leo Spitzer, *Ghosts of Home: The Afterlife of Czernowitz in Jewish Memory* (Berkeley, 2010), 9.
4. http://blog.mayaescobar.com/category/berlins-eruv (accessed 4 August 2012).
5. Like memory, emotion is a dynamic communal and communicative part of human life (see note 10 below). We convey our emotions through written, oral, visual, and somatic expressions. This essay is about expressions of emotion through written language and visual imagery.
6. I am emphasizing the provisional nature of my sketch here because, to the best of my knowledge, no scholarly work exists on Jewish emotions about post-1945 Germany and Poland. In Jewish historiography, I know of emotions being applied to the study of antisemitism. See Uffa Jensen, "Emotions and the History of Modern Antisemitism," Conference Report, H-Soz-u-Kult (June 2012).
7. Jack Kugelmass, "The Rites of the Tribe: The Meaning of Poland for American Jewish Tourists," *YIVO Annual* 21 (1993): 419; Caryn Aviv and David Shneer, *New Jews: The End of the*

Jewish Diaspora (New York, 2005); Jeffrey Shandler, *Adventures in Yiddishland: Postvernacular Language and Culture* (Berkeley, CA, 2006); Rona Sheramy, "From Auschwitz to Jerusalem: Re-enacting Jewish History on the March of the Living," *POLIN: Studies in Polish Jewry* 19 (2007): 307–26; Jackie Feldman, *Above the Death Pits, Beneath the Flag: Youth Voyages to Poland and the Performance of Israeli National Identity* (New York, 2008).

  8. Sidra DeKoven Ezrahi, *Booking Passage: Exile and Homecoming in the Modern Jewish Imagination* (Berkeley, 2000), 219.

  9. Here I am building on the work of Jewish studies scholars, who have uncovered the multiple and fluid geographies of Jewishness by exploring intersections among space, place, belonging, identity, and home. Reflecting on this growing literature, Barbara Mann writes: "There *is* a center, of sorts, though it has not held. And the varieties of Jewish experience that radiate from this fragmented center have produced unpredictable and irregular shapes, irreducible trajectories of their own that emanate far beyond any notion of an original center." Barbara E. Mann, *Space and Place in Jewish Studies* (New Brunswick, NJ, 2012), 3.

  10. I am inspired here by Walter Benjamin's turn to montage as a practice of assembling lesser-known, sometimes forgotten fragments of the past into a textual constellation of multiple and juxtaposing ideas, a creation that resists reduction to linear metaphors of time. As with many of Benjamin's productive ideas, his method of using montage to build a constellation remains obtuse. The central idea, as Martin Jay writes, seems to be "a juxtaposed rather than integrated cluster of changing elements that resist reduction to a common denominator, essential core, or generative first principle." Benjamin had political aspirations for montage; here my aim is to use it to narrate and analyze. Finally, I impose more narrative structure to my fragments than Benjamin probably would, if we take the notes for his *Arcades* project to be any indication of what his textual montage would have looked like. Martin Jay, *Adorno* (Cambridge, MA, 1984), 14–15; Walter Benjamin, *The Arcades Project,* ed. Rolf Tiedemann, trans. Howard Eiland and Kevin McLaughlin (Cambridge, MA, 2002).

  11. What might explain this hypothesized continuity? This question goes far beyond my aim here in this exploratory piece, but two answers seem suggestive. First, Germany and Poland have functioned since the Holocaust as complex emotional spaces—landscapes of alienating ruins and familiar places that have provoked shared feelings across time. Second, individuals express emotions in reciprocal relationship with communal motifs, images, languages, stories, and memories. We are not autonomous emotional beings: where we are located (place), with whom we are interacting (communities), what experiences we have heard or had in the past (memories), and how we are communicating (languages, stories) all shape our feelings in ways that scholars are just now beginning to explore. For recent methodological discussions on studying the history of emotions, see Benno Gammerl, "History of Emotions," *German History* 28, no. 1 (2010): 67–80; Benno Gammerl, "Emotional Styles—Concepts and Challenges," *Rethinking History* 15, no. 2 (2012): 161–75; Jan Plamper, "The History of Emotions: An Interview with William Reddy, Barbara Rosenwein, and Peter Stearns," *History and Theory* 49, no. 2 (2010): 237–65.

  12. *Zarys działalności CKŻP w Polsce za okres od 1 stycznia do 30 czerwca 1946* (Warsaw, 1946). See also Albert Stankowski, "Nowe spojrzenie na statystyki dotyczące emigracji Żydów z Polski po 1944 roku," in *Studia z historii Żydów w Polsce po 1945 r.,* ed. Grzegorz Berendt, August Grabski, and Albert Stankowski (Warsaw, 2000), 103–51.

  13. David Engel, "Patterns of Anti-Jewish Violence in Poland, 1944-1946," *Yad Vashem Studies* (1998): 43–85; Jan Gross, *Fear: Antisemitism in Poland after Auschwitz* (New York, 2006), 35; Andrzej Żbikowski, "Morderstwa popełnianie na Żydach w pierwszych latach po wojnie," in *Następstwa zagłady Żydów. Polska 1944-2010,* ed. Feliks Tych and Monika Adamczyk-Garbowska (Lublin, 2011), 71–93.

  14. On reading Holocaust texts as such, see James E. Young, *Writing and Rewriting the Holocaust: Narrative and the Consequences of Interpretation* (Bloomington, IN, 1988).

  15. Jacob Pat, *Ashes and Fire,* trans. Leo Steinberg (New York, 1947), 13.

  16. Pat, *Ashes and Fire,* 11.

17. Pat, *Ashes and Fire*, 13, 69, 85, 128.
18. Pat, *Ashes and Fire*, 70.
19. Pat, *Ashes and Fire*, 250.
20. Pat, *Ashes and Fire*, 128.
21. Pat, *Ashes and Fire*, 127.
22. Pat, *Ashes and Fire*, 128.
23. Jan Gross with Irena Grudzińska Gross invokes similar uncanny feelings in *Golden Harvest: Events at the Periphery of the Holocaust* (New York, 2012), 3.
24. Sylvie-Anne Goldberg, *Crossing the Jabbok: Illness and Death in Askenazi Judaism in Sixteenth- through Nineteenth-Century Prague*, trans. Carol Cosman (Berkeley, 1997).
25. Alina Skibińska, "Powroty ocalałych," in *Prowincja noc. Życie i zagłada Żydów w dystrykcie warszawskim*, ed., Barbara Engelking, Jack Leociak, and Darius Libionka (Warsaw, 2007), 565–66.
26. As Pat writes: "One cannot help marveling at the inner strength and discipline of those 'first Jews' of Lublin who proclaimed the rebirth of the Jewish people in Poland by creating, during their first hours, this historical commission." Pat, *Ashes and Fire*, 62.
27. Pat, *Ashes and Fire*, 111.
28. Pat, *Ashes and Fire*, 11, 250.
29. Barbara Engelking, *"Szanowny panie Gistapo." Donosy do władz niemieckich w Warszawie i okolicach w latach 1940-1941* (Warsaw, 2003); Engelking, Leociak, and Libionka, *Prowincja noc*; Barbara Engelking, *Jest taki piękny słoneczny dzień... Losy Żydów szukających ratunku na wsi polskiej 1942-1945* (Warsaw, 2011); Jan Grabowski, *"Ja tego Żyda znam!" Szantażowanie Żydów w Warszawie, 1939-1943* (Warsaw, 2004); Jan Grabowski, *Judenjagd. Polowanie na Żydów 1942-1945. Studium dziejów pewnego powiatu* (Warsaw, 2011); Jan Gross, *Neighbors: The Destruction of the Jewish Community in Jedwabne, Poland* (New York, 2002); Alina Skibińska and Jakub Petelewicz, "The Participation of Poles in Crimes Against Jews in the Świętokrzyskie Region," *Yad Vashem Studies* 35, no. 2 (2007): 5–48; Andrzej Żbikowski, ed., *Polacy i Żydzi pod okupacją niemiecką 1939-1945. Studia i Materiały* (Warsaw, 2006), chs. 4–10; Andrzej Żbikowski, *U genezy Jedwabnego: Żydzi na kresach Północno-Wschodnich II Rzeczypospolitej* (Warsaw, 2006); *Zarys krajobrazu. Wieś polska wobec zagłady Żydów 1942–1945* (Warsaw, 2011). For English summations of this outpouring of research from the *Centrum Badań nad Zagładą Żydów*, see the essays in *East European Politics and Societies* no. 25, 3 (2011): 391–580.
30. On lost emotions, see Ute Frevert, *Emotions in History—Lost and Found* (Budapest and New York, 2011).
31. Jack Kugelmass and Jonathan Boyarin, *From a Ruined Garden: The Memorial Books of Polish Jewry*, 2nd ed. (Bloomington, IN, 1998).
32. On the court's visit to Auschwitz, see Devin O. Pendas, *The Frankfurt Auschwitz Trial, 1963-1965: Genocide, History, and the Limits of the Law* (New York, 2006), 168–82.
33. Amos Elon, *Journey through a Haunted Land: The New Germany*, trans. Michael Roloff (New York, 1967), 1–2.
34. Although Elon traveled to East Germany, he spent most of his time in West Germany and he writes most insightfully about it. I have thus decided not to discuss his sections on East Germany.
35. "Ein Gespräch mit Amos Elon—20 Jahre danach," in Amos Elon, *In einem heimgesuchten Land: Reise eines israelischen Journalisten in beide deutsche Staaten* (Nördlingen, 1988), 391.
36. "Ein Gespräch mit Amos Elon," 394.
37. Hannah Arendt, "The Aftermath of Nazi Rule: Report from Germany," *Commentary*, October 1950, 342.
38. Günter Grass, *Die Blechtrommel* (Darmstadt/Berlin/Neuwied am Rhein, 1959).
39. Elon, *Journey*, 13.
40. Elon, *Journey*, 231, 237.
41. Elon, *Journey*, 49.
42. Elon, *Journey*, 166–67.

43. Elon, *Journey*, 43.
44. Ibid., 258.
45. Amos Elon, "The Antagonist as Liberator," *New York Times*, 26 January 1997.
46. Amos Elon, "A German Requiem," *The New York Review of Books*, 15 November 2011.
47. Amos Elon, *Europa bauen, den Wandel gestalten* (Stuttgart, 2004).
48. *Another Road Home*, directed by Danae Elon (Phoenix, AZ, 2005), DVD. My transcription.
49. "Conversations with Contemporary Artists: Yael Bartana," Solomon R. Guggenheim Museum, New York, NY, 24 January 2012 (accessed full video through "Guggenheim videos," YouTube, 15 August 2012). My transcription.
50. "Till Imagination Takes Us Back—A Conversation with Yael Bartana," *Ma'arav*, 29 April 2012 (accessed 28 August 2012).
51. "Till Imagination Takes Us Back."
52. The literature on Germany's memory battles over the past thirty years is enormous. See Atina Grossmann, "The 'Goldhagen Effect:' Memory, Repetition, and Responsibility in the New Germany," in *The "Goldhagen Effect:" History, Memory, Nazism—Facing the German Past*, ed. Geoff Eley (Ann Arbor, MI, 2000), 89–129; Dagmar Herzog, *Sex after Fascism: Memory and Morality in Twentieth-Century Germany* (Princeton, NJ, 2005); Philipp Gassert and Alan E. Steinweis, eds., *Coping with the Nazi Past: West German Debates on Nazism and Generational Conflict, 1955-1975* (New York, 2006); A. Dirk Moses, *German Intellectuals and the Nazi Past* (New York, 2007).
53. Harald Welzer, Sabine Moller, and Karoline Tschuggnall, "*Opa war kein Nazi:" Nationalsozialismus und Holocaust im Familiengedächtnis* (Frankfurt am Main, 2002); Olaf Jensen, *Geschichte machen: Strukturmerkmale des intergenerationellen Sprechens über die NS Vergangenheit in deutschen Familien* (Tübingen, 2004); Robert G. Moeller, "Germans as Victims? Thoughts on a Post-Cold War History of World War II's Legacies," *History & Memory* 17, no. 1/2 (2005): 147–94.
54. "Conversations with Contemporary Artists." My transcription.
55. Michael Meng, *Shattered Spaces: Encountering Jewish Ruins in Postwar Germany and Poland* (Cambridge, MA, 2011), ch. 4.
56. Jack Kugelmass, "Bloody Memories: Encountering the Past in Contemporary Poland," *Cultural Anthropology* 10, no. 3 (1995): 281.
57. Quoted in Laurence Weinbaum, *The Struggle for Memory in Poland: Auschwitz, Jedwabne and Beyond* (Jerusalem, 2001), 35.
58. Philip Roth, *Operation Shylock: A Confession* (New York, 1994), 44.
59. Roth, *Operation Shylock*, 45.
60. Roth, *Operation Shylock*, 46.
61. *And Europe Will be Stunned* (London, 2012), 126.
62. Bartana got lucky in her timing. A year later, the stadium was demolished to build a new one for the Euro 2012.
63. This translation from the Polish is taken from *And Europe Will be Stunned*, 120.
64. "Till Imagination Takes Us Back."

Contributors

Omer Bartov is the John P. Birkelund Distinguished Professor of European History at Brown University. His most recent publications are *Erased: Vanishing Traces of Jewish Galicia in Present-Day Ukraine* (2007), and the co-edited volume *Shatterzone of Empires: Coexistence and Violence in the German, Habsburg, Russian, and Ottoman Borderlands* (2013). He is currently completing a new book, *The Voice of Your Brother's Blood: Buczacz, Biography of a Town*.

Sara Bender is a senior lecturer in the department of Jewish history at the University of Haifa. She is the author of *The Jews of Białystok during World War II and the Holocaust* (2008) and *In Enemy Land: The Jews of Kielce and the Vicinity during World War II—1939–1945* (2012) [Hebrew]. She is the co-editor of the journal *DAPIM—Studies on the Shoah,* and of the multivolume *Encyclopedia of the Righteous Among the Nations: Rescuers During the Holocaust* (2008–). Her research compares the histories of Jewish communities in the Białystok and Radom districts with special focus on Jewish leadership, resistance, and Polish-Jewish relations.

Daniel Blatman is the Max and Rita Haber Professor in Contemporary Jewry and Holocaust Studies at the Hebrew University of Jerusalem. He has published extensively on the history of Polish Jewry in the twentieth century, the Jewish labor movement in Eastern Europe, Polish-Jewish relations during the Holocaust and its aftermath, and Nazi extermination policy. His books include *For Our Freedom and Yours: The Jewish Labor Bund in Poland, 1939-1949* (2003); *En direct du ghetto. La presse clandestine juive dans le ghetto de Varsovie* (2005); and *The Death Marches: The Final Phase of Nazi Genocide* (2010).

Steven Bowman is a Professor of Judaic Studies at the University of Cincinnati. His research interests are centered on Greek and Jewish relations throughout the past three millennia. His books include *Jews in Byzantium, 1204-1453* (1985), *The Holocaust in Salonika: Eyewitness Accounts* (2002), *Jewish Resistance in Wartime Greece* (2006), and *The Agony of Greek Jews, 1940-1945* (2009). He has edited and introduced a number of Greek Holocaust memoirs and studies in *The Sephardi and Greek Holocaust Library*, of which he is editor-in-chief, and has completed an annotated translation of the *Book of Yosippon*.

Tuvia Friling is a senior researcher at the Ben-Gurion Research Institute, at the Ben-Gurion University of the Negev. He was the head of the Ben-Gurion Institute (1993–2001) and the State Archivist of Israel (2001–2004). In 2003–2004 he served as Vice Chairman of the International Commission of the Holocaust in Romania headed by Elie Wiesel. Among his publications are *Arrows in the Dark: David Ben-Gurion, the Yishuv Leadership and Rescue Attempts during the Holocaust* (2005) and *A Jewish Kapo in Auschwitz: History, Memory and the Politics of Survival* (2014).

Alexandra Garbarini is an associate professor of history at Williams College. She is the author of *Numbered Days: Diary Writing and the Holocaust* (2006), and the co-author with Emil Kerenji, Jan Lambertz, and Avinoam Patt of *Jewish Responses to Persecution, volume 2, 1939-1940* (2011). Her current research focuses on European Jewish and non-Jewish responses to mass violence in the decades before the Holocaust.

Norman J.W. Goda is the Norman and Irma Braman Professor of Holocaust Studies at the University of Florida. His books include *Tomorrow the World: Hitler, Northwest Africa and the Path Towards America* (1998); *Tales from Spandau: Nazi Criminals and the Cold War* (2007); and *The Holocaust: Europe, the World, and the Jews* (2013).

Sara R. Horowitz is a professor of comparative literature at York University and the director of the Koschitzky Centre for Jewish Studies. Her publications include *Voicing the Void: Muteness and Memory in Holocaust Fiction* (1997) as well as numerous articles concerning gendered approaches to Holocaust literature and film including "The Literary Afterlives of Anne Frank," in *Anne Frank Unbound: Media, Imagination, Memory*, ed. Barbara Kirschenblatt-Gimblet and Jeffrey Shandler (2010).

Gordon J. Horwitz is an associate professor of history at Illinois Wesleyan University. He is the author of *Ghettostadt: Łódź and the Making of a Nazi City* (2008), chosen as a finalist for the National Jewish Book Award in the category of works on the Holocaust.

Samuel Kassow is the Charles H. Northam Professor of History at Trinity College and has lectured and taught in Mexico, Lithuania, Russia, Poland, and Israel. He is the author of *Students, Professors and the State in Tsarist Russia: 1884-1917* (1989) and *The Distinctive Life of East European Jewry* (2003), and co-editor of *Between Tsar and People* (1993). His most recent book is *Who Will Write our History? Emanuel Ringelblum, the Warsaw Ghetto, and the Oyneg Shabes Archive* (2007). He is a consultant to the Museum of History of the Polish Jews, to open on the site of the former Warsaw Ghetto.

Arieh J. Kochavi is a professor of modern history at the University of Haifa and directs the university's Institute of Holocaust Studies. Among his books in English are *Prelude to Nuremberg: Allied War Crimes Policy and the Question of Punishment* (1998); *Post-Holocaust Politics: Britain, the United States and Jewish Refugees, 1945-1948* (2001); and *Confronting Captivity: Britain, the United States, and their POWs in Nazi Germany* (2005).

Michael Meng is an assistant professor of history at Clemson University. His first book, *Shattered Spaces: Encountering Jewish Ruins in Postwar Germany and Poland*, appeared in 2011 with Harvard University Press. He is also the co-editor, with Erica Lehrer, of the volume *Jewish Space in Contemporary Poland* (2014).

Dan Michman is professor of modern Jewish history and chair of the Finkler Institute of Holocaust Research at Bar-Ilan University. He is also Head of the International Institute for Holocaust Research and Incumbent of the John Najmann Chair of Holocaust Studies at Yad Vashem. His publications deal with a broad variety of aspects of the Shoah and its impact, predominantly with historiography, Jewish Councils, ghettos, religious life, and the post-Holocaust Jewish world.

Bob Moore is professor of twentieth century European history at the University of Sheffield. His books include *Victims and Survivors: the Nazi Persecution of the Jews in the Netherlands, 1940-1945* (1997); *Crises of Empire: Decolonization and Europe's Imperial States* (with Martin Thomas and Larry Butler, 2007); and *Refugees from Nazi Germany and the Liberal European States* (with Frank Caestecker, 2009). He has also edited a number of collections, including *Resistance in Western Europe* (2000) and *Prisoners of War, Prisoners of Peace* (with Barbara Hately, 2005). His latest monograph, *Survivors: Jewish Self-Help and Rescue in Nazi-Occupied Western Europe,* was published by Oxford in 2010.

Renée Poznanski is the Yaakov and Poria Avnon Professor of Holocaust Studies at Ben-Gurion University. Her book *The Jews in France during World War II* (2001) was awarded the Jacob Buchman Prize for the Memory of the Holocaust. Her last book, *Propagandes et persécutions: La Résistance et le "problème juif," 1940–1944* (2008) was awarded the 2009 Henri Hertz prize by the *Chancellerie des Universités de Paris*. During the academic year 2012–2013, she was a fellow at the Radcliffe Institute for Advanced Study at Harvard University, where she worked on a book on The Resistance of the Jews in France.

Timothy Snyder is the Bird White Housum Professor of History at Yale University. The essay published here refers to themes from *Bloodlands: Europe Between Hitler and Stalin* (2010), which was awarded ten prizes, including the Leipzig Award for European Understanding, the Hannah Arendt Prize in Political Thought, the Ralph Waldo Emerson Prize in the Humanities, and the European History Book Award.

Selected Bibliography

Adler, Jacques. *The Jews of Paris and the Final Solution: Communal Response and Internal Conflicts, 1940–1944.* New York, 1987.
Ancel, Jean. *The History of the Holocaust in Romania.* Translated by Yaffah Murciano. Lincoln, NE, 2011.
Aviv, Caryn S., and David Shneer, *New Jews: The End of the Jewish Diaspora.* New York, 2005.
Baldwin, Peter, ed. *Reworking the Past: Hitler, the Holocaust, and the Historians' Debate.* Boston, 1990.
Bankier, David, and Dan Michman, eds., *Holocaust Historiography in Context: Emergence, Challenges, Polemics, and Achievements.* Jerusalem, 2008.
Barkan, Elazar, Elizabeth A. Cole, and Kai Struve, eds. *Shared History—Divided Memory: Jews and Others in Soviet-Occupied Poland, 1939-1941.* Göttingen, 2007.
Bauer, Yehuda. "Jewish Leadership Reactions to Nazi Policies." In *The Holocaust as Historical Experience,* ed. Yehuda Bauer and Nathan Rotenstreich. New York, 1981.
———. *The Death of the Shtetl.* New Haven, CT, 2009.
———. *Rethinking the Holocaust.* New Haven, CT, 2001.
Bartov. Omer. *Erased: Vanishing Traces of Jewish Galicia in Present-Day Ukraine.* Princeton, NJ, 2007.
Bartov, Omer, and Eric D. Weitz, eds. *Shatterzones of Empires: Coexistence and Violence in the German, Habsburg, Russian, and Ottoman Borderlands.* Bloomington, IN, 2013.
Bender, Sara. *The Jews of Białystok During World War II and the Holocaust.* Translated by Yaffa Murciano. Hanover, NH, 2008.
Bender, Sara. *In Enemy Land: The Jews of Kielce and the Vicinity During World War II—1939-1945* [Hebrew]. Jerusalem, 2012.
Benz, Wolfgang, and Juliane Wetzel, eds. *Solidarität und Hilfe für Juden während der NS-Zeit.* 7 vols. Berlin, 1996–2004.
Berg, Nicholas. *Der Holocaust und die westdeutschen Historiker: Erforschung und Erinnerung.* Göttingen, 2003.
Berkhoff, Karel C. *Harvest of Despair: Life and Death in Ukraine under Nazi Rule.* Cambridge, MA, 2004.
———. "Dina Pronicheva's Story of Surviving the Babi Yar Massacre: German, Jewish, Soviet, and Ukrainian Records." In *The Shoah in Ukraine: History, Testimony, Memorialization,* ed. Ray Brandon and Wendy Lower. Bloomington, IN, 2008.
Blatman, Daniel. *The Death Marches: The Final Phase of Nazi Genocide.* Cambridge, MA, 2011.
Blobaum, Robert, ed. *Antisemitism and Its Opponents in Modern Poland.* Ithaca, NY, 2005.
Bloxham, Donald, and A. Dirk Moses, eds. *The Oxford Handbook of Genocide Studies.* Oxford, 2010.
Bolchover, Richard. *British Jewry and the Holocaust.* New York, 1993
Bowman, Steven. *Jewish Resistance in Wartime Greece.* London, 2006.

———. *The Agony of Greek Jews, 1940-1945*. Stanford, CA, 2009.
Brandon, Ray, and Wendy Lower, eds. *The Shoah in Ukraine: History, Testimony, and Memorialization*. Bloomington, IN, 2008.
Brauch, Julia, Anna Lipphardt, and Alexandra Nocke, eds. *Jewish Topographies: Visions of Space, Traditions of Place*. London, 2008.
Brenner, Reeve Robert. *The Faith and Doubt of Holocaust Survivors*. New York, 1980.
Breitman, Richard. *Official Secrets: What The Nazis Planned, What the British and the Americans Knew*. New York, 1998.
Breitman, Richard. and Allan J. Lichtman. *FDR and the Jews*. Cambridge, MA, 2013.
Browning, Christopher R. *Collected Memories: Holocaust History and Postwar Testimony*. Madison, WI, 2003.
———. *Remembering Survival: Inside a Nazi Slave Labor Camp*. New York, 2010.
Budnitskii, Oleg. *Russian Jews Between the Reds and the Whites, 1917-1920*. Translated by Timothy J. Portice. Philadelphia, 2012.
Cesarani, David. *The Jewish Chronicle and Anglo-Jewry*. New York, 1994.
Cesarani, David, and Eric J. Sundquist, eds. *After the Holocaust: Challenging the Myth of Silence*. London, 2012.
Cohen, Asher. "Rescuing Jews: Jews and Christians in Vichy France," *British Journal of Holocaust Education* 3, no. 1 (1994): 4–31.
Cohen, Boaz. *Israeli Holocaust Research: Birth and Evolution*. Translated by Agnes Vazsonyi. New York, 2012.
Comte, Madeleine. *Sauvetages et baptêmes. Les religieuses de Notre-Dame de Sion face à la persécutions des Juifs en France (1940-1944)*. Paris, 2001.
Confino, Alon. *Foundational Pasts: The Holocaust as Historical Understanding*. New York, 2012.
Corni, Gustavo. *Hitler's Ghettos: Voices from a Beleaguered Society 1939-1944*. London, 2003.
Dieckmann, Christoph. *Deutsche Besatzungspolitik in Litauen 1941-1944*. Göttingen, 2011.
Dieckmann, Christoph, and Babette Quinkert, eds. *Im Ghetto 1939-45: Neue Forschungen zu Alltag und Umfeld*. Göttingen, 2009.
Dietsch, Johan. *Making Sense of Suffering: Holocaust and Holodomor in Ukrainian Historical Culture*. Lund, 2006.
Diner, Dan. *Beyond the Conceivable: Studies on Germany, Nazism, and the Holocaust*. Berkeley, CA, 2000.
Dinnerstein, Leonard. *America and the Survivors of the Holocaust*. New York, 1982.
Engel, David. *Historians of the Jews and the Holocaust*. Stanford, CA, 2010.
Farbstein, Esther. *Hidden in Thunder: Perspectives on Faith, Halachah and Leadership during the Holocaust*. Translated by Deborah Stern. Jerusalem, 2007.
Fatal-Knaani, Tikva. *Grodno Is Not the Same*. [Hebrew]. Jerusalem, 2001.
Feldman, Jackie. *Above the Death Pits, Beneath the Flag: Youth Voyages to Poland and the Performance of Israeli National Identity*. New York, 2008.
Finder, Gabriel N., and Alexander V. Prusin, "Collaboration in Eastern Galicia: The Ukrainian Police and the Holocaust," *East European Jewish Affairs* 34, n. 2 (2004): 95–118.
Fink, Carole. *Defending the Rights of Others: The Great Powers, the Jews, and International Minority Protection, 1878-1938*. New York, 2004.
Fogel, Yehezkel, ed. *I Will be Sanctified: Religious Responses to the Holocaust*. Translated by Edward Levin. Northvale, NJ, 1998.
Friedländer, Saul. *Nazi Germany and the Jews: The Years of Persecution, 1933-1939*. New York, 1997.
———. *Nazi Germany and the Jews: The Years of Extermination, 1939-1945*. New York, 2007.
———. "An Integrated History of the Holocaust: Some Methodological Challenges." In *The Holocaust and Historical Methodology*, ed. Dan Stone. New York, 2012.
Friling, Tuvia. *Arrows in the Dark: David Ben-Gurion, the Yishuv Leadership, and Rescue Attempts During the Holocaust*. Translated by Ora Cummings. Madison, WI, 2003.
———. *A Jewish Kapo in Auschwitz: History, Memory, and the Politics of Survival*. Waltham, MA, 2014.

Funkenstein, Amos. *Perceptions of Jewish History.* Berkeley, 1993.
Garbarini, Alexandra. *Numbered Days: Diaries and the Holocaust.* New Haven, CT, 2006.
Garbarini, Alexandra, et al., ed. *Jewish Responses to Persecution*, vol. 2: *1938-1940.* Lanham, MD, 2011.
Geissbühler, Simon. *Blutiger Juli: Rumäniens Vernichtungskrieg und der vergessene Massenmord an den Juden 1941.* Paderborn, 2013.
Gerlach, Christian. *Kalkulierte Morde: Die deutsche Wirtschafts- und Vernichtungspolitik in Weißrußland 1941 bis 1944.* Hamburg, 1999.
Goldberg, Amos. "The Victim's Voice and Melodramatic Aesthetics in History." *History and Theory* 48, no. 3 (2009): 220–37.
Goodman, Nancy R., and Marilyn B. Meyers, eds. *The Power of Witnessing: Reflections, Reverberations, and Traces of the Holocaust.* New York, 2012.
Grabowski, Jan. *Hunt for the Jews: Betrayal and Murder in German-Occupied Poland.* Bloomington, IN, 2013.
Gutman, Yisrael. *The Jews of Warsaw, 1939-1943: Ghetto, Underground, Revolt.* Translated by Ina Friedman. Bloomington, IN, 1982.
Gutman, Yisrael, and Cynthia J. Haft, eds. *Patterns of Jewish Leadership in Nazi Europe, 1933-1945: Proceedings of the Third Yad Vashem International Historical Conference, Jerusalem, April 4-7, 1977.* Jerusalem, 1979.
Gutman, Yisrael, et al., eds. *The Jews of Poland between the Two World Wars.* Hanover, NH, 1989.
Hagen, William W. "Before the 'Final Solution': Toward a Comparative Analysis of Political Anti-Semitism in Interwar Germany and Poland," *Journal of Modern History* 68, no. 2 (1996): 351–81.
———. "The Moral Economy of Popular Violence: The Pogrom in Lwów, November 1918." In *Antisemitism and Its Opponents in Modern Poland,* ed. Robert Blobaum. Ithaca, NY, 2005.
Hartman, Geoffrey H. *The Longest Shadow: In the Aftermath of the Holocaust.* Bloomington, IN, 1996.
Hayes, Peter, and John K. Roth, eds. *The Oxford Handbook of Holocaust Studies.* Oxford, UK, 2010.
Herf, Jeffrey. *The Jewish Enemy: Nazi Propaganda during World War II and the Holocaust.* Cambridge, MA, 2008.
Himka, John-Paul. *Ukrainians, Jews and the Holocaust: Divergent Memories.* Saskatoon, 2009.
———. "Debates in Ukraine over Nationalist Involvement in the Holocaust, 2004-2008," *Nationalities Papers* 39, no. 3 (2011): 353–70.
———. "The L'viv Pogrom of 1941: The Germans, Ukrainian Nationalists, and the Carnival Crowd," *Canadian Slavonic Papers* 53, no. 2–4 (2011): 209–43.
Himka, John-Paul, and Joanna B. Michlic, eds. *Bringing the Dark Past to Light: The Reception of the Holocaust in Postcommunist Europe.* Lincoln, NE, 2013.
Hirsch, Marianne, and Leo Spitzer. *Ghosts of Home: The Afterlife of Czernowitz in Jewish Memory.* Berkeley, CA, 2010.
Horwitz, Gordon J. *Gettostadt: Łódź and the Making of a Nazi City.* Cambridge, MA, 2010.
Horowitz, Sara R. *Voicing the Void. Muteness and Memory in Holocaust Fiction.* New York, 1997.
———. "Gender, Genocide, and Jewish Memory," *Prooftexts* 20, no. 1 (January 2000): 158–90.
———. "The Gender of Good and Evil: Women and Holocaust Memory." In *Gray Zones: Ambiguity and Compromise in the Holocaust and its Aftermath,* eds. Jonathan Petropoulos and John Roth. New York, 2005, 165–78.
Jilge, Wilfried, and Stefan Troebst. "Divided Historical Cultures? World War II and Historical Memory in Soviet and Post-Soviet Ukraine." *Jahrbücher für Geschichte Osteuropas* 54, no. 1 (2006).
Jokusch, Laura. *Collect and Record! Jewish Holocaust Documentation in Early Postwar Europe.* New York, 2012.
Kaplan, Marion A. *Between Dignity and Despair: Jewish Life in Nazi Germany.* New York, 2009.
Kassow, Samuel D. *Who Will Write Our History? Emanuel Ringelblum, the Warsaw Ghetto, and the Oyneg Shabes Archive.* Bloomington, IN, 2007.

Katz, Steven T., Shlomo Biderman, and Gershon Greenberg, eds. *Wrestling with God: Jewish Theological Responses during and after the Holocaust.* New York, 2007.
Kirschner, Robert, ed. *Rabbinic Responsa of the Holocaust Era.* New York, 1985.
Kochavi, Arieh J. *Post-Holocaust Politics: Britain, the United States and Jewish Refugees, 1945-1948.* Chapel Hill, NC, 2001.
Kugelmass, Jack. "The Rites of the Tribe: The Meaning of Poland for American Jewish Tourists." *YIVO Annual* 21 (1993): 395–453.
———. "Bloody Memories: Encountering the Past in Contemporary Poland." *Cultural Anthropology* 10, no. 3 (1995): 279–301.
Kugelmass, Jack, and Jonathan Boyarin, eds. *From a Ruined Garden: The Memorial Books of Polish Jewry,* 2nd ed. Bloomington, IN, 1998.
Kulińska, Lucina, and Adam Roliński, eds. *Kwestia ukraińska i eksterminacja ludności polskiej w Małopolsce Wschodniej w świetle dokumentów Polskiego Państwa Podziemnego 1942-1944.* Kraków, 2004.
Kushner, Tony. *The Holocaust and the Liberal Imagination: A Social and Cultural History.* Cambridge, MA, 1994.
Langer, Lawrence L. *Holocaust Testimonies: The Ruins of Memory.* New Haven, CT, 1991.
Lawson, Tom. *Debates on the Holocaust.* Manchester, 2010.
Lazare, Lucien. *Rescue as Resistance: How Jewish Organizations Fought the Holocaust in France.* New York, 1996.
Levy, Daniel, and Natan Sznaider. *The Holocaust and Memory in the Global Age.* Philadelphia, 2006.
Longerich, Peter. *Holocaust: The Nazi Persecution and Murder of the Jews.* Translated by Shaun Whiteside. New York, 2010.
Löw, Andrea. *Juden im Getto Litzmannstadt: Lebensbedingungen, Selbstwahrnehmung, Verhalten.* Göttingen, 2006.
Marrus, Michael R. *The Holocaust in History.* Hanover, NH, 1987.
Matsas, Michael. *The Illusion of Safety: The Story of the Greek Jews During World War II.* New York, 1997.
Matthäus, Jürgen, ed. *Approaching an Auschwitz Survivor: Holocaust Testimony and Its Transformations.* New York, 2009.
Mendelsohn, Ezra. *The Jews of East Central Europe between the World Wars.* Bloomington, IN, 1983.
Ménager, Camille. *Le Sauvetage des Juifs à Paris: Histoire et Mémoire.* Paris, 2005.
Meng, Michael. *Shattered Spaces: Encountering Jewish Ruins in Postwar Germany and Poland.* Cambridge, MA, 2011.
Michael, Holger. *Zwischen Davidstern und Roter Fahne: Die Juden in Polen im XX. Jahrhundert.* Berlin-Brandenburg, 2007.
Michman, Dan, ed. *Belgium and the Holocaust: Jews Belgians Germans.* Jerusalem, 1998.
———. *Holocaust Historiography: A Jewish Perspective—Conceptualizations, Terminology, Approaches and Fundamental Issues.* London, 2003.
———. "Is There an Israeli School of Holocaust Research?" In *Holocaust Historiography in Context: Emergence, Challenges, Polemics and Achievements,* ed. David Bankier and Dan Michman. Jerusalem, 2008.
———. *The Emergence of Jewish Ghettos During the Holocaust.* New York, 2011.
Milhaud, Fred, and Denise Milhaud, *L'Entraide Temporaire. Sauvetage d'Enfants Juifs sous l'Occupation.* Paris, 1984.
Młynarczyk, Jacek Andrjej, and Jochen Böhler, eds. *Der Judemord in den eingegliederten polnischen Gebieten 1939-1945.* Osnabrück, 2010.
Moore, Bob. *Survivors: Jewish Self-Help and Rescue in Nazi-Occupied Western Europe.* New York, 2010.
Ofer, Dalia. *Escaping the Holocaust: Illegal Immigration to the Land of Israel, 1939-1944.* New York, 1990.
Peled, Yael. *Krakov ha-Yehudit, 1939-1943: Amida, Makhteret, Maavak* [*Jewish Krakow, 1939-193: Resistance, Underground, Struggle*]. Lohamei Hagetta'ot, 1993.

Petropoulos, Jonathan, and John K. Roth, eds. *Gray Zones: Ambiguity and Compromise in the Holocaust and Its Aftermath.* New York, 2006.
Piątkowski, Sebastian. *Dni życia, dni śmierci : ludność żydowska w Radomiu w latach 1918–1950.* Warsaw, 2006.
Pohl, Dieter. *Nationalsozialistische Judenverfolgung in Ostgalizien 1941-1944: Organisation und Durchführung eines staatlichen Massenverbrechens.* Munich, 1996.
Polonsky, Antony. *The Jews in Poland and Russia.* 3 vols. Oxford, UK, 2010–12.
Porat, Dina. *The Blue and Yellow Stars of David: The Zionist Leadership in Palestine and the Holocaust, 1939-1945.* Cambridge, MA, 1990.
———. *The Fall of a Sparrow: The Life and Times of Abba Kovner.* Stanford, CA, 2000.
Poznanski, Renée. *Jews in France During World War II.* Translated by Nathan Bracher. Hanover, NH, 2001.
———. *Propagandes et persécutions: La Résistance et le "probleme juif," 1940-1944.* Paris, 2008.
———. "Rescue of Jews and the Resistance in France: From History to Historiography," *French Politics, Culture and Society* 30, n. 2 (2012): 8–32.
Ranz, John. *Inhumanity: Death March to Buchenwald and the Last Jews of Bendzin.* Bloomington, IN, 2007.
Rayski, Adam. *The Choice of the Jews under Vichy: Between Submission and Resistance.* Notre Dame, IN, 2005.
Redlich, Shimon. *Together and Apart in Brzeżany: Poles, Jews, and Ukrainians, 1919-1945.* Bloomington, IN, 2002.
Reemtsma, Jan Philipp. *Charisma und Terror: Gedanken zum Verhältnis intentionalistischer und funktionalistischer Deutungen der nationalsozialistischen Vernichtungspolitik.* Frankfurt, 1994.
Roseman, Mark. "Holocaust Perpetrators in the Victims' Eyes." In *Years of Persecution, Years of Extermination: Saul Friedländer and the Future of Holocaust Studies,* ed. Christian Wiese and Paul Betts. New York, 2010.
Rosenfeld, Alvin. *A Double Dying: Reflections on Holocaust Literature.* Bloomington, IN, 1980.
———. *The End of the Holocaust.* Bloomington, IN, 2011.
Roskies, David. *Against the Apocalypse: Responses to Catastrophe in Modern Jewish Culture.* Cambridge, MA, 1984.
Rudling, Per Anders. "The OUN, the UPA and the Holocaust: A Study in the Manufacturing of Historical Myths," Carl Beck Papers in Russian and East European Studies, No. 2107. Pittsburgh, 2011.
Saerens, Lieven. *Vreemdelingen in een Wereldstad: Een geschiedenis van Antwerpen en zijn joodse bevolking (1880-1940).* Tielt, 2000.
Samusia, Paweł, and Wiesław Pusia, eds. *Fenomen getta łódzkiego, 1940-1944.* Łódź, 2006.
Sandkühler, Thomas. *"Endlösung" in Galizien: Der Judenmord in Ostpolen und die Rettungsinitiativen von Berthold Beitz, 1941-1944.* Bonn, 1996.
Schreiber, Marion. *The Twentieth Train: The Remarkable Story of the Only Successful Ambush on the Journey to Auschwitz.* London, 2003.
Shandler, Jeffrey. *Adventures in Yiddishland: Postvernacular Language and Culture.* Berkeley, CA, 2006.
Shanes, Joshua. *Diaspora Nationalism and Jewish Identity in Habsburg Galicia.* New York, 2012.
Shapiro, Robert Moses, and Tadeusz Espstein, eds., *The Warsaw Ghetto Oyneg Shabbes-Ringelblum Archive: Catalogue and Guide.* Bloomington, IN, 2010.
Sheramy, Rona. "From Auschwitz to Jerusalem: Re-enacting Jewish History on the March of the Living," *POLIN: Studies in Polish Jewry* 19 (2007): 307–26.
Sinkoff, Nancy. *Out of the Shtetl: Making Jews Modern in the Polish Borderlands.* Providence, RI, 2004.
Sorokina, Marina. "People and Procedures: Toward a History of the Investigation of Nazi Crimes in the USSR," *Kritika* 6, n. 4 (Fall 2005): 797–831.
Snyder, Timothy. *Bloodlands: Europe Between Hitler and Stalin.* New York, 2010.
Steinberg, Maxime. *L'Étoile et le Fusil. Part I: La Question juive, 1940-1942.* Brussels, 1983.

———. *L'Étoile et le Fusil. Part II: 1942, Les cent jours de la déportation des Juifs de Belgique.* Brussels, 1984.
———. *L'Étiole et le Fusil. Part III: La Traque des Juifs, 1942–1944.* 2 vols. Brussels, 1987.
Stone, Dan. *Constructing the Holocaust: A Study in Historiography.* London, 2003.
———. *Histories of the Holocaust.* New York, 2010.
———, ed., *The Holocaust and Historical Methodology.* New York, 2012.
Struve, Kai. "Tremors in the Shatterzone of Empires: Eastern Galicia in Summer 1941." In *Shatterzone of Empires: Coexistence and Violence in the German, Habsburg, Russian, and Ottoman Borderlands,* ed. Omer Bartov and Eric D. Weitz. Bloomington, IN, 2013, 463–84.
Trezise, Thomas. *Witnessing Witnessing: On the Reception of Holocaust Survivor Testimony.* New York, 2013.
Trunk, Isaiah. *Judenrat: The Jewish Councils in Eastern Europe under Nazi Occupation.* New York, 1962.
Tsur, Eli. *Before Darkness Fell: Hashomer Hatzair in Poland and Galicia 1930-1940* [Hebrew]. Sde Boqer, 2006.
Unger, Michal. *Lodz: The Last Ghetto in Poland* [Hebrew]. Jerusalem, 2005.
Vital, David. *A People Apart: The Jews in Europe, 1789-1939.* New York, 1999.
Wasserstein, Bernard. *On the Eve: The Jews of Europe before the Second World War.* London, 2012.
Waxman, Zoë Vania. *Writing the Holocaust: Identity, Testimony, Representation.* New York, 2006.
Wiese, Christian, and Paul Betts, eds. *Years of Persecution, Years of Extermination: Saul Friedländer and the Future of Holocaust Studies.* New York, 2010.
Yagil, Limore. *Chrétiens et Juifs sous Vichy (1940-1944) Sauvetage et désobéissance civile.* Paris, 2005.
Yerushalmi, Yosef Hayim. *Zakhor: Jewish History and Jewish Memory.* Seattle, 1996.
Young, James E. *Writing and Rewriting the Holocaust: Narrative and the Consequences of Interpretation.* Bloomington, IN, 1988.

Index

Page numbers in italics indicate figures and tables.

A

Abraham, Pierre, 212
Adler, Malka, 163
Agnon, Shmuel Yosef, 106, 110, 113–14, 122, 236n21
Aktionen (violent roundups), 80–82, 107, 114–15, *122,* 125n4, 131n47
Alexander, Harold R.L.G., 258
Aleynhilf (Yiddisher Sozyaler Aleynhilf—Żydowska Samopomoc Społeczna), 83, 87n45, 176, 180–81, 184–85, 191n32
Allen, Roger, 255–56
Allen, W. Dennis, 253, 255
Allied POWs and nationals, 255–59
American Jewish Committee, 100–101
American Jewish Congress, 254–55
American Jewish Joint Distribution Committee (JDC), 176, 180, 184, 197, 199–200, 207n30, 254
andartiko (partisan movement), 226, 233–35
Anderman, Janek, 131n47
Anderman, Zeev, 131n47
André, Joseph, 203
Anielewicz, Mordecai, 187
Ansky, S. (Shloyme Zanvl Rappoport), 112, 127n26
antisemitism, 3, 5–8, 21–23, 25–27, 33n31, 220–21
Appleman-Jurman, Alicia, 131n44
Arad, Yitzhak, 6
Arendt, Hannah, 3, 34n44, 47, 51n9, 271

Association des Juifs de Belgique (AJB), 195–96, 198, 206
Atelme, Robert, 160
Auerbach, Rachel, 174, 180–82, 185
Auschwitz, 20–21, 33n29, 80, 84, 140–41, 155–58, 243, 271, 273. *See also* Birkenau
Axis allies and German occupied countries, 26–28, 36n68, 36n74, 37n77, 37n83, 37n85, 255–56

B

Bad Gandersheim, 159–60
Bahn, Mosze Meir, 86n8
Balaban, Meyer, 178, 181
Bandera, Stepan, 115, 117, 121, *121*
Barącz, Sadok, 110
Barash, Efraim, 77, 79, 82–85, 181
Bartana, Yael, 268–69, 274–78
Bartov, Omer, 32n26, 101
Bauer, Yehuda, 6–7, 19, 32nn19–20, 51n12, 131n34, 131n47, 184, 273
Bauman, Zygmunt, 34n44
Beaune-la-Rolande internment camp, 242–43
Begin, Menachem, 225, 249n23
belated memories, 135. *See also* deferred memories
Belgian Comité de Défense des Juifs (CDJ), 195–99, 203–4, 206n4
Belgium: children's escape networks and, 196–98, 203–4; Christians' assistance in, 197–98; family prewar countryside holidays in, 194; organizational connections with non-Jews in, 195–96,

195–99, 206n4, 206n7, 207n19; prewar relations with non-Jews in, 194; religious connections with non-Jews in, 202–4; rescued Jews statistics and, 196–97; resistance in, 195; underworld activities in context of judicial system in, 205, 208n46; underworld connections in, 204–5
Bełżec, 107, 131n47
Bender, Sara, 189
Benjamin, Walter, 279n10
Ben-Sasson, Havi, 187
Berek (pseud.), 144–47, 149
Bergen, Doris, 6
Berger, Gottlob, 258
Berler, Willy, 161
Berman, Adolf, 174, 187
Bessarabia, 253
Bevin, Ernest, 262
Białystok Ghetto, 9, 73–74, 77, 79–85, *80–82,* 140, 181
Biebow, Hans, 59–60, 65–67, 70n18
Bielski, Sonia, 139
Birkenau: child murder in concentration camps and, 137; deportations to, 103n25, 243, 248n10; Eliezer Gruenbaum as Kapo in, 10, 243; evacuation of, 157–58; gold excavations in postwar, 269–70; iconic photograph of gate at, 21; infanticide in, 140; Sonderkommando resistance in, 226, 230–33, 236n24, 236nn26–27. *See also* Auschwitz
Blechhammer, 158
Bloch, Jean Richard, 212
Bloodlands: overview of, 8, 22, 33n39; annihilation of Jews in, 48; apologist dialect and, 44–45, 51n7; critiques of, 22, 33n39, 34n42; death statistics, 40, 41; deportation plan and, 47–48; Final Solution and, 47–48; Holocaust in context of, 21–22, 41, 48, 50n3; ideologies and, 45–46; as Jewish homeland, 46–47; microhistories and, 8, 39–40, 39–44, 42–44, 47, 49–50, 50n1, 50n4; nationalism and, 42–43, 47, 50n3, 50n6, 51n9; Poland and, 40, 46, 50; regime alliances in, 47; regime comparisons in, 48–49, 51nn11–12, 130n42; regime overlap in, 41–43, 47–48, 50n3; regional/macrohistories and, 22, 40, 42–44, 47, 49–50, 50n2, 50n4; temporality and, 45; Ukraine and, 39, 46, 50; universal meaning of Holocaust and, 44; unprecedentedness and, 49, 51n12. *See also* Buczacz
Bloxham, Donald, 4, 19–20, 32n25
Blumenthal, Nachman, 179
Bobyk, Ivan, 120, 125n4, 134n72
Boder, David, 164
Bolchover, Richard, 250
Bolchower, Margarete (Grete) Presser, 98–100, 101, 104n30
Borochov, Ber, 175–76, 179–81, 189n8
Braun, Robert, 104n34
Brenner, Reeve Robert, 104n26
Breslau (Wrocław), 266
Brinker, Menachem, 224
Broszat, Martin, 5, 13n28
Browning, Christopher R., 3, 19, 26, 41, 124n2
Buchenwald, 155, 243
Buczacz: *Aktionen*/violent roundups and, 107, 114–15, *122,* 125n4, 131n47; archives and, 122, 124; Austria and, 112, 128n27; Bandera and, 115, 117, 121, *121;* Bobyk and, 120, 125n4, 134n72; bureaucratic processes and, 107, 124n2; Christians and, 107, 118–20, 122, 126n7, 134n72; communal massacres and, 107, 114–15; Czortków and, 98, 106, *106,* 114–15, 130n43; deportations from, 107, 114, 120, 131n47; diaries and, 109–10; documentation and, 109, 110, 112, 122, 124, 128n27; Fedor Hill and, 114–15, *121, 122, 123,* 133n66; German policemen and, 107, 125n4, 130n43; Germans' protection of Jews and, 115, 118; individual narratives and, 116–18; Jewish cemetery and, 114–15, *122, 122, 123,* 124; Jewish death statistics and, 106, 107, 114–15, 117–18, 130nn41–43, 131n47; Jewish leadership and, 107, 114, 125n4, 131n46, 131nn46–47; Jewish policemen and, 107, 114–15, 131nn46–47; Jewish population in, 107, 114, 124, 125n4, 126n6; Jewish wealth and, 119, 133n63, 133n66; Nazi ideology and, 108–9, 114, 119; Nazi regime and, 114–15, 115–20, 125n4, 130n43, 132n52; OUN and, 113–15, 117, 119, 121,

121, 130n33, 130n43, 134n72; postwar Jewish testimonies and, 109–10, 124; prewar period in, 8–9, 106–14, *111, 112,* 126nn6–7, 126n12; Russia/Soviet Union and, *111,* 111–12, *113,* 114, 115, 117, 119–20, 125n4, 126n12, 128n27, 134n70; single site studies and, 8–9, 106, 108; Sipo and, *106,* 106–7, 114–15; site selection and, 106; summary justice and, 120; unprecedentedness and, 108; UPA and, 115, 117, 119; Yizkor or memorial books and, 110, 120, 127n14. *See also* Bloodlands; Polish non-Jews; Ukrainian non-Jews
Buna-Monowitz, 243
Byrnes, James F., 260

C

Central Jewish Historical Commission, 270, 280n26
Chalfen, Eliasz, 116
Chari, Anatol, 64
Chełmno (Kulmhof), 65, 66–67, 185
children: child resurrection narratives and, 144–49; deportations and, 55–56, 58–61, 59, 66, 70n12, 137; escape networks with non-Jews and, 194–99, 201–4; murder in concentration camps and, 137, 140–41
Christians, 107, 118–20, 122, 126n7, 134n72, 197–98, 202–4, 208n38, 260. *See also* non-Jews
Cohen, Leon, 230–31, 236nn26–27
Cohen, Yisrael, 127n14
colonialism, 21–22, 33nn30–31, 45–46
Comité de Bienfaisance, 200
Comité Inter-Mouvements Auprès d'Evacués (CIMADE), 199–200
communal massacres, 106, 124n1. *See also* Buczacz
comparative history, 9, 73–74
concentration camps: overview of, 152–53; child murder in, 137, 140–41; daily life in, 153–54, 157; death marches in comparison to, 152–53; evacuation of, 156–58; liberation day and, 154–56; mental capitulation in, 159; prisoners in abandoned, 155–56; slave labor, 84, 85, 137; space and, 154, 160–61. *See also specific concentration camps*

Confino, Alon, 3, 58, 69, 102
Corni, Gustavo, 175
Creet, Julia, 140–41
Czech government-in-exile, and pressure groups, 252–53, 261
Czerniaków, Adam, 59, 179–80
Czernowitz, 161, 266
Czortków, 98, 106, *106,* 114–15, 130n43. *See also* Buczacz
Czortków Ghetto, 98

D

Dalairac, François-Paulin, 110
Daniel, Yehiel, 166
Datner, Szymon, 83
Daum, Estera, 59–60, 66
Dawidowicz, Lucy S., 102n3, 181
death marches: overview of, 10, 152–53; concentration camps in comparison to, 152–53; daily life during, 158; escape narratives and, 164–66; evacuation of concentration camps and, 156–58; friends during, 159–60; goals of, 161–62; Greek Jews and, 165–66; guards' compassion during, 161; Jews and, 162–66; liberation day memories and, 155, 166–67; memories of, 153, 156, 166–67; mental capitulation during, 159; Nazi ideology and, 162; non-Jews and, 162, 165, 168n39; population statistics and, 153; postwar testimonies of, 153, 156, 167; preparation for, 157–58; space and, 153, 160–61; survival and, 152–53, 158–59, 162–66
death statistics: Bloodlands, 40, 41; Holocaust core, 21, 33n29; Jews in Buczacz, 106, 107, 114–15, 117–18, 130nn41–43, 131n47; non-Jews, 24, 130n41, 130n43; Romania, 50n3
deferred memories, 135–36, 149
De-Nur, Yehiel (Ka-Tzetnik), 249
Devaux, Théomir, 202
Diamant, Josef, 75
diaries: overview of, 9–10, 92, 94–95, 100–102; analytical readings of, 98, 101; efficacy of representation and, 99, 101–2, 104n34; French Holocaust historiography and, 95–98, 100, 103n15, 103n25; future in context of, 93, 94, 99, 101; historians' distrust and, 92, 102n3; literary devices and

influences on, 98–99; religious beliefs and, 97–98, 104nn26–27; responses to Holocaust and, 96–98, 104nn26–27; secular democracy as immoral and, 96–98; "space of experience" and, 93–94; testimonies in context of, 93; theoretical and methodological issues and, 92–95, 103n10; victim-focused historiography and, 91, 99–100
Dieckmann, Christoph, 51n10
Displaced Persons (DPs), and pressure groups, 250–51, 255–56, 259–62
Displaced Persons Act of 1948, 261–62
Drancy transit camp, 103n25, 216, 218
Dreyfus, Lucien, 95–98, 103n15, 103n25

E
Éclaireurs Israélites de France, 199
economics, in context of Jews, 26–27, 36n70
Eden, Anthony, 256
Efrati/Efrusi, Shimon, 139
Eichengreen Lucille, 62
Eichmann, Adolf, 3, 18, 28, 48, 131n46, 249n21
Eisenbach, Artur, 180
Eisenhower, Dwight D., 258
Elias, Ruth, 141–43, 149
Elon, Amos, 268–69, 271–74, 280n34
emotions, postwar. *See* postwar emotions
Engel, David, 6–7, 101
L'Entreaide Temporaire, 201
escape narratives, 164–66, 185
escape networks. *See* Jewish self-help, and escape networks
Escobar, Maya, 266–67
Eternal Jew, The (film), 174

F
Final Solution of the Jewish Question: Bloodlands and, 47–48; colonialism in context of, 21–22; economics of, 27; final destruction of ghettos and, 83–84; "genocide studies" and, 3; Holocaust core and, 24–25; ideology and, 3, 19, 24, 35n50; non-Jewish death statistics and, 24; unprecedentedness and, 97. *See also* World Jewry annihilation
Flavius Josephus, 226, 227–30, 236n17
Fortunoff Video Archive for Holocaust Testimonies, 4, 109, 135

Fotoamator (film), 59
France: antisemitic legislation and, 209, 213; children's escape networks in, 199, 201–2; deportations from, 209, 213, 218–21, 243–44, 248n10; family prewar countryside holidays in, 194; Franco-Judaism and, 95, 96, 103n15; Holocaust historiography and, 95–98, 100, 103n15, 103n25; organizational connections with non-Jews in, 195, 199–202, 207nn30–31, 208nn33–34; prewar relations with non-Jews in, 194–95; religious connections with non-Jews in, 202, 204, 208n38; resistance in, 195. *See also* Jewish Communists in France
Francs-Tireurs et Partisans de la Main d'Oeuvre Immigrée (FTP-MOI), 214
Frank, Jacques, 218
free loan societies *(gmiles khesed kasses)*, 176, 190n11
Freidländer, Saul, 5–6, 24, 35n50, 58, 69, 70n8
Friedman, Jonathan, 63–64
Friedman, Philip, 4, 5

G
Gelbart, Isidor, 125n4, 130n43
gendered identity, and infanticide, 135, 143–44, 146
Genewein, Walter, 65
genocide, as term of use, 18–21, 29, 31n12, 32n14, 32n20, 32n25, 32n26
Gens, Jacob, 30–31, 181
geographies of Jewishness (transnational perspectives), 19, 21–22, 33n30, 33n39, 267, 275
geopolitics, 2, 12n6, 255–56, 261
Gepner, Abraham, 179–80
Gerlach, Christian, 19
Gerlier, Pierre-Marie, 202
Gerlik, Menachem, 247
Germany, and postwar emotions, 266–67, 271–75, 278, 278nn5–6, 279n9
Gęsiówka, 165–66, 233. *See also* Greek Jews
ghetto experience: overview of, 84–85; *Aktionen*/violent roundups and, 80–82; archives and, 181; comparative history and, 9, 73–74; daily life and, 77–81; deportations and, 80, 83–85; economic

demands by Nazis and, 75–76, 86n8; employment and, 77–81, 83; final destruction and, 81, 83–84; infanticide in, 140; Jewish leadership and, 74–77, 79–80, 82–85, 86n6, 86n8, 86n14, 87n36, 181; Jewish policemen and, 81–82, 87n36; Nazi authorities relations and, 82–83; population statistics, 76, 80; rescue through labor and, 57, 59, 66, 70n13, 79–80, 83; taxes and, 76, 79, 81–82; violence against women and, 62, 64–65. *See also specific ghettos*
Ginsburger, Pierre, 212
Giterman, Yitzhak, 176, 184, 187, 190n11, 191n31
Goldberg, Amos, 103n10
Goldhagen, Daniel Jonah, 3, 124n2, 273
Göring, Hermann, 28, 36n71
Graf, Henri, 157
Grass, Günter, 271, 272
Great Britain, and pressure groups, 11, 214, 250–62
Greek Jews: overview of, 225–26; *andartiko* and, 226, 233–35; Birkenau Sonderkommando resistance by, 226, 230–33, 236n24, 236nn26–27; death marches and, 165–66; Maccabean revolt and, 226, 228, 232, 234; Masada revolt and, 226–30, 232–33, 235n13, 236nn20–21, 236n23; nationalism and, 231–32, 234–35, 236nn28–29
Gripel, Aliza (Rosenwasser), 133n66
Grosman, Haika, 81, 83
Gross, George (Gershon), 130n43, 131n46
Gross, Jan T., 124n1
Grossman, Mendel, 66
Gross-Rosen, 157
Gruenbaum, Eliezer (Leon Berger): biographical information about, 242, 244; Birkenau and, 10, 243–44, 248n10; citizenship issue and, 244; Communist party accusations/exonerations/expulsion and, 243–44, 249n14; death march to Buchenwald, 243; deportations and, 243–44, 248n10; fictional portraits of, 245–46, 249n21; Israeli Defense Forces and, 10, 244; Jewish Communist movement and, 10, 241–44, 246, 248n6; as Kapo in Birkenau, 10, 243; memories and, 10, 241, 244–46; prewar fissures in Jewish society and, 10–11, 241; rehabilitation of reputation and, 10–11, 244–47, 248n2; *Scrolls of Fire* and, 246; Spanish Civil War and, 241, 242, 248n8; ultra-Orthodox community, 241, 245–47; Zionism, 241, 244, 246, 247
Gruenbaum, Eliezer (nephew), 246–47
Gruenbaum, Miriam, 242
Gruenbaum, Yitzhak, 10–11, 241–42, 245–47, 248n2
Gruenbaums, Binyamin-Bengio, 242
Gutman, Yisrael, 66, 67, 102n3, 189

H

Hagen, Wilhelm, 5
halakha (Jewish religious law), 29, 139
Halamajowa, Franciszka, 147
Hambresin, Emile, 196
Handelsman, Marceli, 177
Hanover, Natan, 110
Harff, Barbara, 31n12
HaShomer HaTzair, 242, 246n5
Hasmoneans (Maccabean Revolt), 226, 228, 232, 234
Heiber/Héber, Maurice, 197
Hellendael, Eugene, 196
Herszfeld, Ludwig, 179–80
Hertz, Yvonne, 196
Herzbruck, 161
Heydrich, Reinhard, 28, 45, 252
Hilberg, Raul, 5, 25–26, 63
Hiller, Jakub, 64
Himmler, Heinrich, 24–25, 35n54, 36n56, 45, 162, 257–58
Hirsch, Marianne, 267
Hirschaut, Yekhiel, 188
historiography of Holocaust. *See* Holocaust historiography
Hitler, Adolf: Allied POWs and, 255, 257–58; Bloodlands and, 8, 22; colonialism and, 21, 33n31; ideological decisions of, 2–3; temporality and, 45; World Jewry annihilation and, 24–26, 28, 34n45, 34n47, 36n56, 37n85. *See also* Nazism and ideology
Holländer, Margarete (Grete) Presser Bolchower, 98–102
Holocaust/holocaust: as term of use, 18–19, 31n9, 32n20, 32n25; Bloodlands and, 21–22, 41, 48, 50n3; Jewish behavior during, 174, 180, 186,

191n20; universal meaning of, 32n20, 44, 186, 191n49. *See also* Holocaust historiography

Holocaust (television series), 19

Holocaust core: overview of, 7–8, 17, 30; antisemitism and, 21–23, 25–27, 33n31; Auschwitz-centered view and, 20–21, 33n29; Axis allies and occupied countries' role in context of, 26–28, 36n68, 36n74, 37n77, 37n83, 37n85; colonialism and, 21–22, 33nn30–31; death statistics and, 21, 33n29; economics in context of Jews and, 26–27, 36n70; Final Solution and, 24–25; genocide as term of use and, 18–21, 29, 31n12, 32n14, 32n20, 32n25, 32n26; geographies of Jewishness and, 19, 21, 22, 33n30, 33n39; h/Holocaust as term of use and, 18–19, 31n9, 32n20, 32n25; *Hurban/Churbn* as term of use and, 17–18; Jewish dimension of, 7–8, 22, 33n39, 255; Jewish history and, 23, 29–31, 34n42; Jewish religious life and, 29, 35n55; Jewish self-help and, 29–30; non-Jews and, 18, 24, 31n9; re-identification of Jews and, 26, 36n68; rescuers as non-Jews and Jews and, 30; Shoah as term of use and, 17–18, 21; terminology and, 17–20; universal meaning and, 32n20; unprecedentedness and, 19–20, 32n20; World Jewry annihilation and, 6, 23–29, 34nn44–45, 34n47, 35–36nn54–56, 35n50, 36n68. *See also* Holocaust

Holocaust historiography: overview of, 1; antisemitism and, 3, 5–8; bureaucratic processes and, 3–6; historians' distrust of retrospective testimonies and, 5, 92, 102n3; ideology and, 2–3, 6, 8; Israeli approach to, 5–6, 14n32, 91, 189; Jewish commentators and, 100–101; Jewish history and, 6–7, 173–74; local level studies and, 3–9, 14n32; Nazi films and, 173–74; personal narratives of Jews and, 1, 5–6, 11; responses by Jews and, 7, 97; victim-focused, 4, 63, 91, 99–100, 189; Yizkor or memorial books and, 4; Zionism and, 7

Hungary, 254, 255

Hurban/Churbn (destruction), as term of use, 17–18

I

Independence Front (FI), 195–96, 198

individual narratives or testimonies: collections of, 4; diaries in context of, 93; future in context of, 93; historians' distrust of, 5, 92, 102n3; Holocaust historiography and, 1, 5–6, 11, 63–67; local subjectivity and, 5; memories and, 5–6; by perpetrators, 2, 24; in Soviet Union, 2; statistics on collections of, 4; U.S. geopolitical interests and, 2, 12n6. *See also* diaries; memories; postwar testimonies

infanticide: overview of, 10, 135–37, 149; accidental deaths and, 138, 148; aftereffects in context of resurrection narrative and, 147–49; in Białystok Ghetto, 140; biblical Moses narrative and, 145–46; in Birkenau, 140; child resurrection narratives and, 144–49; child's perspective of resurrection narrative and, 147–49; "choiceless choice" and, 138–39; deferred memories and, 135–36, 149; deliberate deaths and, 138–39; eyewitness narratives and, 139–40; fathers and, 143–47; gendered identity and, 135, 143–44, 146; group pressure and, 138, 148; moral norms and, 139, 148; mothers and, 140–43; mourning deaths and, 143; multi-perspectives on narratives and, 147–48; relatives and, 137–38; as resistance, 139–40, 142; in slave labor camps, 137; survival and, 140, 142–43, 148; traumatic memories and, 138, 140, 143

International Brigades, 241, 242, 248n8

Israel: Holocaust historiography in, 5–6, 14n32, 91, 189; Israeli Defense Forces, 10, 244; Palestinian conflict with, 26, 32n26, 274; postwar emotions in, 267, 278n9; ultra-Orthodox community in, 241, 245–47. *See also* Zionism

J

Jabłónsky, Dariusz, 59

Jakobs-Melkman, Leny, 30–31

Jarecka, Gustawa, 185–86

Jawischowitz, 243

Jewish Agency, 101, 241, 244–45

Jewish cemetery in Buczacz, 114–15, 122, *122, 123,* 124

Jewish commentators, 100–101
Jewish Communist movement, 10, 241–44, 243–44, 246, 248n6, 249n14
Jewish Communists in France: overview of, 10, 209–10, 221–22; activists and, 212–13; antisemitic legislation and, 209, 213; Communist propaganda activites and, 210, 213–14; deportations and, 213, 218–21; Eliezer Gruenbaum and, 242–43; ethnic and political identity in context of, 210, 214–18, 222nn16–17; history of, 210–12; Jewish resistance and, 209–10, 212–18, 222nn16–17; MOI and, 211–12, 214, 218, 221, 222n2; racism and, 220–21; sensation of disbelief and, 213; social welfare and, 213; Solidarité Juive and, 213. *See also* France
Jewish histories of Holocaust, 4–6, 14n32, 91, 102n1, 173–74, 184
Jewish history, 6–7, 23, 29–31, 34n42, 46–47, 174–75, 177–79, 187, 191n31
Jewish identity: ethnic and political, 210, 214–18, 222nn16–17; re-identification and, 26, 36n68
Jewish leadership (Judenrat): in Buczacz, 107, 114, 125n4, 131nn46–47; ghetto experience and, 74–77, 79–80, 82–85, 86n6, 86n8, 86n14, 87n36, 181. *See also specific leaders*
Jewishness, geographies of, 19, 21, 22, 33n30, 33n39
Jewish policemen, 81–82, 107, 114–15, 131nn46–47
Jewish religious beliefs/life: burial practice and, 270; *halakha*/Jewish religious law and, 29, 139; Holocaust core and, 29, 35n55; martyrdom and, 226, 229, 235n11; memories of national disasters and, 224–25; Nazism and, 29, 35n55; resistance and, 225–26, 226–30, 232–34, 235n11, 235n13, 236nn20–21, 236n23; responses to Holocaust and, 97–98, 104nn26–27; ultra-Orthodox community and, 241, 245–47
Jewish Renaissance Movement in Poland (JRMiP), 274, 277
Jewish self-help: Aleynhilf and, 83, 87n45, 176, 180–81, 184–85, 191n32; free loan societies and, 176, 190n11; Nazism and, 29–30, 184
Jewish self-help, and escape networks: overview of, 9, 193, 206; children's escape networks and, 194–99, 201–4; community of non-Jews and, 193–95; family prewar countryside holidays and, 194; organizations of non-Jews and, 195–202, 206n4, 206n7, 207n19, 207nn30–31, 208nn33–34; party affiliations contacts with non-Jews and, 195; prewar relations with non-Jews and, 194–95; religious non-Jews and, 202–4, 208n38; rescued Jews statistics and, 196–97; as resistance, 193, 195; underworld connections and, 204–5. *See also specific organizations*
Jewish society, prewar, 10–11, 175, 182–83, 241
Jewish wealth, 65–66, 119, 133n63, 133n66
Jewish/Yiddish secular culture, 176, 178, 184, 191n42
Jews' responses to Holocaust, 7, 96–98, 104nn26–27
Jokusch, Laura, 4, 101
Jospa, Hertz (Ghert Joseph), 196
Judenrat (Jewish leadership). *See* Jewish leadership (Judenrat)

K

Kagan, Dobcia, 40, 50
Kaplan, Marion A., 7
Karasso, Daisy, 233
Kassow, Samuel, 73, 101
Katyn Massacre, 39, 50, 213
Katz, Yoel, 118
Katzenelson, Yitzhak, 101
Ka-Tzetnik (Yehiel De-Nur), 249
Katzki, Herbert, 200
Kelly, D.V., 253
Kerkhofs, Louis-Joseph, 203
Kershaw, Ian, 25
Kertész, Imre, 154, 155
Khmelnitsky, Bohdan, 110
Khvostenko, Maria Mykhailivna, 119
Kielce Ghetto, 9, 73–79, 81–85, 86n6, 86n8, 86n14, 87n36
Kimmelmann, Abraham, 159
Kitsos, Kapitan (Yitzhak Moshe), 233
Klonicki/Klonymus, Arie, 117

Koninski, Aaron, 182
Korzen, Meir, 178–79
Kosciuszko Uprising monograph, 179, 190n14
Koselleck, Reinhart, 93
Kovner, Abba, 30–31, 236n20
Kovno Ghetto, 137, 139–40
Krasiński, Zygmunt, 110
Krasucki, Henri, 212
Kriegel-Valrimont, Maurice, 212
Kruk, Herman, 181
Krzepicki, Avrom, 185
Kuper, Leo, 124n2
Kushner, Tony, 4

L

Langer, Lawrence, 135–36, 138–40
Langman, Majcher, 243
Lanzmann, Claude, 18, 141–42, 278
Lasch, Karl, 76
Leff, Laurel, 254
Leibovitz, Liel, 236n23
Lemkin, Raphael, 18, 29
Lepkifker, Joseph, 203
Lev, Aba, 112
Leventhal, Nahman, 154
Levi, Primo, 10, 69, 154
Levy, Herman, 76, 79, 82, 83, 85, 87n36
liberalist apologist dialect, 44–45
liberation day memories, 154–56, 166–67
Lichtenstein, Israel, 188
Lichtheim, Richard, 101
Lifton, Robert Jay, 124n2
liquidation. *See* Final Solution of the Jewish Question; World Jewry annihilation
Lithuania, 48, 51n10
local level studies, 3–9, 14n32. *See also* Buczacz
Łódź Ghetto: abusive activities by Nazis in, 64–67; archive of, 181, 184; child deportation policies and, 55–56, 58–61, 59, 66, 70n12; employment and, 79; Final Solution in context of, 57; ghetto experience in context of Rumkowski and, 57; interpersonal relations in, 62, 64; interpersonal relations residents in, 63–64; Jewish policemen in, 64; Jewish wealth and, 65–66; leadership in, 56, 57, 68, 72n59; population of, 80; power in, 57, 62, 64; rescue through labor in, 57, 59, 66, 70n13; sensation of disbelief in, 58–59, 61, 64, 66, 70n8; valuables confiscated and, 65, 66; violence against women in, 62, 64–65. *See also* Rumkowski, Mordechai Chaim
Lorenz, Chris, 17
Löw, Andrea, 62
Lublin, 84, 280n26

M

Maccabean Revolt, 226, 228, 232, 234
macrohistories/regional, 22, 40, 42–44, 47, 49–50, 50n2, 50n4. *See also* local level studies
Mahler, Rafael, 177
Main d'Oeuvre Étrangère (MOE), 195–96, 211
Main d'Oeuvre Immigrée (MOI), 200, 211–12, 214, 218, 221, 222n2
Majdanek, 84, 85
Malkin, Frances [Fay] (Feyge Chashe), 147–49
Maltz, Chaim (Herbert), 147, 149
Maltz, Moshe, 147–48
Maltz, Shmelke, 147–48
Mandelbaum, Israël, 196
Mann, Barbara E., 279n9
Marcus, Yitzhak, 82
Mary—Koszmary (Nightmares) [film], 274, 278
Masada revolt, 226–30, 232–33, 235n13, 236nn20–21, 236n23
mass murder. *See* Final Solution of the Jewish Question; World Jewry annihilation
Mauthausen, 163, 254
Mayer, Saly, 197
Mazower, Mark, 21–22, 51n9
memories: belated, 135; of concentration camps, 154–56; of death marches, 153, 156, 166–67; deferred, 135–36, 149; Eliezer Gruenbaum in context of, 10, 241, 244–46; individual narratives and, 5–6; liberation day, 154–56, 166–67; of national disasters, 224–25; postwar, 267; Ringelblum on, 183; traumatic, 138, 140, 143; Yizkor or memorial books and, 4, 110, 120, 127n14, 271. *See also* postwar testimonies
Mengele, Josef, 141–42

Michman, Dan, 4–5, 8, 14n32, 94, 189
microhistories, 8, 39–40, 42–44, 47, 49–50, 50n1, 50n4. *See also* postwar testimonies; individual narratives
Middle East, 28, 37n85. *See also* Israel; Zionism
Milgram, Stanley, 124n2
Milhaud, Denise, 201–2
Milhaud, Fred, 201–2
Mincer, Joachim, 117–18
Mink, Emanuel, 242
Montgomery, Bernard L., 259–60
Moses, Dirk, 19–20, 32n25, 33n31
Moses biblical narrative, 145–46
Moshe, Yitzhak (Kapitan Kitsos), 233
Mostowicz, Arnold, 59
Mouvement National Contre le Racisme (MNCR or National Movement against Racism), 213, 219
Mum (film), 140
Mur i Wieża (Wall and Tower) [film], 274

N

nationalism: Bloodlands and, 42–43, 47, 50n3, 50n6, 51n9; Greek Jewish, 231–32, 234–35, 236nn28–29; Polish non-Jews', 111–12; Ukrainian non-Jews', 110–15, 117, 119–21, *121,* 126n12, 130n33, 130n43, 134n70, 134n72
Nazism and ideology: annihilation of Jews and, 48; apologist dialectic and, 44, 51n7; Axis allies and occupied countries' role under, 26–28, 36n68, 36n74, 37n77, 37n83, 37n85; in Bloodlands, 41–49, 50n3, 51n7, 51nn11–12; Buczacz narrative and, 108–9, 114, 119; bureaucratic processes and, 3–6, 107, 124n2; colonialism and, 21, 33n31, 45–46; death marches and, 162; death statistics, 41; economics in context of Jews and, 26–27, 36n70; films and, 173–74; Final Solution and, 3, 19, 24, 35n50; German Jewry and, 25–26; German support for, 3; ghettos formation and, 26; Hitler's decisions and, 2–3; Holocaust explanation critique and, 45–46; Holocaust historiography and, 2–3, 6, 8; ideology explanation critique and, 45–46; Jewish religious life and, 29, 35n55; Jewish self-help and, 29–30, 184; Judenrat relations and, 82–83; non-Jews persecuted under, 18, 23, 24, 31n9; perpetrator witnesses, 2, 24; pregnancy policy and, 136–37; redemption and, 23–24; re-identification of Jews under, 26, 36n68; sexual intercourse policy and, 136; temporality and, 45; trials and, 1–2, 12n4, 18, 65, 109–10, 249n21; valuables confiscated and, 65, 66; World Jewry annihilation and, 6, 23–29, 34nn44–45, 34n47, 35–36nn54–56, 35n50, 36n68, 48. *See also* Hitler, Adolf; Nazism
Netherlands, the, 26–27, 36n68, 193, 253–54
Nèvejean, Yvonne, 197
NKVD (Soviet secret police), 39, 115, 130n41, 134n72
Nolte, Ernst, 44, 51n7
non-Jews: children's escape networks with, 194–99, 201–4; Christians and, 107, 118–20, 122, 126n7, 134n72, 197–98, 202–4, 208n38, 260; context of community connections as escape networks with, 193–95; death marches and, 162, 165, 168n39; death statistics for, 24, 130n41, 130n43; deportations from France and, 218–21; DPs and, 259–60; escape networks in context of prewar relations with, 194–95; Holocaust and, 18, 24, 31n9; organizational connections as escape networks with, 195–202, 206n4, 206n7, 207n19, 207nn30–31, 208nn33–34; party affiliations as escape networks with, 195; protection from, 114–15, 118, 130n43, 131nn44–45, 133n63, 161; Quakers and, 199–200, 204; religious connections as escape networks with, 202–4, 208n38; resistance and, 193, 195. *See also* Polish non-Jews; Ukrainian non-Jews in Buczacz
Nordmann, Joë, 10, 212, 215–18, 222nn16–17
No. 4 Street of Our Lady (documentary), 148–49
Nye, Archibald E., 258
Nykerk, Benjamin (Benno), 196, 197

O

Oeuvre des Secours aux Enfants (OSE), 200, 207n30

Oeuvre Nationale de l'Enfance (ONE), 197
Opoczynski, Peretz, 182
Ordnungsdienst (OD), 107, 131nn46–47. *See also* Jewish policemen
Organization of Ukrainian Nationalists (OUN), 113–15, 117, 119, 121, *121*, 130n33, 130n43, 134n72
Oshry, Ephraim, 139
Oyneg Shabes: agenda/mission of, 181, 182, 185; as "alternative community," 184–85; caches of, 174, 183, 186nn5–6; collaborator-participants in, 179, 181–82, 190n27; data collection approach for, 178–79, 183, 189; history of, 9, 173, 181; interethnic conflict and, 185; Jewish histories of Holocaust and, 173–74, 184; Jewish leadership and, 181–82, 184; Jewish/Yiddish secular culture and, 184, 191n42; legacy of, 188–89; organizational structure for, 176, 181; organization of, 173, 181; Polish-Jewish relations and, 177, 183–84; postwar testimonies in comparison to, 183; prewar Jewish society approach and, 175, 182–83; prewar politics and, 179; resistance and, 186; testimonies against perpetrators from, 5; YIVO and, 182, 184, 189n3. *See also* Ringelblum, Emanuel

P

Palestinian conflict, 26, 32n26, 274
Pat, Jacob, 267–71
Patterson, Orlando, 124n2
Pelc, Moshe, 74–76, 83, 85, 86n8
Peled, Yael, 189
Perelman, Chaïm, 196
perpetrators: dehumanization of victims by, 8–9, 105–6; motivations of, 3; testimonies by, 1–2, 12n4, 18, 24, 65, 249n21. *See also* Nazism and ideology
personal narratives. *See* diaries; individual narratives or testimonies; memories; postwar testimonies
Petrykevych, Viktor, 119
Poalei Tziyon/Poale Zion, 175–76, 179–81, 189n8, 191n31, 196, 199
Pohl, Dieter, 130n42
Poland: Bloodlands and, 40, 46, 50; Central Jewish Historical Commission in, 270, 280n26; commemorations by non-Jews in, 21; deportation from, 176; diaries and, 98–100, 101–2, 104n30; government-in-exile from, 252, 261; individual narratives and, 39–40, 50; Jewish commentators and, 100–101; Jewish Communist movement and, 242, 248n6; Jewish postwar population statistics, 268; Jewish religious beliefs and, 242; Kosciuszko Uprising and, 179, 190n14; Kovel synagogue massacre and, 40, 50; mass murders in historical context and, 97; Nazis' invasion of, 27–28; Polish DPs and, 259–60; Polish government-in-exile and, 251–52, 261; Polish-Jewish DPs and, 259–60, 259–61; postwar emotions and, 266–71, 274–78, 278nn5–6, 279n9, 280n26; redemption and, 277; resettlement of Jews to, 274, 276–78; self-help for Jews in, 195–99, 206n4; violence against Jews in, 27, 254, 268, 270; Zionism and, 242. *See also* Bloodlands; Buczacz; ghetto experience; *and specific ghettos*
Polish-American Congress (PAC), 250–51, 260
Polish non-Jews: death statistics in Buczacz, 130n41, 130n43; deportation from Buczacz and, 114, 120; Jews' relations with, 177–79, 183–84, 187–88, 190n14, 192n53; nationalism and, 111–12; population in Buczacz, 107, 122, 126n6; postwar testimonies by, 124, 168n39
politics: geopolitics and, 2, 12n6, 255–56, 261; Jewish identity and, 210, 214–18, 222nn16–17; prewar Jewish, 9, 175–76, 179–80, 187, 189n8, 190n14, 190n22, 190n27, 191n31, 192n53; in U.S., 260–62
Politzer, Georges, 212 13
Pollak, Zofia, 131n45
Polonsky, Antony, 7
Porat, Dina, 236n20
postwar emotions: overview of, 266–67, 266–71, 278, 278nn5–6; admiration for activities, 270, 280n26; anger, 270–71, 276; bewilderment, 272–75; the dead, 269–70; disappointment, 274; discomfort, 272–75; empathy, 270–71, 272–74; fear, 269, 276; geographies of Jewishness and, 267, 279n9; gold

excavations in Birkenau and, 269–70; hope, 274–75; longing, 274–78; memories, 267, 271, 273, 275–76, 278n9; montage-like portrait of, 267–68, 279n10; numbness, 271, 275; resettlement of Jews and, 274, 276–78; sadness, 269; space and, 267, 270, 272, 276, 278, 279n9, 279n11; temporality and, 268, 278, 279n11; Yizkor or memorial books and, 271

postwar testimonies: Buczacz and, 109–10, 124; death marches and, 153, 156, 167; historians' distrust of retrospective, 5, 92, 102n3; Oyneg Shabes in comparison to, 183; Poles and, 124, 168n39; Rumkowski and, 10, 59–60, 62–64, 69; trials and, 1–2, 12n4, 249n21; Ukrainians and, 124

Potocki, Mikołaj, 110

pressure groups: overview of, 11, 214, 250–51; Allied POWs and nationals in context of, 255–59; Christians and, 260; Czech government-in-exile and, 252–53, 261; Displaced Persons Act and, 261–62; DPs and, 250–51, 255, 259–62; geopolitics versus, 255–56, 261; Hungarians representatives and, 254; Jewish dimension of Holocaust and, 255; Jewish organizations and, 254–57; the Netherlands government-in-exile and, 253–54; the Netherlands government-in-exile and, 253–54; PAC and, 250–51, 260; Polish DPs and, 259–60; Polish government-in-exile and, 251–52, 261; Polish-Jewish DPs and, 259–61; politics versus, 260–62; sensation of disbelief and, 254–55; Soviet DPs and, 259; UNWCC and, 255; World Jewry annihilation and, 254–55, 254–56; Zionism in context of DPs and, 255–56, 260–62

Pronicheva, Dina, 2

Pulawer, Moshe, 55–56, 59

Q

Quakers, 199–200, 204

R

racism, 220–21

Rapoport, David, 201, 208n33

Rappoport, Shloyme Zanvl (S. Ansky), 112, 127n26

Reams, Roberts Borden, 255

Red Cross, 197, 201

redemption, 23–24, 188, 277

regional/macrohistories, 22, 40, 42–44, 47, 49–50, 50n2, 50n4. *See also* local level studies

rehabilitation of reputations, 10–11, 244–47, 248n2

religious beliefs/life of Jews. *See* Jewish religious beliefs/life

rescuers, 30. *See also* Jewish self-help, and escape networks

rescue through labor, 57, 59, 66, 70n13, 79–80, 83

resistance: *andartiko* and, 226, 233–35; in Belgium, 195; in Buczacz, 131n47; in France, 195; Greek Jewish, 226, 230–33, 236n24, 236nn26–27; infanticide in context of, 139–40, 142; Jesus Christ and, 228, 235n14; Jewish Communists in France and, 209–10, 212–15; Jewish partisans and, 225, 235n7; Jewish religious beliefs and, 225, 226–30, 232–33, 232–34, 235n13, 236nn20–21, 236n23; self-help as, 193, 195; in Warsaw Ghetto, 186

Reynders, Bruno, 203

Ribbentrop-Molotov Pact, 74

Ricoeur, Paul, 93

Riegner, Gerhardt, 254

Ringelblum, Emanuel: overview of, 9; Aleynhilf and, 176, 180–81, 184–85, 191n32; biographical information about, 113, 175, 186–88; Bundist socialism and, 179, 190n27; capture of, 186–88; free loan societies *(gmiles khesed kasses)*, 176, 190n11; Jewish behavior during Holocaust and, 174, 180, 186, 191n20; as Jewish historian, 174–75, 177–79, 187, 191n31; Jewish/Yiddish secular culture and, 176, 178, 184, 191n42; Kosciuszko Uprising monograph and, 179, 190n14; on memories, 183; Oyneg Shabes organization by, 173, 181; Polish-Jewish relations and, 177–79, 184, 187–88, 190n14, 192n53; prewar Jewish society approach, 175; prewar politics and, 9, 175–76, 179–80, 187, 189n8, 190n14,

190n22, 190n27, 191n31, 192n53; self-help social activism and, 175, 176; on universal meaning of Holocaust, 186, 191n49; YIVO and, 178–79, 181; Zionism and, 175, 187. *See also* Oyneg Shabes

Roberts, Frank, 251, 253, 255

Romanian Jews, 27, 50n3, 255

Roosevelt, Franklin D., 252

Roseman, Mark, 6

Rosenfeld, Oskar, 59, 63–64

Rosenman, Gedaliah, 77

Rosenthal, A. M., 267

Rosenwasser, Aliza (Gripel), 133n66

Rosenzweig, Stefa (Stefania), 244

Roser, Henri, 204

Roskies, David, 101

Rosner, Mina, 131n44

Rossoliński-Liebe, Grzegorz, 130n42

Roth, Philip, 276–77

Rozmarek, Charles, 260

Rue Amelot Committee, 199–201

Rumkowski, Mordechai Chaim: adoption of child by, 62; Biebow and, 59–60, 70n18; characteristics of, 56–57, 68–69; child deportation policy and, 55–56, 58–61, 66, 70n12; critiques of activities and, 57, 68, 72n59; fictional portraits of, 55–56, 61–63, 68–69, 71n29; individual narrative testimonies and, 63–67; interpersonal relations and, 62, 64; leadership and, 56, 57, 68, 72n59; Łódź Ghetto experience in context of, 57; Nazi relations with, 57, 60; postwar Jewish testimonies and, 10, 59–60, 62–64, 69; power and, 57, 62, 64; rescue through labor and, 57, 59, 66, 70n13; sensation of disbelief by, 10, 58–59. *See also* Łódź Ghetto

Russia/Soviet Union: Bloodlands and, 8, 22, 41–43, 47–49, 50n3, 51nn11–12; Buczacz and, *111*, 111–12, *113*, 114, 115, 117, 119–20, 125n4, 126n12, 128n27, 134n70; colonialism and, 46; DPs from, 259; ghettos formation in occupied, 26; ideology and, 46; individual narratives and, 2; liberation of Auschwitz by, 156; World Jewry annihilation and, 27–28. *See also* Bloodlands; Russia; Stalin, Joseph

S

Saint-Cyprien detention camp, 242

Sargent, Orme, 251

Save the Children Fund, 197, 207n19

Schindler, Bruno, 81

Schiper, Yitzhak, 173–74, 177, 178, 181, 187

Schutzpolizei (Schupo), 81

Schwartz, Joseph, 207n31

Scrolls of Fire, 246

Secours d'Hiver (Winter Help), 197

Secours Populaire, 197

Secours Sioniste, 197

secular democracy as immoral, 96–98

Semprun, Jorge, 155

Sem-Sandberg, Steve, 61–63

sensation of disbelief, 6, 10, 58–59, 61, 64, 66, 70n8, 254–55

Sepher Yosippon, 228–30, 232–34, 236n15

Service de Travail Obligatoire (STO), 218–19

Service Social International d'Aide aux Emigrants (SSAE), 201

Shatzky, Jacob, 190n14

Shaw, Martin, 19, 32n14, 32n26

Shikhor, Yitzhak (Szwarc), 131n47

Shoah (documentary), 18, 141–42, 278

Shoah (catastrophe, disaster), as term of use, 17–18, 21

Shoah Visual History Foundation, 4, 109, 136

Shprung, Hadassah, 83

Sicherheitspolizei (Sipo), *106,* 106–7, 114–15

Sierakowiak, David, 63

Sierakowski, Sławomir, 274, 276–78

Siewinski, Antoni, 111–12, 127n24

Sikorski, Władysław, 252

single site studies, 8–9, 106, 108

Slapakowa, Celia, 182, 183

slave labor camps, 84, 85, 137

Slovakian Jews, 255

Smith, Helmut Walser, 3

Sobotnik, Dov Berl, 79

Sociétés de Secours Mutuels, 197

Sofsky, Wolfgang, 153

Solidarité Juive, 195–97, 200, 213

Solomon, Jacques, 212–13

Solski, Adam, 39, 50

Soviet Union. *See* Russia/Soviet Union

space: concentration camps and, 154, 160; death marches and, 153, 160–61; diaries and, 93–94; postwar emotions and, 267, 270, 272, 276, 278, 279n9, 279n11. See also temporality
Spanish Civil War, 241, 242, 248n8
Spielberg-Flitman, Edzia, 118, 133n66
Stalin, Joseph, 8, 22. See also Russia/Soviet Union
Stangl, Franz, 124n2
Stargardt, Nicholas, 103n10
Steinberg, Israel (Alberto Ferrari), 205, 208n46
Stern, Fritz, 267
Stern, Juliette, 208n34
Stone, Dan, 19, 32n17
survival, 140, 142–43, 148, 152–53, 158–59, 162–66
Sutzkever, Avrom, 1–2, 12n4
Szeryński, Józef, 179–80
Szpigiel, Mojżesz, 118
Szwarc, Yitzhak (Shikhor), 131n47

T

Taitelbaum, Yoel, 104n27
Tatz, Colin, 19, 20
Tedeschi, Giuliana, 164
temporality, 45, 268, 278, 279n11. See also space
Tenenbaum, Mordecai, 181
Theresienstadt, 84
transnational perspectives (geographies of Jewishness), 19, 21–22, 33n30, 33n39, 267, 275
Trawniki, 186–87
Treblinka, 80, 84, 124n2, 181–83, 185, 187, 189
Tremback, Julija Mykhailivna, 118–19, 133n63
Truman, Harry S, 260–61
Trunk, Isaiah, 66

U

Ukraine, 39, 46, 50, 120, 134n72. See also Bloodlands; Buczacz
Ukrainian Insurgent Army (UPA), 115, 117, 119
Ukrainian non-Jews in Buczacz: death statistics, 130n41, 130n43; deportation of, 114, 120; narratives of, 120, 134n72; nationalism and, 110–15, 117, 119–21, 121, 126n12, 130n33, 130n43, 134n70, 134n72; policemen or Schuma and, 107, 114, 117–18, 125n4, 130n43, 131n47; population statistics, 107, 126n6; postwar testimonies and, 124; protection of Jews by, 118, 130n43, 131n45, 133n63; violence and, 114–19, 125n4, 130n43, 133nn63–64, 133n66, 253
Unger, Michal, 66, 189
Union des Juifs pour la Résistance et l'Entraide (UJRE), 214
Union Générale des Israélites de France (UGIF), 199–202, 206
United Nations War Crimes Commission (UNWCC), 255
United States: geopolitical interests of, 2, 12n6; Holocaust Memorial Museum in, 4, 109, 174; organizational connections with non-Jews in, 201; postwar emotions in, 267, 278n9; pressure groups and, 11, 250–62; trials in, 2; World Jewry annihilation in context of, 27, 37n80
unprecedentedness, 19–20, 32n20, 49, 51n12, 97

V

van den Berg, Albert, 203
van Praag, Roger, 197
van Roey, Jozef Ernst, 203
Varouh, Joseph, 231
Veldii, Petro, 39, 50
Vergara, Paul, 204
victim-focused historiography, 4, 63, 91, 99–100, 189
Villon, Pierre, 212
Vilna Ghetto, 30–31, 181
violence against Jews: Aktionen/violent roundups and, 107, 114–15, 122, 125n4, 131n47; in the Netherlands, 26, 27, 36n68; in Poland, 27, 254, 268, 270; in Romania, 27, 256; sensation of disbelief and, 6, 10, 58–59, 61, 64, 66, 70n8, 254–55; space in context of, 153–54, 160–61; Ukrainian non-Jews and, 114–19, 125n4, 130n43, 133nn63–64, 133n66; women in ghettos and, 62, 64–65
Visser, Lodewijk E., 27

W

Warsaw Ghetto: Aleynhilf and, 83, 87n45, 176, 180–81, 184–85, 191n32; deportations from, 59, 181–83, 185, 187, 189; Gęsiówka and, 165–66, 233; Jewish leadership in, 59, 179–82, 184; Nazi films of, 173–74; population of, 80; resistance in, 186. *See also* Oyneg Shabes; Ringelblum, Emanuel
Wasser, Bluma, 174
Wasser, Hersh, 174, 190n27
Waxman, Zoë Vania, 93
Weichert, Michael, 83
Werber, Abusz, 196
Werdum, Ulrich von, 110
Wiesenthal, Simon, 113
Winkler, Jerzy, 182
Winter, Jay, 101
Wise, Stephen S., 254
Wisliceny, Dieter, 2, 24
Wizinger, Moshe, 130n43, 131n46
World Jewish Congress (WJC), 254–55
World Jewry annihilation: antisemitism in context of, 3; Bloodlands and, 46–48; debates about reason for, 2–3; final destruction of ghettos and, 83–84; German population support for, 3; local decisions in context of, 3; Nazi ideology and, 6, 23–29, 34nn44–45, 34n47, 35–36nn54–56, 35n50, 36n68; pressure groups in context of, 254–55, 254–56. *See also* Final Solution of the Jewish Question
Wulf, Joseph, 5
Wurmser, André, 212

Y

Yad Vashem, 4, 109, 203
Yeshurun, Sara, 234
YIVO Institute for Jewish Research Archives, 2, 5, 177–78, 178–79, 181–82, 184, 189n3, 236n28
Yizkor (memorial) books, 4, 110, 120, 127n14, 271

Z

Zagan, Shakhne, 187
Zamach (Assassination) [film], 274
Zapp, Paul, 24
Zeisler, Gertrude, 78–79
Zelkowicz, Josef, 61
Zimbardo, Philip, 124n2
Zimmerer, Jürgen, 21
Zionism, 7, 10, 175, 187, 241–42, 244–47, 246n5, 255–56, 260–62. *See also* Israel
Zirpins, Ernst, 65
Zuroff, Rene, 120

MAKING SENSE OF HISTORY
Studies in Historical Cultures
General Editor: Stefan Berger
Founding Editor: Jörn Rüsen

Bridging the gap between historical theory and the study of historical memory, this series crosses the boundaries between both academic disciplines and cultural, social, political and historical contexts. In an age of rapid globalization, which tends to manifest itself on an economic and political level, locating the cultural practices involved in generating its underlying historical sense is an increasingly urgent task.

Volume 1
Western Historical Thinking: An Intercultural Debate
   Edited by Jörn Rüsen

Volume 2
Identities: Time, Difference, and Boundaries
   Edited by Heidrun Friese

Volume 3
Narration, Identity, and Historical Consciousness
   Edited by Jürgen Straub

Volume 4
Thinking Utopia: Steps into Other Worlds
   Edited by Jörn Rüsen, Michael Fehr, and Thomas W. Rieger

Volume 5
History: Narration, Interpretation, Orientation
   Jörn Rüsen

Volume 6
The Dynamics of German Industry: Germany's Path toward the New Economy and the American Challenge
   Werner Abelshauser

Volume 7
Meaning and Representation in History
   Edited by Jörn Rüsen

Volume 8
Remapping Knowledge: Intercultural Studies for a Global Age
   Mihai I. Spariosu

Volume 9
Cultures of Technology and the Quest for Innovation
   Edited by Helga Nowotny

Volume 10
Time and History: The Variety of Cultures
   Edited by Jörn Rüsen

Volume 11
Narrating the Nation: Representations in History, Media and the Arts
   Edited by Stefan Berger, Linas Eriksonas, and Andrew Mycock

Volume 12
Historical Memory in Africa: Dealing with the Past, Reaching for the Future in an Intercultural Context
   Edited by Mamadou Diawara, Bernard Lategan, and Jörn Rüsen

Volume 13
New Dangerous Liaisons: Discourses on Europe and Love in the Twentieth Century
   Edited by Luisa Passerini, Liliana Ellena, and Alexander C. T. Geppert

Volume 14
Dark Traces of the Past: Psychoanalysis and Historical Thinking
   Edited by Jürgen Straub and Jörn Rüsen

Volume 15
A Lover's Quarrel with the Past: Romance, Representation, Reading
   Ranjan Ghosh

Volume 16
The Holocaust and Historical Methodology
    Edited by Dan Stone

Volume 17
What is History For? Johann Gustav Droysen and the Functions of Historiography
    Arthur Alfaix Assis

Volume 18
Vanished History: The Holocaust in Czech and Slovak Historical Culture
    Tomas Sniegon

Volume 19
Jewish Histories of the Holocaust: New Transnational Approaches
    Edited by Norman J.W. Goda

Volume 20
Helmut Kohl's Quest for Normality: His Representation of the German Nation and Himself
    Christian Wicke

Volume 21
Marking Evil: Holocaust Memory in the Global Age
    Edited by Amos Goldberg and Haim Hazan

Volume 22
The Rhythm of Eternity: The German Youth Movement and the Experience of the Past, 1900–1933
    Robbert-Jan Adriaansen

Volume 23
Viktor Frankl's Search for Meaning: An Emblematic 20th-Century Life
    Timothy Pytell

Volume 24
Designing Worlds: National Design Histories in an Age of Globalization
    Edited by Kjetil Fallan and Grace Lees-Maffei

Volume 25
Doing Conceptual History in Africa
    Edited by Axel Fleisch and Rhiannon Stephens

Volume 26
Divining History: Prophetism, Messianism and the Development of the Spirit
    Jayne Svenungsson

Volume 27
Sensitive Pasts: Questioning Heritage in Education
    Edited by Carla von Boxtel, Maria Grever, and Stephen Klein

CPSIA information can be obtained
at www.ICGtesting.com
Printed in the USA
JSHW021354140120
3588JS00004B/44